EYEWITNESS
GETTYSBURG

THE CIVIL WAR'S GREATEST BATTLE

ROD GRAGG

AUTHOR OF *COVERED WITH GLORY*
AND *CONFEDERATE GOLIATH*

REGNERY
HISTORY

Regnery History™ is a trademark of Salem Communications Holding Corporation; Regnery® is a registered trademark of Salem Communications Holding Corporation

First paperback edition published 2016: ISBN 978-1-62157-301-2
Originally published in hardcover, 2013, under the title *The Illustrated Gettysburg Reader*: ISBN 978-1-62157-043-1

Cataloging-in-Publication data on file with the Library of Congress

Published in the United States by
Regnery History
An imprint of Regnery Publishing
A Division of Salem Media Group
300 New Jersey Ave NW
Washington, DC 20001
www.RegneryHistory.com

Manufactured in the United States of America

10 9 8 7 6 5 4 3 2 1

Books are available in quantity for promotional or premium use. For information on discounts and terms, please visit our website: www.Regnery.com.

Distributed to the trade by
Perseus Distribution
250 West 57th Street
New York, NY 10107

For
James Melvin Lindsey IV
"Jate"

CONTENTS

Introduction

"Whatever fatigues and sacrifices we may be called upon to undergo, let us have in view constantly the magnitude of the interests involved, and let each man determine to do his duty, leaving to an all-controlling Providence the decision of the contest." So wrote Major General George Meade upon assuming command of the Federal Army of the Potomac on the eve of the battle of Gettysburg. "No troops could have displayed greater fortitude or better performed the arduous marches of the past ten days," wrote General Robert E. Lee of his Army of Northern Virginia on the march northward to Pennsylvania. Soldiers of both armies would indeed be required to display "fortitude" and endure "fatigues and sacrifices" in the epic struggle that lay ahead.

The three-day battle of Gettysburg would prove to be the largest engagement ever fought in North America and the bloodiest battle of the American Civil War. It would also prove to be the turning point of the war. The battle's importance was immediately obvious to many of its survivors, including both common soldiers and officers. In letters, diaries, official reports, and memoirs, many of them tried to describe what they had seen and endured as the dramatic events of battle unfolded across the Pennsylvania countryside on July 1–3, 1863. Nothing written about the battle of Gettysburg is more powerful or evocative than the words of its eyewitnesses. "Every tree is riddled with bullets," wrote one soldier, "and the dead and wounded lie thick among the rocks." Observed another: "The regimental flags and guidons were plainly visible along the whole line. The guns and bayonets in the sunlight shone like silver."

Their eyewitness accounts are surprisingly descriptive: "There it was again! and again! A sound filling the air above, below, around us, like the blast through the top of a dry cedar or the whirring sound made by the sudden flight of a flock of quail. It was grape and canister...." And at times their words are also astonishingly frank, robbing all romance from the record of war: "an officer [was] sitting with his back to the fence along the Emmitsburg road, having his lower jaw shot clean away; sitting there with staring eyes watching the men as they passed by to the charge." Remarkably, even as they fought to destroy each other, they remained aware that they were Americans all, and did not hesitate to recognize the valor of the enemy. "This was indeed the great slaughter pen on the field of Gettysburg," wrote a Northern soldier of his Southern opponents, "and in it lay hundreds of the brave heroes who an hour before buoyed up with hope and ambition were being led, as they fully believed, to victory...."

Here, in the words of those who lived through the battle of Gettysburg—and some who did not—is an eyewitness history of the Civil War's greatest battle. Forged as it was in the flame of battle by those who were there, and illustrated by period images, it is both authoritative and intimate, fascinating and unforgettable—it is the *Illustrated Gettysburg Reader.*

CHAPTER ONE

"Advance into Pennsylvania"

By late June of 1863, the gentle rains of spring and early warmth of summer had brought a rich green hue to the fields and forests around the southern Pennsylvania town of Gettysburg. A dense green canopy of hardwood trees shaded the rocky crests of Little Round Top and Culp's Hill, and cloaked the steep slope of Herbst Woods. Local waterways such as Willoughby Run, Marsh Creek, and Plum Run flowed briskly through the fields and woodlands that surrounded the town. In between Seminary Ridge and Cemetery Ridge the pastureland was green with grass and clover, marked here and there by pastel-colored patches of wheat, oats, and barley. Baked by the summer sun, the Emmitsburg Road entered town from the south in between rows of weathered wooden fences; to the west, the Chambersburg Turnpike entered town after rising and falling over Herr Ridge and McPherson's Ridge.

It was these two roads, among others, that would soon bring the storm of war to Gettysburg. A medium-sized farm-country town of approximately 2,400 residents, Gettysburg was the county seat of Adams County, and in some ways it appeared similar to the neighboring towns of York and Chambersburg—with the exception of its roads. Gettysburg radiated roads like the spokes of a wheel.

Surrounded by peaceful ridges, fields, and forests, the southern Pennsylvania town of Gettysburg seemed an unlikely site for the Civil War's bloodiest battle.

National Archives

No fewer than ten highways converged on the town—more roadways than found in the state capital of Harrisburg. The convergence of so many highways in Gettysburg made the town a geographic magnet in southern Pennsylvania. As two huge Northern and Southern armies lumbered through the region that summer searching for each other and for a place to do battle, both were drawn to Gettysburg. There they would engage in the greatest battle of the American Civil War.[1]

"We Advanced toward the Potomac"
General Robert E. Lee Launches the Gettysburg Campaign

On the morning of Monday, June 15, 1863, a long, dust-covered column of Confederate cavalry reached the Virginia side of the Potomac River south of Williamsport, Maryland. Uniformed in gray and butternut, the Southern soldiers eagerly spurred their horses down the riverbank and splashed across the wide, shallow Potomac ford toward the Maryland shore and the road to Pennsylvania.

Commanded by Brigadier General Albert G. Jenkins, they comprised the advance guard of General Robert E. Lee's 75,000-man Army of Northern Virginia, which was advancing steadily through Virginia's Shenandoah Valley bound for an invasion of Pennsylvania. There, on Northern soil, Lee hoped to fight and win a decisive battle that would hasten an end to America's bloody Civil War and establish Southern nationhood.

Jenkins's Cavalry Brigade was screening the vanguard of Lee's army—Lieutenant General Richard S. Ewell's Second Army Corps—which a day earlier had defeated and dispersed a Federal garrison of troops at Martinsburg, Virginia. As they forded the Potomac near Williamsport and headed across Maryland toward the Mason-Dixon Line and Pennsylvania, the youthful cavalrymen were in high spirits, bolstered by their recent victory and the knowledge that as they rode into enemy territory, Robert E. Lee's army followed behind them at peak strength.

Among their ranks was a young junior officer, Lieutenant Hermann Schuricht of the 14th Virginia Cavalry, who carefully kept a personal diary during his time in the field. In it, he recorded the opening actions of the Gettysburg Campaign.

Spearheading General Robert E. Lee's 1863 invasion of the North, Confederate cavalry ford the Potomac River in this period newspaper illustration.

Frank Leslie's Illustrated Newspaper

June 15, 1863.—Fatigued, but hopeful, and encouraged by the result of our glorious battle of yesterday at Martinsburg, Virginia, we were called by the sound of the bugle to mount horses. As early as 2 o'clock in the morning we advanced towards the Potomac. We recon- noitered first to "Dam No. 5," and, returning to the road to Williamsport, Maryland, we rapidly moved to the river.

Fording the Potomac, we took possession of Williamsport, and were received very kindly by the inhabitants. Tables, with plenty of milk, bread, and meat, had been spread in the street, and we took a hasty breakfast. Soon after this

With a cigar in his mouth and a Colt revolver in his hand, a young Virginia cavalryman exhibits the bold attitude that typified Southern cavalry.

Library of Congress

we rode towards Hagerstown, Maryland, where we arrived at noon, and were enthusiastically welcomed by the ladies. They made us presents of flowers, and the children shouted, "Hurrah for Jeff. Davis!"

The ladies entreated us not to advance into Pennsyl- vania, where we would be attacked by superior forces. However, we sped on, and when we came in sight of Greencastle, Pennsylvania, General Jenkins divided his brigade in two forces. My company belonged to the troops forming the right wing, and pistols and muskets in hand, traversing ditches and fences, we charged and took the town. The Federal cavalry escaped, and only one lieutenant was captured.

After destroying the railroad depot, and cutting the telegraph wires, the brigade took up its advance to Chambersburg, Pennsyl- vania. No other Confederate cavalry force seems to co-operate with our brigade, numbering about 3,200 officers and men. Our van- guard had several skirmishes with the retreating enemy. On the road we found several partly burned wagons, which they had destroyed;

and at 11 o'clock at night, we entered the city of Chambersburg, and on its eastern outskirts we went into camp.[2]

"As Near Perfection as a Man Can Be"
An Eyewitness Description of Robert E. Lee

In early May of 1863—days after his greatest victory—General Robert E. Lee began planning an invasion of the North. Lee was a Virginian, the fifty-six-year-old commander of the Confederate Army of Northern Virginia. He had been brevetted for gallantry during the Mexican War, and had served as the superintendent of West Point. He was a member of the Virginia aristocracy, the son of an acclaimed Revolutionary War cavalry commander—Lieutenant Colonel Henry "Light-Horse Harry" Lee—and he had served with distinction in the prewar United States Army, rising to the rank of colonel. In the view of many, both Northern and Southern, he was also a military genius. "His name might be Audacity," observed a fellow officer. "He will take more desperate chances, and take them quicker than any other general in this country, North or South...."

Tall, gray-bearded, and dignified, he was a quietly devout Christian. "I am nothing but a poor sinner," he once said, "trusting in Christ alone for my salvation...." He was also an ardent admirer of George Washington. Lee's wife, Mary Anne Custis Lee, was the daughter of Washington's adopted son, and Lee's father had been Washington's wartime subordinate and postwar friend. With such ties to the nation, Lee had come with regret and reluctance to Southern command. He considered slavery to be a "moral & political evil" and described secession as a "calamity," but on the eve of the war he declined an offer to command the principal Northern army. Instead, he resigned his commission in the U.S. Army and returned to his family home on the Virginia side of the Potomac opposite Washington, D.C. "I shall return to my native state," he asserted, "and share the miseries of my people...." When Virginia seceded, he agreed to accept command of the state's troops, and when Virginia joined the Confederacy, he

General Robert E. Lee, commander, Army of Northern Virginia.

became a Confederate general. He held various posts during the first year of the war, eventually serving as the chief military advisor to Confederate President Jefferson Davis.

In June of 1862, he accepted command of the Confederate army defending Richmond, the Confederate capital, which was then threatened by the Federal Army of the Potomac under Major General George B. McClellan. Lee reorganized his forces into the Army of Northern Virginia, and in a series of engagements called the Seven Days Battles, he demolished McClellan's Peninsula Campaign and drove the Federal army away from Richmond. In August of 1862, he boldly moved his army into northern Virginia, where he defeated Major General John Pope and another Federal army at the Battle of Second Bull Run. He subsequently attempted to lead his army on a campaign into Maryland, a potential invasion of the North, but was forced to withdraw following the bloody Battle of Antietam in September of 1862.

In December of that year, he inflicted a disastrous defeat on the Army of the Potomac at the Battle of Fredericksburg. In May of 1863, he once again defeated the Army of the Potomac—this time under the command of Major General Joseph Hooker—at the Battle of Chancellorsville. It was his most heralded victory, but it came at great cost: his invaluable subordinate, Lieutenant General Thomas J. "Stonewall" Jackson, died of complications from wounds suffered at Chancellorsville. "I know not how to replace him," Lee admitted. Shortly thereafter, despite the loss of Jackson, Lee began seriously contemplating and planning a campaign to take the war to the North. It would be risky, but Lee had the confidence and support of his superiors, his officers, and his soldiers. While he was respected and feared in the North, he was *revered* in the South—for his character and devout faith as well as his military genius. Typical of the Southern attitude toward Lee was a description of him recorded in 1863—not by a Southerner, but by a British military observer, Lieutenant Colonel Arthur L. Fremantle.

General Lee is, almost without exception, the handsomest man of his age I ever saw. He is fifty-six years old, tall, broad-shouldered, very well made, well set up—a thorough soldier in appearance; and his manners are most courteous and full of dignity.

He is a perfect gentleman in every respect. I imagine no man has so few enemies, or is so universally esteemed. Throughout the South, all agree in pronouncing him to be as near perfection as a man can be. He has none of the small vices, such as smoking, drinking, chewing, or swearing, and his bitterest enemy never accused him of any of the greater ones. He generally wears a well-worn, long, gray jacket, a high, black felt hat, and blue trousers tucked into his Wellington boots.

I never saw him carry arms; and the only mark of his military rank are the three stars on his collar. He rides a handsome horse, which is extremely well groomed. He himself is very neat in his dress and person, and in the most arduous marches he always looks smart and clean.

In the old army he was always considered one of its best officers; and at the outbreak of these troubles, he was lieutenant-colonel of the 2d cavalry. He was a rich man, but his fine estate was one of the first to fall into the enemy's hands. I believe he has never slept in a house since he commanded in the Virginian army, and he invariably declines all offers of hospitality, for fear the person offering it may afterwards get into trouble for having sheltered the rebel general....

Lieutenant General Thomas J. "Stonewall" Jackson.
Library of Congress

It is understood that General Lee is a religious man, though not so demonstrative in that respect as Jackson; and unlike his late brother in arms, he is a member of the Church of England. His only faults, so far as I can learn, arise from his excessive amiability.[3]

"There Is Always Hazard in Military Movements"

Lee Makes the Case for Invasion of the North

I f the South did not win the war soon, Lee believed, it would not win at all. Despite Southern victories, such as Chancellorsville in the east, Federal amphibious operations and an increasingly effective Northern naval blockade were closing Southern seaports one by one. Meanwhile Northern forces were steadily overrunning the South in the war's Western Theater, with disastrous consequences. Kentucky and most of Tennessee had been conquered and occupied by Northern forces, which now also held most of the Mississippi River, including New Orleans and Memphis. Between the two port cities, a massive Federal army under Major General Ulysses S. Grant threatened the Confederate river bastion of Vicksburg. The fall of Vicksburg would split the South and ensure Federal control of the Mississippi.

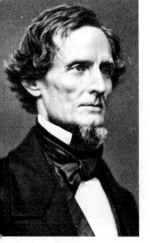

Confederate President
Jefferson Davis.
Library of Congress

Even Confederate victories came at a disturbing price: the Battle of Chancellorsville resulted in 13,000 Southern casualties, for example, and was a sobering reminder that the South was steadily being bled of manpower. The North's superior resources meant that it was just a question of time before the South was defeated. "We should not, therefore, conceal from ourselves that our resources in men are constantly diminishing," Lee advised President Davis in correspondence. On May 14, 1863, Lee left army headquarters near Fredericksburg and traveled down to Richmond to personally meet with Davis,

Confederate Secretary of War James A. Seddon, and Davis's other cabinet officers. For three days, Lee reviewed the existing military situation and possible options. At one point Davis wondered aloud if Lee should send part of his army to the war's Western Theater in order to help defend Vicksburg.

Lee disagreed, believing the South would be best served if he could immediately take the war to the North. A successful invasion of the North would allow Lee to move his army from war-ravaged Virginia and to provision his troops and horses from the rich farmland of Pennsylvania. It could trigger a financial panic in the North, bolster the growing Northern peace movement, demoralize the Northerners, and result in official recognition of the Confederacy by Britain or France. The capture of Washington, Philadelphia, or even Pennsylvania's capital of Harrisburg might be enough to produce a negotiated end to the war and to win Southern Independence. Another Confederate victory such as those at Chancellorsville or Fredericksburg—but on Northern soil—might achieve all of these objectives.

Eventually Davis agreed and issued directives reinforcing Lee's army. On Wednesday, June 3, 1863, Lee ordered the Army of Northern Virginia to begin the march northward. As the great campaign began to unfold, he sent a message from army headquarters to Secretary of War Seddon, summarizing his argument for invasion of the North. "We might hope," Lee observed in an understatement, "to make some impression on the enemy."

———————————

CONFIDENTIAL
HDQRS. ARMY OF NORTHERN VIRGINIA,
June 8, 1863

Honorable JAMES A. SEDDON,
Secretary of War, Richmond, Va.:
SIR: I have had the honor to receive your letter of the 5th....
There is always hazard in military movements, but we must decide
between the positive loss of inactivity and the risk of action.... As

In May of 1863, General Lee met with President Davis and his cabinet here at the Executive Mansion in Richmond—later known as the Confederate White House—to strategize Lee's proposed invasion of the North.

National Archives

far as I can judge, there is nothing to be gained by this army remaining quietly on the defensive, which it must do unless it can be re-enforced. I am aware that there is difficulty and hazard in taking the aggressive with so large an army in its front, intrenched behind a river, where it cannot be advantageously attacked. Unless it can be drawn out in a position to be assailed, it will take its own time to prepare and strengthen itself to renew its advance upon Richmond, and force this army back within the intrenchments of that city.

This may be the result in any event; still, I think it is worth a trial to prevent such a catastrophe. Still, if the Department thinks it better to remain on the defensive, and guard as far as possible all the avenues of approach, and await the time of the enemy, I am ready to adopt this course. You have, therefore, only to inform me.

I think our southern coast might be held during the sickly season by local troops, aided by a small organized force, and the predatory excursions of the enemy be repressed. This would give us an active force in the field with which we might hope to make some impression on the enemy, both on our northern and western frontiers.

Unless this can be done, I see little hope of accomplishing anything of importance.

All our military preparations and organizations should now be pressed forward with the greatest vigor, and every exertion made to obtain some material advantage in this campaign.

I am, with great respect, your obedient servant,

R. E. Lee,

General[4]

"We Whip the Yankees Every Time We Catch up with Them"

The Army of Northern Virginia Readies Itself for Another Victory

"There were never such men in an army before." So said General Robert E. Lee of the troops who comprised his Army of Northern Virginia. "They will go anywhere and do anything if properly led," he observed. Lee was not alone in his opinion. "I believe they will compare favorably with those of the Romans or of Napoleon's Old Guard," concluded one of Lee's colonels. "The army that he has now can not be whipped by anything in Yankeedom."

In preparation for the campaign into Pennsylvania, and in reaction to the loss of "Stonewall" Jackson, Lee reorganized the Army of Northern Virginia from two corps into three corps. The First Corps would be commanded by Lieutenant General James Longstreet; the Second Corps—General Jackson's former corps—would be led by Lieutenant General Richard Ewell; and the Third Corps would be commanded by Lieutenant General Ambrose Powell Hill. The army's artillery was also restructured, and its cavalry division—commanded by Major General J. E. B. Stuart—was reinforced to a troop-strength of about 10,000. Additional reinforcements increased the army to approximately 75,000 men.

Although "as ragged as could be," the soldiers of the Army of Northern Virginia were renowned for their fighting abilities. Said Lee: "There were never such men in an army before."

Library of Congress

Despite his best efforts, Lee knew that the Army of Northern Virginia had its weaknesses. Even with new reinforcements, the army would likely be outnumbered. Providing rations—always a problem for Confederate troops—would remain a challenge. Generals Ewell and Hill had never before held corps command, several division and brigade commanders were novices at their posts, and, most troubling, General Jackson— Lee's "right arm"—was no more.

Lee hoped restructuring the army would minimize the loss of Jackson. Even if some of his commanders were new to their posts, they were all seasoned combat veterans. He expected to amply provision his army from resources in the North, and his troops were used to fighting—and winning—against superior enemy numbers. Lee had confidence in his troops, and—flushed with victories at Chancellorsville and Fredericksburg—they had confidence in themselves and in "Uncle Robert," as some reverently called him. Observed a soldier in a letter home, "We whip the Yankees every time we catch up with them...."

The soldiers in the ranks did not look like a spit-and-polish body of troops. "Their clothing is serviceable," noted an observer, "but there is the usual absence of uniformity as to color and shape of their garments and hats . . . [gray] of all shades, and brown clothing, with felt hats." Some were shoeless. Few had knapsacks. Many wore blankets rolled and looped over one shoulder and around the chest with the ends tied together at the waist. Most "were as ragged as they could be," a veteran would recall, "some with the bottom of their pants in long frazzles, others with their knees sticking out, others out at their elbows, and their hair sticking through holes in their hats." Despite their scruffy appearance, Lee's troops were well-armed with imported British Enfield rifles and captured U.S. Springfields, and they carried themselves with an air of confidence and professionalism—as noted by a Unionist letter writer who had observed the Army of Northern Virginia the year before as it marched through Maryland.

I wish, my dear Minnie, you could have witnessed the transit of the Rebel army through our streets a day or two ago. Their coming was unheralded by any pomp and pageantry whatever. No burst of martial music greeted your ear, no thundering sound of cannon, no brilliant staff, no glittering cortege dashed through the streets; instead came three long, dirty columns that kept on in an unceasing flow.

I could scarcely believe my eyes; was this body of men moving so smoothly along, with no order, their guns carried in every fashion, no two dressed alike, their officers hardly distinguishable from the privates, were these, I asked myself in amazement, were these dirty, lank, ugly specimens of humanity, with shocks of hair sticking through the holes in their hats, and the dust thick on their dirty faces, the men that had coped and encountered successfully, and driven back again and again, our splendid legions with their fine discipline, their martial show and color, their solid battalions keeping such perfect time to the inspiring bands of music?

I must confess, Minnie, that I felt humiliated at the thought that this horde of ragamuffins could set our grand army of the Union at defiance. Why, it seemed as if a single regiment of our gallant boys in blue could drive that dirty crew into the river without any trouble.

As if ready for the march, an unidentified soldier in the Eleventh Virginia Infantry—part of Longstreet's First Corps at Gettysburg—rests on a model 1841 Mississippi rifle. By the summer of 1863, Lee's veteran troops no longer displayed the spit-and-polish look of this new recruit.

Library of Congress

And then, too, I wish you could see how they behaved—a crowd of boys on holiday don't seem happier. They are on the broad grin all the time. Oh! They are so dirty! I don't think the Potomac River could wash them clean; and ragged!—there is not a scarecrow in the corn-fields that would not scorn to exchange clothes with them; and so tattered!—there isn't a decently dressed soldier in their whole army. I saw some strikingly handsome faces though; or, rather, they would have been so if they could have had a good scrubbing.

They were very polite, I must confess, and always asked for a drink of water, or anything else, and never think of coming inside a door without an invitation. Many of them were barefooted. Indeed, I felt sorry for the poor, misguided wretches, for some were limping along so painfully, trying hard to keep up with their comrades. But I must stop. I send this by Robert, and hope it will reach you safely. Write to me as soon as the route is open.

Kate[5]

"A Soldier by Instinct, Intuition and Profession"

In Charge of Stopping Lee's Invasion: General Joseph Hooker

Major General
Joseph Hooker,
commander,
Army of
the Potomac.

Across the Rappahannock River from Fredericksburg and Lee's army lay the Federal Army of the Potomac and its commander, Major General Joseph Hooker. A forty-eight-year-old West Pointer born in Massachusetts, Hooker had distinguished himself in the Mexican War, and in the first two years of the Civil War had risen in rank from brigadier to major general, and from brigade commander to army commander. He was a gifted army organizer and a capable strategist, but his fondness for gambling and camp women showed him to be "wanting in character,"

General Hooker was a good judge of horseflesh, but he severely misjudged Lee's ability to react at the battle of Chancellorsville—with disastrous results.

National Archives

according to one critic, and his enthusiasm for the bottle caused him once to topple from his horse.

Inadvertently but appropriately nicknamed "Fighting Joe" Hooker by the Northern press, he was a bold, aggressive commander whose troops were known for engaging in ferocious fighting and for incurring heavy casualties. He was shamelessly ambitious, often at the expense of other officers. When introduced to President Abraham Lincoln shortly after the Northern loss at the First Battle of Bull Run, he brashly stated, "I am a damned sight better general than you, Sir, had on that field." In late 1862, after a disastrous Federal defeat at the Battle of Fredericksburg, Lincoln promoted Hooker to commander of the Army of the Potomac—even though Hooker had publicly opined that "both the Army and the Government needed a Dictator." Said Lincoln, "What I now ask of you is military success, and I will risk the dictatorship."

In the spring of 1863, Hooker launched a bold offensive that caught Lee off guard. "My plans are perfect," he boasted, "and when I start to carry them out, may God have mercy on General Lee, for I will have none." However, it was Hooker who would need mercy; on May 1–4, 1863, Lee inflicted a humiliating defeat on Hooker and his army at the Battle of Chancellorsville. With his reputation as battered as his troops, Hooker put his army into lines north of Fredericksburg and waited for Lee's next move. The defeat at Chancellorsville, admitted one of Hooker's subordinates, "has shaken the confidence of the army." Another described Hooker as the object of "universal disgust among the officers," while another critic branded him "a used-up man."

In early June of 1863, as Lee readied his army for the march northward, Hooker was still commander of the Army of the Potomac—and still had his supporters. One of them was his chief of staff, Major General Daniel Butterfield, who recorded a glowing profile of "Fighting Joe" and his martial attributes.

His magnificent physique and genial bearing with his magnetic influence over his command soon became apparent. It contradicted

the effect of reckless statements of his personal habits and character. From a long service with him and every opportunity to judge and know by personal observation, I denounce these statements as false.... Fearless in the expressions of his opinions and his criticisms, he gave offence often without intending offence, but claiming, when remonstrated with concerning it, that the expression

At field headquarters near Fredericksburg in 1863, General Hooker's staff officers pretend to enjoy a smoke and a drink for the photographer.

of a truthful opinion was the duty of a patriot and the privilege of a gentleman. We can overlook these expressions from their sincerity and lack of malignity, and the bitter hostility they brought him.

Outspoken and fearless in speech—in conduct vigilant—wonderfully skilled in strategy, his troops soon learned that no soldier's life would be uselessly imperilled through his orders, and that no personal peril must forbid or endanger the accomplishment of a necessary military purpose, or the winning of a battle....

In the conception of military operations, Hooker was audacious, original, acute; In executing them he was energetic, yet circumspect and prudent. He was severe in discipline, exacting in his demands upon officers and men; lofty in his ideal of the soldier's intrepidity, fortitude, earnestness and zeal, yet, he was generous in praise, quick to see and recognize ability and merit, as well in the ranks of his adversary as in his own.

A soldier by intuition, instinct and profession. Hooker's sword was adorned by the best accomplishments known to the art of war. His character thoroughly military. He was fit for command. He was proud of the profession of arms. He brought to it the highest accomplishments of a soldier. His manner and bearing were distinguished, yet urbane and gentle. His temper was quick, yet forgiving. He was gracious to junior officers and prompt to recognize merit.

Diligent and punctilious in the discharge of duty. Toward all under his command he was exacting in discipline, inexorable to the laggard, prodigal in praise to the zealous and diligent. He always bowed to superior power with the same loyalty that he demanded from his own troops. He never sulked in his tent when summoned to battle. He was a patriot.[6]

"I Am Inclined to Think That We Shall Have to Acknowledge Their Independence"

The Army of the Potomac Yearns for Leadership and Victory

As Lee's Confederates began easing out of their lines to begin the march northward, approximately 85,500 Federal soldiers in the Army of the Potomac were encamped and entrenched just a few miles away on the

north side of the Rappahannock River near Fredericksburg. The army had been whittled down from more than 120,000 troops due to the casualties at Chancellorsville as well as the expiration of troop enlistments. Even so, it remained numerically superior and its ranks were packed with superbly equipped, battle-tested troops—"the finest army on the planet," Hooker had once stated.

Despite its strengths in June of 1863, the Army of the Potomac was beset by leadership crises. In less than one year, the army had been headed by three different commanders, a situation stemming from the fact that the army had been repeatedly defeated by Robert E. Lee and the Army of Northern Virginia. In response to the Northern defeat at First Bull Run in the summer of 1861, Union forces organized the Army of the Potomac outside Washington and entrusted command to Major General George B. McClellan. After months of building and drilling, McClellan had crafted the newly established army into an operation far superior to the previously vanquished Northern army of amateurs.

With President Lincoln increasingly impatient for action, McClellan moved the army by water to Virginia and launched his Peninsula Campaign, designed to capture Richmond and bring a swift end to the war in the summer of 1862.

Parked hub-to-hub near army lines on the eve of Gettysburg, an abundance of supply wagons waits to serve the well-equipped Army of the Potomac—"the finest army on the planet."
Library of Congress

Instead, after pushing to within sight of Richmond's church spires, he and the Army of the Potomac were bested by Lee and were forced to fall back to the Washington area. In September of 1862, after Lee defeated another Federal army under General John Pope at the Battle of Second Bull Run, McClellan and the Army of the Potomac fought Lee's army to a standstill at the Battle of Antietam. Although he had stopped Lee's advance across Maryland at Antietam, McClellan was removed from army command for failing to pursue and destroy the retreating Confederate army.

McClellan's replacement, Major General Ambrose E. Burnside, proved to be a calamity as a commander, ineptly ordering a series of futile frontal assaults against Lee's entrenched lines at the Battle of Fredericksburg in December of 1862—with almost 13,000 casualties. Lincoln removed Burnside and replaced him with Hooker, who capably reorganized and reinvigorated the army after its demoralizing defeat at Fredericksburg—only to lead it the humiliating loss at Chancellorsville.

Now, as the enemy began unfolding an invasion of the North, the soldiers of the Army of the Potomac—the principal Northern army in the East—displayed

Huddled on pew benches hauled from a Virginia church, off-duty soldiers from the Army of the Potomac take a moment in the Southern sun to mend uniforms, write letters and read newspapers.

mixed attitudes concerning the army's ability to win. Some remained confident. "You can whip them time and again," a Massachusetts soldier observed, "but the next fight they go into, they are in good spirits, and as full of pluck as ever.... Some day or other we shall have our turn." Some were embittered. "We have got just enough men now to get licked every time," a Michigan infantryman groused, "especially if the officers get drunk every time." Others, such as Private John P. Sheahan, a twenty-one-year-old cavalryman from Maine, had come to believe that a Southern victory was inevitable. In a letter written between the battles of Fredericksburg and Chancellorsville, he shared his grim prediction with his father.

Camp Near Bell Plain
March 2nd 1863

My Dear father
As I have got a few moments to spare I will improve them by writing you a few lines. We are having easier times now than we have had since the battle. We have not been on picket since a fortnight ago or more. Most of our company is down to Bell Plain Landing to work. I was down but had to come up. I was chafed so badly I can hardly walk now....

Well what do you think of the Conscription? Does is look as tho' the war was going to end by next fall? I think not. The south are determined to have their Independence and they will have it.

And no soldier in the Army of the Potomac doubts but what they will get it.

Some argue that they have not got the means to carry on the war. But how did we carry on a war with England the most powerful of European nations for seven long years? We were fighting for our independence and we were bound to have it cost what it may and we got it and so in my opinion will they.

I should be exceedingly sorry to see our country divided and I do not think there is many more willing to do more for their country than I am, but I am almost inclined to think that we shall have to acknowledge their independence.

I must write Mary a letter so I will close this. Give Mary her letter as soon as you can and don't open it. Now mind what I tell you.

[John][7]

A fresh-faced soldier from the Second Corps of the Army of the Potomac. In June of 1863, the army was burdened by multiple commanders and repeated defeats, but it would soon fight on Northern soil for the first time.

Library of Congress

CHAPTER TWO

"Look at Pharaoh's Army Going to the Red Sea"

═══════════

By June 4, 1863, two of Lee's three corps were on the road. General A. P. Hill's Third Corps was ordered to remain in line below Fredericksburg for more than a week afterward in order to keep Federal forces unaware of Lee's actions. Lee planned to concentrate most of his forces west of Fredericksburg at Culpeper Courthouse, then move his army into the Shenandoah and march northward toward Maryland and Pennsylvania. Lee positioned Major General J. E. B. Stuart and the army's 10,000-man cavalry division near Culpeper Courthouse to screen Lee's army as the invasion unfolded.[1]

With weapons shouldered, marching Confederate infantry take up the "route step."

Battles and Leaders of the Civil War

"Clouds of Dust Mingled with the Smoke of Discharging Firearms"

Federal and Confederate Cavalry Clash at Brandy Station

While waiting for orders to proceed northward, General Stuart staged two impressive grand cavalry reviews, which included a viewing audience of invited guests brought by train from Richmond. The second review attracted the attention of the Federal cavalry as well as General Hooker, who believed the event was the beginning of a major Confederate cavalry raid. To stop it, he dispatched the Army of the Potomac's cavalry corps—more than 8,000 strong—backed by artillery and infantry. It was led by the army's new cavalry commander, Brigadier General Alfred Pleasonton, a seasoned cavalry

As Lee assembled his army for the march northward, Federal cavalry launched a surprise attack on his cavalry at the battle of Brandy Station.

Library of Congress

officer. On June 9, 1863, the day after Stuart's second cavalry review, Pleasonton launched a pre-dawn surprise attack on Stuart's cavalry division.

The Battle of Brandy Station, as the engagement would come to be known, was the largest cavalry battle of the Civil War and involved more than 20,000 troops. It was a classic cavalry contest, fought with sabers as well as carbines, and lasted almost the entire day. At one point, as Pleasonton's Federal cavalry fought to capture a critical section of high ground called Fleetwood Hill, they appeared on the verge of victory—only to be repulsed by Stuart's horse artillery. The battle ended in a tactical draw, and Northern casualties outnumbered Southern losses 936 to 523.

Nevertheless, the Federal horse soldiers had shown themselves to be the equals of the lauded Confederate cavalry—and General Stuart had been surprised and humiliated. A vivid account of the Battle of Brandy Station was preserved in a journal kept by one of Stuart's artillerymen, Private George Neese, a gunner in Chew's Artillery Battery.

━━━━━━━━━━━━━━━━━━━━━

When the first inauspicious boom of cannon rolled over the fields from our rear … it was like an electric shock which first stuns, then reanimates, and in less time than it takes to relate it our cavalry was rushing toward the enemy in our rear, with nerves and courage strung to the highest pitch—every man determined to do or die. We followed close after them with the battery at a double-quick gallop. The dust in the road was about three inches deep, and in our hurried movement my mule fell down and rolled over me, and I over him, both of us wallowing in three inches of dust, and for once I and my mule favored and looked alike so far as color was concerned. By the time I got my mule up and I was mounted again the battery had disappeared in a thick cloud of flying dust.

The body of Yankee cavalry—General Gregg's division—that appeared in our rear crossed the Rappahannock at Kelly's Ford about seven miles below Beverly Ford, and moved up on this side of the river, striking the Orange and Alexandria Railroad at Brandy Station, then advanced in our rear. Nearly a mile from Brandy Station and in the direction of Beverly Ford is Fleetwood Heights, a prominent hill jutting boldly out from the highland on the west to an almost level plain on the east and south. The enemy in our rear had already gained the heights and were strongly posted on the crest, with a line of cavalry and a battery of artillery not far away ready to open fire, when our cavalry arrived in sight of the formidable hill that was crowned with threatening danger and almost ready to burst into battle.

There was not a moment to lose if our cavalry expected to gain the heights from the enemy's grasp and possession, and hold them,

Brigadier General Alfred Pleasonton, mounted here on a handsome, well-groomed horse, took command of the Army of the Potomac's cavalry corps on the eve of Brandy Station.

Library of Congress

and it had to be done instantly and by a hand-to-hand and hill-to-hill conflict. The decision for a saber charge was consummated in a moment, and our cavalry gallantly dashed up the slope of Fleetwood, with gleaming sabers, and charged the formidable line of cavalry that had opened a terrific fire from the crest of the hill. Then commenced the hand-to-hand conflict which raged desperately for awhile, the men on both sides fighting and grappling like demons, and at first it was doubtful as to who would succumb and first cry enough; but eventually the enemy began to falter and give way....

They rallied twice after their line was broken the first time, and heroically renewed the struggle for the mastery of the heights, but in their last desperate effort to regain and hold their position our cavalry met the onset with such cool bravery and rigid determination that the enemy's overthrow and discomfiture was so complete that they were driven from the hill, leaving three pieces of their artillery in position near the crest of the heights and their dead and wounded in our hands. When we arrived with our battery on top of Fleetwood the Yanks had already been driven from the hill and were retreating across the plain toward the southeast. Squadrons and regiments of horsemen were charging and fighting on various parts of the plain, and the whole surrounding country was full of fighting cavalrymen ...

Clouds of dust mingled with the smoke of discharging firearms rose from various parts of the field, and the discordant and fearful music of battle floated on the thickened air ... The charmed dignity of danger that evinces and proclaims its awe-inspiring presence by zipping bullets, whizzing shell, and gleaming sabers lifted the contemplation of the tragical display from the common domain of grandeur to the eloquent heights of sublimity. Stirring incidents and exciting events followed one another in quick succession, and no sooner was the enemy dislodged in our rear, than a heavy force that had been fighting us all morning advanced on our front, with cavalry and artillery. Their batteries at once opened a severe fire on our position, to which we immediately replied. Then the hardest and liveliest part of the artillery fighting commenced in earnest, and the thunder of the guns roared fiercely and incessantly for several hours....

One shell exploded fearfully close to me and seriously wounded two of my cannoneers and raked the sod all around me. For about three long hours whizzing shot, howling shell, exploding shrapnel, and screaming fragments filled the air that hung over Fleetwood Heights with the music of war. After a severe cannonading for several hours the fire of the Yankee battery slackened, and soon after ceased altogether, and the battery abandoned their position and withdrew their guns beyond the range of our fire.

Just before the Yankee battery ceased firing a large body of Yankee cavalry moved in solid column out in the open field about a mile and a half from our position. They remained there about two hours in a solid square, for the purpose, we supposed, of making a desperate charge on the hill and our battery, if their battery would have succeeded in partially silencing our guns. After the enemy's battery ceased firing Captain Chew ordered me to get ready to fire canister, and if the Yankee cavalry attempted to charge us I must reserve my fire until they charged to within three hundred yards of my gun, then open fire with canister, carefully aim at the horses' knees and fire as rapidly as possible. But after threateningly menacing our position for about two hours, the immense host of Yankee horsemen in our immediate front withdrew from the field, disappeared in a woods, and I saw them no more, for soon afterwards the battle ended, and the enemy retreated and recrossed the river. Several times during the day I saw General Stuart, when the battle raged the fiercest, dash with his staff across the field, passing from point to point along his line, perfectly heedless of the surrounding danger.

The Yanks cruelly rushed us out of camp this morning before breakfast, consequently we had nothing to eat during the whole day until after dark this evening, and strange to say I did not experience any hunger until after the battle was over ... We were on the field twelve hours, and during that time I fired my faithful gun one hundred and sixty times. This evening just before the battle closed, with the last few shots we fired I saw the fire flash from the cascabel of my gun, and I found that it was disabled forever—burnt entirely out at the breach ... The enemy's forces we fought to-day were under the command of General Pleasanton. He had three divisions of cavalry, with a complement of artillery—six batteries, I think— the whole backed by two brigades of infantry. His forces recrossed the river this evening and General Stuart held the battle-field.[2]

"The Roadsides Were Soon Lined with Stragglers"

Lee's Army Struggles with Heat and Rain on the March

On Wednesday, June 10, 1863, Lee's army left Culpeper Courthouse, heading north toward Maryland and Pennsylvania. The troops of General Richard Ewell's Second Corps were in the lead, screened in front by Jenkins's cavalry brigade. General James Longstreet's First Corps troops followed, and five days later, on June 15, the soldiers of the Third Corps under General A. P. Hill set up camp near Fredericksburg and joined the march. The army entered Virginia's Shenandoah Valley on selected roads through the mountain passes and marched northward—"down the Valley," as locals called it—advancing toward the Potomac River and the Maryland border. To protect the army's rear as it advanced, Lee dispatched forces to defeat or drive away Federal garrisons at Winchester and Martinsburg, which they did efficiently, capturing large numbers of prisoners, supplies, and ordnance. Meanwhile, General J. E. B. Stuart's cavalry corps guarded the army's rear and right flank.

Hungry Confederate soldiers take a break from the march to enjoy corn confiscated from a roadside cornfield.

Battles and Leaders of the Civil War

As they took up the "route step"—a steady, measured marching pace—Lee's soldiers knew they were heading toward the North and toward battle, even if they did not know their exact destination. "Some think we are going to Maryland," one wrote home, "but we don't know." Penned another, "I must confess it seems to me ... that it would be quite as well to concentrate everything in the valley of Va. and advance on Philadelphia." Other soldiers wrote to loved ones what they knew might be final farewells. "If I never see you again my prayer is to meet you in heaven," one man corresponded to his wife. "Take good care of my little girl and train her to love God...."

Lee's march occurred during a sweltering summer heat wave, which cloaked the marching columns in clouds of dust and left the roadsides lined with exhausted, sweating soldiers. Some even died of heatstroke. "It looked hard to see so many men lying on the side of the road almost smothering with heat," one soldier wrote. "May the Good Lord take care of the poor soldiers." In some areas along the route, the severe heat was interrupted by thunderstorms, which brought different but equal misery to the troops. Virginia soldier George S. Bernard, a private in Lee's Third Corps, would later pen a memoir of the march based on a detailed journal he kept.

Wednesday, June 17.— Started this morning about 10 o'clock and marched the first three or four miles very rapidly. The weather to-day excessively hot and straggling commenced very early. The roadsides were soon lined with stragglers, many of whom were completely exhausted by the heat, many suffering from and some dying, it was said, with sunstroke. When the brigade made its first halt to rest, it was a mere skeleton of what it was when it started, so many were behind. About sunset the division went into camp … at night the heat was so great that it was difficult to sleep.

Friday, June 19.—Started about sunrise and halted about midday on a high hill within a mile of and overlooking the village of Front Royal [Warren] county, having crossed the Blue Ridge at Thornton Gap. The scenery along the route was exceedingly beautiful—in some places very wild. We were struck with the luxuriant richness of the country on both sides of the mountains. How it

As depicted in this period sketch, Virginia's Shenandoah Valley offered a sheltered highway from Virginia into Maryland and Pennsylvania.

Library of Congress

contrasted with the worn out and devastated country to which we had so long been accustomed! About 4 o'clock P.M. our march is resumed. We pass through the town of Front Royal, our bands playing and the men cheering as the ladies wave their handkerchiefs to us.

Saturday, June 20—Last night was very bad on the men in consequence of the heavy rain. Just as my messmate and myself had about fallen asleep the water from the soft and wet ground where our bed was made soaked through our underlying oil cloth and blanket, and through the thick sleeves of my woolen shirt and coat, and reaching my skin thus reminded me of the uncanny condition of things. We at once got up and found it raining a little, but some of the men had already begun to make fires from the rails of a neighboring fence. To one of these fires we repaired and spent the remainder of the night alternately drying and warming one side of our clothes and bodies whilst the other side was getting a fresh wetting from the falling rain.

31

Sunday, June 21—This morning one day's rations of corn bread issued to us. The country through which we are now marching is very beautiful. The lands very fine. The roads are general macadamized roads, made with limestone, which abounds in this region.

[Tuesday,] June 23—Left our camp near Berryville about 12-1/2 P.M., yesterday, passed through Berryville and halted about sunset about three miles from Charlestown, marching 9 miles. Started again this morning soon after daylight, marched through Charlestown and halted a few minutes ago, 11 A.M., at this place, having marched about 12 miles. Berryville is an ugly little place, but Charlestown on the other hand is quite pretty. The ladies of the latter place turned out in large numbers to see us. I scarcely ever before heard such cheering as the boys gave this morning.

Wednesday, June 24.—On Picket near Shepherdstown. Last evening about sunset our regiment was ordered on picket, and is now on duty about 3/4 of a mile east of the point we left, and in the direction of Harper's Ferry. Everything quiet last night. We heard yesterday that Gen. Lee has issued very stringent orders to secure respect for private property when we get into the enemy's country. We are all still utterly ignorant of Gen. Lee's design in making this move, but the army was never in better spirits or more confident of success.[3]

"We Crossed the River in Primitive Style"

Lee's Army Leaves the South Behind and Advances toward Pennsylvania

Preceded by Jenkins's cavalry, troops from Lee's Second Corps began crossing the Potomac River on June 15, followed, over the course of more than a week, by the rest of the army. The bridges spanning the Potomac in the region had been burned earlier in the war, so the Army of Northern Virginia crossed the river at long-standing fords near Williamsport, Maryland, and Shepherdstown, Virginia. Although claimed by the Confederacy, Maryland was firmly secured in the Union by Federal forces, and Lee's troops viewed fording the Potomac into Maryland as symbolically crossing into enemy country. Twenty-eight-year-old Julius Lineback, a musician in the 26th North Carolina Infantry, recorded his regiment's crossing in his personal diary.

June 25th—We made an early start again. Sam still being and I not at all well. The colonel ordered that in the future as we were going into camp, we should play, "The Campbells Are Coming" and "The Girl I Left Behind Me" when leaving. Soon we came to the Potomac River, which was pretty wide and a halfthigh deep. Taking off our shoes, socks, pants and drawers, we made a comical looking set of men. Many did not take the trouble of undressing even partially.

Just as I reached the Maryland side of the river, I stumbled and fell on my knees, doing involuntary homage to the state. When we were again dressed, one of the men asked us to play "Maryland, My Maryland."

For nineteen-year-old Private Thomas Perrett, a soldier in Lineback's regiment, the amusing image of thousands of naked soldiers wading through the

Lee's soldiers doff uniforms and equipment to ford the Potomac River.

Battles and Leaders of the Civil War

This 1863 sketch by artist Alfred Waud depicts troops of Lee's army as they appeared while crossing the Potomac near Williamsport, Maryland.
Library of Congress

river in "primitive style" was not the overwhelming memory he would retain from the event. Instead, what he would never forget was the rough, plaintive chorus of "Maryland, My Maryland" sung by legions of young Southern soldiers as they stepped onto the Maryland shore.

> We marched on to the Potomac near Shepherdstown, where we crossed the river in primitive style and stopped on the Maryland side to adjust deranged apparel and get the Regiment in line. While here in waiting, some soldier boys strike up the song "My Maryland," and by inspiration it is taken up by many voices and sung with much fervor and pathos.
>
> This incident has lingered with me all through long years as the sad memory of a trouble dream. Many of my comrades, companions of my youth, were then looking for the last time upon the receding shores of their beloved Southland, and were marching away to meet a soldier's fate and fill and unmarked grave. As the last song floats away and dies in echo on the bosom of the river, we take up the line of march again....[4]

"Look at Pharaoh's Army Going to the Red Sea"

Lee's Army Encounters a Land of Plenty in Pennsylvania

By June 27, all three corps of Lee's 75,000-man army had crossed the Mason-Dixon Line into Pennsylvania—on Northern soil. "They came in close marching order," a Northern civilian would later remember. "Many were ragged, shoeless, and filthy, [but] all were well-armed and under perfect discipline." Unlike much of war-torn Virginia, the Pennsylvania countryside was green and flourishing as it neared harvest time—"overflowing with wealth & fatness," noted a young Southerner. "Our men have purchased vast numbers of chickens, ducks, pigs, and lots of butter, milk and honey, at Yankee prices," reported another, "paying for them with Confederate money."

As the dust-covered Confederate legions tramped through the small hamlets of south-central Pennsylvania—each "a little one-horse town," in the words of one Southern soldier—they were viewed with a mixture of curiosity, fear, and hostility by Northern civilians. "We find the people here cowed by the presence of our army," one of Lee's soldiers observed. "The men are cringing, cowardly scoundrels and perfect dollar worshippers. Some of the women are spirited and

In this nineteenth century postwar photograph, Pennsylvania farmers near Gettysburg gather their hay harvest much as they did in the summer of 1863.

Library of Congress

Confederate foragers round up horses, cattle, and other livestock in Pennsylvania—paid for with Confederate money.

Leslie's Illustrated

spunky...." One bold Northern woman yelled out at the passing Rebels, "Look at Pharaoh's army going to the Red Sea." Another taunted, "What rags and tatters!" to the passing troops. "Very true, very true," shouted a Southern soldier in response, "but we always put on our worst duds when we start out to butcher"—a reply that caused the female heckler to visibly pale.

"I felt when I first came here, that I would like to revenge myself upon these people for the desolation they have brought upon our own beautiful home," a Confederate officer wrote his wife, "yet I could not find it in my heart to molest them." Horses, mules, cattle, and supplies were officially commandeered for Lee's army in large quantities, but were usually paid for—in Confederate currency or promissory notes. Railroad tracks, bridges, trestles, an ironworks, and other designated military targets were destroyed—largely by Major General Jubal Early's division of advance guard troops, who, at one point, formed a bucket brigade to extinguish fires that had spread to civilian structures. "With the exception of a few instances," a Pennsylvania civilian observed, "private houses were not entered with hostile intent. I must say that from all the conceptions from history of the desolation of an invading army ... this invasion of our State widely differed."

The difference may have been the result of Lee's orders, which commanded his troops to respect private property and maintain discipline in the ranks, and which were generally enforced by his officers. For example, General Order Number 73 stipulated that the Army of Northern Virginia "make war only upon armed men."

Headquarters, Army of Northern Virginia
General Order, No. 73
Chambersburg, Pennsylvania, June 27, 1863

Thirsty Southern soldiers take a break from the march to haul water from a farmhouse well.

National Archives

The commanding general has observed with marked satisfaction the conduct of the troops on the march, and confidently anticipates results commensurate with the high spirit they have manifested. No troops could have displayed greater fortitude or better performed the arduous marches of the past ten days. Their conduct in other respects has with few exceptions been in keeping with their character as soldiers, and entitles them to approbation and praise. There have however been instances of forgetfulness on the part of some, that they have in keeping the yet unsullied reputation of the army, and that the duties expected of us by civilization and Christianity are not less obligatory in the country of the enemy than in our own.

The commanding general considers that no greater disgrace could befall the army, and through it our whole people, than the perpetration of the barbarous outrages upon the unarmed, and defenceless and the wanton destruction of private property that have marked the course of the enemy in our own country. Such proceedings not only degrade the perpetrators and all connected with them, but are subversive of the discipline and efficiency of the army, and destructive of the ends of our present movement.

It must be remembered that we make war only upon armed men, and that we cannot take vengeance for the wrongs our people have suffered without lowering ourselves in the eyes of all whose abhorrence has been excited by the atrocities of our enemies, and offending against Him to whom vengeance belongeth, without whose favor and support our efforts must all prove in vain.

The commanding general therefore earnestly exhorts the troops to abstain with most scrupulous care from unnecessary or wanton injury to private property, and he enjoins upon all officers to arrest and bring to summary punishment all who shall in any way offend against the orders on this subject.

R. E. Lee

General[5]

"He Acts like a Man without a Plan"

General Hooker Resigns Command of the Army of the Potomac

President Lincoln urged General Hooker to attack Lee's army while it was on the march. On June 14, the president sent Hooker a telegram, noting that Lee's army was then stretched from Fredericksburg through the Shenandoah Valley and almost to Maryland—and was surely vulnerable to attack.

In happier times, General Joseph Hooker, seated second from right, posed for a group photograph with his staff prior to his resignation from command. National Archives

"If the head of Lee's army is at Martinsburg and the tail of it on the Plank road between Fredericksburg and Chancellorsville," Lincoln wrote, "the animal must be very slim somewhere. Could you not break him?" Hooker, however, was still unnerved and indecisive from his humiliating defeat by Lee at the Battle of Chancellorsville. "He acts like a man without a plan and is entirely at a loss what to do," one of Hooker's staff confided to his diary. "He knows that Lee is his master & is afraid to meet him in fair battle."

President Abraham Lincoln, summer of 1863.

Library of Congress

Hooker dutifully put the Army of the Potomac on the march, heading northward on a route that shielded Washington, D.C., from attack, but for two weeks he did little more than trail Lee. Fretting that he was outnumbered, he exaggerated the size of Lee's army to more than 100,000 troops. He also grew increasingly resentful to questions and proposals from his immediate superior, General in Chief Henry W. Halleck, and even from President Lincoln. "The nature of the control to be exercised by me I would like to have distinctly and clearly fixed and understood," he grumbled to Halleck at one point.

Finally, on June 27, 1863, after Halleck had advised him to include protection of the Federal garrison at Harpers Ferry in his plans, Hooker peevishly tendered his resignation. Instead of offering reassurances, the General in Chief simply forwarded Hooker's request to President Lincoln, reprinted below.

Sandy Hook, June 27, 1863, 1 p.m.
Major General H.W. Halleck,
General-in-Chief:

My original instructions require me to cover Harper's Ferry and Washington. I have now imposed upon me, in addition, an enemy in my front of more than my numbers. I beg to be understood, respectfully but firmly, that I am unable to comply with this condition, with the means at my disposal, and earnestly request that I may at once be relieved from the position I occupy.

Joseph Hooker,
Major-General.

Washington, D.C.,
June 27, 1863, 8 p.m.
Major General Hooker,
Army of the Potomac:

Your application to be relieved from your present command is received. As you were appointed to this command by the President, I have no power to relieve you. Your dispatch has been duly referred for Executive action.

H.W. Halleck,
General-in-Chief[6]

"Meade Will Fight Well on His Own Dunghill"

The Army of the Potomac Gets a New Commander

President Lincoln quickly relieved General Hooker of command, acting within hours of receiving the general's request. He worried aloud about changing commanders on the eve of what was certain to be a major battle. "While crossing a stream," he observed, "it is too late to change horses." He considered Hooker to be "a beaten general," however, and seized the opportunity to remove him as army commander. But who could he name as a replacement? Including Hooker, three high-ranking officers now had been appointed—and removed—as heads of the Army of the Potomac.

Several officers were considered, but Lincoln settled on Major General George Gordon Meade, a bewhiskered, balding forty-seven-year-old corps commander. A West Pointer who had served in the Seminole and Mexican Wars, Meade was not a standout leader or a particularly original commander, but he was experienced, capable, and disciplined. He had been seriously wounded in the Peninsula Campaign the previous summer, but he had recovered sufficiently enough to hold important commands at Fredericksburg and at Chancellorsville. Furthermore, the Army of the Potomac faced imminent battle in Pennsylvania—the general's home state. Meade, Lincoln predicted, "will fight well on his own dunghill."

Although typically reserved in nature, Meade had a white-hot temper when under pressure. "I have seen him so cross and ugly that no one dared speak to him," one of his staff officers confided, and his troops referred to him as "a damned old goggle-eyed snapping turtle." The official news of his promotion reached Meade at his corps headquarters tent in the middle of the night. When the officer bearing it awakened him, Meade actually thought he was being removed from command for some unbeknownst reason. Upon learning that he had received a promotion, he initially argued that he was not the best choice for the position. Finally, he agreed to take the command—with reluctance. "Well," he stated, "I've been tried and condemned without a hearing, and I suppose I shall have to go to the execution." On June 28, 1863, he issued his first order as commander of the Army of the Potomac.

Normally quiet and reserved, General George Meade could at times exhibit the temper that earned him the reputation of a "damned old goggle-eyed snapping turtle."
Library of Congress

Headquarters of the Army of the Potomac
General Order, No. 66
June 28, 1863

By direction of the President of the United States, I hereby assume the command of the Army of the Potomac. As a soldier, in obeying

Posed before his headquarters tent in polished, knee-high boots, General Meade called Pennsylvania his home, prompting President Lincoln to speculate that Meade would "fight well on his own dunghill."

National Archives

this order, an order totally unexpected and unsolicited, I have no promises or pledges to make.

The country looks to this army to relieve it from the devastation and disgrace of a hostile invasion. Whatever fatigues and sacrifices we may be called upon to undergo, let us have in view constantly the magnitude of the interests involved, and let each man determine to do his duty, leaving to an all-controlling Providence the decision of the contest.

It is with just diffidence that I relieve, in the command of this army, an eminent and accomplished soldier, whose name must ever appear conspicuous in the history of its achievements; but I rely upon the hearty support of my companions in arms to assist me in the discharge of the duties of the important trust which has been confided to me.

George G. Meade,
Maj.-Gen. Commanding.[7]

"We Endure the Fatigues of the March Well"

The Army of the Potomac Moves to Overtake the Enemy

On his first day as army commander, General Meade received confirmation that the bulk of Lee's army had crossed into Pennsylvania. Where was Lee heading? Harrisburg? Philadelphia? Or, would he turn and advance on Baltimore or even on Washington? Meade took immediate action. He organized his new staff and gave orders to get the full army moving toward Pennsylvania in pursuit of Lee's forces. He also dispatched the provost guard and a force of cavalry to Frederick, Maryland—twenty-five miles below the Pennsylvania border. There, a lapse in military discipline had turned the army's advance guard loose in the town bars, resulting in scores of soldiers "lying about the streets, on the doorsteps, under fences, in the mud, dead drunk...."

The next morning, June 29, 1863, the Army of the Potomac was on the march, moving northward despite rain showers and muddy roads that slowed progress. As he pushed to overtake the invading Confederates and shield Washington, D.C., Meade's no-nonsense discipline reduced drinking, looting, and straggling within the army. His plan was to put the army in a position to block the Confederate advance across Pennsylvania while safeguarding Washington. "My endeavor will be in my movements to hold my force well together," he telegraphed General in Chief Halleck, "with the hope of falling upon some portion of Lee's army in detail."

As they advanced northward across Maryland toward Pennsylvania, Meade's army troops appeared to be in "fine spirits." Among their ranks was Captain Samuel W. Fiske of the 14th Connecticut Infantry, who recorded an account of the Federal march.

Twenty-two-year-old Charles Wellington Reed, a soldier in the 9th Massachusetts Light Artillery Battery, sketched the troops of the Army of the Potomac on their march to overtake Lee's army.

There is a deal of romance about this business of war. We lay us down at night under heaven's glorious canopy, not knowing if at any moment the call to arms may disturb our slumbers. We wake at réveille, cook and eat our scanty breakfast, thankful if we have any to dispose of in that way. At the bugle-call, we strike tents, put on our harness and packs, and start off, not knowing our direction, the object of our march, or its extent; taking every thing on trust, and enjoying as much as possible the varied experience of each passing hour; and ready for a pic-nic or a fray, a bivouac, a skirmish, a picket, a reconnoissance, or a movement in retreat.

There is no life in which there is more room for the exercise of faith than in this same soldierly life of ours,—faith in our own good right arms, and in the joint strength and confidence of military discipline; faith in the experience and watchfulness of our tried commanders (happy if they be not tried and found wanting); faith in the ultimate success of our country's good and holy cause; faith in the overruling care and protection of Almighty Jehovah, who holdeth the movements of armies and nations, as also the smallest concerns of private individuals, in his hand.

Our marches for the last few days have been through the most lovely country, across the State of Maryland to the east of Frederick City. There is not a finer cultivated scenery in the whole world, it

*seems to me; and it was almost like getting to Paradise from—
another place; the getting-out of abominable, barren, ravaged Old
Virginia, into fertile, smiling Maryland. It is a cruel thing to roll the
terrible wave of war over such a scene of peace, plenty, and fruitful-
ness; but it may be that here on our own soil, and in these last
sacrifices and efforts, the great struggle for the salvation of our
country and our Union may successfully terminate.*

*Poor Old Virginia is so bare and desolate as to be only fit for a
battle-ground; but it seems that we must take our turn too, in the
Northern States, of invasion, and learn something of the practical
meaning of war in our own peaceful communities. I sincerely hope
that the scare up in Pennsylvania isn't going to drive all the people's
wits away, and prevent them from making a brave defense of homes,
altars, and hearths.*

*When I read in a paper, today, of the "chief burgess" of York
pushing out eight or ten miles into the country to find somebody to
surrender the city to, I own to have entertained some doubts as to
the worthiness and valor of that representative of the dignity of the
city. It would be well for the citizens of Pennsylvania to remember
that Lee's soldiers are only men, after all, and that their number is
not absolutely limitless, and that they have not really the power of
being in a great many places at the same time....*

*Our boys come back out of Pennsylvania with no very exalted
opinion of the German inhabitants of that portion of the State we
visited, or of the German regiments in our army of defenders. The
people seem to be utterly apathetic as to our great national struggle, and careless of every thing but their own property. If each old
farmer's henroost and cabbage-patch could only be safe, little
would he care for the fate of the country, or the success of our
army....*

*We of the unfortunate "grand army," to be sure, haven't much
reason to make large promises; but we are going to put ourselves
again in the way of the Butternuts, and have great hopes of*

retrieving, on our own ground, our ill fortune in the last two engagements, and, by another and still more successful Antietam conflict, deserve well of our country. Our troops are making tremendous marches some of these days just past; and, if the enemy is anywhere, we shall be likely to find him and feel of him pretty soon. For sixteen days we have been on the move, and endure the fatigues of the march well.

There is much less straggling, and much less pillaging, than in any march of the troops that I have yet accompanied. Our men are now veterans, and acquainted with the ways and resources of campaigning. There are very few sick among us. The efficient strength, in proportion to our numbers, is vastly greater than when we were green volunteers. So the Potomac Army, reduced greatly in numbers as it has been by the expiration of the term of service of so many regiments, is still a very numerous and formidable army.[8]

By summer of 1863, the Army of the Potomac was composed largely of veterans "acquainted with the ways and resources of campaigning."

National Archives

"Should Any Person Find This Body"

Troops on Both Sides Prepare for What Lies Ahead

Most soldiers in both armies were combat veterans—they had "seen the elephant," as initiation to combat was called. By the time they neared Gettysburg, most realized a major battle was likely. "June 30 finds us at Cashtown, Penn.," a Southern soldier noted in his journal. "Here we hourly expect a fight. The enemy being near." With battle believed to be imminent, they prepared themselves, checking their consciences as well as their weapons. As he approached Gettysburg in a column of marching troops, one soldier noticed how the road beneath his feet was littered with playing cards. They had apparently been discarded by repentant troops. The road to war, he concluded, was paved with upturned faces—kings, queens, jacks, and jokers. Another soldier noticed the serious expressions on the faces of his fellow troops and realized it was the look of "men who are about to face death."

In this sketch by *Harper's Weekly* combat artist Alfred Waud, troops of the Army of the Potomac pack up and prepare to resume the march. Both armies were composed of combat veterans, and most realized what lay ahead.

Library of Congress

A common practice for a soldier heading into battle was to attach a scrap of paper bearing his name as well as the name and address of his next of kin to his uniform. Twenty-four-year-old Matthew Marvin, a sergeant in the 1st Minnesota Infantry, prepared for battle by folding up a wad of U.S. currency and tucking it into his leather-bound pocket diary. Then, on the diary's inside front cover, he penciled this plea, offering to pay the stranger who found his body if he would notify Marvin's parents of his death.

Gettyiesburg Pa

Should any person find this on the body of a soldier on the field of battle or by the roadside they will confer a lasting favor on the parents of its owner by sending the book & pocket purse & silver finger ring on the left hand. Taking their pay for the trouble out of the Greenbacks herein inclosed.

Mat

To Seth Marvin, Esq, St. Charles, Kane Co. Ill.[9]

Although his regiment would suffer horrible casualties at Gettysburg, Sergeant Marvin would survive—along with the message he intended as a post-mortem plea for help.

CHAPTER THREE

"Into the Jaws of the Enemy"

eneral Lee had a serious problem: most of his cavalry was missing. It was Sunday, June 28, 1863, and otherwise the invasion appeared to be progressing as Lee had hoped. Out in front, the army's Second Corps under Lieutenant General Ewell was spread out across Pennsylvania in two columns: Major General Jubal Early's division had passed through the city of York and was nearing the Susquehanna River, while Ewell and the rest of his corps approached Harrisburg—which Lee had ordered him to capture. In Harrisburg, state employees hurriedly packed up official records, while panicky refugees crowded city streets with overloaded wagons—brimming with "beddings, tables, chairs, their wives and children perched on the top; kettles and pails dangling beneath." In faraway Philadelphia, scores of worried citizens frantically dug earthworks, while to the south in Baltimore, city authorities had ordered all black residents— both free and slave—to go to working digging defensive trenches.

Meanwhile, Lee had established his tent headquarters in a grove of trees just east of Chambersburg, Pennsylvania. There, and at the village of Cashtown farther to the east, he had concentrated the bulk of his army. He planned to

Major General J. E. B.
Stuart leads his
Confederate cavalry
on a raid.

Library of Congress

move the army's other two corps across Pennsylvania to join Ewell's troops at Harrisburg. Since crossing the Potomac, however, he had not heard from General J. E. B. Stuart and the army's cavalry. Without scouting reports from his cavalry, Lee had no reliable intelligence on the location and strength of Federal forces.

Finally, on Sunday night, a reconnaissance report arrived. A mysterious figure was escorted to Lee's headquarters tent—a civilian spy named James Harrison, who had been hired by General Longstreet. Through Harrison, Lee learned that the Army of the Potomac was trailing the Confederate army into Pennsylvania, and that General Hooker had been replaced by General Meade. Lee knew of the new commander and respected him. "General Meade will commit no blunder in my front," he commented, "and if I make one will make haste to take advantage of it."

The new information proved extremely valuable, but what would Lee do to obtain reconnaissance tomorrow—depend on a single spy? Without Stuart and the cavalry, the eyes of the army, it was as if Lee's troops were marching blindly through enemy country.[1]

"We Rode, Rode, Rode"

General Stuart Leads Lee's "Lost" Cavalry on a Grand Raid

While Lee suffered from the absence of reliable intelligence, Major General J. E. B. Stuart was leading the bulk of the army's cavalry on a grand raid around the rear of the Federal army. At age thirty, James Ewell Brown Stuart—nicknamed "Jeb" for his initials—was bright, energetic, and flamboyant. A red-bearded West Pointer from Virginia, he had fought Indians in prewar

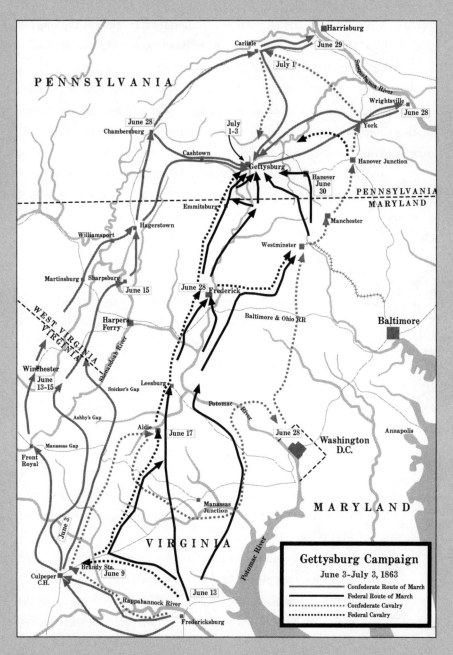

In June of 1863, the Army of Northern Virginia slipped away from
its lines near Fredericksburg, Virginia, and marched northward toward
Pennsylvania—trailed to the east by the Army of the Potomac.

Based on a map by Hal Jespersen,
www.CWmaps.com

Kansas—where he had married the post commander's daughter—and sported thigh-high cavalry boots, a yellow sash, a red-lined cape, and a plumed hat.

A brilliant cavalry commander, he had experienced a meteoritic rise in Confederate service from lieutenant colonel to major general and commander of Lee's 10,000-man cavalry division—all in the course of a single year. Under Stuart's direction, the cavalry had become an invaluable asset to Lee's army. Stuart had distinguished himself in the Seven Days Battles, at Second Bull Run, and at Chancellorsville, where he had discovered the weaknesses in Hooker's troop dispositions that had led to the humiliating Federal defeat. His greatest fame arose from a series of bold raids he had conducted, including two in which he had led his cavalry entirely around the Army of the Potomac while it was under General McClellan's command.

Lee relied on Stuart's cavalry as the eyes of his army, and looked upon the young officer with almost father-like affection. "I can scarcely think of him without weeping," he would say after Stuart was killed in action in 1864. At the Battle of Brandy Station, Stuart had been taken by surprise by the enemy attack, leaving him embarrassed and highly motivated to restore his reputation. On June 25, 1863, Stuart set out with his cavalry on a raid around the rear of the Federal army. It was the kind of spectacular ride that had earned him glory in the past. He rode from Virginia through Maryland and deep into Pennsylvania, before Lee's summons to rejoin the army reached him at Carlisle.

The raid captured more than a hundred enemy wagons laden with supplies and took more than 400 prisoners, but it deprived Lee of critically needed cavalry protection and intelligence on the eve of battle. It was—in the words of a Lee aide— merely "a useless, showy parade." Captain John Esten Cooke, Stuart's chief of ordnance and a novelist-turned-soldier, recorded a colorful account of Stuart's controversial raid.

Major General J. E. B. Stuart, the commander of Lee's cavalry, here poses for a photograph attired in his customary uniform, which includes a red-lined cape, a yellow sash, thigh-high cavalry boots, and a plumed hat.

Library of Congress

When Lee's army advanced into Pennsylvania, Stuart took the army's cavalry on a raid around the vanguard of the Federal army, leaving Lee without reliable reconnaissance.

Battles and Leaders of the Civil War

"Ho! for the Valley!" There could certainly be no doubt about the General's meaning. He had turned his horse toward the Ridge. "Ho! for the Valley!" indicated his intended line of march; he, like myself, was going to see his good friends all in that land of lands along the Shenandoah.... General Stuart had scarcely got out of sight of the village, when he was riding rapidly eastward, in a direction precisely opposite to the Blue Ridge. The General had practised a little ruse to blind the eyes of the Cross-Roads villagers—was doubling on the track; he was going after General Hooker, then in the vicinity of Manassas, and thence—whither?

We bivouacked by the roadside under some pines that night.... The bugle sounded; we got into the saddle again; the columns moved; and that evening we had passed around Manassas, where Hooker's rear force still lingered, and were approaching Fairfax Station through the great deserted camps near Wolf Run Shoals. The advance pushed on through the wild and desolate locality, swarming with abandoned cabins and army débris; and soon we had reached the station, which is not far from the [Fairfax]

Court-House.... It was impossible to forbear from laughing at the spectacle which the cavalry column presented. Every man had on a white straw hat, and a pair of snowy cotton gloves. Every trooper carried before him upon the pommel of his saddle a bale of smoking tobacco, or a drum of figs; every hand grasped a pile of ginger-cakes....

Soon the column was again moving steadily towards the Potomac.... We reached at nightfall an elevation not far from the Great Falls.... The broad river glittered in the moon, and on the bright surface was seen the long, wavering line of dark figures, moving "in single file;" the water washing to and fro across the backs of the horses, which kept their feet with difficulty. The hardest portion of the task was crossing the cannon of the horse-artillery. It seemed impossible to get the limbers and caissons over without wetting, and so destroying the ammunition; but the ready brain of Stuart found an expedient. The boxes were quickly unpacked; every cavalry-man took charge of a shell, case, or solid shot with the fixed cartridge; and thus held well aloft, the precious freight was carried over dry.... The river was crossed; also the Chesapeake and Ohio canal, by a narrow bridge; and the cavalry halted for brief rest....

The column moved at dawn toward the "undiscovered land" of Star-and-Stripe-dom, in a northern direction toward Rockville, [Maryland]. It was not long before we came on the blue people. "Bang! bang! bang!" indicated that the advance guard was charging a picket; the shots ended; we pushed on, passing some dead or wounded forms, bleeding by the grassy roadside; and the town of Rockville came in sight. The present writer pushed on after the advance guard, which had galloped through, and riding solus

With an Adams revolver tucked in his belt and a sword at the ready, farmboy David Thatcher, nineteen, projects a formidable image as a private in the 1st Virginia Cavalry—which went to Gettysburg with J. E. B. Stuart.

along a handsome street, came suddenly upon a spectacle which was truly pleasing. This was a seminary for young ladies, with open windows, open doors—and doors and windows were full and running over with the fairest specimens of the gentler sex that eye ever beheld. It was Sunday, and the beautiful girls in their fresh gaily colored dresses, low necks, bare arms, and wildernesses of braids and curls, were "off duty" for the moment, and burning with enthusiasm to welcome the Southerner....

Stuart did not tarry. In war there is little time for gallant words, and news had just reached us from the front which moved the column on like the sound of the bugle. This news was that while we approached Rockville from the south, a mighty train of nearly two hundred [Federal] wagons—new, fresh-painted, drawn each by six sleek mules, as became the "Reserve Forage Train" of the Department at Washington—had in like manner approached from the east, intent on collecting forage. Stuart's face flushed at the thought of capturing this splendid prize; and shouting to a squadron to follow him and the main column to push on, he went at a swift gallop on the track of the fleeing wagons.... The immense train was seen covering the road for miles. Every team in full gallop, every wagon whirling onward, rebounding from rocks, and darting into the air,—one crashing against another "with the noise of thunder"....

Stuart burst into laughter, and turning round, exclaimed: "Did you ever see anything like that in all your life!" ... Soon they were all stopped, captured, and driven to the rear by the aforesaid cursing drivers, now sullen, or laughing like the captors. All but those overturned. These were set on fire, and soon there rose for miles along the road the red glare of flames, and the dense smoke of the burning vehicles. They had been pursued within sight of Washington, and I saw, I believe, the dome of the capitol. That spectacle was exciting—and General Stuart thought of pushing on to make a demonstration against the defences. This, however, was given up; and between the flames of the burning wagons we pushed back to Rockville, through which the long line of captured vehicles, with their sleek, rosetted mules, six to each, had already defiled, amid the shouts of the inhabitants. Those thus "saved" were about one hundred in number.

The column moved, and about ten that night reached Brookville, where the atmosphere seemed Southern, like that of Rockville, for a bevy of beautiful girls thronged forth with baskets of cakes, and bread and meat, and huge pitchers of ice-water.... At Brookville some hundreds of prisoners—the greater part captured by General Wickham in a boat at the Potomac—were paroled and started for Washington, as an act of humanity.... Moving steadily on, the column approached Westminster, and here Fitz Lee, who was in advance, found the enemy drawn up in the street. A charge quickly followed, carbines banged, and the enemy gave way.... The net results of the capture of the place were—one old dismounted gun of the "Quaker" order on a hill near the cavalry camp aforesaid, and a United States flag taken from the vault of the Court-House....

We left the town that night, bivouacked in the rain by the roadside, pushed on at dawn, and were soon in Pennsylvania.... We were enemies here, but woman, the angelic, still succoured us; woman, without shoes or stockings often, and speaking Dutch, but no less hospitable. One of them presented me with coffee, bread spread with "apple-butter"—and smiles.... The horses were appropriated; but beyond that nothing—the very necks of the chickens went unwrung.... As we approached Hanovertown, we stirred up the hornets.... The enemy, who were drawn up in the outskirts of the town.... A heavy line was seen advancing, and soon this line pushed on with cheers to charge the artillery on the heights.... Breathed's fire, however, repulsed the charge; and as night drew on, Stuart set his column in motion....

We rode, rode, rode—the long train of wagons strung out to infinity, it seemed.... At daylight we reached the straggling little village of Dover, where more prisoners were paroled; thence proceeded through a fine country ... and at night reached [the Federal army post at] Carlisle, which General Stuart immediately summoned to surrender by flag of truce. The reply to this was a flat refusal from General Smith; and soon a Whitworth gun in the town opened, and the Southern guns replied. This continued for an hour or two, when the U. S. barracks were fired, and the light fell magnificently upon the spires of the city, presenting an exquisite spectacle....

Any further assault upon Carlisle was stopped by a very simple circumstance. General Lee sent for the cavalry. He had recalled Early from York; moved with his main column east of the South Mountain, toward the village of Gettysburg; and Stuart was wanted.[2]

"Into the Jaws of the Enemy"
A Confrontation Develops at Gettysburg

On Monday morning, June 30, General Lee issued new orders from his headquarters in Chambersburg. Now aware of the Federal army's general location, Lee revised his strategy. No longer did he plan to move on Harrisburg, fight a battle somewhere nearby, or move against Washington or Philadelphia. His new strategy involved positioning his army on General Meade's route of march and forcing a confrontation shortly thereafter—to fight the major battle on Northern soil that he sought. He dispatched couriers to recall Ewell's corps from Harrisburg and the Susquehanna River back to the Chambersburg-Cashtown area. Without cavalry reconnaissance, Lee was unsure exactly where the opposing armies would collide, but he believed the battle would be fought near York, or, more likely, to the east of Cashtown near

On June 30, 1863, General Henry Heth sent Confederate troops through the village of Cashtown toward Gettysburg, looking for shoes and Federal troops. They encountered none of the former, but plenty of the latter.

Library of Congress

the crossroads town of Gettysburg. "To-morrow, gentlemen," he told his staff officers on Monday, "we will not move to Harrisburg as we expected, but will go over to Gettysburg and see what General Meade is after."

Meanwhile, Brigadier General James J. Pettigrew, a brigade commander in General A. P. Hill's Third Corps, set out on a reconnaissance-in-force from Cashtown to Gettysburg under orders from his division commander, Major General Henry Heth—who had directed him to "search the town for army supplies (shoes especially)." Composed of several infantry regiments, a battery of field artillery, and a small train of wagons, Pettigrew's troops advanced on Gettysburg from the west, along the Chambersburg Turnpike—until they sighted Federal cavalry just outside of town.

Pettigrew called in his skirmishers and fell back to Cashtown, where he reported the presence of enemy troops in Gettysburg. General Heth forwarded the report to General Hill, but both officers dismissed Pettigrew's account. They concluded that the blue-uniformed force of troops seen by Pettigrew was a local home guard unit or just a wandering cavalry patrol—but was *not* the advance guard of the Army of the Potomac. As part of the concentration of Lee's army, General Hill's corps was scheduled to march to Gettysburg the following day, so Hill ordered Heth and his division to lead the way. Heth, in turn, issued orders for Brigadier General James J. Archer and his brigade to head up the march to Gettysburg the next day—July 1, 1863.

First Lieutenant Louis G. Young, an aide to General Pettigrew, had accompanied the reconnaissance to Gettysburg and was alarmed at the apparent "spirit of disbelief" that led Generals Heth and Hill to disregard Pettigrew's warning. The Northern cavalry sighted at Gettysburg was the spearhead of the Army of the Potomac, Young believed, and he feared that the "blindness" of his superiors would cause Lee's army to stumble unprepared into "the jaws of the enemy." Young later transcribed an account of the day's events.

———————————

Hill's Corps had arrived at Cashtown, about eight miles west of Gettysburg, on 29 June. On the following morning General Pettigrew was ordered by General Heth, his division commander, to go to Gettysburg with three of his four regiments present, three field pieces of the Donaldsonville Artillery, of Louisiana, and a number of wagons, for the purpose of collecting commissary and quartermaster stores for the use of the army. General Early had levied on Carlisle, Chambersburg and Shippensburg, and had found no difficulty in having his requisitions filled. It was supposed that it would be the same at Gettysburg. It was told to General Pettigrew that he might find the town in possession of a home guard, which he would have no difficulty in driving away; but if, contrary to expectations, he should find any organized troops capable of making resistance, or any portion of the Army of the Potomac, he should not attack it. The orders to him were peremptory, not to precipitate a fight. General Lee with his columns scattered, and lacking the information of his adversary, which he should have had from his cavalry, was not ready for battle—hence the orders.

On the march to Gettysburg we were passed by General Longstreet's spy who quickly returned and informed General Pettigrew

that [Brigadier General John] Buford's Division of [Federal] cavalry—estimated at three thousand strong—had arrived that day
and were holding the town. This report was confirmed by a Knight
of the Golden Circle who came out for the purpose of giving us
warning. Buford's presence made it evident that the Army of the
Potomac, or at least a portion of it, was not far off, and General
Pettigrew sent immediately to General Heth, a report of what he
had learned and asked for further instructions. The message
received in reply, was simply a repetition of the orders previously
given coupled with an expression of disbelief as to the presence of
any portion of the Army of the Potomac.

As the presence of Buford's Cavalry was certain, and it would
not be possible for him to enter Gettysburg without a fight, which
he was forbidden to make, General Pettigrew withdrew from before
Gettysburg. This he did, not as was reported to General Lee,
"because he was not willing to hazard an attack with the single
brigade," (he had only three regiments of his brigade) ... General
Pettigrew was willing to make the attack had not his orders forbidden it. Buford's Cavalry followed us at some distance, and Lieutenant Walter H. Robertson and I, of Pettigrew's staff, remained in the
rear to watch it. This we easily did, for the country is rolling, and
from behind the ridges we could see without being seen and we had
a perfect view of the movements of the approaching column. Whenever it would come within three or four hundred yards of us we
would make our appearance, mounted, and the column would halt
until we retired. This was repeated several times. It was purely an
affair of observation on both sides and the cavalry made no effort
to molest us....

Blindness in part seemed to have come over our commanders,
who, slow to believe in the presence of an organized army of the
enemy, thought there must be a mistake in the report taken back
by General Pettigrew, but General Heth asked for and obtained

The Chambersburg Turnpike approached Gettysburg from the west over a series of ridges. Here, on this side of town, the battle of Gettysburg would be ignited when advance elements of the opposing armies clashed with each other.

National Archives

permission to take his division to Gettysburg on the following day, for the purpose of reconnoitering, and of making the levy which had been the object of the expedition on the day before. Neither General Heth nor General Hill believed in the presence of the enemy in force, and they expressed their doubts so positively to General Pettigrew that I was called up to tell General Hill what I had seen while reconnoitering the movements of the force which had followed us from Gettysburg. As a staff officer with General Pender, I had served under General Hill in the seven days fights around Richmond and at Cedar Run, and because I was well known to General Hill, General Pettigrew supposed that my report might have some weight with him.

Yet, when in answer to his inquiry as to the character of the column I had watched I said their movements were undoubtedly those of well-trained troops and not those of a home guard, he replied that he still could not believe that any portion of the Army of the Potomac was up; and in emphatic words, expressed the hope that it was, as this was the place he wanted it to be. This spirit of unbelief had taken such hold, that I doubt if any of the commanders of brigades, except General Pettigrew, believed that we were marching to battle, a weakness on their part which rendered them unprepared for what was about to happen.

General Archer with his Tennessee Brigade, was to lead, and General Pettigrew described to him minutely the topography of the country between Cashtown and Gettysburg, and suggested that he look out for a road that ran at right angles to the one we were on, and which might be used by the enemy to break into his line of march. And, as he had carefully observed the configuration of the ground in the vicinity of the town, told General Archer of a ridge some distance out of Gettysburg on which he would probably find the enemy, as this position was favorable for defense.

General Archer listened, but believed not, marched on unprepared, and was taken by surprise.... For want of faith in what had been told, and a consequent lack of caution, the two leading brigades of Heth's Division marched into the jaws of the enemy, met with disaster, and, contrary to General Lee's wish, brought on an engagement with the Army of the Potomac before we were ready, and precipitated one of the greatest battles of modern times.[3]

"Union Cavalry Began to Arrive in the Town"

Gettysburg Attracts the Opposing Armies like a Magnet

General George Meade and much of the Federal army were still on the march in Maryland on June 30. Meade had hoped to establish a defensive position along Pipe Creek near the Maryland village of Taneytown, and to draw Lee into battle there. Instead, like Lee, his strategy changed. Now, on the last day of June, he planned to advance the Army of the Potomac into Pennsylvania,

Federal cavalry
stir up dust on a
Pennsylvania road.
On June 30, the Army
of the Potomac's 1st
Cavalry Division
reached Gettysburg.

*Battles and Leaders
of the Civil War*

searching for the Confederate army while moving toward Harrisburg. He had put the left wing of the army under the command of Major General John Reynolds, with orders to advance toward Gettysburg and its network of roads. Reynolds led his three corps into Pennsylvania on the thirtieth.

Commanded by Brigadier General John Buford, the army's 1st Cavalry Division, scouting in advance of Reynolds's force, reached Gettysburg on the afternoon of June 30. Several days before, General Early's Confederates had passed through the town on their journey eastward—stopping long enough to empty many shelves in the town's stores—and now Gettysburg's residents feared the arrival of more Southern troops. Seeing scores of blue-uniformed horsemen on their streets brought welcome relief to most of Gettysburg's residents, who cheered the passing columns. One who watched the procession with excitement was a fifteen-year-old girl named Tillie Pierce Alleman, who would never forget the day the Northern army arrived in her town.

---

*A little before noon on Tuesday, June 30th, a great number of
Union cavalry began to arrive in the town. They passed northwardly along Washington Street, turned toward the west on*

On June 30, a dusty column of Federal horse soldiers— Buford's Cavalry— passed through this Gettysburg neighborhood, heading to the west in search of the Confederate army.

National Archives

reaching Chambersburg Street, and passed out in the direction of the Theological Seminary.

It was to me a novel and grand sight. I had never seen so many soldiers at one time. They were Union soldiers and that was enough for me, for I then knew we had protection, and I felt they were our dearest friends. I afterwards learned that these men were Buford's cavalry, numbering about six thousand men.

A crowd of "us girls" were standing on the corner of Washington and High Streets as these soldiers passed by. Desiring to encourage them, who, as we were told, would before long be in battle, my sister started to sing the old war song, "Our Union Forever." As some of us did not know the whole of the piece we kept repeating the chorus.

Thus we sought to cheer our brave men; and we felt amply repaid when we saw that our efforts were appreciated. Their countenances brightened and we received their thanks and cheers. After the battle some of these soldiers told us that the singing was very good, but that they would have liked to have heard more than the chorus.

The movements of this day in addition to what we beheld a few days previous, told plainly that some great military event was coming pretty close to us. The town was all astir and every one was anxious. Thus in the midst of great excitement and solicitude the day passed. As we lay down for the night, little did we think what the morrow would bring forth.[4]

"You Will Have to Fight like the Devil"
General Buford's Federal Cavalry Claims the High Ground at Gettysburg

Brigadier General John Buford was only thirty-seven years old when he led his cavalry division into Gettysburg, yet his troops called him "Old Steadfast." The nickname came from Buford's dependability and calm demeanor under fire. Born in Kentucky and raised in Illinois, Buford was the latest in a line of family members serving in the military, including a grandfather who had fought in the Revolution under cavalry commander "Light Horse Harry" Lee—Robert E. Lee's father. A West Point graduate, Buford had been forged and hardened by fighting the Sioux, Comanche, and Apache on the Western frontier. His family owned slaves and his cousin was a Confederate general, but Buford had cast his lot with the Union. En route to Gettysburg, he had hanged a suspected Southern spy from a roadside tree—leaving the man's naked corpse swinging from a tree limb.

He had begun the war posted at a desk in Washington, but he earned a brigadier's commission and distinguished himself at the Battle of Second Bull Run, where he was wounded and mistakenly reported as killed in action. Unlike "Jeb" Stuart, he had no inclination to be a dashing cavalier. Tough, seasoned, and capable, he received command of a cavalry brigade, further displayed his competence at Chancellorsville, and achieved promotion to division command.

Described by a contemporary as "the soldier, par excellence," Buford had the ability to comprehend critical military situations, and had a knack for recognizing the advantages of different terrain.

When some of his patrolling cavalry sighted General Pettigrew's Confederates while on their reconnaissance-in-force on June 30, Buford did not delude himself with any "spirit of unbelief." Instead, he immediately notified his superiors that the Confederate army was in the vicinity of Gettysburg, and provided a precise, pinpointed location of the enemy—a tactical advantage Lee desperately wanted yet still lacked. And so the Federal Army of the Potomac hastened toward Gettysburg on a collision course with the Confederate Army of Northern Virginia.

Tough, seasoned, and savvy, Brigadier General John Buford immediately spotted the defensive advantages that Gettysburg's terrain offered the Federal army. He also understood what lay ahead: "You will have to fight like the devil," he told his troops.

Library of Congress

Equally important, Buford grasped the opportunities offered by the terrain surrounding Gettysburg. To protect Gettysburg's critically important intersecting roads, he posted dismounted cavalry armed with rapid-fire carbines on the west side of town—the direction from which he expected Lee's army to advance. There, a series of high ridges—Herr Ridge, McPherson's Ridge, and Seminary Ridge—offered good ground for defense. In town, Cemetery Hill and adjacent Cemetery Ridge, which extended a mile or so southward, offered a strong fallback position if needed.

On the ridges to the west of Gettysburg, facing Cashtown and Chambersburg, Buford chose to make a stand. Gettysburg, he believed, would be the location of the great battle that was certain to occur soon. "The enemy must know the importance of this point and will strain every nerve to secure it," he told a subordinate that day, "and if we are able to hold it we will do well." Lieutenant Aaron Jerome, a young Signal Corps officer attached to Buford's cavalry, accompanied Buford to Gettysburg on June 30, and penned an account of Buford's critical actions that day.

Gettysburg's
Lutheran Seminary
towers above the tree
line in this 1863
photograph.
In order to scout
the advancing
Confederate army,
General Buford
scaled its cupola.

Library of Congress

Buford marched into Gettysburg with his division on the afternoon of June 30th, and, passing through the town, [Colonel William] Gamble's Brigade encamped on the Cashtown road, while [Colonel Thomas] Devin's Brigade encamped on the road to Mummasburg. Gamble scouted toward Chambersburg, while Devin scouted the country toward Carlisle as far as Hunterstown, capturing a number of Rebel stragglers, from whom important information was elicited. On the night of the 30th, General Buford spent some hours with Colonel Tom Devin, and while commenting upon the information brought in by Devin's scouts, remarked that "the battle would be fought at that point," and that "he was afraid it would be commenced in the morning before the infantry would get up." These are his own words. Devin did not believe in so early an advance of the enemy, and remarked that he would "take care of all that would attack his front during the ensuing twenty-four hours." Buford answered: "No you won't. They will attack you in the morning and

With their horses held in the rear, Buford's cavalrymen fought on foot, using their breech-loading, rapid-fire carbines to slow the Confederate advance until the Federal army could arrive in force.

Battles and Leaders of the Civil War

they will come booming—skirmishers three deep. You will have to fight like the devil to hold your own until supports arrive. The enemy must know the importance of this position and will strain every nerve to secure it, and if we are able to hold it we will do well."

Upon his return, he ordered me, then first lieutenant and signal officer of his division, to seek out the most prominent points and watch everything; to be careful to look out for camp-fires, and in the morning for dust. He seemed anxious, more so than I ever saw him.[5]

"I Was Ignorant of What Force Was at or near Gettysburg"

The Opposing Armies Collide at Gettysburg on July 1

On the morning of Wednesday, July 1, 1863, General Henry Heth took his division to Gettysburg, marching along the Chambersburg Turnpike from the division's encampment near Cashtown. Heth had requested to lead General A. P. Hill's Third Corps on its march toward Gettysburg, claiming that he hoped to find footwear for his troops in town. "If there is no objection," he had told Hill, "then I will take my division tomorrow and go to Gettysburg and get those shoes." Hill had agreed, but had reminded Heth of General Lee's orders not to provoke battle with the enemy until all of Lee's army was reunited. "Do not bring on an engagement," Hill had warned Heth.

General Heth, new to division command, was an affable thirty-seven-year-old Virginian—known to his friends as "Harry"—and had graduated last in his class at West Point. As a captain in the prewar U.S. Army, he had fought Indians on the Western frontier, and he had quickly earned a brigadier's commission in Confederate service. He had commanded his brigade capably at Chancellorsville, and now he held a new post as commander of one of the three divisions in Hill's corps. Some viewed him as courageous; others saw him as impulsive.

On the road to Gettysburg, Heth's powerful reconnaissance-in-force was led by Brigadier General James J. Archer's brigade of Alabama and Tennessee troops, followed by General Joseph R. Davis's brigade of Mississippians and North Carolinians, and was supported by a battalion of artillery under Major William J. Pegram. Following in reserve were Brigadier General Pettigrew's brigade of North Carolinians and Colonel John M. Brockenbrough's brigade of Virginians. Farther back, available if needed, were Major General William Dorsey Pender's division and more artillery.

About three miles west of Gettysburg on the Chambersburg Turnpike, Heth's Confederate skirmishers encountered General John Buford's Federal cavalry pickets and both sides opened fire. It was shortly after eight o'clock. The Federal pickets fell back, and Heth's troops continued their advance along the pike. At about nine-thirty, they encountered a battle line of dismounted cavalry atop Herr Ridge, who were armed with rapid-fire breech-loading carbines. It was Colonel William Gamble's 1st Cavalry Brigade, backed by a battery of Federal artillery.

Although he had graduated last in his class at West Point, General "Harry" Heth was viewed as a capable, experienced officer. The Gettysburg Campaign, however, was his first engagement as a division commander.
Library of Congress

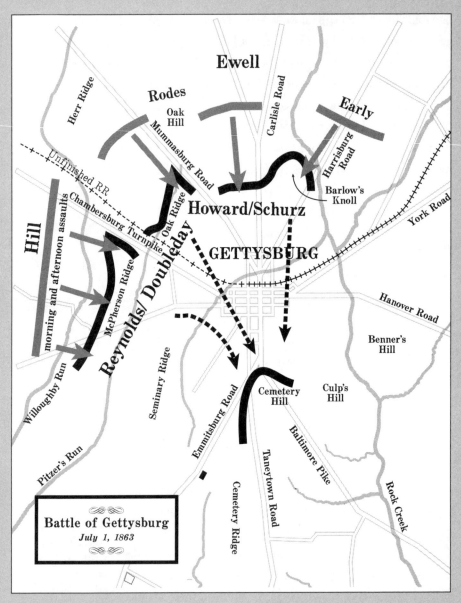

Ewell

Rodes

Herr Ridge

Oak Hill

Carlisle Road

Early

Mummasburg Road

Unfinished R.R.

Harrisburg Road

Howard/Schurz

Barlow's Knoll

York Road

Hill

Chambersburg Turnpike

Oak Ridge

morning and afternoon assaults

GETTYSBURG

McPherson Ridge

Reynolds/ Doubleday

Hanover Road

Seminary Ridge

Benner's Hill

Willoughby Run

Emmitsburg Road

Cemetery Hill

Culp's Hill

Pitzer's Run

Battle of Gettysburg
July 1, 1863

Cemetery Ridge

Taneytown Road

Baltimore Pike

Rock Creek

On Gettysburg's first day of battle, a morning clash escalated into serious fighting west of the town along both sides of the Chambersburg Turnpike. Based on a map by Hal Jespersen, www.CWmaps.com

When confronted by serious fire, Heth's Confederates deployed on both sides of the road—with Archer's Brigade advancing on the right and Davis's Brigade approaching on the left. Buford's 1,600 front-line troops laid down a stiff fire, but they could not repel Heth's division, soon supported by effective fire from Pegram's artillery, so they fell back across a local creek, Willoughby Run, and withdrew to the next ridge—McPherson's Ridge. There, at Buford's direction, they redeployed and unleashed a fierce fire. Despite General Heth's orders to "not bring on an engagement," the battle of Gettysburg had begun. Months later, in an official army report, Heth would try to explain the events that triggered the fighting.

━━━━━━━━━━━━━━━━━━━━

Headquarters, Heth's Division
Camp near Orange Court-House
September 13, 1863.

I have the honor to report the operations of my division from June 29 until July 1, including the part it took in the battle of Gettysburg (first day), July 1.

The division reached Cashtown, Pa., on June 29. Cashtown is situated at the base of the South Mountain, on the direct road from Chambersburg, via Fayetteville, to Gettysburg, and 9 miles distant from the latter place.

On the morning of June 30, I ordered Brigadier-General Pettigrew to take his brigade to Gettysburg, search the town for army supplies (shoes especially), and return the same day. On reaching the suburbs of Gettysburg, General Pettigrew found a large force of cavalry near the town, supported by an infantry force. Under these circumstances, he did not deem it advisable to enter the town, and returned, as directed, to Cashtown. The result of General Pettigrew's observations was reported to Lieutenant-General Hill, who reached Cashtown on the evening of the 30th.

A light force of Federal artillery supported Buford's cavalry as it attempted to hold back the Confederate advance. The "demonic 'whir-r-r' of the rifled shot ... filled the air," an eyewitness would recall.

Battles and Leaders of the Civil War

On July 1, my division, accompanied by Pegram's battalion of artillery, was ordered to move at 5 a. m. in the direction of Gettysburg. On nearing Gettysburg, it was evident that the enemy was in the vicinity of the town in some force. It may not be improper to remark that at this time—9 o'clock on the morning of July 1—I was ignorant what force was at or near Gettysburg, and supposed it consisted of cavalry, most probably supported by a brigade or two of infantry.

On reaching the summit of the second ridge of hills west of Gettysburg, it became evident that there were infantry, cavalry, and artillery in and around the town. A few shot from Pegram's battalion (Marye's battery) scattered the cavalry vedettes....

My division, now within a mile of Gettysburg, was disposed as follows: Archer's brigade in line of battle on the right of the turnpike; Davis' brigade on the left of the same road, also in line of battle; Pettigrew's brigade and Heth's old brigade (Colonel Brockenbrough commanding), were held in reserve. Archer and Davis were now directed to advance, the object being to feel the enemy; to make a forced reconnaissance, and determine in what force the enemy were—whether or not he was massing his forces on Gettysburg. Heavy columns of the enemy were soon encountered....

I am, very respectfully, your obedient servant,

H. Heth, Major-General[6]

"We Must Hold This Position"

Federal Cavalry and Artillery Fight a Fierce Delaying Action

As General Heth's infantry troops advanced toward McPherson's Ridge on both sides of the Chambersburg Pike, General Buford's Federal cavalry stood its ground and poured fire into the advancing Southern ranks. Heth initially believed his division faced Northern militia troops, who would break as the fighting intensified. The Federal fire did not slacken, however, and Heth's troops also began to suffer casualties from enemy artillery fire.

Deployed across McPherson's Ridge in support of Buford's dismounted cavalry was Battery A of the 2nd U.S. Artillery. Commanded by Lieutenant John H. Calef, Battery A was equipped with six three-inch, long-range rifled field pieces. Calef had just finished his breakfast that morning when General Buford ordered the battery into action. He deployed his guns atop the ridge on both sides of the pike. Below him to the west, the Confederate army hastened its advance through fields and patches of woods along the road. To his rear, past the local Lutheran Seminary—an imposing brick structure topped by a cupola— lay the town of Gettyburg.

Calef knew his battery was the only Federal artillery on the field. The rest of the Army of the Potomac was on the way, but it fell to Calef's artillery and to Buford's cavalry to hold off the advancing enemy until the army could arrive. "Calef held his own gloriously [and] worked his guns deliberately," General Buford would later report, "with great judgment and skill, and wonderful effect on the enemy." Years later, Lieutenant Calef would recall that tense, deadly morning.

The morning of the eventful 1st of July came bright and hot. After breakfast I had ordered my horse and was prepared to make a hasty inspection of Gettysburg, there to make some purchases for our mess, when an orderly from General Buford galloped up with the information that the enemy were advancing and to prepare for action at once. It was thirty-one years before I made that contemplated visit to Gettysburg. In an incredibly short time our bivouac was broken and baggage and caissons sent to the rear.

Colonel Gamble, commanding the brigade, instructed me to select my own position, which I did on a crest in advance of the one we had occupied during the night. Leveling the intervening fences, the battery moved forward to the position selected, which was a good one for artillery.... It was part of General Buford's plan to cover as large a front as possible with my battery (his only artillery) for the purpose of deceiving the enemy as to his strength. He therefore instructed me to post two guns on the right of the pike, two on the left and the remaining two still further to the left, where the Eighth New York Cavalry was covering the left flank. It was just at the right of the guns last mentioned, in a corner of the woods, that General Reynolds was killed a few minutes later.

I had scarcely completed the posting of this left section when Lieutenant Roder opened on the right of the pike, his left piece being the opening gun, directed against a column beyond Willoughby's Run, where our cavalry, dismounted, was stoutly resisting the advance of Hill's infantry. The other guns now opened, which drew the artillery of the enemy, and my four guns on the right were soon hotly engaged with Pegram's and McIntosh's battalions of artillery, numbering from twenty-seven to thirty guns.

Seeing the battery so greatly outnumbered, I directed the firing to be made slowly and deliberately and reported to Buford what was in my front. The battle was now developing, and the demonic "whir-r-r" of the rifled shot, the "ping" of the bursting shell and the wicked "zip" of the bullet, as it hurried by, filled the air. While riding to the guns on the left I met General Buford,

In the summer of 1862, the officers of Battery A, 2nd U.S. Artillery, stood beside the muddied wheels of a field piece—its swab, sponge, rammer, and grease bucket in place and ready for action. A year later, Battery A would fire some of the opening shots at the battle of Gettysburg.

Library of Congress

accompanied by a bugler only, and calmly smoking his pipe. He had just made an inspection of the field and remarked: "Our men are in a pretty hot pocket, but, my boy we must hold this position until the infantry come up; then you withdraw your guns in each section by piece, fill up your limber chests from the caissons and await my orders." Just as he finished speaking a shell burst so near to us that both of our horses reared with fright, but all escaped injury.

By this time the wounded were being brought to the rear and temporary field-hospitals were established in the vicinity of the Seminary. Here also were my caissons. As I joined the left guns again there came out of the McPherson woods in our front a double line of battle in gray, and not over a thousand yards distant. It was Archer's brigade, and their battle-flags looked redder and bloodier in the strong July sun than I had ever seen them before....[7]

"He Fell from His Horse Dead"

Federal Troops under General John Reynolds Rush into Gettysburg

Major General John F. Reynolds turned down the opportunity to command the Federal Army of the Potomac on the eve of Gettysburg. In an irony of war, however, he found himself the senior officer on the field when the battle began.

Wikimedia Commons

Major General John F. Reynolds hurried his horse through the streets of Gettysburg, followed by his mounted staff officers. They were riding toward the west side of town where heavy firing could be heard in the distance. Tall, slim, and dark-eyed, with a neatly trimmed beard and mustache, Reynolds rode like an expert horseman, having honed his skills while fighting Indians in the West. An 1841 graduate of West Point, he had been twice decorated for actions in the Mexican War and had served as commandant of cadets at West Point. Promoted to brigadier general at the beginning of the war, he had been a division commander in some of the war's bloodiest fighting.

The forty-two-year-old officer had recently turned down command of the Army of the Potomac, even though many—including General Meade—believed Reynolds was the most qualified officer to lead the army. He had no desire to take the command that had been unsuccessfully held by so many other officers, and now, in the irony of war, he performed the role of senior officer on the field at Gettysburg. As commander of the left wing of Meade's army, Reynolds had been up since 4:00 a.m., leading the army's First and Eleventh Corps toward Gettysburg. He knew the road well as he was a native of nearby Lancaster. He had moved forward at a comfortable pace—until a courier had brought a desperate-sounding dispatch from General Buford at Gettysburg, reporting his cavalry was being pressed by a large force of Confederate troops. Reynolds forwarded the news to General Meade in the rear, and hurried to Gettysburg.

There, he found Buford in the midst of a heated fight. "What's the matter, John?" he asked. Realizing his outnumbered cavalrymen were about to be overwhelmed, Buford replied, "The Devil's to pay." With his typical competence, Reynolds took command, and as soon as his troops arrived he began deploying them on McPherson's Ridge—just as Buford's defensive line began to break. The infantry hurriedly took up positions in long lines on both sides of the Chambersburg Turnpike, and began unleashing volley fire into Heth's Confederates as they slowly advanced up McPherson's Ridge. Reynolds also introduced fresh artillery in order to reinforce Calef's guns, and the battle increased in intensity.

"Forward men," Reynolds shouted to the blue-uniformed troops, "forward for God's sake and drive those fellows out of those woods." Then the general suddenly toppled off his horse. He had been hit in the back of the head by Confederate volley fire or by a well-aimed sharpshooter's round. It was a fatal wound: General John F. Reynolds was dead. The critical moment of his death would be recounted later by his orderly, Sergeant Charles Veil.

Alfred R. Waud, a *Harper's Weekly* war artist embedded with the Federal army, used eyewitness reports to sketch this image of General Reynolds at the moment he was shot from his horse. Library of Congress

Herbst Woods, a local woodlot, shades a portion of McPherson's Ridge in this 1863 photograph. While deploying Federal troops, General Reynolds was shot and killed in the edge of these trees.

National Archives

The Genl ordered our troops to advance near to the top of the ridge and lay down—as they advanced up the ridge the enemy advanced up the other side of the ridge, and both lines met near the top of the ridge. The action had now Commenced in real earnest. The Genl road along in rear of our line towards the woods on our left (Called I believe McPhersons, though I heard while in Gettysburg that they belonged to Mr. Herbst). As he rode along he saw the enemy advancing through the woods, facing the Cashtown Road.

The Genl saw at a glance that something desperate must be done or our troops would be entirely flanked as there was a Reg't comeing [sic] down, from the Seminary—(was but a short distance from the woods)—was the 19th Indiana—belonging to Brig on left of Cashtown Road—but had by some means got in rear) He ordered it to "Forward into line" at a double quick and ordered them to charge into the woods, leading the Charge in person; the Regiment Charged into the woods nobly, but the enemy was too strong, and they had to give way to the right. The enemy still pushed on, and was now not much more than 60 paces from where the Gen'l. was. Minnie Balls were flying thick.

The Genl. turned to look towards the Seminary, (I suppose to see if the other troops were comeing on,) as he did so, a Minnie Ball Struck him in the back of the neck, and he fell from his horse dead. He never spoke a word, or moved a muscle after he was struck. I have seen many men killed in action, but never saw a ball do its work so instantly as did the ball which struck General Reynolds, a man who knew not what fear or danger was, in a word, was one of our very best Generals. Where ever the fight raged the fiercest, there the General was sure to be found, his undaunted Courage always inspired the men with more energy & courage. He would never order a body of troops where he had not been himself, or where he did not dare to go. The last words the lamented General spoke were—"Forward men forward for God's sake and drive those fellows out of those woods," (meaning the enemy).

When the General fell the only persons who were with him was Capt's Mitchell, & Baird, and myself. When he fell we sprang from our horses, the Gen'l. fell on his left side, I turned him on his back, glanced over him but could see no wound escept [sic] a bruise above his left eye. We were under the impression that he was only stunned, this was all done in a glance. I caught the Genl. under the arms, while each of the Capt's. took hold of his legs, and we commenced to carry him out of the woods towards the Seminary. When we got outside of the woods the Capt's. left me to carry the word to the next officers on Command, of his death. I in the meantime got some help from some of the orderlies who came up about this time, & we carried the body towards the Seminary, really not knowing where to take it to, as the enemy appeared to be comeing in on our right and left.

When we arrived at the Seminary I concluded to carry the body to the Emmitsburg Road & done so, Carrying it to Mr George's house, (a small stone house). As we were laying him down, I first found the wound in the back of the neck. I then saw that the Genl was dead. I also almost forgot to tell you that in crossing the fields between the woods where he was killed & the Semy, he gasped a little and I thought was comeing to his senses. We stopped a moment & I gave him a drop of water from a canteen but he would not drink, it was his last struggle. I have often wondered why it was that the wound did not bleed. I think now that he must have bled inwardly. When we arrived at Mr. George's house I sent for an ambulance and Mr. Rosengarten & myself went into town to try & get a coffin, but did not succeed. The only thing that we could get was a box from the marble cutters this was too short, so we knocked one end of it out & lay the body in this....[8]

War may have seemed far away when Major General Abner Doubleday and his wife, Mary Hewitt Doubleday, struck a pose in Matthew Brady's Washington, D.C., studio—the general in his dress uniform and she in cloaked finery. In stark contrast, Doubleday inherited a field command on Gettysburg's first day in the midst of smoke, fire, and death.

Library of Congress

"This Raised a Terrible Rebel Yell"

Archer's and Davis's Brigades Press the Federal Line

As General Reynolds's body was carried to the rear, his troops were pouring fire into the Confederate forces advancing up McPherson's Ridge on both sides of the Chambersburg Pike. General James J. Archer's brigade moved forward on the right of the road, advancing through open fields and a stand of timber called Herbst Woods, while General Joseph R. Davis's brigade fought its way up the ridge on open ground on the left side of the road. Facing them were

First Corps troops from the Army of the Potomac under Major General Abner Doubleday, who assumed command when Reynolds fell.

The troops were from Brigadier General James I. Wadsworth's division, which was composed of two brigades: troops from Wisconsin, Indiana, and Michigan under Brigadier General Solomon Meredith, and New Yorkers, Pennsylvanians, and Indianans commanded by Brigadier General Lysander Cutler. Meredith's Brigade battled Archer's Alabama and Tennessee Confederates, while Cutler's Brigade engaged Davis's Mississippians and North Carolinians. On the Federal right, Cutler's troops were taking a beating, but the Midwesterners defending the Federal left were largely veteran troops, and their reputation as tenacious fighters had earned them the nickname the "Iron Brigade." They were also called the "Black Hat Brigade" because they wore the formal 1858 U.S. Army black dress hat.

Brigadier General James J. Archer was known as the "Little Gamecock" for his courage in combat—but at Gettysburg he became the first general from Lee's army to be captured by the enemy.

Library of Congress

They stubbornly resisted Archer's troops as the Confederates ascended McPherson's Ridge, and slowly began to drive them back down the ridge. Through the haze of battle smoke cloaking the ridge, Archer's men could see the Iron Brigade's black hats and realized the men were seasoned combat veterans and not mere militia. "There are those damned black hatted fellows again!" one shouted above the racket of battle. "T'aint no militia. It's the Army of the Potomac!" Under the pressure of the Iron Brigade's counterattack, the Confederate right collapsed, and Archer's troops retreated back to Herr Ridge. General Archer was captured and sent to the Federal rear, where he encountered General Doubleday, who had been his classmate at West Point. "Good morning, Archer!" Doubleday cheerfully pronounced. "How are you? I'm glad to see you!" Glumly, Archer replied, "Well, I am not glad to see you by a damn sight."

Private William H. Moon, a member of the color guard in the 13th Alabama Infantry, recalled that first morning at Gettysburg, as Archer's Brigade advanced toward McPherson's Ridge.

———————————

We had been in line of battle but a short time after our battery took position until the order was given: "Forward!" As we debouched into the open field, a Federal battery ... saluted us with a shower of shells. Our line of advance placed the 13th on a direct line between the Federal and Confederate batteries. The descent to Willoughby Run is a gradual slope with a dip about one hundred and fifty yards from the Run, so our battery could not engage the Federal guns until we had gone about a half mile down the slope. As soon as we were below the range of our guns, they fired a volley at the Federal battery, and I thought it the sweetest music I had ever heard as the balls went whizzing just above our heads.

At the second volley from our battery, I saw one of the Federal guns topple and fall to the ground. This raised a terrible Rebel yell all along the line. I was color guard on the left of the color bearer, Tom Grant. He was a big, double-jointed six-footer, and, having that morning [partaken] freely of Pennsylvania rye or apple joice [sic], he was waving the flag and holloaing [sic] at the top of his voice, making a fine target while the shells were flying thick around us. I said: "Tom, if you don't stop that I will use my bayonet on you." Just them a fusillade of rifle balls from the Federals greeted us, and Tom needed no further admonition from me.

We were now in easy range of the Federals across the Run, who were firing on us, but not advancing. We continued to advance, but in a walk, loading and firing as we went, until we reached a strip of low land along the Run. There we were protected from the fire of the enemy by an abrupt rise across the Run in our front. We halted

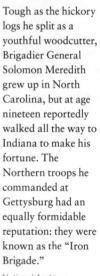

to reform, reload, catch our breath, and cool off a little. It was but nine o'clock in the morning and hot, hotter, hottest!

While we were engaged, the Tennesseans on our left advanced through a copse which ran up a ravine, spreading out into a fan shape as it neared the top of the ridge. They were hotly engaged at close quarters, the Yanks charging them in column, the Tennesseans lying on their backs to load and whirling over to fire. At this stage, Colonel George ... rode down the line to the right and requested General Archer or Colonel Akin—they were close together—to left wheel the 13th Alabama Regiment so as to cross fire on the Federals in front of the Tennesseans.

This move placed the right of our regiment on or near the crest of the ridge and about seventy-five yards from the blue coats, into whom we were pouring volley after volley as fast as we could shoot. We were rather enjoying the fray when the order was given to, "fall back to Willoughby Run...."[9]

Tough as the hickory logs he split as a youthful woodcutter, Brigadier General Solomon Meredith grew up in North Carolina, but at age nineteen reportedly walked all the way to Indiana to make his fortune. The Northern troops he commanded at Gettysburg had an equally formidable reputation: they were known as the "Iron Brigade."

National Archives

"The Honors Were with the Boys in Blue"

The Army of the Potomac Wins the Opening Round

General Davis's Mississippi and North Carolina troops appeared to be holding their own. While Archer's brigade retreated from McPherson's Ridge, Davis's troops—advancing on the north side of the Chambersburg Turnpike—met the Federal troops of Cutler's Brigade with well-timed volleys that staggered the blue line. Stunned, Cutler's troops broke and fell back. The Southerners then surged forward in an attempt to turn the Federal right flank.

As disaster unfolded on the Federal side, Lieutenant Colonel Rufus R. Dawes, commanding a Federal reserve force behind McPherson's Ridge, received a frantic call to shore up the breaking line. Dawes commanded the Iron Brigade's 6th Wisconsin Infantry as well as about one hundred other "Black Hat" troops, and he promptly led them into the fight.

The Black Hats reinforced Cutler's Brigade, reversed the Federal retreat, and sent Davis's Confederates reeling back down McPherson's Ridge. Several hundred of them sought shelter in a nearby railroad cut—a gorge dug for an unfinished railroad on the north side of the Chambersburg Turnpike. There, they were quickly surrounded by Federal troops—trapped like sheep in a pen—and immediately threw down their weapons in surrender. In the Confederate rear, General Heth managed to stop the retreat and reform the survivors of his two battered brigades. He also dispatched a courier to his superior, General A. P. Hill, reporting the situation and requesting instructions. Despite General Lee's orders to avoid a general engagement, Heth had not only opened a battle—he was also *losing* it.

Held in reserve in the early fighting on July 1, Lieutenant Colonel Rufus R. Dawes and his 6th Wisconsin Infantry were later rushed into battle—just in time to turn back a Confederate surge.

Library of Congress

Captain J. V. Pierce of the 147th New York Infantry, a regiment in Cutler's Brigade, was engaged in the fighting with Davis's Confederates, and later penned an account of the struggle.

I moved my men forward a few yards further to the crest of the ridge with the men of Company C, and discovered a line of Confederate skirmishers on our front, advancing from the valley up a slope towards a rail fence, firing as they advanced into Hall's Battery, while the battery was fighting for dear life. A detachment of Confederates gathered in a fence corner, a short distance beyond the [railroad] cut. I immediately ordered, "Left oblique, fire." Several rounds were fired into the skirmish lines; it became too hot for them, and I saw them return down the hill, with several of their number stretched on the hillside. [Captain Daniel] Hall's Battery had been fighting that skirmish line in a death grapple. "Artillery against skirmishers is like shooting mosquitoes with a rifle." The Confederate skirmishers had the best of it up to the time the left of the One hundred and forty-seventh Regiment opened on them. The moment the battery was relieved from the force of the attack it began to limber to the rear, and as the Confederate skirmishers fell back, the battery disappeared in a cloud of dust on the Chambersburg Pike. While this was taking place on the left, the battle reopened on the right with redoubled fury, and the cry came down the line, "They are flanking us on the right...." I saw an officer ride down from Oak Hill in our rear, and wave his cap in retreat. To venture into this maelstrom between the railroad cut and that fence on the right was death.... Closer pressed the enemy. A regiment—the Fifty-fifth North Carolina—was pressing far to our right and rear, and came over to the south side of the rail fence. Their colors drooped to the front. An officer in front of the centre corrected the alignment as if passing in review. It was the finest exhibition of discipline and drill I ever saw....

As I started with my men to the rear I found Edwin Aylesworth mortally wounded, who begged me not to leave him. I stopped, and with Sergt. Peter Shuttz, assisted him to his feet, and tried to carry him; but I could not, and had to lay him down. His piteous appeal, "Don't leave me, boys," has rung in my ears and lived in my memory these five and twenty years. Sergeant Shuttz was killed soon after near Oak Ridge. The time spent in assisting Aylseworth delayed me, so I was among the last to leave the field.

Finding the enemy so close upon us and the way open—the route we came in by—I followed several of my men into the railroad cut. A squad of Confederates were at the west end of the cut, behind

Stunned by searing fire from the 6th Wisconsin, scores of Confederates from Davis's Brigade sought shelter in a deep railroad cut alongside the Chambersburg Pike—and found themselves trapped like sheep in a pen.

Adams County Historical Society

some rails, and as we struck the bottom of that railroad cut, they saluted us with all their guns, and each one loaded with a bullet. I did not stay to dispute possession, for they evidently intended "to welcome us Yanks with bloody hands to hospitable graves," and I climbed up the rocky face of the cut, on the south side, and made my way with many of our men across the meadow between the railroad cut and the Chambersburg Pike....

Lieutenant Colonel Rufus R. Dawes, commander of the 6th Wisconsin Infantry, later described how his Black Hat troops reversed the Federal retreat and defeated Davis's Confederate brigade.

We could see that the thin regiments of Cutler's brigade, beyond the turnpike, were being almost destroyed. The rebel line swayed and bent, and the men suddenly stopped firing and ran into the railroad cut, which is parallel to the Cashtown turnpike. I now ordered the men to climb over the turnpike fences and advance upon them. I was not aware of the existence of a railroad cut, and mistook the maneuver of the enemy for a retreat, but was soon undeceived by the heavy fire which they began at once to pour upon us from their cover in the cut. Capt. John Ticknor, a dashing soldier, one of our finest officers, fell dead while climbing the second fence, and others were struck, but the line pushed on.

When over the fences and in the field, and subjected to an infernal fire, I saw the 95th New York Regiment coming gallantly into line upon our left. I did not then know or care where they came from, but was rejoiced to see them. Farther to the left was the 14th Brooklyn Regiment, but we were ignorant of the fact. The 95th New York had about 100 men in action. Maj. Edward Pye appeared to be in command. Running hastily to the major, I said, "We must charge," and asked him if they were with us. The gallant major replied, "Charge it is," and they were with us to the end. "Forward, charge!" was the order given by both the major and myself.

We were now receiving a fearfully destructive fire from the hidden enemy. Men who had been shot were leaving the ranks in crowds. Any correct picture of this charge would represent a V-shaped crowd of men with the colors at the advance point, moving firmly and hurriedly forward, while the whole field behind is streaming with men who had been shot, and who are struggling to the rear or sinking in death upon the ground. The only commands I gave, as we advanced, were "Align on the colors! Close up on that color! Close up on that color!" The regiment was being broken up so that this order alone could hold the body together. Meanwhile the colors were down upon the ground several times, but were raised at once by the heroes of the color guard. Not one of the guard escaped, every man being killed or wounded. Four hundred and twenty men started as a regiment from the turnpike fence, of whom 240 reached the railroad cut, . . .

Every officer proved himself brave, true, and heroic in encouraging the men to breast this deadly storm, but the real impetus was the eager, determined valor of the men who carried muskets in the ranks. *The rebel colors could be seen waving defiantly just above the edge of the railroad cut. A heroic ambition to capture it took possession of several of our men. Corporal Eggleston, of Company H, a mere boy, sprang forward to seize it, and was shot dead the moment his hand touched the colors. Private Anderson, of his company, furious at the killing of his brave young comrade, recked little for the rebel colors, but he swung aloft his musket and with a terrific blow split the skull of the rebel who had shot young Eggleston.... Into this deadly melee rushed Corp. Francis A. Waller, who seized and held the rebel battle-flag....*

My first notice that we were immediately upon the enemy was a general cry from our men of: "Throw down your muskets. Down with your muskets." Running quickly forward through the line of men, I found myself face to face with at least a thousand rebels, whom I looked down upon in the railroad cut, which was here about four feet deep. Adjutant Brooks, equal to the emergency, had quickly placed men across the cut in position to fire through it. I shouted: "Where is the colonel of this regiment?" An officer in gray, with stars on his collar, who stood among the men in the cut, said: "Who are you?" I said: "I am commander of this regiment. Surrender, or I will fire on you." The officer replied not a word, but promptly handed me his sword, and all his men, who still held them, threw down their muskets.... It was a short, sharp, and desperate fight, but the honors were with the boys in blue.[10]

CHAPTER FOUR

"We Must Fight a Battle Here"

About midday on July 1, the vicious fighting that had covered McPherson's Ridge with smoke and fallen bodies abruptly ceased. The battered survivors of General Davis's brigade were now back inside the Confederate rear line on Herr Ridge, catching their breath and counting their depleted numbers. Meanwhile, scores of their fellow soldiers were trudging to the Federal rear, without weapons, as prisoners of war. General Archer's surviving troops were being reformed in the Confederate rear—minus their commander: General Archer had become the first general officer in Lee's army to be captured by the enemy. Both sides now stepped back from the morning's fierce first combat and reformed their ranks. Both sides tended to their wounded. Both sides waited for reinforcements to arrive. And both sides expected to resume the battle.

In Gettysburg Major General Oliver O. Howard arrived at the head of the Federal army's Eleventh Corps and took command of Federal forces until General Meade could reach the battle with the rest of the army. "General Reynolds is dead," Howard was told bluntly, "and you are the senior officer on the field." A quick look at the field told Howard that General Buford's

Left: Major General A. P. Hill, commander of Lee's Third Corps, was known for his red shirts and decisive action. On July 1, 1863, it was his decision to allow a Confederate reconnaissance-in-force to go forward that ignited the battle of Gettysburg.
Library of Congress

Right: Major General Oliver O. Howard was a corps commander in the Army of the Potomac, and had been passed over when a new commander was chosen. When he reached Gettysburg on July 1, he was greeted with blunt news: General Reynolds was dead, and he was now the senior Federal commander on the field.
National Archives

stubborn defense of Gettysburg's westside ridges and General Reynolds's "bold front"—as Howard put it—had given the Federal army the advantage of choosing the battlefield. Howard left the army's First Corps troops in line on the western side of Gettysburg, and he deployed most of the Eleventh Corps troops in a defensive battle line on the northern side of town, along a ridgeline called Oak Ridge.

Back on Herr Ridge, General Heth also had to make critical decisions in the absence of his army's commander. He had been ordered not to fully engage the enemy yet, but his trip to Gettysburg had triggered a serious battle with the Army of the Potomac. So what to do now? He decided that "the safe and soldierly thing to do"—as one man put it—was to keep his troops in a line of battle, supported by artillery and prepared to resume the attack, while he summoned instructions from his immediate superior, General A. P. Hill. The general arrived on Herr Ridge in the early afternoon. Partial to long locks and red calico shirts, Ambrose Powell Hill was cocky and impulsive to some, but most were inclined to admit that he was a bold, brilliant officer. At times, his potential was undermined by poor health—the effects of a much-regretted case of venereal disease contracted while he was a cadet at West Point. Even as he stepped down from the saddle, Hill appeared pale and sickly. Upon consulting with Heth, he reached a conclusion: they would wait on General Lee.[1]

"The Enemy Poured into Us a Withering Fire"
The Battle Resumes with Increased Ferocity

Lee and his staff reached the Confederate line on Herr Ridge soon after General Hill. Lee appeared concerned, even frustrated. He had stated his intention not to engage in battle before his forces were fully reunited, but serious fighting had occurred outside Gettysburg. What should he do now? Despite the morning's setback, Hill's corps was in line and ready for battle, but Longstreet's corps was still spread out on the Chambursburg Turnpike to the west, and Ewell's corps had not yet arrived from the north. Meanwhile, Lee had still heard nothing from Stuart's cavalry and was thus still suffering from limited reconnaissance. "In the absence of reports from him, I am in ignorance as to what we have in front of us here," Lee admitted to a subordinate. "It may be the whole Federal army, or it may be only a detachment. If it is the whole Federal force we must fight a battle here."

General Hill advised Lee that his corps, largely replenished with fresh troops, was ready to once again assault the Federal line on McPherson's Ridge, but still Lee waited. Until more of his army arrived, he did not want to engage the enemy again. Then, at about two-thirty in the afternoon, on the faraway ridges to the north, lines of Confederate troops began spilling out of the woods and deploying for battle. It was Ewell's corps—two divisions thus far—who had been recalled by Lee from York and from Carlisle. Leading the troops, General Ewell saw Federal forces advancing toward Oak Ridge, believed this to be an attack, and ordered Major General Robert Rodes to put his 8,000-man division into battle. A graduate of Virginia Military Institute, the thirty-four-year-old Rodes was an aggressive, capable combat commander who had so distinguished himself at Chancellorsville that on his deathbed, General "Stonewall" Jackson had recommended the valiant commander for promotion. As his artillery unlimbered and opened fire, Rodes rushed his troops into action.

It was a costly assault. General John Buford's Federal cavalry had alerted General Howard of Ewell's approach, so Federal forces were not taken by surprise. Rodes's attack struck between the right flank of the Federal First Corps and the left flank of the Federal Eleventh Corps and encountered fierce resistance. A brigade of Alabama troops commanded by Colonel Edward A. O'Neal was stunned by well-aimed Federal volley fire and was driven back with severe casualties. Nearby, a brigade of North Carolinians commanded by Brigadier General Alfred Iverson stumbled into the killing zone set up by a brigade of Federal First Corps troops under Brigadier General Henry Baxter. A tough former California gold miner and veteran army officer, Baxter deployed his troops behind a stone wall alongside the Mummasburg Road, and delivered such savage fire that Iverson's brigade was almost annihilated.

General Robert E. Lee hoped to avoid battle until all of his forces were on hand and ready to engage. However, when he saw an opportunity for victory at Gettysburg, he took it.

National Archives

A U.S. senator's son who had fought Comanche and Kiowa warriors in the prewar U.S. Army, Iverson was a competent and courageous officer who had shown his mettle on various fields of fire during the Civil War. On this day at Gettysburg, however, he succumbed to an extreme case of combat fatigue and stayed back while his troops engaged in battle—perhaps affected by a near-death experience at Chancellorsville where he had been shot in the groin. His men were sent forward without skirmishers—and fell into General Baxter's deadly trap. A Federal soldier later counted seventy-nine dead North Carolina soldiers lying in a straight row. "They had all evidently been killed by one volley of musketry," he reported, "and they had fallen in their tracks without a single struggle." Of approximately 1,400 soldiers in Iverson's Brigade, more than 800 were killed, wounded, or captured. When

General Iverson learned what had become of his brigade, he broke down into hysterics.

A survivor of Iverson's Brigade, Sergeant H. C. Wall of the 23rd North Carolina Infantry, would later recall the horror of that afternoon assault on Oak Ridge.

Leaving Carlisle on Tuesday, the last day of June, we marched swiftly southward. Cherries were ripe along the rock-walled lanes. Bringing camp hatchets out, fruit ladened limbs were severed and we regaled ourselves as we swung onward. The spirit and morale of the army were then superb. Many German-descended members of our regiment ... were in this region amid, or not far from, their kin. From here their ancestors had emigrated to North Carolina about one hundred years before. But I doubt if many of them thought of it at that time. Little did the families at the separation imagine that the descendants of the emigrants should in a generation or two return as invaders to the old home....

Sounds of strenuous battle reached us early on the morning of Wednesday, 1 July, as we pressed forward towards Gettysburg.... Our brigade (Iverson's) led Ewell's corps and was the first to become engaged as he hurried forward to succor A. P. Hill, then hard pressed. At Willoughby Run our Field Officers dismounted. Approaching from the north by the Heidelburg road till within about a mile of the field of battle, we were filed off by the right flank to the Mummersburg road. As we emerged from the woods and moved down the slope to the latter road twenty pieces of artillery opened on us with grape, from the left, inflicting some loss.

A flint-hard Northern combat commander, Brigadier General Henry J. Baxter had been seriously wounded three times before Gettysburg. On the battle's first day, his extensive combat experience showed itself.

Library of Congress

93

The Mummersburg road here runs east and west. Very close to the road on the south side stands the Forney house.... Along the path or eastern side of the field and on a ridge ran a stone fence, which formed part of the enemy's line. Behind this fence, alone, lay hidden from view, more men than our assaulting column contained. A body of woods extended from the southeastern corner of the field for about two hundred yards along its southern side.

The brigade about 1,450 strong, advanced under artillery fire through the open grass field in gallant style, as evenly as if on parade. But our brigade commander (Iverson) after ordering us forward, did not follow us in that advance, and our alignment soon became false. There seems to have been utter ignorance of the force crouching behind the stone wall. For our brigade to have assailed such a stronghold thus held, would have been a desperate undertaking. To advance southeast against the enemy, visible in the woods at that corner of the field, exposing our left flank to an enfilading file from the stronghold was fatal. Yet this is just what we did. And unwarned, unled as a brigade, went forward Iverson's deserted band to its doom. Deep and long must the desolate homes and orphan children of North Carolina rue the rashness of that hour.

When we were in point blank range of the dense line of the enemy rose from its protected lair and poured into us a withering fire from the front and both flanks.... This effected, the enemy moving under cover of the ridge and woods, disposed his forces to enfilade our right from the woods just as our left was enfiladed from the stone fence.

Pressing forward with heavy loss under deadly fire our regiment, which was the second from the right, reached a hollow

An aggressive, capable combat officer, Major General Robert Rodes was used to winning. On Gettysburg's first day, however, he and his Southern soldiers were surprised by the fierce resistance they received from Federal troops on the north side of town.

Rubenstein Rare Book and Manuscript Library, Duke University *or low place, running irregularly north, east and southwest through the field. We were then about eighty yards from the stone fence to the left and somewhat further from the woods to the right, from both of which, as well as from the more distant corner of the field in our front, poured down upon us a pitiless rifle fire.*

Unable to advance, unwilling to retreat, the brigade lay down in this hollow or depression in the field and fought as best it could. Terrible was the loss sustained, our regiment losing the heaviest of all in killed, as from its position in line the cross enfilading fire seems to have been the hottest just where it lay. Major C. C. Blacknall was shot through the mouth and neck before the advance was checked. Lieutenant-Colonel R. D. Johnson was desperately, and Colonel D. H. Christie mortally wounded, as the line lay in the bloody hollow. There, too, fell every commissioned officer save one....

The carnage was great along our whole line which, except the Twelfth Regiment on the right, was at the mercy of the enemy....

The wary foe aware of this, swarmed over the wall and rushed down upon our weakened line. Leaving the wounded they drove off with bayonets and clubbed muskets 49 prisoners and carried our flag with them.... General Rodes said that Iverson's men fought and died like heroes. When the brigade went from its position in the hollow its dead and wounded lay in distinctly marked line of battle from one end to the other.

Among the regiments pouring fire into Iverson's Brigade was the 97th New York Infantry. Captain Isaac Hall of Company A never forgot how Iverson's men "kept bravely on" in the face of devastating fire—until finally crushed by it. Two decades later, Hall's emotionally raw memories would yet remain.

Iverson's Brigade of North Carolina troops was almost annihilated in the first day's fighting at Gettysburg, and two of its regiments had their battle flags captured by Federal forces.

Harper's Weekly

The 97th New York, following the 12th Massachusetts, halted in rear or east of this wall and fronted left, and a regiment, or part of another regiment, to the left of the 97th, fronted the same way, thus covering the front of the balance of the brigade. This wall afforded no protection, but the land, for a short distance to the front, rose gradually and then fell off to a gradual slope on the other side, so that our regiments in rear of the wall and a little back from it were hid, even while standing, from the observation of any force that might approach over the narrow meadow in their front....

Iverson's brigade, by some means unobserved, appeared suddenly in our front. From the left of Baxter's line they came sweeping up, with a yell, obliquely upon Baxter's left. They were met by a withering fire, but they kept bravely on, and seemed about to engulf his left flank, when their flank was struck by the fire of our regiment and by the regiment on our immediate left. The determined spirit of these regiments, wrought up to the highest pitch, smarting as they were under the fire of a concealed foe, was with difficulty held in check till the opportune moment should arrive. But, when it did arrive, a flame of fire in which every shot seemed to take a toll burst upon the flank of the Confederate line.

It staggered, halted, and was swept back as by an irresistible current into a gully running diagonally to our front and perhaps 300 yards from our line. Under cover of this natural entrenchment these troops first began to open fire upon us, but some displayed white flags, and Lieutenant Colonel Spofford, of our regiment a gallant and intrepid officer, who remained mounted on the left, taking in the situation and the high spirit of the regiment without waiting for orders, said: "Boys of the 97th, let us go for them and capture them." The first intimation I had of his intent was a cheer from the left, and looking in that direction I found the colors already over the wall and the color company following with ringing cheers.

I hastened my company forward, and on a bound between the lines we were upon them. We took about 400 prisoners officers and men and two regimental flags of North Carolina troops. One flag (the 20th North Carolina) was captured by Sergeant Sylvester Riley of company C ... Some of the Confederates escaped, but most of them surrendered without leaving the ditch.... On that day the 97th New York had ten officers killed and wounded out of twenty-tour, and the rank and file suffered in about the same proportion. My only lieutenant, Wm. J. Morrin, was killed during that charge, and my sword-scabbard, which I had taken from my belt and held in my right hand, by stopping a bullet, saved my thigh and perhaps my life. The color-bearer, James Brown, fell shot through the head, but a corporal of the color-guard, James B. McClerran, picked up the colors and brought them off the field.... [2]

Nineteen-year-old Lieutenant Bayard Wilkeson here directs the fire of a battery of Federal artillery, which temporarily slowed the Confederate attack on Gettysburg's north side. Shot from the saddle and seriously wounded, Wilkeson amputated his own leg with a pocketknife.

Battles and Leaders of the Civil War

"His Guns Are Fired with Precision and Effect"

A Youthful Federal Officer Makes a Daring, Fatal Stand

While the Federal infantry fought stubbornly to turn back Ewell's attacking Confederates on the north side of Gettysburg, they were supported by Federal artillery—including Battery G of the 4th U.S. Artillery. One of five artillery batteries attached to the Eleventh Corps, the battery was commanded by a nineteen-year-old junior officer, Lieutenant Bayard Wilkeson, who had left a prominent upstate New York family to enter the army at age sixteen. Ironically, Bayard's father, Samuel Wilkeson, was a *New York Times* war correspondent attached to the Federal army at Gettysburg.

As the fighting intensified on the ridges north of Gettysburg, Wilkeson's artillery battery was deployed in a dangerously exposed position. Mounted on horseback beside his guns—and exhibiting what one admirer called a "fearless demeanor"—Wilkeson directed a ferocious fire against the advancing South-erners. To stop him, more than half a dozen Confederate gun crews trained their fire on his battery. He and sixteen of his gun crewmen quickly went down. Shot out of his saddle, Wilkeson found himself with a leg that he knew was mangled beyond repair. He used his officer's sash as a tourniquet to stop the bleeding, then calmly amputated his own leg with a pocketknife.

His valiant efforts were not enough to save his life, however, and he died a few hours later. Before death occurred, he was carried to a makeshift hospital in Gettysburg's nearby poorhouse—known as the Almshouse. There he encountered a senior Federal officer, who knew at a glance the young lieutenant's wound was fatal. "I met Wilkeson being carried to the rear by his men on a stretcher," the officer would later recall. "One leg had been cut off at the knee by a cannon shot. He spoke to me and was cheerful and hopeful."

Another journalist, Charles Carleton Coffin of the *Boston Journal*, a com-petitor with Wilkeson's father, would later record young Wilkeson's story in an account of the battle.

━━━━━━━━━━━━━━━━━━━━━━━

The only battery which could be spared on the Union side for the right of the line was G, Fourth United States, commanded by Lieu-tenant Wilkeson, who had placed four of his light 12-pounders on a knoll overlooking a wide reach of fields on both sides of Rock Creek, and two pieces nearer the town, by the Almshouse, under Lieutenant Merkle. The Seventeenth Connecticut, and Twenty-fifth, Seventy-fifth, and One Hundred and Seventh Ohio, consti-tuted the brigade of General Ames, assigned to hold this important position, with no reserve that could be called upon in the hour of need. Von Gilsa, along Rock Creek, must hold the flank. The artil-lery duel began, between Wilkeson, with four pieces, and twelve guns on the part of the Confederates. Wilkeson was supported by the Seventeenth Connecticut regiment.

It was a trying situation for the cannoneers of the Union battery. Their commander, to encourage them, to inspire them with his own lofty spirit, sat upon his horse, a conspicuous figure, calmly directing the fire of the pieces. He rode from piece to piece, his horse upon the walk. Shells were bursting amid the guns; shot from rifled cannon cut the air or ploughed the ground, from cannon not half a mile away, upon a hill much higher than that which he occupied. This young lieutenant bore an honored name—Bayard Wilkeson—a family name, given him in part, also, by his parents out of their admiration for the great Chevalier of France, the knight of other days, whose character was without a stain, whose life was above reproach.

This self-possessed lieutenant from New York, animated by an unquenchable patriotism, became a soldier at sixteen, received his commission when he was but seventeen, and was not then nineteen years of age. His first battle was Fredericksburg. For six months he had been commander—his captain engaged elsewhere. So admirable the discipline and efficient the battery under the instruction of this boy-lieutenant that it had been accorded the post of honor—the right of the line. It is a brave spirit that can look out composedly upon the scene in a contest so unequal, but his guns are fired with precision and effect.

A rifled cannon-shot strikes his right leg, crushing the bones and mangling the flesh. His soldiers lay him upon the ground. With composure he ties his handkerchief around it, twists it into a tourniquet to stop the flow of blood, then with his own hand and knife severs the cords and tendons, and, sitting there, tells his cannoneers to go on with their fire—a bravery unsurpassed even by that of the Chevalier of France.... Faint and thirsty, he sends a soldier with his canteen to fill it at the Almshouse well. When the man returns, a wounded infantryman whose life is ebbing away, beholding the canteen, exclaims, "Oh, that I could have but a swallow!"...
"Drink, comrade, your necessities are greater than mine," so Bayard

Wilkeson, with like unselfishness, courtesy, and benevolence, replies, "Drink, comrade; I can wait." In the consuming thirst and fever of approaching death the infantryman drains the canteen of its contents.

When it was seen that the line must retire, Wilkeson allowed himself to be carried to the Almshouse hospital, which, a few minutes later, was within the advancing lines of the Confederates, and where, during the night, for want of attention, he died. Dead—but his heroism, sense of duty, responsibility to obligation, devotion, and loyalty remain....

Wilkeson's journalist father located his son's body in the Gettysburg poorhouse, and brought it home to New York for burial. He closed his *New York Times* report on the battle of Gettysburg with a lament that surely reflected the hearts of countless grieving American families, Northern and Southern, during the war.

I rise from a grave whose wet clay I have passionately kissed, and I look up and see Christ spanning this battle-field with his feet and reaching fraternal and lovingly up to heaven. His right hand opens the gates of Paradise—with his left he sweetly beckons to these mutilated, bloody, swollen forms.[3]

"Everybody Was Then Running for the Rear"
Federal Troops Break and Run on Gettysburg's First Day

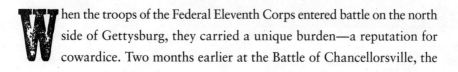

hen the troops of the Federal Eleventh Corps entered battle on the north side of Gettysburg, they carried a unique burden—a reputation for cowardice. Two months earlier at the Battle of Chancellorsville, the

The open fields and rolling ridges north of Gettysburg became the scene of desperate, bloody fighting on the afternoon of July 1.

Library of Congress

troops of the Eleventh Corps had been leisurely cooking supper in camp when "Stonewall" Jackson's screaming Confederates burst out of the woods in a surprise assault—panicking the shocked Federals and stampeding them into retreat. More than half of the regiments in the Eleventh Corps were composed of German immigrants, and, while other Federal troops broke and ran as well, many in the army blamed "the Germans" for the humiliating defeat at Chancellorsville. When the Eleventh Corps deployed on the Federal right flank against Ewell's Confederates, they did so with a tarnished reputation.

Commanding the Eleventh Corps troops at Gettysburg was Major General Carl Schurz, who had been elevated to corps command when General Howard assumed overall command of Federal forces pending General Meade's arrival. Schurz, also a German immigrant, was a "political general," who had limited military experience and colossal political clout. In the 1860 presidential election, he had recruited hundreds of thousands of German-American voters for Lincoln, and had been rewarded with a diplomatic post in Spain, followed by a general's commission in the army. Now he was leading the Eleventh Corps at Gettysburg.

On the afternoon of July 1, Ewell's Confederates poured out of the woods north of Gettysburg in two divisions. General Rodes's division, attacking from the Confederate right, was initially stalled by the effective Federal fire—especially against Iverson's Brigade. Rodes's attack was followed on the Confederate left with an assault by General Jubal Early's division—which had greater success. Early's troops reached the field at about four o'clock and piled into the Federal right flank, manned by Schurz's Eleventh Corps. The fighting was close-up and bloody. "The combatants approached each other until they were scarcely more than seventy-five yards apart," a Federal officer later recalled.

The Eleventh Corps troops fought fiercely at first, but then they broke and fled. Almost 40 percent of the corps was killed, wounded, or captured. The retreat occurred due to sheer "overwhelming force," concluded the Federal chief of artillery, Brigadier General Henry J. Hunt. Less charitable was Brigadier General Francis C. Barlow, a battle-hardened twenty-eight-year-old Eleventh Corps division commander, who dismissed the German-American troops as "miserable creatures" and accused them of panicking, as they had done at Chancellorsville. Barlow himself, however, earned a significant share of the blame for the collapse of the Federal line on Gettysburg's north side and the resulting retreat of the Eleventh. For reasons that apparently seemed prudent to him at the time, Barlow moved his brigade to Blocher's Knoll—later renamed Barlow's Knoll—a position that lay in advance of the Federal line. The movement left his brigade isolated and exposed, allowing it to be flanked, and the Federal line broke. According to Barlow, his troops could have repelled the enemy. Instead, he claimed, they panicked and fled, precipitating the collapse of the Eleventh Corps line. "Everybody," he reported, "was then running to the rear."

Federal artillery forces, such as Captain Hubert Dilger's Battery I of the 1st Ohio Light Artillery, attempted to stall the Confederate advance and cover the Federal retreat, but nothing stopped the flood of men in blue from surging back toward town. Captain Alfred Lee was a company commander in the 82nd Ohio Infantry, which was attached to the Eleventh Corp's 3rd Division under Brigadier General Alexander Schimmelfennig. Captain Lee survived Gettysburg, and penned a personal memoir of the Eleventh Corp's determined defense—as well as its collapse.

A prominent German-American political leader, Major General Carl Schurz's support for President Lincoln had earned him an ambassadorship and an officer's commission in the army. At Gettysburg, he was put in command of the Federal Eleventh Corps, which held huge numbers of German immigrants—and a stigma of failure.

Reminiscences by Carl Schurz

Filing from the road into the open fields beyond the town, our troops immediately went into position. The regiments being formed into solid squares by "doubling on the centre," ours was placed in support of Dilger's battery, which had already commenced firing. The return fire of the rebel guns was lively, and their shot and shell ricochetted [sic] splendidly over the open fields. While the regiment was taking its position, a corporal of my company was struck by one of these missiles and thrown prostrate. Directly another soldier was struck, and the regiment, being unable to return fire, slightly shifted its position. Then the rolls were called, and the men quietly responded to their names amid the boom of cannon and the screech of exploding shells.

The enemy's masses were seen conspicuously ranging themselves along the slopes of Seminary Ridge, while the columns of the First Corps appeared on our left front, moving up firmly to the attack. As the combatants neared each other, random shots cracked spitefully, and were quickly followed by crashing volleys. In a few minutes the rebels, who had yielded at the first onset, were seen scampering to the rear like frightened sheep. A loud cheer followed this success, and officers who had watched the movement through their glasses declared that we were "getting along splendidly." But the enemy had strong reserves, and soon rallied. In fact, it began to be suspected that we were being cunningly dallied with by a greatly superior force, with the design of decoying our left wing beyond supporting distance, while our right might, in the mean time, be circumvented and overwhelmed. Such a scheme, if successful, would not only effect the overthrow of our little army, but would completely separate it from its slender reserves on Cemetery Hill.

The impression that such a design was being attempted was soon confirmed by a report from the skirmish-line that the enemy, in heavy masses, was endeavoring to turn our right flank. The nature of the ground favored this attempt, since the woods and ravines on that flank afforded a mask to the movement. It was evident that our brigade commander realized this new and dangerous situation of affairs. His face grew pale and distressed. To every mind, indeed, it was apparent that a great crisis had come,—that the enemy must be met, and met at once,—and it was rashly resolved that we should go and meet him half-way in the open plain

Accordingly, the troops changed front, and a general advance of the line through the open fields began. Fences that might have served in the construction of a breastwork were thrown down in a twinkling, and absolutely nothing remained to screen our line from the crossfire that now poured upon it from flank and front. The enemy's batteries swept the plain completely from two or three different directions, and their shells plunged through our solid squares, making terrible havoc. Yet the line swept steadily on, in almost perfect order. Gaps made in the living mass by the cannon-shot were closed again as quickly and quietly almost as though nothing particular had happened, and the men were really less nervous under the ordeal of this fire than they had been during their inactive support of the artillery.

The gray lines of the Confederates now began to be unmasked from the ravine and to deploy themselves on the level surface of the plain. They belonged to Ewell's—formerly Stonewall Jackson's— corps and were old acquaintances. Their movements were firm and steady, as usual, and their banners, bearing the blue Southern cross, *flaunted impudently and seemed to challenge combat. On they came, one line after the other, in splendid array. Up to this time scarcely a musket-shot had been fired; but now our solid squares deployed, and the men were ordered to "let them have it." Quick as a flash the compliment was returned; bullets hummed about our ears like infuriated bees, and in a few minutes the meadow was strewn with arms and accoutrements, with the wounded and the dead.*

The combatants approached each other until they were scarcely more than seventy-five yards apart, and the names of battles printed on the Confederate flags might have been read, had there been time to read them. Quickly our line became thinned to a mere shadow of its former self, and the field-officers, by the killing or disabling of their horses, were every one dismounted. The troops on our right were outflanked and driven back, and, there being no reserves, no alternative remained but to withdraw. The enemy did not venture to charge, but maintained a severe fire, to which our response in the act of falling back was necessarily feeble. Forgetful that I had in my belt a good revolver, with five good loads in it, I picked up a musket and asked a soldier for a cartridge. He gave me one, remarking as he did so that he did not think it would "go," as his ammunition had been dampened by the rain. My next impulse was to load the musket and get at least one parting shot at the enemy. While I was thus engaged, a stalwart young fellow dropped at my side, and cried, "Oh, help me!" Having taken my hand, he struggled to rise, but could not, and, finding his efforts unavailing, murmured, "Oh, I'm gone! just leave me here."

A moment or two later I too felt the sting of a bullet, and fell benumbed with pain. It was an instantaneous metamorphosis from strength and vigor to utter helplessness. The man nearest me, being called to for assistance, replied by a convulsive grasp at the spot where a bullet that instant struck him. He passed on, limping as he went, and in a few minutes more the last blue blouse had disappeared, and the field swarmed with gray Confederates. Of twenty-two commissioned officers and two hundred and thirty-six men constituting our regiment as it went into this action, only three officers and eighty-nine men came out of it. The rest were mostly killed and wounded. The musketry-firing having slackened, the enemy's line of battle now came forward in fine style, preceded by skirmishers. The crimson flags were flaunted more impudently than ever, and the entire Confederate force breathed exultation and defiance. Some of the victors seemed disposed to be even savage. A wounded man lying near me, who had raised himself on his elbow, probably to get an easier posture, was assailed with a volley of curses by a stalwart soldier in gray, who ordered him to lie down instantly, on pain of being shot dead. The soldier held his musket at a ready, evidently intending to execute his threat if not summarily obeyed.

The rebel skirmish-line now passed me, and one of the skirmishers, a gentle-faced young man, came near. He had obtained the sword of a Union officer, and carried it swinging to the belt which was thrown over his neck. To the inquiry whether the Union wounded were going to be molested, he replied, "No; you need not be afraid. Ten minutes ago I would have shot you in a minute; but now that you are a prisoner you shall not be disturbed...." The Confederate infantry now faced by its right flank, and moved off in that direction. I rejoiced at this, for I now felt at liberty to look about me. The whole field was strewn with the prostrate bodies of men in blue. Almost my first glance discovered, not far away, a well-known face.

A former artillery officer in the German army, Captain Hubert Anton Casimir Dilger commanded Battery I of the 1st Ohio Light Infantry. At Chancellorsville, he had directed his guns to cover the retreat of the Federal Eleventh Corps; at Gettysburg, he did so again.

Library of Congress

It was that of our adjutant, Lieutenant B——. Pierced by two musket-balls, he had fallen from his horse, which galloped away, but fell, like its rider, before getting out of range. "Is that you, lieutenant?" He replied only by a look, expressive at once of recognition and of agony. I was about to make further inquiry, when I was interrupted by a rebel battery, which came up at a brisk canter and unlimbered its guns where we lay. They seemed to be about to commence firing on the town, through which our troops were yet retreating.

Some of the artillerymen having noticed the danger I was in of being trampled by the horses, two of them very gently removed me to a place of greater safety. Supporting my arms on the friendly shoulders of these men and listening to their rough words of sympathy, I could not but feel that they were, after all, both fellow-men and fellow-countrymen, and wonder how we could be, or rather have been, such deadly enemies. They next brought Lieutenant B——., and laid him near me. His sufferings were terrible, and his cries of pain agonizing to listen to. The Confederate artillerymen spoke to him sympathizingly, and their bronzed faces expressed sincere compassion. They endeavored to arrange for him an easy posture, but in vain: all postures were alike painful. They procured water, which he demanded incessantly, but it served only as an emetic. Nothing could alleviate his intense thirst, aggravated as it was alike by the fever of his wounds and by the excessive heat of the sun.

It was now five o'clock in the afternoon. The fighting had mostly ceased; the artillerymen were summoned away, and the columns of the Confederate infantry quietly filed off to their different stations in front of Gettysburg. Calm settled upon the ensanguined field where so lately the whirlwind of battle had arisen and spent itself. Except the moaning of the wounded and their cries for assistance, there was little to disturb the evening quiet. Here and there a rebel soldier sauntered about in quest of plunder, or, as sometimes happened, on a mission of mercy, refreshing the wounded with water from his canteen, and saying to them with looks of pity how sorry he was that "you-uns were all out here against us this way...."

The declining sun neared the verge of the horizon, and the clouds that hung about its disk were magnificently tinged with golden light. Their parted volumes disclosed a shining vista ending in serene effulgence, beyond which the eye could not pierce. It was not difficult to imagine that along this luminous path the souls of heroes and martyrs were ascending from the bitter cross of the battlefield to the crown of immortality and infinite peace....[4]

"With a Ringing Yell, My Command Rushed upon the Union Right"

A Stunning Southern Attack Collapses the Federal Right Flank

When General Early's division of Confederates struck the Federal right flank north of town, they were led by a brigade of troops under Brigadier General John Brown Gordon. The thirty-one-year-old Georgian was not a professional soldier; he had been a lawyer, a newspaper reporter, and a coal mine boss before creating his own company—the Raccoon Roughs—from the Deep South hill country. He had proven himself to be a superb commander—rising from major to brigadier—and was praised by his superiors and troops alike. He was also fearless in battle: at Antietam he was wounded five times, and nearly drowned in his own blood from a head wound. He recovered and returned to the army in time for Lee's invasion. He had a commanding presence—six feet tall and powerfully built—and at Gettysburg he rode into battle on a magnificent black stallion.

Gordon's brigade consisted of six regiments of veteran Georgia troops, 1,200 strong, at the head of Early's division. The Georgians arrived at Gettysburg on the Heidlersburg Road, coming from the direction of Harrisburg, and were preceded by a deadly accurate Confederated artillery barrage. They deployed through the fields and dealt the Eleventh Corps and the Federal right flank a smashing blow. After initial stubborn resistance—under pressure from Early's other three brigades and a renewed surge by General Rodes's division—the Federal ranks on the right collapsed like falling dominoes. Some troops panicked, but most did not—at least at first. There was just a progressive collapse of the Federal battle line, which sent a rolling blue tide of Northern troops spilling across the fields north of Gettysburg toward the town.

At thirty-one, Brigadier General John Brown Gordon sported a French-style goatee—and a reputation as a fierce fighter. On the afternoon of July 2, he and his brigade of 1,200 Georgians smashed into the Federal far right flank.

National Archives

As the Federals began retreating, Gordon's troops and various others followed in immediate pursuit, igniting a panic among the increasingly frantic troops of the Eleventh Corps. Then, to Gordon's surprise, he received orders from General Ewell to halt the advance. Gordon initially resisted the order, and later stated that he wished he had never obeyed it. The Army of the Potomac, he believed, was on the verge of defeat. Like other Southern commanders, Gordon later admitted that at Gettysburg he yearned for the presence and leadership of "Stonewall" Jackson. But Jackson was gone. Decades afterward in his memoirs, Gordon chronicled his brigade's role in the breaking of the Federal right flank.

Returning from the banks of the Susquehanna, and meeting at Gettysburg, July 1, 1863, the advance of Lee's forces, my command was thrown quickly and squarely on the right flank of the Union army. A more timely arrival never occurred. The battle had been raging for four or five hours. The Confederate General Archer, with a large portion of his brigade, had been captured. Heth and Scales,

Confederate generals, had been wounded. The ranking Union commander on the field, General Reynolds, had been killed, and Hancock was assigned to command. The battle, upon the issue of which hung, perhaps, the fate of the Confederacy, was in full blast.

The Union forces, at first driven back, now re-enforced, were again advancing and pressing back Lee's left and threatening to envelop it. The Confederates were stubbornly contesting every foot of ground, but the Southern left was slowly yielding. A few moments more and the day's battle might have been ended by the complete turning of Lee's flank. I was ordered to move at once to the aid of the heavily pressed Confederates. With a ringing yell, my command rushed upon the line posted to protect the Union right.

Here occurred a hand-to-hand struggle. That protecting Union line once broken left my command not only on the right flank, but obliquely in rear of it. Any troops that were ever marshalled would, under like conditions, have been as surely and swiftly shattered. There was no alternative for Howard's men except to break and fly, or to throw down their arms and surrender. Under the concentrated fire from front and flank, the marvel is that any escaped.

In the midst of the wild disorder in his ranks, and through a storm of bullets, a Union officer was seeking to rally his men for a final stand. He, too, went down, pierced by a Minie ball. Riding forward with my rapidly advancing lines, I discovered that brave officer lying upon his back, with the July sun pouring its rays into his pale face. He was surrounded by the Union dead, and his own life seemed to be rapidly ebbing out. Quickly dismounting and lifting his head, I gave him water from my canteen, asked his name and the character of

A top Harvard graduate with ties to Boston intelligentsia, Brigadier General Francis Barlow had been endorsed for promotion by the likes of Ralph Waldo Emerson and Nathaniel Hawthorne. At Gettysburg, he was wounded and left for dead by his troops.

National Archives

his wounds. He was Major-General Francis C. Barlow, of New York, and of Howard's corps. The ball had entered his body in front and passed out near the spinal cord, paralyzing him in legs and arms. Neither of us had the remotest thought that he could possibly survive many hours.

I summoned several soldiers who were looking after the wounded, and directed them to place him upon a litter and carry him to the shade in the rear. Before parting, he asked me to take from his pocket a package of letters and destroy them. They were from his wife. He had but one request to make of me. That request was that if I should live to the end of the war and should ever meet Mrs. Barlow, I would tell her of our meeting on the field of Gettysburg and of his thoughts of her in his last moments. He wished me to assure her that he died doing his duty at the front, that he was willing to give his life for his country, and that his deepest regret was that he must die without looking upon her face again.

I learned that Mrs. Barlow was with the Union army, and near the battle-field. When it is remembered how closely Mrs. Gordon followed me, it will not be difficult to realize that my sympathies were especially stirred by the announcement that his wife was so near him. Passing through the day's battle unhurt, I despatched [sic] at its close, under flag of truce, the promised message to Mrs. Barlow. I assured her that if she wished to come through the lines she should have safe escort to her husband's side. In the desperate encounters of the two succeeding days, and the retreat of Lee's army, I thought no more of Barlow, except to number him with the noble dead of the two armies who had so gloriously met their fate. The ball, however, had struck no vital point, and Barlow slowly recovered, though this fact was wholly unknown to me....

On the first day neither General Early nor General Ewell could possibly have been fully cognizant of the situation at the time I was ordered to halt. The whole of that portion of the Union Army in my front was in inextricable confusion and in flight. They were necessarily in flight, for my troops were upon the flank and rapidly sweeping down the lines. The firing upon my men had almost ceased. Large bodies of the Union troops were throwing down their arms and surrendering, because in disorganized and confused masses they were wholly powerless either to check the movement or return the fire. As far down the lines as my eye could reach, the Union troops were in retreat. Those at a distance were still resisting, but giving ground, and it was only necessary for me to press forward in order to insure the same results which invariably follow such flank movements. In less than one-half hour my troops would have swept up and over those hills, the possession of which was of such momentous consequence.

It is not surprising, with a full realization of the consequences of a halt, that I should have refused at first to obey the order. Not until the third or fourth order of the most peremptory character reached me, did I obey. I think I should have risked the consequences of disobedience even then, but that the order to halt was accompanied with the explanation that General Lee, who was several miles away, did not wish to give battle at Gettysburg....

No soldier in a great crisis ever wished more ardently for a deliverer's hand than I wished for one hour of Jackson, when I was ordered to halt. Had he been there, his quick eye would have caught at a glance the entire situation, and instead of halting me, he would have urged me forward and have pressed the advantage to the utmost, simply notifying General Lee that the battle was on, and he had decided to occupy the heights. Had General Lee himself been present this would undoubtedly have been done.

Grievously wounded and left for dead by his troops, General Barlow eventually recovered and returned to command. After the war, General Gordon often told his story of assisting the wounded young officer—and how the two eventually became friends. According to Gordon, both he and Barlow mistakenly thought the other had been killed in the war, until they were introduced by a mutual friend in a postwar meeting. "Nothing short of an actual resurrection from the dead could have amazed either of us more," he wrote.[5]

"Covered with Glory"

General Lee Renews the Confederate Assault on McPherson's Ridge

From his position atop Herr Ridge on the west side of Gettysburg, General Robert E. Lee could see the smoke and dust arising on the distant ridges and fields north of town. The troops from Ewell's corps were pressing the enemy. A new attack on the Federal left might win the day for the South. Standing beside Lee, as he silently studied the fighting, was his First Corps commander, General Hill, along with General Heth, who had redeployed his division since its setback earlier that day. Finally Lee turned to the two officers and issued an order: put in Heth's division.

Opposite Herr Ridge to the east, across Willoughby Run, the Federal left extended in a battle line along McPherson's Ridge. It was still primarily defended by Brigadier General Solomon Meredith's Iron Brigade of Midwesterners from Wisconsin, Michigan, and Indiana. On the brigade's right—just south of the Chambersburg Turnpike—troops of the 2nd and 7th Wisconsin were deployed—mainly in open fields along the ridge. In the middle of the line, the 24th Michigan was posted in the sprawling stand of timber known as Herbst Woods, and to the left—also in the woods—were the troops of the 19th Indiana. Defending the brigade's far right and left flanks were troops from Pennsylvania and New York, supported by scattered sections of field artillery. Heth's Confederates

attacked at about two-thirty in the afternoon, splashing through Willoughby Run and advancing under fire up the slopes of McPherson's Ridge. On the Confederate left, closest to the Chambersburg Turnpike, was a brigade of Virginians commanded by Colonel John M. Brockenbrough. On the Confederate right were the battered survivors of General Archer's Brigade, and in the middle was Brigadier General James J. Pettigrew's brigade of North Carolinians.

The fighting on McPherson's Ridge was a bloodbath. Entire regiments on both sides were shredded in face-to-face combat. The timber-shaded slopes of Herbst Woods and the fields on both sides were left carpeted with the bodies of young men from North Carolina, Michigan, Virginia, Indiana, and Wisconsin. The greatest glory—and the greatest gore—occurred at the center of the battle lines, where troops of the 26th North Carolina battled the Iron Brigade's 24th Michigan and 19th Indiana. By some accounts, no fewer than fourteen color-bearers were shot down in the 26th North Carolina, and nine in the 24th Michigan. Of the 800 officers and troops

Named for local farmer John Herbst, Herbst Woods extended from Willoughby Run up the slope of McPherson's Ridge to its crest. Its leafy hardwoods created a pleasant, shady grove—an unlikely looking site for a bloodbath.

Library of Congress

in the 26th North Carolina who had ascended McPherson's Ridge, only 212 survived unharmed—a 73-percent casualty rate. By battle's end, the 26th North Carolina would incur a greater casualty rate than any regiment at Gettysburg—85 percent—and the casualty rate of the 24th Michigan would not be much less. As the opposing forces whittled each other down to nearly nothing, the Black Hats of both the 24th Michigan and the 19th Indiana were finally forced to concede ground along with the rest of the Iron Brigade. They did so begrudgingly, continuing their disciplined fire even as they were driven back through the woods and into the fields to their rear. Analyzing the battle from a distance, Brigadier General James J. Pettigrew observed the Iron Brigade's line breaking and dispatched Captain Westwood W. McCreery to the commander of the 26th North Carolina: "Tell him," Pettigrew said, "his regiment has covered itself with glory today."

As its ranks were shredded in Herbst Woods, the 26th North Carolina Infantry fell under the command of a former Tarheel farmer—Lieutenant Colonel John R. Lane. Courageously, Lane led the regiment's survivors in a renewed charged—until knocked flat by a bullet to the head.

Courtesy of J. R. Gorrell

Commanding the 26th North Carolina was twenty-one-year-old Colonel Henry "Harry" K. Burgwyn, who was mortally wounded after retrieving the regiment's fallen battle flag. After Burgwyn was shot down, command of the 26th North Carolina fell to Lieutenant Colonel John R. Lane, a tall, stocky North Carolina farmer-turned-soldier with a chest-length black beard. Raising the regiment's bloody battle flag above him, Lane led the regiment's battered survivors forward as they forced the retreat of the Iron Brigade. Then, he too, was shot down by a well-aimed round to the back of the head, which dropped him—in the words of a bystander—"as limber as a rag." Remarkably, Lane survived, and would eventually rejoin the regiment. Decades later, as a prosperous North Carolina horse-trader and real estate broker, he would return to Gettysburg on the battle's fortieth anniversary and deliver a speech that eloquently recalled the horrors and the heroism on McPherson's Ridge that afternoon in 1863.

Forty years ago—who can realize it?—forty years ago, on the 1st of July at 10 o'clock a. m., our regiment lay over there facing McPherson's hill, in line of battle. How the heart of the old soldier, especially the old officer, returns with affection and pride to his old regiment. What a magnificent body of men it was! I see them now. In the center with the first glow of youth on his cheek was the gallant Col. Henry King Burgwyn. His eye was aflame with the ardor for battle. Near him was his lieutenant colonel, commanding the right, and Maj. John T. Jones commanding the left. These officers had put their souls into the training of the soldiers and were now waiting the issue of battle with full confidence in their courage and proficiency....

May I mention some of the things that went to make them good soldiers? In the first place the soldiers came of good blood. I do not mean that their parents were aristocratic—far from it; many of them never owned a slave. They were the great middle class that owned small farms in central and western North Carolina; who earned their living with honest sweat and owed not any man. They were good honest American stock, their blood untainted with crime, their eyes not dimmed by vice. These boys had grown up on the farm and were of magnificent physique. Their life between the plow handles, and wielding the axe had made them strong. They had chased the fox and the deer over hill and valley and had gained great power of endurance that scorned winter's cold—or the parching heat of a July sun. Again these men, many of them without much schooling, were intelligent, and their life on the farm, and in the woods had taught them to be observant and self-reliant. They were quick to see, quick to understand, quick to act.

Again, every one of them had been trained from boyhood to shoot a rifle with precision. Gen. Pettigrew, observing the deadly execution of the muskets on this field, remarked that the Twen-

On the afternoon of July 2, Confederate troops from General A. P. Hill's corps swarmed through the fields and timber that covered McPherson's Ridge, driving Federal troops from the ridge and back through Gettysburg.

Battles and Leaders of the Civil War

ty-sixth shot as if shooting squirrels. Again these men were patriots; they loved their country, they loved liberty. Their forefathers had fought the British at King's Mountain and Guilford Court House. They had grown up to love and cherish their noble deeds. Now every man of them was convinced that the cause for which he was fighting was just; he believed that he owed allegiance first to his home and his State. He was standing to combat an unjust invader. Finally, these men had native courage—not the loud mouthed courage of the braggart—but the quiet, unfaltering courage that caused them to advance in the face of a murderous fire....

 All this time the enemy were moving with great rapidity. Directly in our front across the wheat field was a wooded hill (McPherson's Woods). On this hill the enemy placed what we were afterwards informed was their famous "Iron Brigade." They wore tall, bell-crowned black hats, which made them conspicuous in the line. The sun was now high in the heavens.... Suddenly, about 2 *p.m. there came down the line the long-awaited command "Atten-tion." The time for this command could not have been more inop-portune. Our line had inspected the enemy and we knew the desperateness of the charge we were to make. But with the greatest quickness the regiment obeyed. All the men were up at once and ready, every officer at his post. Col. Burgwyn in the centre, Lieut. Col. Lane on the right; Major Jones on the left. Our gallant stand-ard bearer, J. H. Mansfield, at once stepped to his position—four paces to the front, and the eight color guards to their proper places.*

At the command "Forward March" all to a man stepped off apparently as willingly and as proudly as if they were on review. The enemy at once opened fire, killing and wounding some, but their aim was rather too high to be effective. All kept the step and made as pretty and perfect a line as regiment ever made, every man endeavoring to keep dressed on the colors. We opened fire on the enemy. On and on we went, our men yet in perfect line, until we reached the branch (Willoughby's Run) in the ravine. Here the briers, reeds and underbrush made it difficult to pass. There was some crowding in the center, but the right and left crossed the stream where they struck it. The enemy's artillery (Cooper's Bat-tery) on our right got an enfilade fire. Our loss was frightful. But our men crossed in grand order and immediately were in proper position again and up the hill we went firing now with better exe-cution.

The engagement was becoming desperate. It seemed as if the bullets were as thick as hailstones in a storm. At his post on the right of the regiment and ignorant as to what was taking place on the left, Lieut. Col. Lane hurries to the center. He is met by Col. Burgwyn, who informs him "it is all right in the center and on the left: we have broken the first line of the enemy." The reply comes, "We are in line on the right, Colonel." At this time the colors have been cut down ten times, the color guard all killed or wounded. We have now struck the second line of the enemy where the fighting is the fiercest and the killing the deadliest. Suddenly Captain W. W. McCreery, assistant inspector general of the brigade, rushes forward and speaks to Col. Burgwyn. He bears him a message. "Tell him," says General Pettigrew, "his regiment has covered itself with glory today."

Delivering these encouraging words, Capt. McCreery, who has always contended that the 26th would fight better than any other regiment in the brigade, seizes the fallen flag, waves it aloft and advancing to the front, is shot through the heart and falls, bathing the flag in his life's blood. Lieut. George Wilcox of Co. "H." now rushes forward and pulling the flag from under the dead hero, advances with it. In a few steps he also falls with two wounds in his body. The line hesitates; the crisis is reached; the colors must advance. The gallant Burgwyn leaps forwards, takes them up and again the line moves forward. He, turning again from the right Lieut. Col. Lane sees Col. Burgwyn advancing with the colors. At this juncture, a brave private, Franklin Honeycutt of Union county, takes the colors and Burgwyn turns. Lane again reports all well on the right. Burgwyn delivers Pettigrew's message. At that instant he falls with a bullet through both lungs, and at the same moment brave Honeycutt falls dead only a few steps in advance.

Colonel Samuel J. Williams and the 19th Indiana Infantry defended a portion of Herbst Woods on the afternoon of July 1. "Boys," Williams shouted to his men, "we must hold our colors on the line, or lie here under them."

U.S. Army Military History Institute

Then indeed was our situation desperate. The flag was down, the line is halting, the enemy are strengthening their line and firing upon our men with murderous effect, and more than all the youthful commander has fallen, and all the responsibility falls upon the youthful shoulders of his successor. Bowing by the side of the fallen youth, Lieut. Col. Lane stops for a moment to ask: "My dear colonel, are *you severely hurt?" A bowed head and a motion to the left side and a pressure of the hand is the only response; but "he looked as pleasantly as if victory were on his brow." Reluctantly leaving his dying commander to go where duty calls him Lieut. Col Lane hastens to the right, meets Capt. McLauchlin, of Company K, tells him of Gen. Pettigrew's words of praise, but not of his colonel's fall. He gives the order: "Close your men quickly to the left. I am going to give them the bayonet." Gallant Capt. McLauchlin! In a few minutes he is so seriously wounded that his services to the Confederacy are lost.*

Col. Lane hurries to the left and gives similar orders and returns to the center. During this time the battle has been raging fiercely. Our captains have been coolly giving their orders. "Shoot low, men," and the men have been busy, but they have suffered dreadfully. After the battle Gen. Heth saw the line of those who fell at this time and remarked that the fallen were in line as if on dress parade. When Col. Lane returns he finds the colors still down. Col. Burgwyn and the brave Franklin Honeycutt lying by them. Now or never the regiment must advance.

He raises the flag. Lieut. Blair of Company I, rushes out, saying: "No man can take those colors and live." Lane replies, "It is my time to take them now," and shouting at the top of his voice while advancing with the flag, says: "Twenty-sixth, follow me." The men answer with a yell and press forward. Several lines of the enemy have given away, but a formidable line yet remains, which seems determined to hold its position. Volleys of musketry are fast thinning out those left; only a skeleton line now remains. To add to the horrors of the scene the battle smoke has settled down over the combatants making it almost as dark as night. But these men are undaunted. They never tire; their muscles are made of iron. With a cheer they greet every order to advance. They rush on and upward; now they reach the summit of the hill; the last line of the enemy gives way and suddenly retires.

Just as the last shots are firing, a sergeant—in the Twenty-fourth Michigan... lingers to take a farewell shot, with his last cartridge, and resting his musket on a tree he awaits his opportunity. When about thirty steps distant, as Col. Lane turns to cheer his regiment, a ball fired by his brave and resolute adversary strikes him in the back of the neck, just below the brain, crashes through his jaw and mouth, and for the fourteenth and last time the colors are down. They are taken from the hand of the fallen Lane by S. W. Brewer, the gallant captain of Company E, and the remnants of the regiment under command of Maj. J. T. Jones presses on to the Seminary, where the few survivors are relieved by Pender's Division. The red field is won....

Long after Gettysburg, when Colonel Lane was an aging Confederate veteran, he was introduced to a Chicago pharmaceutical executive named Charles H. McConnell, who turned out to be the sergeant in the 24th Michigan who had shot him in the final moments of the 26th's assault on McPherson's Ridge. "I thank God I did not kill you," McConnell told Lane. For the rest of their lives they remained friends.[6]

"He Was the Youngest Colonel I Ever Saw"

The "Boy Colonel of the Confederacy" Falls on McPherson's Ridge

The commander of the 26th North Carolina, Colonel Henry K. "Harry" Burgwyn, issued his first orders to the troops of that regiment as a young man of nineteen. It was the summer of 1861, and Burgwyn was a teenage major and drillmaster at Camp Carolina on the outskirts of Raleigh, North Carolina. The son of a prominent North Carolina planter and state official, Burgwyn was exceptionally bright and mature for one so young. He was an honors graduate from the University of North Carolina, which he had entered at age sixteen, and was also a distinguished alumnus of VMI. None other than General "Stonewall" Jackson, his former VMI instructor, had endorsed him as "a high-toned Southern gentleman" known for "the highly practical as well as scientific character of his mind." When North Carolina joined the Confederacy and began raising troops, Burgwyn was made drillmaster at the capital city's sprawling camp of instruction—all of this by age nineteen.

As a drillmaster, he marched and drilled the boisterous young recruits incessantly, determined to instill discipline and obedience in the ranks. His zeal for perfection led many of the independent-minded recruits to despise him, and when he became lieutenant colonel and second in command of the 26th North Carolina, some soldiers swore they would just as soon shoot Burgwyn as they would the Yankees. That attitude changed, however, when the regiment saw its first combat at the Battle of New Bern. There, the troops of the 26th were almost trapped and captured by victorious Federal forces, and narrowly escaped only through the discipline instilled in them by their demanding young drillmaster. Afterward Burgwyn was revered by his troops, and, in 1862, he was promoted to colonel and commander of the regiment—at age twenty. When he led the regiment into battle at Gettysburg, Burgwyn was only twenty-one, and would become known as the "Boy Colonel of the Confederacy."

At Gettysburg, the 26th North Carolina marched into battle as if on parade, advancing unflinchingly through killing fire up the wooded slopes of McPherson's Ridge and into the guns of the 19th Indiana and 24th Michigan. As the hard-fighting Black Hats of the Iron Brigade tore huge gaps in the 26th's battle lines, the North Carolinians demonstrated why the 26th was renowned as the best-drilled regiment in the Confederate army: they halted under fire, closed the gaps, dressed their ranks, and resumed their

Born in Massachusetts, Colonel Henry K. Burgwyn was raised in North Carolina and sided with the south. At age nineteen, he was a graduate of the University of North Carolina and the Virginia Military Institute—and at twenty-one, he led the 800-man 26th North Carolina Infantry Regiment into battle at Gettysburg.

Southern Historical Collection, University of North Carolina assault. At the peak of the battle, as his depleted regiment drove the Iron Brigade's line to the breaking point, Colonel Burgwyn was shot down with a mortal wound. As the regiment pressed on under Lieutenant Colonel Lane, some of the regiment's men moved Burgwyn to the rear, where he died. One of the soldiers who assisted Burgwyn, Private William M. Cheek, would later preserve a record of the last moments in the life of the "Boy Colonel."

———————————————

It was in the first day's fight at Gettysburg. Our regiment had been formed in line of battle and advanced a considerable distance towards the Federal lines. Our colors were very prominent in the center. Time after time they were shot down by the hot fire of infantry and artillery, and in all they fell fifteen times, sometimes the staff being broken and sometimes a color-bearer being shot down. The color-sergeant was killed quite early in the advance and then a private of F company took the flag. He was shot once, but rose and went on, saying, "Come on, boys!" and as the words left his lips was again shot down, when the flag was taken by Captain McCreery, who was killed a moment or two later.

Then Colonel Burgwyn himself took the colors and as we were advancing over the brow of a little hill and he was a few feet in advance of the center of the regiment, he was shot as he partly turned to give an order, a bullet passing through his abdomen. He fell backwards, the regiment continuing its advance, Lieutenant-Colonel John R. Lane taking command and at the same time taking the flag from Colonel Burgwyn. In a moment, it seemed, he was shot, and then Captain W. S. Brewer, of my company, took the flag and carried it through the remainder of the advance, Major John Jones having then assumed command of the regiment.

Our regiment was recalled and retired. I was knocked down by the explosion of a shell, which injured my eyesight somewhat, but soon rose and as myself and some comrades went back, I saw

Colonel Burgwyn being carried off the field by two soldiers, named Ellington and Staton, who were using one of their blankets for that purpose. Colonel Burgwyn asked me, whom he recognized as being a member of his command, to help carry him off the field, and I at once gave my aid.

We carried him some distance towards the place where our line of battle had been formed, and as we were thus moving him a lieutenant of some South Carolina regiment came up and took hold of the blanket to help us. Colonel Burgwyn did not seem to suffer much, but asked the lieutenant to pour some water on his wound. He was put down upon the ground while the water was poured from canteens upon him. His coat was taken off and I stooped to take his watch, which was held around his neck by a silk cord. As I did so the South Carolina lieutenant seized the watch, broke the cord, put the watch in his pocket and started off with it.

I demanded the watch, telling the officer that he should not thus take away the watch of my colonel, and that I would kill him as sure as powder would burn, with these words cocking my rifle and taking aim at him. I made him come back and give up the watch, at the same time telling him he was nothing but a thief, and then ordering him to leave, which he did. In a few moments Colonel Burgwyn said to me that he would never forget me, and I shall never forget the look he gave me as he spoke these words.

We then picked him up again and carried him very close to the place where we had been formed in line of battle. Captain Young, of General Pettigrew's staff, came up and expressed much sympathy with Colonel Burgwyn. The latter said that he was very grateful for the sympathy, and added, "The Lord's will be done. We have gained the greatest victory in the war. I have no regret at my approaching death. I fell in the defense of my country."

About that time a shell exploded very near us and took off the entire top of the hat of Captain Brewer, who had joined our party.

*I left and went to search for one of our litters, in order to place
Colonel Burgwyn upon it, so as to carry him more comfortably and
conveniently. I found the litter with some difficulty, and as the
bearers and myself came up to the spot where Colonel Burgwyn
was lying on the ground, we found that he was dying. I sat down
and took his hand in my lap. He had very little to say, but I remember that his last words were that he was entirely satisfied with
everything, and "The Lord's will be done." Thus he died, very
quietly and resignedly. I never saw a braver man than he. He was
always cool under fire and knew exactly what to do, and his men
were devoted to him. He was the youngest colonel I ever saw....[7]*

"They Came On...Yelling like Demons"

The Iron Brigade Is Finally Forced to Retreat

Colonel Henry A. Morrow, commander of the 24th Michigan, felt he had
no other option—his men had to fall back due to what he considered
"overpowering" pressure. Begrudging every step, they backed out of
Herbst Woods and off of McPherson's Ridge, firing at the advancing Confederates practically every step of the way. The entire Iron Brigade was falling

Pressed by the
Confederates of
General A. P. Hill's
Third Corps in the
afternoon fighting of
July 1, Federal troops
begrudgingly gave up
their hard-fought line
on McPherson's
Ridge and fell back
through town to
Cemetery Ridge.

*Battles and Leaders
of the Civil War*

back, along with the Federal troops on their flanks. Near the Lutheran Seminary on Seminary Ridge, they attempted to form a new line of defense, but it was a futile attempt. As they retreated, however, they made the victorious Confederates pay a steep price. When Lee ordered in his reserve troops—Major General William Dorsey Pender's division—they were raked by Federal artillery fire. Observed a Confederate eyewitness, "The earth just seemed to open up and take in that line...." Even so, it was not enough to stop the Federal collapse. As the Federal Eleventh Corps troops fled into Gettysburg from the north, the soldiers of the Federal First Corps also began retreating into town from the west—although they did so with much more discipline than the Eleventh Corps troops.

No troops from either side had fought harder than the men of the Iron Brigade, who had contested every foot of ground they had yielded on McPherson's Ridge. Colonel Morrow believed that the 24th Michigan, despite being forced to retreat, had fought gallantly. Morrow, a prewar army officer and a former Detroit judge, had been instrumental in raising his regiment back home in Michigan. Tall, stocky, and given to mutton-chop whiskers, he was a native Virginian, but he was a staunch Union man—as he had proved this day. The 24th Michigan had entered battle with 496 officers and troops; after the morning and afternoon fighting, fewer than a hundred remained unhurt.

Morrow was not among those uninjured—after retreating from the woods, he had been grazed and stunned by a bullet, then had been taken prisoner. He would escape and return to his regiment, however, and in the months following the event, he would write a detailed official report, describing the 24th Michigan's actions on McPherson's Ridge on July 1 and praising his courageous Black Hats—both the living and the dead.

Hdqrs. First Brig., First Div., First Army Corps
Culpeper, Va.,
February 22, 1864.

Captain: have the honor to submit the following report of the part taken by the Twenty-fourth Michigan Volunteers in the battle of Gettysburg, July 1, 1863.... The brigade changed front forward on first battalion, and marched into the woods known as McPherson's woods, and formed in line of battle, the Nineteenth Indiana being on the left of the Twenty-fourth Michigan and the Seventh Wisconsin on its right. In executing this movement, my lieutenant-colonel and adjutant were severely wounded, and did not afterward rejoin the regiment, the former having lost a leg, and the latter being severely wounded in the groin....

Born in Virginia, Colonel Henry A. Morrow had relocated to Michigan as a young man, and sided with the North. The regiment he commanded—the 24th Michigan Infantry—engaged the 26th North Carolina in Herbst Woods, and both were whittled down to nearly nothing.

U.S. Army Military History Institute

The enemy advanced in two lines of battle, their right extending beyond and overlapping our left. I gave direction to the men to withhold their fire until the enemy should come within short range of our guns. This was done, but the nature of the ground was such that I am inclined to think we inflicted but little injury on the enemy at this time. Their advance was not checked, and they came on with rapid strides, yelling like demons. The Nineteenth Indiana, on our left, fought most gallantly, but was overpowered by superior numbers, the enemy having also the advantage of position, and, after a severe loss, was forced back.

The left of my regiment was now exposed to an enfilading fire, and orders were given for this portion of the line to swing back, so as to face the enemy, now on this flank. Pending the execution of this movement, the enemy advanced in such force as to compel me to fall back and take a new position a short distance in the rear. In the meantime I had lost in killed and wounded several of my best officers and many of my men. Among the former were Captain William J. Speed, acting major, and Lieutenant Dickey, a young officer of great promise. Charles Ballou, my second color-bearer, was killed here.

The second line was promptly formed, and we made a desperate resistance, but the enemy accumulating in our front, and our losses being very great, we were forced to fall back and take up a third position beyond a slight ravine. My third color-bearer, Augustus Ernest, of Company K, was killed on this line. Maj. E. B. Wight, acting lieutenant-colonel, was wounded at this time and compelled to leave the field. By this time the ranks were so diminished that scarcely a fourth of the forces taken into action could be rallied. Corpl. Andrew Wagner, Company F, one of the color guard, took the colors, and was ordered by me to plant them in a position to which I designed to rally the men. He was wounded in the breast and left on the field. I now took the flag from the ground, where it had fallen, and was rallying the remnant of my regiment, when Private William Kelly, of Company E, took the colors from my hands, remarking, as he did so, "The colonel of the Twenty-fourth shall never carry the flag while I am alive." He was killed instantly. Private Lilburn A. Spaulding, of Company K, seized the colors and bore them for a time.

Subsequently I took them from him to rally the men, and kept them until I was wounded. We had inflicted severe loss on the enemy, but their numbers were so overpowering and our own losses had been so great that we were unable to maintain our position, and were forced back, step by step, contesting every foot of ground, to the barricade. I was wounded just before reaching the barricade, west of the seminary building, and left the field. Previous to abandoning our last position, orders were received to fall back, given, I believe, by Major-General Doubleday. The command of the regiment now

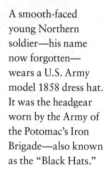

A smooth-faced young Northern soldier—his name now forgotten—wears a U.S. Army model 1858 dress hat. It was the headgear worn by the Army of the Potomac's Iron Brigade—also known as the "Black Hats."

Library of Congress

Stripped of their footwear—probably by shoeless Confederates—Federal dead await burial in a Gettysburg field. Heavy casualties within the Iron Brigade left McPherson Ridge cluttered with the bodies of Federal troops.

Library of Congress

devolved upon Capt. Albert M. Edwards, who collected the remnant of it, and fell back with the brigade to Culp's Hill, which it held for the two succeeding days.

Shortly after I was wounded, Captain Edwards found the colors in the hands of a wounded soldier, who had fallen on the east side of the barricade. He was reclining on his right side, and was holding the colors in his left hand. I have not been able to ascertain the name of this brave soldier in whose paralyzed hands Captain Edwards found the flag. Captain Edwards describes him as being severely wounded, and he is, therefore, probably among our dead. His name may forever be unknown, but his bravery will never die. Captain Edwards behaved very gallantly at this time in rallying the men under a murderous fire. The field over which we fought, from our first line of battle in McPherson's woods to the barricade near the seminary, was strewn with the killed and wounded. Our losses were very large, exceeding, perhaps, the losses sustained by any one regiment of equal size in a single engagement of this or any other war.…

During the battle of the 1st instant, the regiment lost in killed four color-bearers—Abel G. Peck, Charles Ballou, Augustus Ernest, *and William Kelly. During the engagement of the 1st, the flag was carried by no less then nine persons, four of the number having been killed and three wounded. All of the color guard were killed or wounded.... Of the killed nothing less can be said than that their conduct in this memorable battle was brave and daring, and was creditable alike to themselves and the service. It will not be disparaging to his brave comrades who fell on this terrible but glorious day to say that Captain Speed's death was a severe loss to the service and an almost irreparable one to his regiment. He was amiable, intelligent, honorable, and brave, and was universally respected and esteemed by all who knew him. Captain O'Donnell was a young officer who had given strong proofs of courage and capacity, and whose death was deeply deplored in the regiment.*

Lieutenant Wallace served in the Peninsular Campaign under General McClellan, and lost an eye at the battle of Fair Oaks. He was a brave officer, an honorable man, and a good disciplinarian. Lieutenant Dickey joined the regiment in the capacity of commissary sergeant, and for his integrity, capacity, and attention to business was promoted to the rank of sergeant-major, and thence to a second lieutenancy. He had given great promise for future usefulness and distinction. He was the first commissioned officer of the regiment killed at Gettysburg. Lieutenants Grace, Humphreville, Safford, and Shattuck were distinguished in the regiment for their attention to duty, for the amiability of their manners, and for their unflinching courage in battle. Lieutenant Grace was one of the bravest men I ever knew. The remains of Captain Speed and Lieutenants Wallace and Safford were conveyed to Michigan by their friends, for interment, but the remains of the other officers sleep, with the brave non-commissioned officers and privates who fell that day, in the cemetery in which a grateful nation will, at no distant period, erect a mausoleum to perpetuate the memories of its defenders....

When the Federal line broke on the afternoon of July 1, Federal troops on the north and west sides of Gettysburg retreated into town across these fields.

National Archives

I have the honor to be, captain, your obedient servant,

Henry A. Morrow,

Colonel, Twenty-fourth Michigan Volunteers.[8]

"Gettysburg Was Fully in the Enemy's Possession"

The Army of the Potomac Flees through Gettysburg in Retreat

A fter the Iron Brigade and other First Corps troops reformed on Seminary Ridge, they received orders to retreat again—this time all the way into Gettysburg. There, they found the streets crowded with panicky Eleventh Corps troops. Lee had won the first day of battle on July 1 with two well-coordinated afternoon attacks—one on the north side of town and the other on the west side. He had managed to assemble about 23,000 troops in battle compared to 18,800 Federal troops, which erased the Army of the Potomac's numerical superiority. The arrival of Ewell's corps from the north was perfectly timed and proved critical to the defeat of the Eleventh Corps. On the west side of town, both Northern and Southern troops had fought courageously, but Lee's troops had prevailed—and now, from two directions, pursued the defeated Federals into Gettysburg.

As the battle spilled into town, scores of Southern soldiers advanced from street to street. Some Federal troops attempted to fight back; others ran or hid—mainly the panicked troops of the Eleventh Corps. "Away went guns and knapsacks and they fled for dear life," observed a Federal army surgeon. "The rebels coolly and deliberately shot them down like sheep. I did not see an officer attempt to rally them or check them in their headlong retreat." Earlier that day as he arrived in Gettysburg, General Howard had spotted Cemetery Hill—named for a sprawling town graveyard atop it—and the mile-long ridge that extended from it southward out of town. Immediately recognizing its potential strategic importance, he established his headquarters on the hill and positioned a division of troops and two batteries of artillery there as a rallying point if it was so needed.

It was. As the first Federal troops came streaming into town in retreat, Major General Winfield Scott Hancock arrived on horseback from the south. General Meade had rushed him to Gettysburg with orders to take command of Federal forces there—even though General Howard outranked Hancock. At his temporary headquarters south of Gettysburg at Taneytown—where he had been directing Federal troops to the battle—General Meade had received a grim dispatch from General Buford: "General Reynolds was killed early this morning. In my opinion, there appears to be no directing person." In response, Meade sent word to Hancock, who was farther up the road, to take charge at Gettysburg.

Hancock was the right choice to bring order to chaos. A native Pennsylvanian, he had been accepted into West Point at age fifteen, graduating in the class of 1844. He was brevetted for his conduct in the Mexican War, gained experience fighting the Seminole Indians in Florida, and had held several postings in the West. In the Peninsula Campaign, as well as at Antietam, at Fredericksburg, and at Chancellorsville, he had held important combat commands—and in two years he had risen in rank from captain to major general. Just weeks earlier, he had been issued command of the Army of the Potomac's Second Corps. At about four o'clock on July 1, he arrived at Gettysburg—attired in a clean white shirt—and promptly took charge. Although humiliated by having to yield command

Known for his clean white shirts and commanding presence, Major General Winfield S. Hancock took decisive action on July 1, halting the Federal retreat and placing the army in a strong defensive position.

National Archives

to a subordinate, General Howard did so gracefully. General Doubleday appeared less graceful—until Hancock's barked orders at him—then all three took action to rally the defeated Federal army.

Hancock further secured Cemetery Hill, deployed troops atop Culp's Hill—another nearby rocky, wooded eminence—and put the retreating Federal troops in a defensive battle line southward along Cemetery Ridge. Hancock's commanding presence and decisive action soothed the anxious Federal troops, who obediently moved into line and began piling rocks and fence rails into breastworks. Howard's earlier decision to secure Cemetery Hill, coupled with Hancock's handling of the defeated Federal troops, saved the Federal army.

The demoralizing panic that began to seize many Federal soldiers was observed by eighteen-year-old Henry Jacobs, a student at Gettysburg's Lutheran Seminary. Earlier in the day, young Jacobs had watched those same troops advance confidently through town.

A strange and awful spectacle followed in those same streets at 4 o'clock in the afternoon. Overwhelmed, beaten, completely routed in their conflict with Ewell's command, they fled back through the town in wild disorder. There were 2,500 men made prisoners in the streets before our eyes. Our family now took to the cellar, where a window afforded a partial view. In the rear of the fleeing, routed troops the artillery lingered, turning now and then to fire a deterring shot, and, as best it might, protect the despairing *retreat. But the Confederates kept at their very backs. As I stared from the window, I saw a Union soldier running, his breath coming in gasps, a group of Confederates almost upon him. He was in full flight, not turning or even thinking of resistance. But he was not surrendering, either. "Shoot him! Shoot him!" yelled a pursuer. A rifle cracked and the fugitive fell dead at our door. One after another fell that way in the grim chase from the Carlisle road.*

There came a lull in the stream of runners and their hunters. Then came a thunderous pounding fell upon our door by fists and boots. I ran upstairs. One of our own [Pennsylvania] Bucktails named Burlingame, wounded in the leg was there supported by a group of his comrades who would not desert him, and demanded shelter. We took him in, with two of the others, who said they would stay with him. Half an hour later a detail of Confederates arrived and insisted on searching the house. It was impossible to conceal the wounded man. They found him in father's study! His comrades they ferreted out of the cellar. Those they took with them, prisoners; but Burlingame they allowed to remain with us because of his wounds....

With two Colt revolvers tucked in his belt and a pipe in his mouth, a New York soldier strikes a jaunty pose. At Gettysburg, the Army of the Potomac's Eleventh Corps included troops from eleven New York infantry regiments and two New York artillery batteries.

Library of Congress

By 5 o'clock that Wednesday afternoon Gettysburg was fully in the enemy's possession. Dole's brigade of the Rodes division in Ewell's corps quartered itself in our immediate neighborhood. They tore down all our fences to let the troops pass readily; but the harshest critic would find it difficult to find fault with their conduct. They were Georgians, all gentlemanly, courteous and as considerate of the townspeople as it was possible for men in their position to be. The next morning after they had breakfast, I saw a whole crew of them reading from their pocket testaments. Of course, they breathed

*fire and fury at their foes; they were full of what they were going to
do to the hated North; but they were kindly, courteous, Christian
gentlemen, none the less.*

*The evening of the battle's first day fell very quiet and still. The
college and the seminary were crowded with wounded. But it
seemed as though a merciful hush had been laid on the warring
passions of mankind....*

———

In contrast to some of the Eleventh Corps troops, Colonel Rufus Dawes of
the 6th Wisconsin Infantry led his Black Hats through the Gettysburg streets
with measured discipline. All around him, however, he saw signs of panic and
fear. Years later, he would describe the retreat through Gettysburg.

*The streets were jammed with crowds of retreating soldiers, and
with ambulances, artillery, and wagons. The cellars were crowded
with men, sound in body, but craven in spirit, who had gone there
to surrender. I saw no men wearing badges of the first army corps
in this disgraceful company. In one case, these miscreants, mistaking us for the rebels, cried out from the cellar, "Don't fire, Johnny,
we'll surrender."*

*These surroundings were depressing to my hot and thirsty men.
Finding the street blocked, I formed my men in two lines across it.
The rebels began to fire on us from houses and cross-lots. Here came
to us a friend in need. It was an old citizen with two buckets of fresh
water. The inestimable value of this cup of cold water to those true,
unyielding soldiers, I would that our old friend could know.*

*After this drink, in response to my call, the men gave three cheers
for the good and glorious cause for which we stood in battle. The
enemy fired on us sharply, and the men returned their fire, shooting
wherever the enemy appeared. This firing had a good effect. It*

cleared the street of stragglers in short order. The way being open I marched again toward the Cemetery Hill. The enemy did not pursue; they had found it dangerous business....

If fresh troops had attacked us then, we unquestionably would have fared badly. The troops were scattered over the hill in much disorder, while a stream of stragglers and wounded men pushed along the Baltimore Turnpike toward the rear. But this perilous condition of affairs was of short duration. There was no appearance of panic on the Cemetery Hill. After a short breathing spell my men again promptly responded to the order to "fall in." Lieutenant Rogers brought us orders from General Wadsworth, to join our own brigade, which had been sent to occupy Culp's Hill.

As we marched toward the hill our regimental wagon joined us. In the wagon were a dozen spades and shovels. Taking our place on the right of the line of the brigade, I ordered the regiment to intrench. The men worked with great energy. A man would dig with all his strength till out of breath, when another would seize the spade and push on the work. There were no orders to construct these breastworks, but the situation plainly dictated their necessity. The men now lay down to rest after the arduous labors of this great and terrible day.

Sad and solemn reflections possessed, at least, the writer of these papers. Our dead lay unburied and beyond our sight or reach. Our wounded were in the hands of the enemy. Our bravest and best were numbered with them. Of eighteen hundred men who marched with the splendid brigade in the morning, but seven hundred were here. More than one thousand men had been shot. There was to us a terrible reality in the figures which represent our loss. We had been driven, also, by the enemy, and the shadow of defeat seemed to be hanging over us....[9]

"It Was a Moment of Most Critical Importance"

A Confederate Opportunity to Attack the Weakened Federal Army is Rejected

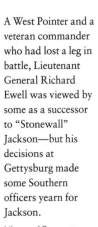

A West Pointer and a veteran commander who had lost a leg in battle, Lieutenant General Richard Ewell was viewed by some as a successor to "Stonewall" Jackson—but his decisions at Gettysburg made some Southern officers yearn for Jackson.

Library of Congress

As Federal troops scrambled through town heading for Cemetery Hill, Gettysburg's town square filled with victorious, celebrating Confederate soldiers. To many, it appeared as if "Uncle Robert"—as Lee's troops reverently called him—had prevailed again, and had won the great victory on Northern soil that might spur an end to the war and establish Southern nationhood. Others were not so certain—not yet. General Ewell's subordinates—Generals Rodes, Early, Gordon, and others—were restless and impatient to follow up on the victory and move against the enemy troops amassing around Cemetery Hill and the ridge running south from it—to break the Army of the Potomac before its defeated troops could be rallied and reorganized. General Ewell, however, would not take action.

At forty-six, Ewell was bearded, balding, profane, and witty. A West Pointer who had fought the Mexicans at Churubusco and fought the Apache out West, he was known to be a dependable, courageous combat officer. He had been a division commander under "Stonewall" Jackson, and now commanded Jackson's former troops as a corps commander. "Old Bald Head"—as he was known in the ranks—had lost his right leg at Second Bull Run and wore a wooden replacement. Riding through Gettysburg with General Gordon, Ewell was hit by a stray bullet which struck his wooden leg. "Are you hurt, sir?" Gordon quickly asked. "No, no, I'm not hurt," Ewell joked. "It don't hurt to be shot in a wooden leg." To his thinking, he had sound reasons for not attacking Cemetery Hill: his available troops were battered from the day's brutal fighting, their momentum had been slowed by the street fighting in town, and some of his corps—Major General Edward Johnson's division—had not yet arrived. Furthermore, General Lee's most recent orders directed him to attack "if practicable"—and to Ewell, a follow-up assault was not "practicable."

Another subordinate, the feisty sixty-one-year-old Major General Isaac Trimble, would later state that he offered to personally lead an attack on Federal positions assembling near Culp's Hill. "Give me a Brigade and I will engage to take that hill," he reportedly urged Ewell. When Ewell said nothing in reply, Trimble cried in frustration, "Give me a good regiment and I will do it!" Yet Ewell ignored him. Some officers, including the aggressive Jubal Early, supported Ewell's decision, but his reluctance to attack made others yearn for "Stonewall" Jackson and his irrepressible hammer-like attacks. They believed a priceless opportunity to decisively defeat the Federal army was wasted. "Oh," said one, "for the presence and inspiration of 'Old Jack' for just one hour!" By the time Lee could consult with General Ewell in person, everyone agreed that it was too late to mount an attack. In the gathering darkness, the sound of spades breaking earth could be heard from the direction of Cemetery Hill—the Federal army was digging in for another day's fighting.

Sixty-one-year-old Major General Isaac Trimble urged General Ewell to follow up on the Confederate first-day victory and attack the defeated Federal army while it was weak. "Give me a good regiment and I will do it!" Trimble vowed, but Ewell declined.

Wikimedia Commons Images

Captain James Power Smith, a twenty-seven-year-old *aide-de-camp* to Ewell, witnessed the controversy. A Presbyterian preacher's son and a seminary graduate, Smith had been an aide to "Stonewall" Jackson, enjoying a relationship that some described as akin to that of a father and son. After Jackson's death, Smith became an aide to General Ewell and served under him at Gettysburg. Years later, he would pen an account of the events surrounding Ewell's decision not to attack the defeated and weakened Army of the Potomac.

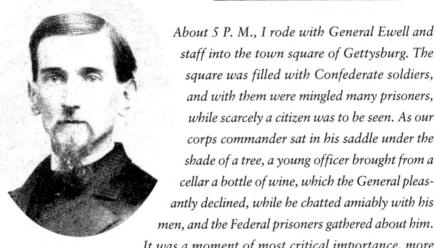

Captain James P. Smith had served as a chief aide to General Jackson, before accepting a similar post with General Ewell. Observing Ewell's decision not to attack the defeated Federals, Smith concluded, "Whatever the opportunity was, it was lost."

Photographic History of the Civil War

About 5 P. M., I rode with General Ewell and staff into the town square of Gettysburg. The square was filled with Confederate soldiers, and with them were mingled many prisoners, while scarcely a citizen was to be seen. As our corps commander sat in his saddle under the shade of a tree, a young officer brought from a cellar a bottle of wine, which the General pleasantly declined, while he chatted amiably with his men, and the Federal prisoners gathered about him. It was a moment of most critical importance, more evidently critical to us now, than it would seem to any one then. But even then, some of us who had served on Jackson's staff, sat in a group in our saddles, and one said sadly, "Jackson is not here."

Our corps commander, General Ewell, as true a Confederate soldier as ever went into battle, was simply waiting for orders, when every moment of the time could not be balanced with gold. General Early and General Rodes came with great earnestness and animation to tell of the advanced position. They desired General Lee to be informed that they could go forward and take Cemetery hill if they were supported on their right; that to the south of the Cemetery there was in sight a position commanding it which should be taken at once; and I was sent by General Ewell to deliver the message to the commanding general.

I found General Lee quite well to the right, in an open field, with General Longstreet, dismounted, and with glasses inspecting the position to the south of Cemetery hill. When I delivered my message, General Lee gave me his glasses and said that the elevated position in front was he supposed the commanding position of which Early and Rodes spoke, that some of "those people" were there (a few mounted men, apparently reconnoitering), that he had no force on the field with which to take that position; and turning to Longstreet asked where his troops were, and expressed the wish that they might be brought immediately to the front. General Longstreet replied that his front division, McLaws, was about six miles away, and then was indefinite and noncommittal.

General Lee directed me to say to General Ewell that "he regretted that his people were not up to support him on the right, but he wished him to take the Cemetery hill if it were possible; and that he would ride over and see him very soon." Whatever the opportunity was, it was lost. Early and Rodes were ready for the assault; A. P. Hill felt the losses in his command and waited for third division, Anderson's, and General Ewell, waiting for his third division, Johnson's, and diverted by a false alarm on his left, lacked initiative and looked for instructions from his commander.... As the sun went down, Edward Johnson arrived on the northwest of the field. General Lee came over and conferred with Generals Ewell, Early and Rodes, outside of the town, on the Carlisle road. All had abandoned attack for that evening....

As Lee gave up his hope for a climactic, decisive attack on the defeated Federal forces, the exhausted troops of the Army of the Potomac began to bed down on Cemetery Hill and along Cemetery Ridge. They had been rallied and redeployed—but they were minus almost 4,000 of their fellow soldiers. That many troops were now behind Confederate lines as prisoners of war—a number comparable to an entire division. Another 5,000 were dead or wounded. Among the Federal troops on Cemetery Ridge struggling to gain a few hours of sleep, an unknown number of them were demoralized by the day's defeat. "What added to our uneasiness," an Iron Brigade veteran would candidly recall, "was the fact that the rebs might clean out the Army of the Potomac and take Washington, then 'Old Abe' and the country were gone for certain." The first day's fighting at Gettysburg had not concluded as either army commander—neither Meade nor Lee—had hoped. But on the night of July 1, both yearned for a decisive victory the next day.[10]

CHAPTER FIVE

"He Is There and I Am Going to Attack Him"

At daylight on Thursday, July 2, General George Meade stood atop Cemetery Hill on the edge of Gettysburg. Nearby, at the entrance to the town graveyard, a cemetery sign boasted an old and, now, an ironic warning: "All persons found using fire-arms in these grounds will be prosecuted with the utmost rigor of the law." Regardless, Meade was at Gettysburg, and he was ready to fight. He had been up all night. Accompanied by his staff, he had ridden up from his Taneytown headquarters during the night, and had reached Gettysburg shortly before midnight. He had been unsure where the expected battle would actually occur, so had remained at Taneytown while dispatching troops to Gettysburg. When Meade realized that Gettysburg was actually the site of the confrontation, he had dispatched General Hancock to take charge, and then had set out on horseback for the battle. At Gettysburg, even in the dark of night, he could see the distant Confederate campfires flickering to the west on Seminary Ridge. He was pleased with how Hancock had rallied the defeated troops, and he approved of the defensive line that Hancock and Howard had anchored at Cemetery Hill, atop Culp's Hill, and along Cemetery Ridge.

By now, most of the Army of the Potomac had arrived at or had almost reached Gettysburg—except for the Federal Sixth Corps, which was still on the march but was not far away. Meade established his headquarters in a two-room whitewashed farmhouse just behind Cemetery Ridge on Taneytown Road, just south of town. There, he conferred with his commanders and engineers. He was thoroughly businesslike, certain that the life-and-death struggle between the two armies would happen here at Gettysburg, and soon. He considered taking the offensive, but decided against it: he saw the Federal line that Hancock had organized as too strong to abandon—better to fortify it and wait for Lee to attack him, Meade concluded. If necessary, he thought, he could always assume the offensive—especially if Lee attempted to withdraw and move against Washington. The natural lay of the land now occupied by his troops was ideal for defense, and Meade gave orders to strengthen and bolster the defensive line set up by Hancock.[1]

General Meade reached Gettysburg shortly before midnight on July 1. He spent the rest of the night examining his army's positions and developing a plan of battle.

National Archives

"I Feel Fully the Responsibility Resting Upon Me"

General Meade Adopts a Defensive Strategy

General Meade surveyed his lines again at midday on July 2, and reassured himself that his army now had "a strong position for defensive," as he put it. Federal forces were deployed on the south side of Gettysburg in a line shaped like a giant, inverted fishhook. The point of the hook was at Culp's Hill, a 140-foot-high, boulder-strewn, heavily wooded hill that lay just southwest of town. The hook curved around the adjacent Cemetery Hill to the west of Culp's

Hill, and the shank extended southward from Cemetery Hill in the north along Cemetery Ridge for more than a mile to the eye of the fishhook—the base of two large, rocky, and heavily forested hills known to locals as Little Round Top and Big Round Top.

Almost the entire Federal line lay on high ground, and Meade's infantry fortified the line by piling up rocks into stone walls, reinforced in many places with wooden fence rails filched from farmers' fields. Federal forces rolled their field artillery into position at excellent locations—high ground with clear fields of fire overlooking the enemy's likely assault routes. Meanwhile, in the distant tree line to the west—almost a mile away across the Emmitsburg Road—Southern forces were deployed in a long line of battle, extending southward from Gettysburg along Seminary Ridge. By midday, almost all of the Army of the Potomac had reached Gettysburg—only the massive Sixth Corps lagged behind, and it too was nearing Gettysburg. Meade had established an artillery reserve behind Cemetery Ridge, and, farther back, a wagon park to keep the army's supply wagons close at hand, but with quick access to the Baltimore Pike.

And now he waited. If the enemy did not attack, he would take up the offensive and order the army to make an assault. In the afternoon, reports from his signal station atop Big Round Top and elsewhere indicated movement against both of his flanks. It was just a question of time, he believed, until the Confederates came his way. He dispatched an official update to General in Chief Henry W. Halleck in Washington. In it, he lightly passed over the previous day's near-disastrous defeat—two corps had to "fall back from the town," he stated—and advised Halleck (and President Lincoln) of his defensive strategy. He also noted that he was awaiting "the attack of the enemy."

Back in Washington, President Lincoln waited in the War Department telegraph office for news from the Army of the Potomac. General Meade's July 2 message from Gettysburg admitted that the army had been forced to "fall back" the day before. National Archives

Headquarters Near Gettysburg, Pa.,
July 2, 1863—3 p. m.
Maj. Gen. H. W. Halleck

General-in-Chief:
    I have concentrated my army at this place to-day. The Sixth Corps is just coming in, very much worn out, having been marching since 9 p. m., last night.
    The army is fatigued. I have to-day, up to this hour, awaited the attack of the enemy, I having a strong position for defensive. I am not determined, as yet, on attacking him till his position is more developed. He has been moving on both my flanks, apparently, but it is difficult to tell exactly his movements. I have delayed attacking, to allow the Sixth Corps and parts of other corps to reach this place and to rest the men. Expecting a battle, I ordered all my trains to the rear. If not attacked, and I can get any positive information of the position of the enemy which will justify me in so doing, I shall attack. If I find it hazardous to do so, or am satisfied the enemy is endeavoring to move to my rear and interpose between me and Washington, I shall fall back to my supplies at Westminster. I will endeavor to advise you as often as possible. In the engagement yesterday the enemy concentrated more rapidly than we could, and toward evening, owing to the superiority of numbers, compelled the Eleventh and First Corps to fall back from the town to the heights this side, on which I am now posted. I feel fully the responsibility resting upon me, but will endeavor to act with caution.

Geo. G. Meade
Major General[2]

"The Enemy Is There and I Am Going to Attack Him"

Lee Decides to Take the Offensive at Gettysburg

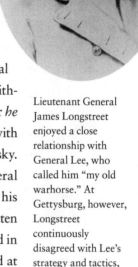

eneral Robert E. Lee had also slept little. He too was up long before daylight on the morning of July 2—and he, too, had decided his strategy: he would take the offensive and attack the enemy. The night before, he had established his tent headquarters near a stone and frame house on Gettysburg's west side. By then, in his typical decisive fashion, he had weighed his options: he could withdraw his army; he could wait for the Federals to attack—or *he* could attack. With his heavily-laden supply wagons, and with the Federal army pressing his rear, withdrawal would be risky. His army was living off the land, and to wait for a Federal attack meant that rations would be quickly depleted and his army potentially weakened. His men had thoroughly beaten the Army of the Potomac in their last three encounters, and in two of the three contests—the first day at Gettysburg and at Chancellorsville—he had won by taking the offensive. He also had serene confidence in his troops—"There were never such men in an army before," he had said, and they had grown accustomed to winning. Lee believed the wisest course of action at Gettysburg was to attack—and to do so immediately.

Lieutenant General James Longstreet enjoyed a close relationship with General Lee, who called him "my old warhorse." At Gettysburg, however, Longstreet continuously disagreed with Lee's strategy and tactics, and later claimed that Lee "seemed under a subdued excitement."
Library of Congress

His second-in-command at Gettysburg, Lieutenant General James Longstreet, disagreed. "Old Pete," as his troops called him, had not been enthusiastic about an invasion of the North. Instead, he had advised taking part of Lee's army and sending it by train to the war's Western Theater, where it might help relieve the vitally important Confederate bastion at Vicksburg on the Mississippi, which was under relentless attack by Federal forces under Major General

Ulysses S. Grant. His proposal had not been accepted, and after Lee's first day victory at Gettysburg, Longstreet had pressed hard for Lee to take the defensive, wait for the enemy to attack, and let the Federals expend themselves the way they had been defeated at Fredericksburg. Lee disagreed. "Gentlemen," he had told Longstreet and others the night before, "we will attack the enemy in the morning as early as practicable." Now, in a pre-dawn conference with Lee and others on Seminary Ridge, Longstreet argued for a flanking movement that could force the Federals to retreat. Lee again disagreed. "No," he had declared earlier, "the enemy is there and I am going to attack him there." Lee believed the wisest course of action was to strike the Federal army and shatter it before it could be fully concentrated. He wanted to attack the left side of the Federal line, turn it, and roll it up. He wanted Longstreet to direct the attack. And he wanted it done quickly.

Longstreet *would* direct the Confederate assault that day—and it would be launched against the Federal left—but it would *not* happen quickly. At times, James Longstreet could be a brilliant commander—Lee called him "my old war-horse"—and the two operated closely together. "The relations between [Lee] and Longstreet are quite touching," the British observer Fremantle noted, "they are almost always together." Tall, dark-haired, with a thick, chest-length beard, Longstreet was a South Carolinian raised in Georgia, who had achieved academic success as a West Point cadet. He had been wounded and decorated for bravery in the Mexican War, had served on the Western frontier, and had quickly risen to major general in Confederate service. At Second Bull Run, Lee had allowed him to delay an attack in order to concentrate his troops, and Longstreet had delivered a stunning success. "Longstreet is a Capital soldier," Lee once told Confederate president Jefferson Davis.

Despite his abilities, Longstreet was viewed by some as arrogant, and if he felt rebuffed he could be moody and glum—an attitude that may have begun when three of his children died of scarlet fever in 1862. On the second day at Gettysburg, he moved slowly to execute Lee's orders. The delays were unavoidable, Longstreet's supporters would claim, caused by a long, circuitous marching route that Longstreet was compelled to take in order to prevent Federal forces from detecting his movements. Critics, however, would accuse him of pouting and moving leisurely because he disagreed with Lee's plans—thus undermining Lee's strategy. Longstreet would stir further controversy after the war by writing about Gettysburg in a manner that many Southerners viewed as critical and disrespectful of Lee—and doing so after Lee's death when rebuttal was impossible. Longstreet's postwar comments may have been self-serving, but resentment toward him in the South may also have been fueled by his postwar political connections with the Republican Party.

In the five years that Lee would live after the war, he would barely say anything to defend his actions at Gettysburg. Longstreet, however, would later detail his objections to Lee's strategy in various publications, including in *The Annals of the War*, published by the *Philadelphia Weekly Times*.

Longstreet, posing with an ornate timepiece in this postwar image, was faulted by critics for taking too much time to deploy his troops at Gettysburg. In his memoirs, he would claim that he urged Lee to employ defensive tactics in the battle.

National Archives

When I overtook General Lee, at five o'clock that afternoon [of July 1], he said, to my surprise, that he thought of attacking General Meade upon the heights the next day. I suggested that this course seemed to be at variance with the plan of the campaign that had been agreed upon before leaving Fredericksburg. He said: "If the enemy is there to-morrow, we must attack him." I replied: "If he is there, it will be because he is anxious that we should attack him—a good reason, in my judgment, for not doing so." I urged that we should move around by our right to the left of Meade, and put our army between him and Washington, threatening his left and rear, and thus force him to attack us in such position as we might select. I said that it seemed to me that if, during our council at Fredericksburg, we had described the position in which we desired to get the two armies, we could not have expected to get the enemy in a better position for us than that he then occupied; that he was in strong position and would be awaiting us, which was evidence that he desired that we should attack him. I said, further, that his weak point seemed to be his left; hence, I thought that we should move around to his left, that we might threaten it if we intended to maneuvre [sic], or attack it if we determined upon a battle.

I called his attention to the fact that the country was admirably adapted for a defensive battle, and that we should surely repulse Meade with crushing loss if we would take position so as to force him to attack us, and suggested that, even if we carried the heights in front of us, and drove Meade out, we should be so badly crippled that we could not reap the fruits of victory; and that the heights of Gettysburg were, in themselves, of no more importance to us than the ground we then occupied, and that the mere possession of the ground was not worth a hundred men to us. That Meade's army, not its position, was our objective.

General Lee was impressed with the idea that, by attacking the Federals, he could whip them in detail. I reminded him that if the Federals were there in the morning, it would be proof that they had their forces well in hand, and that with Pickett in Chambersburg, and Stuart out of reach, we should be somewhat in detail. He, however, did not seem to abandon the idea of attack on the next day. He seemed under a subdued excitement, which occasionally took possession of him when "the hunt was up," and threatened his superb equipoise. The sharp battle fought by Hill and Ewell on that day had given him a taste of victory. Upon this point I quote General Fitzhugh Lee, who says, speaking of the attack on the 3d: "He told the father of the writer [his brother] that he was controlled too far by the great confidence he felt in the fighting qualities of his people, who begged simply to be 'turned loose,' and by the assurances of most of his higher officers...."

When I left General Lee on the night of the 1st, I believed that he had made up his mind to attack, but was confident that he had not yet determined as to when the attack should be made.... General Lee never, in his life, gave me orders to open an attack at a specific hour. He was perfectly satisfied that, when I had my troops in position, and was ordered to attack, no time was ever lost. On the night of the 1st I left him without any orders at all.

On the morning of the 2d, I went to General Lee's headquarters at daylight, and renewed my views against making an attack. He seemed resolved, however, and we discussed the probable results. We observed the position of the Federals, and got a general idea of the nature of the ground. About sunrise General Lee sent Colonel Venable, of his staff, to General Ewell's headquarters, ordering him to make a reconnoissance [sic] of the ground in his front, with a view of making the main attack on his left. A short time afterward he followed Colonel Venable in person. He returned at about nine o'clock, and informed me that it would not do to have Ewell open the attack. He, finally, determined that I should make the main attack on the extreme right. It was fully eleven o'clock when General Lee arrived at this conclusion and ordered the movement. In the meantime, by General Lee's authority, Law's Brigade, which had been put upon picket duty, was ordered to rejoin my command, and, upon my suggestion that it would be better to await its arrival, General Lee assented. We waited about forty minutes for these troops, and then moved forward.

A delay of several hours occurred in the march of the troops. The cause of this delay was that we had been ordered by General Lee to proceed cautiously upon the forward movement, so as to avoid being seen by the enemy. General Lee ordered Colonel Johnston, of his engineer corps, to lead and conduct the head of the column. My troops, therefore, moved forward under guidance of a special officer of General Lee, and with instructions to follow his directions. I left General Lee only after the line had stretched out on the march, and rode along with Hood's Division, which was in the rear. The march was necessarily slow, the conductor frequently encountering points that exposed the troops to the view of the signal station on Round Top.

At length the column halted. After waiting some time, supposing that it would soon move forward, I sent to the front to inquire the occasion of the delay. It was reported that the column was awaiting the movements of Colonel Johnston, who was trying to lead it by some route by which it could pursue its march without falling under view of the Federal signal station. Looking up toward Round Top I saw that the signal station was in full view, and, as we could plainly see this station, it was apparent that our heavy columns was seen from their position, and that further efforts to conceal ourselves would be a waste of time.

I became very impatient at this delay, and determined to take upon myself the responsibility of hurrying the troops forward. I did not order General McLaws forward, because, as the head of the column, he had direct orders from General Lee to follow the conduct of Colonel Johnston. Therefore, I sent orders to Hood, who was in the rear and not encumbered by these instructions, to push his division forward by the most direct route, so as to take position on my right. He did so, and thus broke up the delay. The troops were rapidly thrown into position, and preparations were made for the attack....[3]

"I Saw That This Was the Key of the Whole Position"

Federal Forces Scramble to Secure Little Round Top

Without reconnaissance from General Stuart's cavalry, which was still unaccounted for, Lee had limited knowledge of the terrain and of Federal deployments. He did not realize the full extent of the Federal defensive line, believing—incorrectly—that its extreme left flank stopped near a field of wheat that lay east of the Emmitsburg Road. At the time, the line extended to the base of Little Round Top. Lee's plan of attack called for Longstreet to strike the Federal left flank where Lee believed it ended—at the wheat field—turn the enemy flank and then attack northward, rolling up the Federal battle line back toward Gettysburg. Meanwhile, from the northern end of the Confederate line, troops from General A. P. Hill's corps would make a secondary attack on Cemetery Ridge so that the Federal army would be smashed between two hammer-like blows.

As the twin attacks began, according to Lee's instructions, General Ewell would move his corps against Culp's Hill and Cemetery Hill from the north, and apply pressure to keep General Meade from shoring up the Federal left flank with troops from his right flank. If given the opportunity, Ewell needed to make a full-force attack on Culp's Hill and on Cemetery Hill. It was a complicated plan, requiring coordinated timing and the kind of shock-force attack that had been executed for Lee in the past by "Stonewall" Jackson. But Lee did not have Jackson at Gettysburg.

Lee wanted the attack launched *en echelon*—one brigade after another striking the Federal line, beginning on the Federal left, gathering strength,

A former U.S. Army engineer and West Point mathematics instructor, Brigadier General Gouverneur K. Warren was Chief Topographical Engineer for the Army of the Potomac. He had served the army well at Chancellorsville, but his most valuable service came at Gettysburg.

National Archives

Although not as high as neighboring Big Round Top, its commanding view made Little Round Top a perfect site for artillery. Both armies coveted the boulder-cluttered 150-foot-high landmark, also known locally as Sugar Loaf Hill, but it was successfully occupied and held by the Federal army.

rolling it up—and he wanted it made before the enemy's troops were fully in place or reinforced. Longstreet's corps was still arriving at Gettysburg, so, to make the attack, Lee and Longstreet chose two divisions of troops available to them—one commanded by Major General Lafayette McLaws and the other led by Major General John Bell Hood. For whatever reasons, Longstreet did not get his troops deployed for the attack as quickly as Lee had hoped. Not until late in the afternoon did he have Hood's and McLaws's divisions in place and ready to strike.

At four o'clock, with Longstreet's artillery laying down a cover fire, Hood's division advanced toward the Round Tops on the Confederate right flank, intending to strike and turn the Federal left flank as planned. The actual route of attack would take McLaws's division across the Emmitsburg Road, through a peach orchard and a wheat field, and toward the southern end of Cemetery Ridge, while Hood's division would cross a creek called Plum Run, move through a formidable cropping of huge boulders known locally as Devil's Den, then ascend or go around Big and Little Round Tops and turn the Federal left flank.

As the Confederate attack began to unfold, General Meade held a battlefield conference with his top commanders. The conference abruptly concluded at the sound of the Confederate cannonading, and Meade hurriedly mounted his horse and headed toward the Federal left flank to reconnoiter. With him rode Brigadier General Gouverneur K. Warren, Chief Topographical Engineer for the Army of the Potomac. While checking on the deployment of his troops, particularly an authorized realignment by Major General Daniel Sickles, Meade became concerned that Little Round Top and its commanding summit had not been properly secured. He directed Warren to see to it, and the general ascended the wooded peak with his engineering staff and orderlies. Once there, Warren realized Little Round Top dominated the lower end of the Federal line. He realized it should be made anchor of the Federal line on Cemetery Ridge; its commanding view made it ideal for Federal artillery. If captured by Lee's army, however, Confederate artillery could ravage the entire Federal line. Frantically, he summoned Federal troops, who deployed on the hill barely in time to secure it.

While not solely responsible for saving Little Round Top for Meade's army, Warren's decisive action proved invaluable. Nine years after the battle, he chronicled his role in the events.

━━━━━━━━━━━━━━━━

Just before the action began in earnest, on July 2d, I was with General Meade, near General Sickles, whose troops seemed very badly disposed on that part of the field. At my suggestion, General Meade sent me to the left to examine the condition of affairs, and I continued on till I reached Little Round Top. There were no troops on it, and it was used as a signal station. I saw that this was the key of the whole position, and that our troops in the woods in front of it could not see the ground in front of them, so that the enemy would come upon them before they would be aware of it.

The long line of woods on the west side of the Emmitsburg road (which road was along a ridge) furnished an excellent place for the enemy to form out of sight, so I requested the captain of a rifle battery just in front of Little Round Top to fire a shot into these woods. He did so, and as the shot went whistling through the air the sound

In this nineteenth century artwork, General Warren stands atop Little Round Top and studies the distant Confederate lines with his field glasses. Warren realized the critical military value of the peak and took decisive action to save it for Federal forces.

Battles and Leaders of the Civil War

of it reached the enemy's troops and caused every one to look in the direction of it. This motion revealed to me the glistening of gun-barrels and bayonets of the enemy's line of battle, already formed and far outflanking the position of any of our troops; so that the line of his advance from his right to Little Round Top was unopposed. I have been particular in telling this, as the discovery was intensely thrilling to my feelings, and almost appalling.

I immediately sent a hastily written dispatch to General Meade to send a division at least to me, and General Meade directed the Fifth Army Corps to take position there. The battle was already beginning to rage at the Peach Orchard, and before a single man reached Round Top the whole line of the enemy moved on us in splendid array, shouting in the most confident tones. While I was still all alone with the signal officer, the musket-balls began to fly around us, and he was about to fold up his flags and withdraw, but remained, at my request, and kept waving them in defiance.

Seeing troops going out on the Peach Orchard road, I rode down the hill, and fortunately met my old brigade. General Weed, commanding it, had already passed the point, and I took the responsibility to detach Colonel O'Rorke, the head of whose regiment I struck, who, on hearing my few words of explanation about the position, moved at once to the hill-top. About this time First Lieutenant Charles E. Hazlett of the Fifth Artillery, with his battery of rifled cannon, arrived. He comprehended the situation instantly and planted a gun on the summit of the hill. He spoke to the effect that though he could do little execution on the enemy with his guns, he could aid in giving confidence to the infantry, and that his battery was of no consequence whatever compared with holding the position. He stayed there till he was killed. I was wounded with a musket-ball while talking with Lieutenant Hazlett on the hill, but not seriously; and, seeing the position saved while the whole line to the right and front of us was yielding and melting away under the enemy's fire and advance, I left the hill to rejoin General Meade near the center of the field, where a new crisis was at hand....

"Are You Not Too Much Extended, General?"

The Controversial "Sickles's Salient" Puts the Federal Battle Line at Risk

Forty-three-year-old Major General Daniel Sickles was used to doing things his way. When General Meade told Sickles, an army corps commander, to put his Third Corps into line on Cemetery Ridge just north of Little Round Top, he obeyed—at first. Sickle's corps had arrived on the battlefield the night before and on July 2 had deployed alongside General Hancock's Second Corps troops. However, when Sickles studied his position that afternoon, he decided

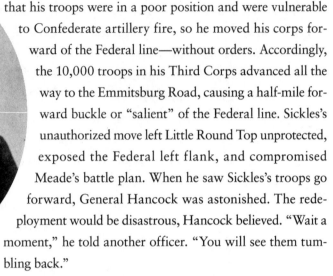

Major General Daniel Sickles commanded the Federal Third Corps at Gettysburg. Flamboyant and prone to controversial action, he advanced his portion of the Federal defensive line without orders, making it vulnerable to attack.

Library of Congress

that his troops were in a poor position and were vulnerable to Confederate artillery fire, so he moved his corps forward of the Federal line—without orders. Accordingly, the 10,000 troops in his Third Corps advanced all the way to the Emmitsburg Road, causing a half-mile forward buckle or "salient" of the Federal line. Sickles's unauthorized move left Little Round Top unprotected, exposed the Federal left flank, and compromised Meade's battle plan. When he saw Sickles's troops go forward, General Hancock was astonished. The redeployment would be disastrous, Hancock believed. "Wait a moment," he told another officer. "You will see them tumbling back."

Sickles was accustomed to controversy. A former New York politician and U.S. congressman, he was known for his outlandish behavior. His reputation had been tarred by charges of embezzlement, swindles, and adultery. As a member of the New York state legislature, he had earned an official censure for parading a notorious prostitute into the legislative chamber. On the eve of the Civil War, his scandalous behavior had attracted national attention when he shot and killed Philip Barton Key, the son of the composer of the National Anthem, for committing adultery with his wife. Defended by Washington attorney Edwin M. Stanton, who would later become his boss as U.S. Secretary of War, Sickles claimed to be momentarily deranged by his rage, and became the first American acquitted on grounds of temporary insanity. His political connections as a Northern Democrat earned him an officer's commission, and he became cronies with General Hooker and his staff, rising to the rank of major general and becoming a corps commander by the time of Chancellorsville. There, his corps had been ravaged by Confederate artillery fire—and his unauthorized redeployment at Gettysburg might have been an attempt to avoid such a disaster again.

General Meade was shocked to find Sickles's troops so far out front of the Federal line. When Sickles tried to explain that he had made the unsanctioned move in search of higher ground, Meade reportedly replied, "General Sickles ... if you keep on advancing you will find constantly higher ground all the way to the mountains." Sickles offered to order his troops back to their original position in the line, but it was too late—the Confederate attack was upon him. Sickles's troops fought fearlessly, and Sickles lost a leg in battle that day, but his decision to move his corps to what became known as "the Sickles's Salient" would remain controversial. In 1864, he defended his actions in testimony before Congress's powerful Joint Committee on the Conduct of the War. At about the same time, the influential *New York Herald* newspaper published an anonymous article by a writer dubbing himself "Historicus," which exonerated Sickles and disparaged General Meade. The article provoked a national controversy, and some of Meade's officers publicly rebutted the article, which one dismissed as "pure invention."

It was widely believed that "Historicus"—General Sickles's anonymous defender in the *Herald*—was actually General Sickles, secretly making a clever public defense of his actions at Gettysburg. Below is an excerpt of the controversial newspaper article.

———

To the Editor of the Herald:

... General Meade broke up his quarters at Taneytown, as he states, at 11 p.m. on Wednesday, and reached Gettysburg at 1 a.m. Thursday, July 2. Early in the morning he set to work examining the position of the various army corps. It is hardly true to say that he imitated the example of all prudent commanders on the eve of a battle, and made a complete survey of the ground he occupied.

It was on these occasions that the genius of the first Napoleon revealed itself; for at a glance he saw the advantages of his own position and the assailable point of the enemy. It seems that General Lee was somewhat more astute than Meade in this, for in his report he states what he deemed "the most favorable point" for his attack. "In front of General Longstreet" (opposite our left wing).... It is not to be supposed that General Meade refused to see this; but as he makes no mention of it in his report, I propose, for the sake of the future historian of the battle, to tell what I know about it.

Near this important ground was posted the valiant Third Corps, and its commander, General Sickles, saw at once how necessary it was to occupy the elevated ground in his front toward the Emmitsburg road, and to extend his lines to the commanding eminence known as the Round Top, or Sugar Loaf hill. Unless this were done, the left and rear of our army would be in the greatest danger. Sickles concluded that no time was to be lost, as he observed the enemy massing large bodies of troops on their right (our left). Receiving no orders, and filled with anxiety, he reported in person to General Meade, and urged the advance he deemed so essential. "O," said Meade, "generals are all apt to look for the attack to be made where they are."

Whether this was a jest or a sneer Sickles did not stop to consider, but begged Meade to go over the ground with him instantly; but the commander-in-chief declined this on account of other duties. Yielding, however, to the prolonged solicitations of Sickles, General Meade desired General Hunt, chief of artillery, to accompany Sickles, and report the result of their reconnaissance. Hunt concurred with Sickles as to the line to be occupied—the advance line from the left of the Second Corps to the Round Top hill—but he declined to give any orders until he had reported to General Meade, remarking, however, that he (General Sickles) would doubtless receive orders immediately.

Two p.m. came, and yet no orders. Why was this? Other orders than those expected by General Sickles were, it appears, in preparation at headquarters. It has since been stated, upon unquestionable authority, that General Meade had decided upon a retreat, and that an order to withdraw from the position held by our army was penned by his chief of staff, General Butterfield, though happily its promulgation never took place. This order is probably on record in the Adjutant-General's Office.

Meanwhile the enemy's columns were moving rapidly around to our left and rear. These facts were again reported to headquarters, but brought no response. Buford's cavalry had been massed on the left, covering that flank with outposts, and videttes [sic] were thrown forward on the Emmitsburg road. While awaiting the expected orders, Sickles made good use of his time in leveling all the fences and stone walls, so as to facilitate the movements of his troops and to favor the operations of the cavalry. What, then, was the surprise of Sickles to see of a sudden all the cavalry withdrawn, leaving his flank entirely exposed! He sent an earnest remonstrance to General Meade, whose reply was that he did not intend to withdraw the cavalry, and that a part of this division (Buford's) should be sent back. It never returned. Under these circumstances, Sickles threw forward three regiments of light troops as skirmishers and for outpost duty.

The critical moment had now arrived. The enemy's movements indicated their purpose to seize the Round Top hill; and this in their possession, General Longstreet would have had easy work in cutting up our left wing. To prevent this disaster, Sickles waited no longer for orders from General Meade, but directed General Hobart Ward's brigade and Smith's battery (Fourth New York) to secure that vital position, and at the same time advancing his line of battle about 300 yards, so as to hold the crest in his front, he extended his left to support Ward and cover the threatened rear of the army.

These dispositions were made in the very face of the enemy, who were advancing in columns of attack, and Sickles dreaded lest the conflict should open before his dispositions were completed. At this juncture he was summoned to report in person at headquarters, to

General Sickles would lose a leg in the battle, donate it to a Washington, D.C., museum, and visit it regularly for years to come.

National Archives

attend a council of corps commanders. His preparations were of such moment and the attack so near, that General Sickles delayed attending the council, while giving all his attention to the carrying out of his orders.

A second peremptory summons came from General Meade, and leaving his unfinished task to the active supervision of General Birney and General Humphreys, Sickles rode off to the rear to headquarters. Before he had reached there, the sound of cannon announced that the battle had begun. Hastening rapidly on, he was met by General Meade at the door of his quarters, who said, "General, I will not ask you to dismount; the enemy are engaging your front; the council is over." It was an unfortunate moment, as it proved, for a council of war.

Sickles, putting spurs to his horse, flew back to his command, and, finding that Graham's brigade was not advanced as far as he desired, he was pushing that brigade and a battery forward about 100 yards, when General Meade at length arrived on the field. The following colloquy ensued, which I gathered from several officers present: "Are you not too much extended, general?" said Meade. "Can you hold this front?" "Yes," replied Sickles, "until more troops are brought up; the enemy are attacking in force, and I shall need support." General Meade then let drop some remark showing that his mind was still wavering as to the extent of ground covered by the Third Corps. Sickles replied, "General, I have received no orders. I have made these dispositions to the best of my judgment. Of course, I shall be happy to modify them according to your views."

"No," said Meade, "I will send you the Fifth Corps, and you may send for support from the Second Corps." "I shall need more *artillery," added Sickles. "Send to the Artillery Reserve for all you want," replied Meade; "I will direct General Hunt to send you all you ask for." The conference was then abruptly terminated by a heavy shower of shells, probably directed at the group, and General Meade rode off. Sickles received no further orders that day.*

There is no doubt, I may venture to add, that Sickles' line was too much extended for the number of troops under his command; but his great aim was to prevent the enemy getting between his flank and the Round Top alluded to. This was worth the risk, in his opinion, of momentarily weakening his lines. The contest now going on was of the most fierce and sanguinary description. The entire right wing of the enemy was concentrated on the devoted Third Corps. ... It was now pretty clear that General Meade had awakened to the fact which he treated with such indifference when pressed on him by Sickles in the morning—that our left was the assailable point, if not the key to our position....

It is to be hoped that the above narrative will be regarded as dispassionate, as it is meant to be impartial. Some slight errors may have crept in; but this may possibly stimulate others to come forward with a rectification. Had General Meade been more copious in his report and less reserved as to his own important acts, the necessity for this communication would not have existed.

HISTORICUS.[4]

"Fix Bayonets, My Brave Texans!"
Lee's Second Day Attack Opens against the Federal Left Flank

As Longstreet's two divisions—Hood's and McLaws's—prepared to attack the Federal left flank shortly before four o'clock, General Longstreet realized that the Federal line was much longer than Lee and he had thought it to be. He could see that it extended beyond the wheat field and the peach orchard all the way to Little Round Top and Big Round Top. General Hood realized the mistake as well, and feared that advancing up the Emmitsburg Road would expose his troops to crushing enemy fire. Better to attack the extreme left flank of the enemy's line, he believed—to go around the Round Tops and attack the Federal rear. He sent a dispatch to Longstreet, urging a change in orders. Longstreet refused: it was past time to attack, and he would not change General Lee's orders. Hood protested further— until Longstreet finally rode over and told him face-to-face, "We must obey the orders of General Lee." Hood finally went forward, but not according to plan. He gave up his plan to march around the two big hills and attack the Federal rear, but, despite orders, he refused to send his troops up the Emmitsburg Road to what he believed was certain destruction. Instead, he sent them straight for the Round Tops.

A blond-bearded, towering giant of a man, Confederate Major General John Bell Hood was known as an aggressive combat commander. Eventually, he would lose the use of an arm and a leg, and would ride into battle tied to his saddle.

Rubenstein Rare Books and Manuscript Library, Duke University

Major General John Bell Hood had a reputation as a skilled commander and a fierce fighter. Some thought he was a Texan because he had made a name for himself commanding Lone Star troops in what was known as the Texas Brigade. He was actually a Kentucky doctor's son, a West Pointer, who had served under General Lee in Texas when Lee acted as a lieutenant colonel in the prewar 2nd U.S. Cavalry. Hood went from service in Texas into Confederate service, experiencing a steady rise in rank from brigadier to major general as he distinguished himself in the Seven Days Battles, at Second Bull Run, and at Antietam. A sad-eyed, long-faced, thirty-two-year-old blond-bearded giant of a man, he would plunge into battle with no hesitation, and the fact that his men would willingly go with him was a tribute to his leadership. Eventually, he would lose the use of an arm and a leg, and would go into battle anyway— roped to his saddle. One of those grievous wounds befell him at Gettysburg.

When the time came to launch the attack on the afternoon of July 2, he sat on horseback in front of his division, which was lined up in the woods opposite the Round Tops. The troops remained quiet—veteran fighters from Alabama, Georgia, Arkansas, and Texas—as they awaited the order to attack. Hood was facing the soldiers of his former Texas brigade. He, too, was quiet, then he stood up in his stirrups—six-feet-two, towering above the men in gray and butter-nut—and shouted an order: "Fix bayonets, my brave Texans; forward and take those heights!" A Texas officer shouted back, "Follow the Lone Star Flag to the top of the mountain!" And then they were off. His troops surged forward, some moving through boulder-strewn Devil's Den, pushing General Sickles's Federal troops backward; some advancing through the woods in between the Round Tops; others climbing up and over Big Round Top to advance on Little Round Top. Almost immediately General Hood was wounded—hit by a fragment from an exploding artillery shell. His left arm was crippled and he was out of the fight, but his troops went forward without him.

In a postwar letter to General Longstreet in 1875, Hood would recall the second day at Gettysburg and his futile attempt to get Longstreet to change orders and redirect the assault around the Round Tops toward the Federal rear.

─────────

New Orleans, La.,
June 28th, 1875.

General James Longstreet:—
General, I have not responded earlier to your letter of April 5th, by reason of pressure of business, which rendered it difficult for me to give due attention to the subject in regard to which you have desired information....
I arrived with my staff in front of the heights of Gettysburg shortly after daybreak, as I have already stated, on the morning of the 2d of July. My division soon commenced filing into an open field near me, where the troops were allowed to stack arms and rest until further orders. A short distance in advance of this point, and during the early part of that same morning, we were both

engaged in company with Generals Lee and A. P. Hill, in observing the position of the Federals. General Lee—with coat buttoned to the throat, sabre-belt buckled round the waist, and field glasses pending at his side—walked up and down in the shade of the large trees near us, halting now and then to observe the enemy. He seemed full of hope, yet, at times, buried in deep thought. Colonel Freemantle, of England, was ensconced in the forks of a tree not far off, with glass in constant use, examining the lofty position of the Federal Army.

General Lee was, seemingly, anxious you should attack that morning. He remarked to me, "The enemy is here, and if we do not whip him, he will whip us." You thought it better to await the arrival of Pickett's Division—at that time still in the rear—in order to make the attack; and you said to me, subsequently, whilst we were seated together near the trunk of a tree: "The General is a little nervous this morning; he wishes me to attack; I do not wish to do so without Pickett. I never like to go into battle with one boot off."

Thus passed the forenoon of that eventful day, when in the afternoon—about 3 o'clock—it was decided to no longer await Pickett's Division, but to proceed to our extreme right and attack up the Emmetsburg road. McLaws moved off, and I followed with my division. In a short time I was ordered to quicken the march of my troops, and to pass to the front of McLaws.

This movement was accomplished by throwing out an advanced force to tear down fences and clear the way. The instructions I received were to place my division across the Emmetsburg road, form line of battle, and attack. Before reaching this road, however, I had sent forward some of my picked Texas scouts to ascertain the position of the enemy's extreme left flank. They soon reported to me that it rested upon Round Top Mountain; that the country was open, and that I could march through an open woodland pasture around Round Top, and assault the enemy in flank and rear; that their wagon

At Gettysburg Hood and his troops launched Lee's attack on the Federal left flank. Edwin Forbes, a field artist for *Leslie's Illustrated* at Gettysburg, sketched it as it appeared from the summit of Little Round Top.

Library of Congress

trains were packed in rear of their line, and were badly exposed to our attack in that direction. As soon as I arrived upon the Emmetsburg road, I placed one or two batteries in position and opened fire. A reply from the enemy's guns soon developed his lines. His left rested on or near Round Top, with line bending back and again forward, forming, as it were, a concave line, as approached by the Emmetsburg road. A considerable body of troops was posted in front of their main line, between the Emmetsburg road and Round Top Mountain. This force was in line of battle upon an eminence near a peach orchard.

I found that in making the attack according to orders, viz.: up the Emmetsburg road, I should have first to encounter and drive off this advanced line of battle; secondly, at the base and along the slope of the mountain, to confront immense boulders of stone, so massed together as to form narrow openings, which would break our ranks and cause the men to scatter whilst climbing up the rocky precipice. I found, moreover, that my division would be exposed to a heavy fire from the main line of the enemy in position on the crest of the high range, of which Round Top was the extreme left, and, by reason of the concavity of the enemy's main line, that we would be subject to a destructive fire in flank and rear, as well as in front; and deemed it almost an impossibility to clamber along the boulders up this steep and rugged mountain, and, under this number of cross fires, put the enemy to flight. I knew that if the feat was accomplished, it must be at a most fearful sacrifice of as brave and gallant soldiers as ever engaged in battle.

The reconnoissance [sic] of my Texas scouts and the development of the Federal lines were effected in a very short space of time; in truth, shorter than I have taken to recall and jot down these facts, although the scenes and events of that day are as clear to my mind as if the great battle had been fought yesterday. I was in possession of these important facts so shortly after reaching the Emmetsburg road, that I considered it my duty to report to you, at once, my opinion that it was unwise to attack up the Emmetsburg road, as ordered, and to urge that you allow me to turn Round Top, and attack the enemy in flank and rear. Accordingly, I despatched a staff officer, bearing to you my request to be allowed to make the proposed movement on account of the above stated reasons. Your reply was quickly received, "General Lee's orders are to attack up the Emmetsburg road." I sent another officer to say that I feared nothing could be accomplished by such an attack, and renewed my request to turn Round Top. Again your answer was, "General Lee's orders are to attack up the Emmetsburg road." During this interim I had continued the use of the batteries upon the enemy, and had become more and more convinced that the Federal line extended to Round Top, and that I could not reasonably hope to accomplish much by the attack as ordered. In fact, it seemed to me the enemy occupied a position by nature so strong—I may say impregnable—that, independently of their flank fire, they could easily repel our attack by merely throwing and rolling stones down the mountain side, as we approached.

A third time I despatched one of my staff to explain fully in regard to the situation, and suggest that you had better come and look for yourself. I selected, in this instance, my adjutant-general, Colonel Harry Sellers, whom you know to be not only an officer of great courage, but also of marked ability. Colonel Sellers returned with the same message, "General Lee's orders are to attack up the Emmetsburg road." Almost simultaneously, Colonel Fairfax, of your staff, rode up and repeated the above orders.

After this urgent protest against entering the battle at Gettysburg, according to instructions—which protest is the first and only one I ever made during my entire military career—I ordered my line to advance and make the assault.

As my troops were moving forward, you rode up in person; a brief conversation passed between us, during which I again expressed the fears above mentioned, and regret at not being allowed to attack in flank around Round Top. You answered to this effect, "We must obey the orders of General Lee." I then rode forward with my line under a heavy fire. In about twenty minutes, after reaching the peach orchard, I was severely wounded in the arm, and borne from the field.

With this wound terminated my participation in this great battle. As I was borne off on a litter to the rear, I could but experience deep distress of mind and heart at the thought of the inevitable fate of my brave fellow-soldiers, who formed one of the grandest divisions of that world renowned army; and I shall ever believe that had I been permitted to turn Round Top Mountain, we would not only have gained that position, but have been able finally to rout the enemy.

I am, respectfully, yours,

J. B. Hood[5]

"Confusion Reigned Everywhere"

Longstreet's Assault on the Federal Left Opens with a Shaky Start

When twenty-seven-year-old Brigadier General Evander M. Law saw the assault route his troops were supposed to follow on July 2—exposed along the Emmitsburg Road—he changed it. Instead, they charged toward Little Round Top.

Photographic History of the Civil War

At four o'clock on July 2, five regiments of Alabama troops led Hood's division forward. Collectively, they comprised Law's Brigade of Hood's division—Longstreet's First Corps—and they were commanded by Brigadier General Evander M. Law of South Carolina. A twenty-seven-year-old graduate of The Citadel Military College in South Carolina, he had practiced law and taught school before moving to Alabama and starting a military academy. When the war began, he converted his academy's cadets into a company of Confederate troops, became their captain, rose to colonel and to commander of the 4th Alabama Infantry, and wound up as a brigadier general in Hood's division—still leading Alabama troops. Despite his rangy build and a French-style goatee, Law had a boyish face—but there was nothing lacking in his fortitude. He had a horse shot from under him at Fredericksburg, and General Hood had personally commended him for bravery.

As Lee's mighty *en echelon* attack began to unfold that afternoon, Law saw the same problem that alarmed Hood: he did not want to take his troops up the Emmitsburg Road and subject them to almost certain devastating flank fire. So he did not; instead, he ordered them to advance straight on through Devil's Den and toward Little Round Top. Joining them were the troops of two more brigades—Arkansans, Texans, and Georgians under Brigadier Generals Jerome B. Robertson and Henry L. Benning.

A young Confederate soldier from Hood's division, killed by Federal fire, lies among the maze of boulders in Devil's Den.

Library of Congress

Ahead of them, defending the left flank of Sickles's line, was a brigade of Federal troops commanded by Brigadier General John Henry Hobart Ward—troops from New York, Maine, Pennsylvania, and Indiana. They ferociously resisted Law's Confederates, fighting in the bizarre maze of giant boulders in Devil's Den and pouring down fire from the base of Little Round Top. Ward ordered his men to hold their fire until the Confederates were only 200 yards away—until they could "plainly see the enemy." It was "desperate tenacious fighting," in the words of a Federal survivor. After more than an hour of combat, and in danger of being surrounded, the Federals defending Devil's Den finally retreated back toward Cemetery Ridge and toward Little Round Top, leaving what some called "the Slaughter Pen" in the possession of Hood's Confederates. It would become a post for Confederate sharpshooters intent on picking off Federal officers atop Little Round Top.

One of Hood's Texans fighting his way through Devil's Den at the base of Little Round Top was Private "Val" Giles, a twenty-one-year-old soldier in the 4th Texas Infantry. For the rest of his life he would remember the smoke, yells, blood, and confusion of that afternoon assault, and before his death in 1915, he recorded this memoir.

General Hobart Ward commanded a brigade of Northern troops who battled Hood's Southerners in Devil's Den and at the foot of the Round Tops. Don't fire until you can "plainly see the enemy," Hobart ordered.

Library of Congress

It was nearly five o'clock when we began the assault against the enemy that was strongly fortified behind logs and stones on the crest of a steep mountain. It was more than half a mile from our starting point to the edge of the timber at the base of the ridge, comparatively open ground all the way. We started off at quick time, the officers keeping the column in pretty good line until we passed through a blossoming peach orchard and reached the level ground beyond. We were now about 400 yards from the timber. The fire from the enemy, both artillery and musketry, was fearful.

In making that long charge, our brigade got jammed. Regiments lapped over each other, and when we reached the woods and climbed the mountains as far as we could go, we were a badly mixed crowd.

Confusion reigned everywhere. Nearly all our field officers were gone. Hood, our Major General, had been shot from his horse. He lost an arm from the wound. Robertson, our Brigadier, had been carried from the field. Colonel Powell of the Fifth Texas was riddled with bullets. Colonel Van Manning of the Third Arkansas was disabled, and Colonel B. F. Carter of my Regiment lay dying at the foot of the mountain.

The side of the mountain was heavily timbered and covered with great boulders that had tumbled from the cliffs above years before. These afforded great protection to the men.

Every tree, rock and stump that gave any protection from the rain of Minié balls that were poured down upon us from the crest above us, was soon appropriated. John Griffith and myself pre-empted a moss-covered old boulder about the size of a 500-pound cotton bale.

By this time order and discipline were gone. Every fellow was his own general. Private soldiers gave commands as loud as the officers. Nobody paid any attention to either. To add to this confusion, our artillery on the hill to our rear was cutting its fuse too short. Their shells were bursting behind us, in the treetops, over our heads, and all around us.

Nothing demoralizes troops quicker than to be fired into by their friends. I saw it occur twice during the war. The first time we ran, but at Gettysburg we couldn't.

This mistake was soon corrected and the shells burst high on the mountain or went over it.

Major Rogers, then in command of the Fifth Texas Regiment, mounted an old log near my boulder and began a Fourth of July speech. He was a little ahead of time, for that was about six thirty on the evening of July 2d.

Of course nobody was paying any attention to the oration as he appealed to the men to "stand fast." He and Captain Cousins of the Fourth Alabama were the only two men I saw standing. The balance of us had settled down behind rocks, logs, and trees. While the speech was going on, John Haggerty, one of Hood's couriers, then acting for General Law, dashed up the side of the mountain, saluted the Major and said: "General Law presents his compliments, and says hold this place at all hazards." The Major checked up, glared down at Haggerty from his' perch, and shouted: "Compliments, hell! Who wants any compliments in such a damned place as this? Go back and ask General Law if he expects me to hold the world in check with the Fifth Texas Regiment!"

The Major evidently thought he had his own regiment with him, but in fact there were men from every regiment in the Texas Brigade all around him.

From behind my boulder I saw a ragged line of battle strung out along the side of Cemetery Ridge and in front of Little Round Top.... We could hear the Yankee officer on the crest of the ridge in front of us cursing the men by platoons, and the men telling him to go to a country not very far away from us just at that time. If that old Satanic dragon has ever been on earth since he offered our Saviour the world if He would serve him, he was certainly at Gettysburg that night....

The advance lines of the two armies in many places were not more than fifty yards apart. Everything was on the shoot. No favors asked, and none offered.

My gun was so dirty that the ramrod hung in the barrel, and I could neither get it down nor out. I slammed the rod against a rock a few times, and drove home ramrod, cartridge and all, laid the gun on a boulder, elevated the muzzle, ducked my head, hollered "Look out!" and pulled the trigger. She roared like a young cannon and flew over my boulder, the barrel striking John Griffith a smart whack on the left ear. John roared too, and abused me like a pickpocket for my carelessness. It was no trouble to get another gun there. The mountainside was covered with them....[6]

"The Blood Stood in Puddles on the Rocks"

The 15th Alabama Infantry Is Bled White on the Slopes of Little Round Top

While the troops of Hood's division were fighting their way through the jumble of boulders in Devil's Den, General Law ordered Colonel William C. Oates, commander of the 15th Alabama Infantry, to take his regiment—which was flanked on the left by the 47th Alabama under Lieutenant Colonel Michael J. Bulger—and suppress enemy fire coming from the lower slopes of Big Round Top. The fire was coming from a detachment of the 2nd U.S. Sharpshooters, who were armed with rapid-fire Sharps rifles. Oates immediately led his men toward the source of the fire—a typical act for the bold young officer. Born to a poor family on a hardscrabble farm in south-eastern Alabama, he received scant education and fled the state at age sixteen following a brush with the law. After stints as a deckhand, house-painter, and gambler, he earned enough money to attend school, became a teacher and, eventually, a lawyer in Abbeville, Alabama. When the war began, he raised an infantry company, served under "Stonewall" Jackson in his 1862 Valley Campaign, and was colonel and commander of the 15th Alabama by age twenty-seven.

Forced to flee Alabama as a teenaged lawbreaker, Colonel William C. Oates eventually became an Alabama teacher, lawyer, and commander of the 15th Alabama Infantry—which attacked the Federal far left flank at Gettysburg.
Wikimedia Commons Images

Oates and his regiment had marched about twenty-five miles earlier that day to reach Gettysburg and had to be tired, but they pressed onward up Big Round Top's steep, forested slopes as the Sharpshooters withdrew before them. Oates wanted to occupy Big Round Top and to haul artillery to its summit, but his orders commanded him to advance and take Little Round Top. The Alabamians came off the big hill, crossed a rocky stretch of woodland, began moving up the boulder-strewn southern slope of Little Round Top—and received a shock-force blast of enemy fire at close range. The volley dropped scores of men and stunned the rest. It was delivered from a makeshift wall of piled-up rocks by troops of the 20th Maine Infantry—part of the Federal Fifth Corps—which had reached the southern slope of Little Round Top only minutes earlier.

When General Warren sent for troops to secure Little Round Top, just as the Confederate assault on the Federal left commenced—the call was taken up by Colonel Strong Vincent, who commanded a brigade of troops from Pennsylvania, New York, Michigan, and Maine—soldiers of Major General George Sykes's Fifth Corps. A Pennsylvania native and a Harvard graduate who disguised his youthfulness with a bushy set of mutton-chop whiskers, Vincent—age twenty-six—was the youngest brigade commander in the Army of the Potomac. Upon learning of the firing on Fort Sumter, he had set aside a law career in order

Little Round Top, on the left, and Big Round Top, on the right, anchored the southern end or far left flank of the Federal line on Cemetery Ridge. As they came off Big Round Top and approached the smaller hill, the troops of the 15th Alabama were stunned by a blast of Federal volley fire.

Library of Congress

to join the army and had seen his share of bloody combat. He reacted quickly when he heard the frantic call for troops to hold Little Round Top. Backed by a section of artillery under Lieutenant Charles Hazlett, Vincent hustled his brigade into line on the western slope of Little Round Top—just in time to be attacked by a large force of Hood's Confederates, who had pushed through Devil's Den. It was composed of another Alabama regiment from Law's brigade and two regiments of Texas troops from Brigadier General Jerome B. Robertson's brigade. The three regiments—all from Hood's Divison—had fought their way through Devil's Den and were advancing on the left of Oates's and Bulcher's regiments.

Strong's brigade met them head-on, beginning with a counter-charge by the 140th New York Infantry under Colonel Patrick H. O'Rorke, which staggered Robertson's Texans. Colonel Strong hastily set up a firing line, striding up and down giving orders, but he was soon struck down with a mortal wound. Just as Strong's brigade appeared on the verge of being overwhelmed, another Fifth Corps brigade arrived and poured fire into the bloodied Texans. Commanded by Brigadier General Stephen H. Weed, it, too, had been summoned by General Warren and showed up just in time to turn back the Confederate assault on Little Round Top's western slope. It was a costly victory: Federal casualties were heavy, and included the twenty-nine-year-old Weed, who fell dead from a head wound. Hazlett, the artillery commander, and Colonel O'Rorke of the 140th New York were also killed in action.

Meanwhile, on the south slope of Little Round Top—the extreme left flank of the Federal line—a bloody drama was being played out between the 15th Alabama and the 20th Maine. Repeatedly, Oates's Alabama troops assaulted the men from Maine, and repeatedly, the Alabamians were driven back. Finally, exhausted and dehydrated, with their numbers severely reduced, they gave up the fight for Little Round Top. Decades later in the *Southern Historical Society Papers*, Oates would record a vivid account of his assault against the extreme left flank of the Federal line—and the 20th Maine. As excerpted here, it begins with the Alabamians ascending Big Round Top.

I continued to advance straight up the southern face of Round Top. My men had to climb up, catching to the bushes and crawling over the immense boulders, in the face of an incessant fire of their enemy, who kept falling back, taking shelter and firing down on us from behind the rocks and crags that covered the mountain side thicker than grave stones in a city cemetery. My men could not see their foe, and did not fire, except as one was seen here and there, running back from one boulder to another. In this manner I pressed forward until I reached the top and the highest point on top of Round Top. Just before reaching this point, the Federals in my front as suddenly disappeared from my sight as though commanded by a magician. From the top of the mountain a Federal soldier could not be seen, except a few wounded and dead ones on the ground over which we had advanced. Here I halted and permitted my men to lie down to rest....

I think not more than five minutes after I halted, Captain Terrell, A. A. G. to General Law, rode up and inquired why I had halted. I told him that the position I then occupied was, in my opinion, a very important one, and should be held by us. He informed me that the order was to press forward. I replied that some of my men, from heat and exhaustion, were fainting, and could fight a great deal better after a few minutes rest, and inquired for General Law. He then informed me that General Hood was wounded and that Law, who was the senior brigadier, was in command of the division, and was along the line somewhere to the left, and said that General Law's order was for me and Colonel Bulger to lose no time, but to press forward and drive the enemy before us as far as possible. To move then was against my judgment. I felt confident that General Law did not know my position, or he would not order me from it. . . .

But notwithstanding my conviction of the importance of holding Round Top and occupying it with artillery ... I considered it to be my duty to obey the order communicated to me by the latter, who was a trustworthy and gallant officer. I ordered my line forward, and passed to the left oblique entirely down the northern or northeastern side of Round Top without encountering any opposition whatever. After I had reached the level ground in rear of Vincent's Spur, in plain view of the Federal wagon trains, and within two hundred yards of an extensive park of Federal ordnance wagons, which satisfied me that I was then in the Federal rear, advancing rapidly, without any skirmishers in front, I saw no enemy until within forty or fifty steps of an irregular ledge of rocks—a splendid line of breastworks formed by nature, running about parallel with the front of the Forty-seventh Alabama and my two left companies, and then sloping back in front of my center and right at an angle of about thirty-five degrees. Our foes, who had so suddenly and mysteriously disappeared from Round Top, had evidently fallen back to a second line behind this ledge, and now, unexpectedly to us, this double line poured into us the most destructive fire I ever saw.

Our line halted, but did not break. As men fell their comrades closed the gap, returning the fire most spiritedly. I soon discovered that the left of the Forty-seventh Alabama was disconnected—I know not how far—from the right of the Fourth Alabama, and consequently the Forty-seventh was outflanked on its left, and its men were being mowed down like grain before the scythe. Just at this time Lieutenant-Colonel Bulger, a most gallant old gentleman over sixty years of age, commanding the Forty-seventh Alabama, fell severely wounded, and soon afterwards his regiment, after behaving most gallantly and sustaining heavy losses, broke and in confusion retreated back up the mountain.

Just as the left of the Forty-seventh regiment was being driven back, I ordered my regiment to change direction to the left, swing around and drive the Federals from the ledge of rocks, partly for

On the summit of Little Round Top, troops of the 140th New York Infantry under Colonel Patrick O'Rorke hurriedly gathered rocks and piled them into makeshift breastworks.
Library of Congress

179

the purpose of enfilading their line and relieving the Forty-seventh. My men obeyed, and advanced about half way to the enemy's position, but the fire was so destructive that my line wavered like a man trying to walk against a strong wind, and then, slowly, doggedly, gave back a little. Then, with no one upon the right or left of me, my regiment exposed, while the enemy was still under cover, to stand there and die was sheer folly; either to retreat or advance became a necessity.

My Lieutenant-Colonel, J. B. Feagin, had lost his leg; the heroic Captain Ellison had fallen, while Captain Brainard, one of the bravest and best officers in the regiment, in leading his company forward, fell, exclaiming: "Oh God! that I could see my mother," and instantly expired. Lieutenant John A. Oates, my beloved brother, was pierced through by eight bullets, and fell mortally wounded. Lieutenants Cody, Hill and Scoggin were killed, and Captain Bethune and several other officers were seriously wounded, while the hemorrhage of the ranks was appalling. I again ordered the advance, and knowing the officers and men of that gallant old regiment, I felt sure that they would follow their commander anywhere in the line of duty, though he led them to certain destruction. I passed through the column waiving my sword, rushed forward to the ledge, and was promptly followed by my entire command in splendid style.

We drove the Federals from their strong defensive position; five times they rallied and charged us—twice coming so near that some of my men had to use the bayonet—but vain was their effort. It was our time now to deal death and destruction to a gallant foe, and the account was speedily settled with a large balance in our favor; but this state of things was not long to continue. The long blue lines of Federal infantry were coming down on my right and closing in on my rear, while some dismounted cavalry were closing

the only avenue of escape on my left, and had driven in my skirmishers. I sent my Sergeant-Major with a message to Colonel
Bowles, of the Fourth Alabama, to come to my relief. He returned
and reported the enemy to be between us and the Fourth Alabama,
and swarming up the mountainside. By this time.... the Fifteenth
Alabama had infantry to the right of them, dismounted cavalry to
the left of them, infantry in front of them and infantry in rear of
them.

With a withering and deadly fire pouring in upon us from every
direction, it seemed that the entire command was doomed to
destruction. While one man was shot in the face, his right hand or
left hand comrade was shot in the side or back. Some were struck
simultaneously with two or three balls from different directions.
Captains Hill and Park suggested that I should order a retreat; but
this seemed impracticable. My dead and wounded were then greater
in number than those still on duty. Of 644 men and 42 officers, I
had lost 343 men and 19 officers. The dead literally covered the
ground. The blood stood in puddles on the rocks. The ground was
soaked with the blood of as brave men as ever fell on the red field of
battle. I still hoped for reinforcements. It seemed impossible to
retreat; I therefore replied to my captains: "Return to your companies; we will sell out as dearly as possible." Hill made no reply, but
Park smiled pleasantly, gave me the military salute, and replied: "All
right, sir."

On reflection, however, a few moments later, I did order a
retreat, but did not undertake to retire in order. I had the officers
and men advised that when the signal was given every one should
run in the direction from whence we came, and halt on the top of
the mountain. When the signal was given, we ran like a herd of wild
cattle right through the line of dismounted cavalrymen. Some of my
men as they ran through, seized three or four of the cavalrymen by

181

the collar and carried them out prisoners. On the top of the mountain I made an attempt to halt and reform the regiment, but the men were helping wounded and disabled comrades, and scattered in the woods and among the rocks, so that it could not be done....[7]

"We Had Held the Ground–'At All Costs'"

The 20th Maine Successfully Defends the Federal Extreme Left Flank

Colonel Joshua Lawrence Chamberlain, commander of the 20th Maine Infantry, was a theologian and college professor, not a professional soldier. He was a natural leader, however, as he demonstrated on the rocky, wooded slope of Little Round Top.

National Archives

When Colonel Strong Vincent assigned the 20th Maine to its place on Little Round Top—defending the extreme left flank of the Federal line—he emphasized the critical importance of the position to the regiment's commander, Colonel Joshua Lawrence Chamberlain. "I place you here!" Vincent stated emphatically. "This is the left of the Union line." Chamberlain later said that he felt as if Vincent was explaining the importance of the Ten Commandments, so explicit was he on the consequences of defeat. He charged Chamberlain's force, numbering about 360 men, with keeping any Confederate attack from turning the Federal left flank, which could destroy the Federal line and lose the battle for the Union. "You understand," Vincent forcefully told him. "You are to hold this ground at all costs."

"I did understand," Chamberlain would later observe, "but I had more to learn about costs." Learning proved central to Chamberlain's life: he was a college professor and theologian, and not a professional soldier. The thirty-four-year-old Maine native was an alumnus of Bowdoin College and of Bangor Theological Seminary, married to a minister's daughter, had fathered five children, and was fluent in ten languages. When he joined the army in 1862, he had walked away from a prestigious professorship at Bowdoin, where he taught "revealed and natural religion," foreign languages, rhetoric, and a variety of other courses. He and the 20th Maine had undergone a bloody baptism by fire at the Battle of Fredericksburg, and, due to his natural leadership abilities, received promotion to colonel and to regimental commander less than two months before Gettysburg.

The "costs" Chamberlain discovered on the south slope of Little Round Top were calculated in blood. Although outnumbered, he and the 20th Maine withstood the repeated assaults against their line by the hard-fighting 15th Alabama under Oates and by some of the veteran troops of the 47th Alabama. After turning back one assault after another, the 20th was low on ammunition and men, and was in danger of being overwhelmed by the enemy. In a desperate gamble, Chamberlain ordered a sweeping bayonet charge, which shocked and turned back the exhausted Alabamians. "We had held the ground," Chamberlain would later recall, "at all costs."

Forty years after Gettysburg, Chamberlain would be awarded the Congressional Medal of Honor for displaying "daring heroism and great tenacity" that chaotic afternoon on Little Round Top. On the fiftieth anniversary of the battle, he wrote a detailed memoir of the 20th Maine's defense of Little Round Top for *Hearst's Magazine*.

Thick groups in gray were pushing up along the smooth dale between the Round Tops in a direction to gain our left flank. There was no mistaking this. If they could hold our attention by a hot fight in front while they got in force on that flank, it would be bad for us and our whole defence. How many were coming we could not know. We were rather too busy to send out a reconnoissance. If a strong force should gain our rear, our brigade would be caught as by a mighty shears-blade, and be cut and crushed. What would follow it was easy to foresee. This must not be. Our orders to hold that ground had to be liberally interpreted. That front had to be held, and that rear covered. Something must be done,—quickly and coolly. I called the captains and told them my tactics: to keep the front fire at the hottest, without special regard to its need or immediate effect, and at the same time, as they found opportunity, to take side steps to the left, coming gradually into one rank, file-closers and all. Then I took the colors with their guard and placed them at our extreme left, where a great boulder gave token and support; thence bending back at a right angle the whole body gained ground leftward and made twice our original front. And were not so long doing it. This was a difficult movement to execute under such a fire, requiring coolness as well as heat. . . .

The roar of all this tumult reached us on the left, and heightened the intensity of our resolve. Meanwhile the flanking column worked around to our left and joined with those before us in a fierce assault, which lasted with increasing fury for an intense hour. The two lines met and broke and mingled in the shock. The crush of musketry gave way to cuts and thrusts, grapplings and wrestlings. The edge of conflict swayed to and fro, with wild whirlpools and eddies. At times I saw around me more of the enemy than of my own men; gaps opening, swallowing, closing again with sharp convulsive energy; squads of stalwart men who had cut their way through us, disappearing as if translated. All around, strange, mingled roar— shouts of defiance, rally, and desperation; and underneath, murmured entreaty and stifled moans; gasping prayers, snatches of Sabbath song, whispers of loved names; everywhere men torn and broken, staggering, creeping, quivering on the earth, and dead faces with strangely fixed eyes staring stark into the sky. Things which cannot be told—nor dreamed. . . .

In the very deepest of the struggle while our shattered line had pressed the enemy well below their first point of contact, and the *struggle to regain it was fierce, I saw through a sudden rift in the thick smoke our colors standing alone. I first thought some optical illusion imposed upon me. But as forms emerged through the drifting smoke, the truth came to view. The cross-fire had cut keenly; the center had been almost shot away; only two of the color-guard had been left, and they fighting to fill the whole space; and in the center, wreathed in battle smoke, stood the Color-Sergeant, Andrew Tozier. His color-staff planted in the ground at his side, the upper part clasped in his elbow, so holding the flag upright, with musket and cartridges seized from the fallen comrade at his side he was defending his sacred trust in the man-ner of the songs of chivalry....*

Brigade Commander Strong Vincent posted the 20th Maine to the south side of Little Round Top—the far left flank of the Federal line. "You are to hold this ground at all costs," he ordered Chamberlain.

Pennsylvania State Archives

When that mad carnival lulled—from some strange instinct in human nature and without any reason in the situation that can be seen—when the battling edges drew asunder, there stood our little line, groups and gaps, notched like saw-teeth, but sharp as steel, tem-pered in infernal heats like a magic sword of the Goths. We were on the appointed and entrusted line. We had held ground—"at all costs!" But sad surprise! It had seemed to us we were all the while holding our own, and had never left it. But now that the smoke dissolved, we saw our dead and wounded all out in front of us, mingled with more of the enemy. They were scattered all the way down to the very feet of the baffled hostile line now rallying in the low shrubbery for a new onset. We could not wait for this. They knew our weakness now. And they were gathering force. No place for tactics now! The appeal must be to primal instincts of human nature!

Low on ammunition after repelling repeated assaults, the troops of the 20th Maine charged down Little Round Top's boulder-littered slope with fixed bayonets. The 15th Alabama vainly "tried to make a stand amidst the trees and boulders...."

Library of Congress

"Shall they die there, under the enemy's feet, and under your eyes?" Words like those brokenly uttered, from heart to heart, struck the stalwart groups holding together for a stand, and roused them to the front quicker than any voice or bugle of command. These true-hearted men but a little before buffeted back and forth by superior force, and now bracing for a dubious test, dashed down the death-strewn slope into the face of the rallied and recovering foe, and hurled them, tore them from above our fallen as the tiger avenges its young. Nor did they stop till they had cleared the farthest verge of the field, redeemed by the loving for the lost—the brave for the brave.

Now came a longer lull. But this meant, not rest, but thought and action. First, it was to gather our wounded, and bear them to the sheltered lawn for saving life, or peace in dying; the dead, too, that not even our feet should do them dishonor in the coming encounter. Then—such is heavenly human pity—the wounded of our Country's foes; brothers in blood for us now, so far from other caring; borne to like refuge and succor by the drummer-boys who

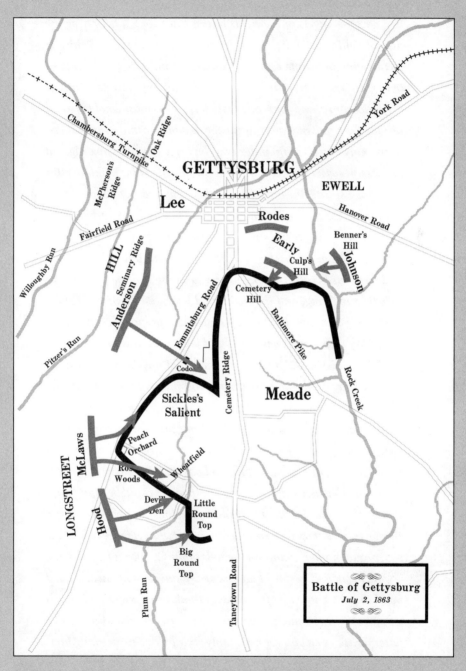

Battle of Gettysburg, July 2, 1863. Based on a map by Hal Jespersen, www.CWmaps.com

had become angels of the field. In this lull I took a turn over the dismal field to see what could be done for the living, in ranks or recumbent; and came upon a manly form and face I well remembered. He was a sergeant earlier in the field of Antietam and of Fredericksburg; and for refusing to perform some menial personal service for a bullying quartermaster in winter camp, was reduced to the ranks by a commander who had not carefully investigated the case. It was a degradation, and the injustice of it rankled in his high-born spirit. But his well-bred pride would not allow him to ask for justice as a favor. I had kept this in mind, for early action. Now he was lying there, stretched on an open front where a brave stand had been made, face to the sky, a great bullet-hole in the middle of his breast, from which he had loosened the clothing, to ease his breathing, and the rich blood was pouring in a stream. I bent down over him. His face lightened; his lips moved. But I spoke first, "My dear boy, it has gone hard with you. You shall be cared for!" He whispered, "Tell my mother I did not die a coward!" It was the prayer of home-bred manhood poured out with his life-blood. I knew and answered him, "You die a sergeant. I promote you for faithful service and noble courage on the field of Gettysburg!" This was all he wanted. No word more. I had him borne from the field, but his high spirit had passed to its place. It is needless to add that as soon as a piece of parchment could be found after that battle, a warrant was made out promoting George Washington Buck to sergeant in the terms told him; and this evidence placed the sad, proud mother's name on the rolls of the Country's benefactors.

As for myself, so far I had escaped. How close an escape I had had I did not know till afterwards. I think I may mention here, as a psychological incident, that some years after the war, I received a letter written in a homely but manly style by one subscribing himself "a member of the Fifteenth Alabama," in these words:

"Dear Sir: I want to tell you of a little passage in the battle of Round Top, Gettysburg, concerning you and me, which I am now glad of. Twice in that fight I had your life in my hands. I got a safe place between two big rocks, and drew bead fair and square on you. You were standing in the open behind the center of your line, full exposed. I knew your rank by your uniform and your actions, and I thought it a mighty good thing to put you out of the way. I rested my gun on the rock and took steady aim. I started to pull the trigger, but some queer notion stopped me. Then I got ashamed of my weakness and went through the same motions again. I had you, perfectly certain. But that same queer something shut right down on me. I couldn't pull the trigger, and gave it up,—that is, your life. I am glad of it now, and hope you are. Yours truly."

I thought he was that, and answered him accordingly, asking him to come up North and see whether I was worth what he missed. But my answer never found him, nor could I afterwards.

The silence and the doubt of the momentary lull were quickly dispelled. The formidable Fifteenth Alabama, repulsed and as we hoped dispersed, now in solid and orderly array—still more than twice our numbers—came rolling through the fringe of chaparral on our left. No dash; no yells; no demonstrations for effect; but settled purpose and determination! We opened on them as best we could. The fire was returned, cutting us to the quick. The Forty-Seventh Alabama had rallied on our right. We were enveloped in fire, and sure to be overwhelmed in fact when the great surge struck us.... Already I could see the bold flankers on their right darting out and creeping catlike under the smoke to gain our left, thrown back as it was. It was for us, then, once for all. Our thin line was broken, and the enemy were in rear of the whole Round Top defense—infantry, artillery, humanity itself—with the Round Top and the day theirs.

Now, too, our fire was slackening; our last rounds of shot had been fired; what I had sent for could not get to us. I saw the faces of my men one after another, when they had fired their last cartridge, turn anxiously towards mine for a moment; then square to the front again. To the front for them lay death; to the rear what they would die to save. My thought was running deep. I was combining the elements of a "forlorn hope," and had just communicated this to Captain Spear of the wheeling flank, on which the initiative was to fall. Just then—so will a little incident fleck a brooding cloud of doom with a tint of human tenderness—brave, warm-hearted Lieutenant Melcher, of the Color Company, whose Captain and nearly half his men were down, came up and asked if he might take his company and go forward and pick up one or two of his men left wounded on the field, and bring them in before the enemy got too near. This would be a most hazardous move in itself and in this desperate moment, we could not break our line. But I admired him. With a glance, he understood, I answered, "Yes, sir, in a moment! I am about to order a charge!"

Not a moment was to be lost! Five minutes more of such a defensive, and the last roll-call would sound for us! Desperate as the chances were, there was nothing for it, but to take the offensive. I stepped to the colors. The men turned towards me. One word was enough—"BAYONET!" It caught like fire, and swept along the ranks. The men took it up with a shout,—one could not say, whether from the pit, or the song of the morning star.... The grating clash of steel in fixing bayonets told its own story; the colors rose in front; the whole line quivered for the start; the edge of the left-wing ... swooped down upon the serried host—down into the face of half a thousand! Two hundred men!

It was a great right wheel. Our left swung first. The advancing foe stopped, tried to make a stand amidst the trees and boulders; but the frenzied bayonets pressing through every space forced a constant settling to the rear. Morrill with his detached company and the remnants of our valorous sharpshooters who had held the enemy so long in check on the slopes of the Great Round Top, now fell upon the flank of the retiring crowd, and it turned to full retreat—some up amidst the crags of Great Round Top, but most down the smooth vale towards their own main line on Plum Run. This tended to mass them before our center. Here their stand was more stubborn. At the first dash the commanding officer I happened to confront, coming on fiercely, sword in one hand and big navy revolver in the other, fires one barrel almost in my face; but seeing the quick saber-point at his throat, reverses arms, gives sword and pistol into my hands and yields himself prisoner. I took him at his word, but could not give him further attention. I passed him over into the custody of a brave sergeant at my side, to whom I gave the sword as emblem of his authority, but kept the pistol with its loaded barrels, which I thought might come handy soon, as indeed it did.

Ranks were broken; many retired before us somewhat hastily; some threw their muskets to the ground—even loaded; sunk on their knees, threw up their hands, calling out, "We surrender. Don't kill us!" As if we wanted to do that! We kill only to resist killing. And these were manly men, whom we would befriend, and by no means kill, if they came our way in peace and good will. Charging right through and over these, we struck the second line of the Forty-seventh Alabama doing their best to stand, but offering little resistance. Their Lieutenant-Colonel as I passed—and a fine gentleman was Colonel Bulger—introduced himself as my prisoner, and as he was wounded, I had him cared for as best we could. Still swinging to the right as a great gate on its hinges, we swept the front clean of assailants. We were taking in prisoners by scores—more than we could hold, or send to the rear, so that many made final escape up Great Round Top. Half way down to the throat of the vale I came upon Colonel Powell of the Fourth Alabama, a man of courtly bearing, who was badly wounded. I sent him to the Eighty-third Pennsylvania, nearest to us and better able to take care of him than we were.

When we reached the front of the Forty-fourth New York, I thought it far enough. Beyond on the right the Texas Brigade had rallied or rendezvoused, I took thought of that. Most of the fugitives before us, rather than run the gantlet of our whole brigade, had taken the shelter of the rocks of Great Round Top, on our left, as we now faced. It was hazardous to be so far out, in the very presence of so many baffled but far from beaten veterans of Hood's renowned division. A sudden rush on either flank might not only cut us off, but cut in behind us and seize that vital point which it was our orders and our trust to hold. But it was no light task to get our men to stop. They were under the momentum of their deed. They thought they were "on the road to Richmond." They had to be reasoned with, persuaded, but at last faced about and marched back to that dedicated crest with swelling hearts. Not without sad interest and service was the return. For many of the wounded had to be gathered up. There was a burden, too, of the living. Nearly four hundred prisoners remained in our hands—two for every man of ours. Shortly the twilight deepened, and we disposed ourselves to meet any new assault that might come from the courage of exasperation. But the attack was not renewed....[8]

CHAPTER SIX

"Advance, Colonel, and Take Those Colors"

A s the afternoon of July 2 wore on, Longstreet's second-day attack moved forward *en echelon*, from south to north, targeting the left side of the Federal line. Federal troops defending Little Round Top and Sickles's Salient took the first blows, then—unfolding with mounting pressure—the Confederate attack moved up the Federal line toward its center. At dusk, it would also include assaults on the Federal far right flank. The second day's fighting was a massive clash of arms: approximately 22,000 assaulting Confederate troops battled some 40,000 Federal defenders over the course of three hours. It yielded a bloody harvest—more than 15,000 dead and wounded. Upon reflection, General Longstreet would view the July 2 Confederate attack on the Federal left as "the best three hours' fighting ever done...." A Federal officer who saw his regiment almost destroyed would be more personal in his assessment, saying simply, "men fell fast at every stride."[1]

"The Men Must See Us Today"
A Bloody Give-and-Take near Devil's Den

A s the battle lines of Hood's division advanced toward the far left flank of the Federal line with flags flying, Captain James E. Smith of the 4th Independent Battery of New York Light Artillery watched them approach. Smith commanded a battery of long-range Parrott rifled artillery, posted on and around the southern end of Houck's Ridge—a rise of ground on the north side of Devil's Den. Heading straight for Smith's guns were parts of two brigades of Hood's division—soldiers from Texas and from Arkansas under Brigadier General Jerome Robertson and Georgia troops under Brigadier General Henry Benning. As the Confederates advanced, Smith's New Yorkers opened a furious artillery fire. It tore huge gaps in the ranks of gray and butternut—but they dressed their lines, filled in the gaps, and continued advancing.

"Give them shell! give them shot!" Smith yelled to his gun crews. "Damn them, give them anything!" The Southerners took their losses—horrible losses— and kept coming. As they neared Smith's artillery, his gun crews were running low on ammunition. Desperate, Smith turned toward the line of Federal infantry supporting his battery and yelled, "For God's sake, men, don't let them take my guns away from me!" Closest was the 124th New York Infantry—troops

Boulders and bodies litter the base of Little Round Top, where Confederates of Hood's division engaged in brutal combat with troops defending the left flank of the Federal line.

Library of Congress

from Sickles's Third Corps—who hailed from New York's Orange County and dubbed themselves the "Orange Blossoms." They were commanded by Colonel Augustus Van Horne Ellis, a tough, profane New Yorker, who had given up a law practice before the war to seek adventure in California and on the high seas. Now he had more adventure than he could possibly want, as Hood's Confederates swarmed up the rise toward his position. To rally his troops, Ellis had his horse brought forward, and climbed into the saddle over the protests of another officer, who knew it would make him a conspicuous target. Ellis insisted. "The men must see us today," he proclaimed.

Ellis and his "Orange Blossoms" fought fiercely—at one point turning back the oncoming Confederates with a bayonet charge. In the end, the Southerners would take Devil's Den and the high ground beside it, as well as three of Smith's precious Parrotts—but nothing more. The "Orange Blossoms" would help preserve the Federal left flank, although not without a great loss of blood. Of the 279 officers and troops who held the line, 90 became casualties that afternoon. Among the wounded was Ellis's second in command, Lieutenant Colonel Francis M. Cummins. Among the dead was another chief subordinate, Major James Cromwell—and Colonel Ellis, who was shot from the saddle in the heat of battle. Captain Charles Weygant, a survivor of that harrowing afternoon, would later describe the desperate, bloody defense waged by Colonel Ellis and his "Orange Blossoms."

***

At about three P. M. a dozen Confederate batteries opened upon us in a most furious manner, and Smith's guns in our rear, and a number of Federal batteries in the vicinity, forthwith began to reply. Presently long solid lines of infantry appeared advancing directly against us.... "At length the enemy appeared in heavy columns of battalion advancing on us from the opposite slope. As we held the position by a single line of battle unsupported, the enemy's superiority in numbers, as seen at a glance, seemed overwhelming. As they approached they deployed in four distinct lines of battle, and came *resolutely on under a rapid fire from our batteries. All seemed lost but in the steady lines of the Third corps not a man flinched, and among them all, none were more ready for the fierce encounter than Major Cromwell...."*

When the enemy's advance line drew near the base of the hill we were on, it appeared to almost halt for a minute, and then started rapidly forward again, and with fierce yells began ascending the slope; and there was heard an opening crash of riflery all along our front, which was the death knell of hundreds; yet on, on they came, but very slowly, only a few feet at a time. Now Cromwell hurries to Colonel Ellis, who stands behind the color company and asks him to order a charge; but the Colonel shakes his head and tells the Major to go back to his place again.

Now the enemy has been brought to a stand, but he is only a few rods away. Again Cromwell walks toward Ellis. This time he is accompanied by Adjutant Ramsdell. Once more he requests the Colonel to charge, and is again told to go back to the left of the regiment; yet a moment later their horses are brought up and ... they mount. The Major's only reply is, "The men must see us to-day," and he rides slowly to and wheels his horse about in rear of the centre of the left wing; where with drawn sword and eyes fixed on the Colonel, he impatiently awaits his superior's pleasure.

Presently Ellis by a simple nod gives the desired permission; at which Cromwell waves his sword twice above his head, makes a lunge forward, shouts the charge, and putting spurs to his horse, dashes forward through the lines. The men cease firing for a minute and with ready bayonets rush after him. Ellis sits still in his saddle and looks on as if in proud admiration of both his loved Major and gallant sons of Orange, until the regiment is fairly under way, and then rushes with them into the thickest of the fray.

The conflict at this point defies description. Roaring cannon, crashing riflery, screeching shots, bursting shells, hissing bullets, cheers, shouts, shrieks and groans were the notes of the song of death which greeted the grim reaper, as with mighty sweeps he leveled down the richest field of scarlet human grain ever garnered on this continent. The enemy's line, unable to withstand our fierce onset, broke and fled, and Cromwell—his noble face flushed with victory, and his extended right arm waving his flashing sabre— uttered a shout of triumph. But it had barely escaped his lips when the second line of the foe poured into us a terrible fire which seemed in an instant to bring down a full quarter of our number.

Once more we hear our beloved Cromwell's shout, and once again we see, amid the fire and smoke, his noble form and flashing blade; but the next instant his brave heart is pierced by a rebel bullet, his right arm drops powerless, his lifeless body falls backward from his saddle, and loud above the din of battle we hear Ellis shout, "My God! My God, men! Your Major's down; save him! save him." Again the onset of Orange County's sons becomes irresistible, and the second line of the foe wavers and falls back; but another and solid line takes its place, whose fresh fire falls with frightful effect on our now skeleton ranks. So terrible is it that two-thirds of the artillerymen in our rear are either killed or wounded, and the balance driven from their guns, by the shells and bullets which pass over and through our line.

A tough, foul-mouthed New Yorker, Colonel Augustus Van Horne Ellis led the 124th New York Infantry into battle on horseback. "The men must see us today," he gallantly announced. Soon afterwards, he took a bullet in the forehead.

Library of Congress

Lieutenant Colonel Cummins, with the experience and eye of an old soldier, realizes that a skirmish line without reserves, be the men who compose it never so brave, must eventually be swept away by a continually renewed solid battle line, and unwilling the regiment should be disgraced by the loss of guns it is expected to protect, attempts to get them started to the rear, and while in the act is so badly injured by a shell—which striking a gun-carriage hurls it against him—that he is carried from the field. But our brave Ellis yet remains, now seen in bold relief, now lost amid the clouds of powder smoke. A moment longer the central figure, he directs his regiment. Again the rebel line begins to waver and we see his proud form rise in his stirrups; his long sharp sword is extended upward, a half uttered order escapes his lips, when suddenly his trusty blade falls point downward, his chin drops on his breast, and his body with a weave pitches forward, head foremost among the rocks; at which his wounded beast rears and with a mad plunge dashes away, staggering blindly through the ranks of the foe, who is now giving ground again, firing wildly as he goes.

But we are too weak to follow him, yet with desperate effort the Orange Blossoms struggle forward and gather up such as they may of the wounded, and with them and the bodies of Ellis and Cromwell, we fall slowly and mournfully back to the main line, from which we never should have advanced—and there reform our shattered bleeding ranks, and prepare to receive as best we may the next onset of the foe. Three times we have beaten him back, but now we are exhausted....

General Sickles has been seriously wounded. Birney now commands our corps, Ward our division, Berdan our brigade, and I find myself, who twenty minutes before was fourth officer in rank, in command of what is left of our regiment. The battle has now become general, and is raging nearly all along the line. Three hundred cannon are rending the air and shaking the earth. From every knoll and hill-top, in front and rear, there come flashes of fire, and buffing clouds of smoke.

Our immediate foes keep up a brisk fire but do not again attempt to ascend the hill in front of us. My ten little companies, now numbering but a trifle over a hundred, all told, are gathered together in little squads like picket posts along the front they are yet expected to hold; but their deliberate aim is not without its effect on the solid Confederate battle line at the foot of the hill below them.... The slope in front was strewn with our dead, and not a few of our severely wounded lay beyond the reach of their unscathed comrades, bleeding, helpless, and some of them dying.... The lifeless remains of Ellis and Cromwell were now lying on a huge boulder but a few yards in our rear, and in plain sight of all those remaining in our battle line, who chanced to look that way.

But the gallant boys fought on. If there were any cowards in our ranks when the battle began they were not there then. Every few moments a man would drop a rifle which had become clogged or so hot that he could not hold it steadily, and bidding those beside him be careful where they fired, rush forward and pick up, in place of it, one that had fallen from the hands of a dead or wounded comrade.

Presently the foes in our front slackened their fire, and turning for a moment to view the bodies of our late leaders, I saw the brains protruding from a small round hole in Ellis' forehead, and discovered glistening on Cromwell's blood-stained breast a gold locket, which I knew contained the portrait of one who but a few moments before was his beloved young wife, but then alas! though she suspected it not—his widow.

As I wheeled about toward the regiment, I heard some one ahead of me say, "they are advancing," and glancing to the left saw that the 40th New York was retiring before a heavy battle line, and that a column of the foe had already moved past their flank. The 99th Pennsylvania too was giving ground. The next instant an aide rode up, (Captain Cooney, I think it was) with orders to fall back without a moment's delay.... As soon as I could get these men together, I started with them after the regiment which was now some distance away, but the enemy had in the mean time advanced

to the top of the ledge our regiment had occupied, and it was by
mere chance that we escaped capture....

The active part that the 124th was to play in this great three
days' battle, had now been performed. Moving to a piece of woods
about a mile in the rear of the Union battle line, we prepared, and
with saddened hearts and gloomy thoughts, quietly partook of our
evening meal....[2]

"O, the Awful, Deathly Surging Sound of Those Little Black Balls"

McLaws's Confederates Are Pummeled by Federal Artillery Fire

It was almost five-thirty when General McLaws sent his division into the battle—one brigade after another against the Federal line to the north of Hood's attack. Major General Lafayette McLaws was a short, stout Georgian—another West Pointer with ample experience in the Mexican War and on the Western frontier. He was late getting his troops up for battle, and debate would continue for generations to come whether the delay was his fault or Longstreet's. To McLaws, it was Longstreet's failure. "General Longstreet is to blame for not reconnoitering the ground," he confided in a letter to his wife, "and for persisting in ordering the assault when his errors were discovered.... I consider him to be a humbug—a man of small capacity, very obstinate, not at all chivalrous, exceedingly conceited and totally selfish."

Despite McLaws's resentment of Longstreet, when his troops went forward, they did so with ferocious enthusiasm and a bloodcurdling Rebel Yell. First, three brigades advanced into battle—Brigadier General J. B. Kershaw's South Carolinians, Georgia troops led by Brigadier General Paul J. Semmes (brother of Raphael Semmes, the famous commander of the CSS *Alabama*), and a reserve brigade of Georgians led by Brigadier General William T. Wofford. They rushed the protruding angle of Sickles's unauthorized line, which was deployed just east of the Emmitsburg Road and north of Devil's Den in a peach orchard and a field of wheat.

Obscure cropland before the battle, the two landmarks would be forever known as *the* Wheatfield and *the* Peach Orchard due to the bloody, furious combat that enveloped them on the afternoon of July 2. Defending the Peach Orchard and the Wheatfield were troops of Major General David B. Birney's division—a brigade of Pennsylvania infantry commanded by Brigadier General Charles K. Graham and a brigade of troops from Michigan, Maine, New York, and Pennsylvania under Colonel P. Régis de Trobriand. Birney's men fought tenaciously, but at this point much of the bloody work of defending the Federal line was accomplished by the Federal artillery. The fighting intensified quickly both in the Wheatfield and the Peach Orchard, as the Confederate brigades piled into the smoky, deadly chaos with both sides killing each other in close quarters and almost face-to-face in places.

On the Federal side, while his troops were engaged in the Peach Orchard, General Graham was struck down by a head wound, left for dead by his soldiers, and captured by the Confederates. General Sickles, meanwhile, was struck by a Confederate shell fragment, which mangled his right leg and knocked him off his horse. The flamboyant general quickly wrapped a saddle strap around his thigh as a tourniquet. As a show of defiance and to boost troop morale, he puffed away on a cigar as stretcher-bearers bore him to the rear. On the Southern side, General Semmes had no opportunity for such heroics. He, too, was shot down, toppled from his horse by the searing Federal fire. He would not live long enough to think about troop morale or to congratulate his famous sea-faring brother: his wound was mortal.

Major General Lafayette McLaws's attack on the Federal left was ferocious— but it was late. Some faulted McLaws, but he blamed Longstreet: "I consider him to be a humbug," he stated.

Library of Congress

As the Confederate *en echelon* attack piled one brigade after another into battle, the Federal line crumbled at the Sickles's Salient and did indeed "come tumbling back" in retreat as General Hancock had predicted. A huge gap opened in Sickles's section of the line near the Peach Orchard, threatening the entire Federal line on Cemetery Ridge. Bolstered by Wofford's Brigade, sent in from reserve, McLaws's Confederates appeared on the verge of breaking the Federal line that afternoon as they pushed through the Peach Orchard, through Rose Woods, and across the Wheatfield. They were stopped short of Cemetery Ridge, however, by skillful, deadly fire from the Federal artillery and by the timely arrival of Federal reinforcements—the newly arrived Sixth Corps, other troops pulled from the right side of the Federal line, and, especially, the Pennsylvania Reserve Division under Brigadier General Samuel W. Crawford. The surging Southern tide was finally slowed, stopped, and reversed—and the hard-fighting Confederates reluctantly fell back from the Federal left to a line that extended along part of the Emmitsburg Road and through Devil's Den.

A civil engineer before the war, Brigadier General Charles K. Graham helped lay out New York City's sprawling Central Park. In a much smaller spot at Gettysburg—the deadly Peach Orchard—he was wounded and captured by the enemy.

Library of Congress

At the forefront of the afternoon struggle on the Federal left flank was Private John Coxe of the 2nd South Carolina Infantry, which belonged to Kershaw's Brigade and McLaws's division. From his home in California a half-century later, Coxe would craft a vivid account of the gory contest in the Peach Orchard and in the Wheatfield.

At Gettysburg, I was a private in Company B, 2nd South Carolina Volunteers, Kershaw's Brigade, McLaws's Division, Longstreet's Corps.... Soon after sunrise [on July 2] we were called into ranks and marched slowly forward on the pike. Just before reaching the seminary we passed a brigade cooking breakfast on the left of the pike, and some of the men told us that they were in the fight on the day before. Coming to the foot of the seminary hill, we debouched to the right down a slight declivity and soon afterwards reached Willoughby Run in the woods directly west of the seminary. Here we halted and lay around for at least two hours, during which Gen. A. P. Hill and staff rode over from the west of the Run and then slowly on up through the woods toward the seminary. General Hill was an interesting personality. A slight but very pleasant smile seemed to light up his face all the time, while his eagle eyes took in everything about him. His flowing whiskers were red, but his hair was a little darker....

At last we were brought to attention and marched in column through open woods down the east side of the Run. Proceeding about half a mile, another halt was called and we lay around another hour. Meanwhile we hear desultory picket firing in the distance to our left. With several others I walked to the left about one hundred yards to an opening in the woods. We looked across a field and road and saw the famous peach orchard beyond. To the right of the orchard and farther away we saw two cone-shaped hills partly covered with scrubby timber. These were the now celebrated Round Tops, the smaller of the two being on the left. The field to the right of the peach orchard extended as far as we could see from that point. The light skirmishing was going on in the peach orchard, which was so densely green that we couldn't see the men of either party. We were sharply called back to ranks and cautioned not to expose ourselves to the view of the enemy.

Soon after this, hearing a noise in the rear, we looked and saw General Hood at the head of his splendid division riding forward parallel to us about fifty yards to the left. This explained our last halt. Hood, who had marched to Gettysburg in the rear of McLaws, was to take position on our right and therefore on the extreme Confederate right. Why this great loss of time at that important juncture to get Hood and his artillery on the extreme right and thus delay the battle of the 2nd of July could never be understood by us private soldiers, but General Longstreet was responsible for it, doubtless believing that it would be better to have the great fighter Hood on his right. But, in fact, it was a very bad error for two reasons—namely, it allowed the Federals time to bring up tremendous forces of arms to meet us, and as it happened, Hood was wounded and disabled right at the beginning of his fight on the extreme right.

It seemed to take an age for Hood's men and train of artillery to pass us, and when finally it did get by, our division followed, Semmes' Brigade leading. But it didn't take us long to reach the open near the Emmitsburg Pike and in plain view of both Round Tops and the peach orchard. I looked and saw a Yankee flag waving signals from the apex of Little Round Top. Indeed, we were so much exposed to view that the enemy had no trouble counting the exact numbers under Hood and McLaws. However, we were placed behind a stone fence along the west side of the pike and ordered to lie down. Immediately in our front and to the left, extending to the peach orchard, was an open field, then mostly in buckwheat. At the farther side of this field and in front of the Round Tops was a thick woods, mostly of heavy oaks.

About fifteen field guns under Cabell were brought up and unlimbered on the pike in front of an oak grove a little to our right, and a little later a Federal battalion of many guns galloped from the woods into the field near the peach orchard and somewhat to the left of our front, followed by a heavy Federal line of battle, but the latter soon after about-faced and returned to the woods. The Federal batteries quickly deployed and unlimbered guns, but didn't open fire. By this time, the sun was observed to be getting down toward the top of South Mountain to the west and to our rear. Then suddenly we heard Hood's cannon under Latimer open on the right and the furious reply of the Federal guns. Then pretty soon a few sharp bugle noises were heard and then boom! boom! boom! blasted away Latimer's guns at the Federal batteries near the peach orchard.

The Yankees were ready and replied with spirit and in less time than it takes to tell it our ears were deafened by the noise of the guns and exploding shells. A little to the right I saw General Longstreet and staff dismounted behind the stone fence watching the effects of our shots through their field glasses. I don't know how long this awful cannonade lasted (probably twenty minutes), but as it began to slacken we were ordered to scale the stone fence behind which we were standing. This was quickly done, and then we were on the Emmitsburg Pike. On the other side of the pike was another stone fence to cross, and this done, there was no other important obstacle between us and the enemy.

The cannonade suddenly ceased, and then we would hear Hood's small arms fighting on the right in terrible crashes and roars. Our line, formed in perfect order of battle, faced a little to the left so as to sweep the Federal batteries near the peach orchard. Just before the order, "Forward, march!" was given I saw General Kershaw and staff immediately in our rear dismounted. About halfway from our start at the pike to the Federal batteries was a little downgrade to a small depression. We went along in perfect order, the 13th South Carolina being on our right. As yet we could see no Federal infantry because it was covered by the wood in the rear of the batteries, but we saw plainly that their artillerists were loading their guns to meet our assault, while their mounted officers were dashing wildly from gun to gun, apparently to be sure that all were ready.

Just before reaching the depression already mentioned, a Confederate battery on the pike somewhat to our left opened fire, and I heard one of our men say, "That will help us out," believing as we all did that its fire was against the Federal guns in our front. But alas! The next moment we saw that its fire was directed at a point further to the left in the peach orchard. Well, just as our left struck the depression in the ground, every Federal cannon let fly at us with grape. O, the awful deathly surging sounds of those little black balls as they flew by us, through us, between our legs, and over us! Many, of course, were struck down, including Captain Pulliam, who was instantly killed. Then the order was given to double-quick, and we were mad and fully determined to take and silence those batteries at once.

We had gotten onto the level land of the Federal guns when the next fusillade of grape met us. We were now so close to the Federal gunners that they seemed bewildered and were apparently trying to get their guns to the rear. But just then—and ah me! To think of it makes my blood curdle even now, nearly fifty years afterward—the insane order was given to "right flank." Of course no one ever knew who gave the order or any reason why it was given. General Kershaw denied being responsible for it, but somebody must have been. Why, in a few moments the whole brigade was jumbled up in a space less than a regiment behind a rocky, heavily wooded bluff with the right flank in the air, close to that historic scarecrow, the Devil's Den and also little Round Top, quite near, with our left flank disconnected and wholly unsupported for a mile or more. We were truly "in a box," liable to be captured or annihilated at any moment.

It was some time until the Federals who had partly charged turned loose all their guns upon the woods over our heads. My! How the trees trembled and split under the incessant shower of shot and shell! But we were well protected from the front of the rocky bluff, and only a few men were injured by falling limbs. However,

A U.S. Army veteran, Brigadier General William T. Wofford of Georgia had opposed secession, but joined the Confederate army anyway. Confederate troops fighting in the Peach Orchard and Wheatfield were inspired by his leadership—but it was not enough.

Photographic History of the Civil War

it wasn't long till the Federal infantry in great force advanced to the rim of the buff and began to pour lead down upon us; but they soon found out that bullets could go uphill with death to their songs as well as downhill, so they dared not rush down upon us. It soon became evident, though, that they were taking steps to flank us as both ends. About that time Charley Markley, of my company, was killed, a ball piercing his forehead. Many others fell, but our "spunk" was up to white heat, and we didn't care but made up our minds to die right there to the last man if necessary.

We fought in that position for nearly half an hour, when to our surprise the thunder and roar of the Federal cannons and musketry in our front suddenly stopped, and the next moment we heard a tremendous Rebel cheer, followed by an awful crash of small arms, coming through the woods on our left front and from the direction of the peach orchard. Then one of our officers shouted and said, "That's help for us! Spring up the bluff, boys!" And we did so. Meanwhile, the crash of small arms and Rebel yells on the left increased. As we reached open ground over the bluff, we saw the Federal artillery we had charged deserted and almost perfect Confederate lines of battle just entering the woods, hotly engaging and driving the Federal infantry.

"Who is that?" shouted an officer. But before we had time to think of getting an answer, an officer galloped from the right of the advancing line and ordered us to join his right and go forward. And that officer was Brig. Gen. William T. Wofford. Until that moment we didn't know that when the division advanced from the Emmitsburg Pike, Wofford's Brigade had been held in reserve on the pike near the peach orchard.... When Wofford ordered us to join his right and rush forward, a tremendous Rebel yell went up from our powder-choked throats. Wofford took off his hat and, waving it at us, turned back and charged along his line to the left. And here was seen how the right sort of officer can inspire his men to accomplish

Confederate troops—likely from Georgia and South Carolina—await burial near the edge of the blood-soaked Peach Orchard.

Library of Congress

next to superhuman results. *Always Wofford rode right along with his men during a fight, continually furnishing examples and cheering them with such words as, "Charge them, boys."... Those who saw it said they never saw such a fine military display as Wofford's line of battle as it advanced from the pike. He went right for those Federal cannons that were firing at us. Nor did it take him long to reach those batteries and smash them even before the gunners had time to turn their guns upon him.*

Rushing over the artillery, he kept right on and tackled the Yankee infantry in the woods beyond. And his assault was so sudden and quickly executed that the Federal lines of infantry were smashed and gave way at every point in Wofford's way; and as the remnant of Kershaw's Brigade, combined with Wofford's splendid body of men, rushed along through the woods, all the Federal supports met the same fate of their first line. It became a regular rout, and while the panic-stricken enemy fell by the scores and hundreds, Wofford lost only a few men.

Emerging from the woods on the other side, we drove the enemy across a wheat field and on to the western slopes of Little Round Top, up which they scampered in great disorder. While crossing the wheat field I looked along their line both ways, but saw no other troops. At that time, and while putting on a cap for another shot, a bullet from Little Round Top tore open my right shirtsleeve from wrist to elbow, but I wasn't hurt much. At the farther edge of the wheat field we were met by shots from Federal cannon on the apex of Little Round Top, but all went high over us. Of course every one of us expected to go right on and capture that famous hill, which at that time seemed easy to do; but Wofford, seeing that night was near and that there were no supports on right or left or in the rear, ordered a halt, and after surveying the hill through his field glasses ordered us to about face and fall back across the wheat field and into the woods from which we had so recently driven the enemy. And, strange to say, when we ceased firing not another gun was heard on that part of the field during the remainder of that 2nd of July. The wheat field and woods were blue with dead and wounded Federals. At the edge of the woods we met McLaws and cheered him, and he seemed well pleased with the evidences of our victory lying around him.

I felt sorry for the wounded enemy, but we could do little to help them. Just before dark I passed a Federal officer sitting on the ground with his back resting against a large oak tree. He called me to him, and when I went he politely asked me to give him some water. There was precious little in my canteen, but I let him empty it. His left leg was crushed just above the ankle, the foot lying on the ground sidewise. He asked me to straighten it up in a natural position and prop it with rocks, and as I did so I asked him if the movement hurt him. "There isn't much feeling in it just now," he replied quietly. Then before leaving him I said, "Isn't this war awful?" "Yes, yes," said he, "and all of us should be in a better business."

He wore long red whiskers and was large and fine-looking. I shall never forget his profuse thanks for the little service I was able to render him. Our lines were established at the west rim of the woods leading to the wheat field. There we built fires, and from haversacks of the dead enemy all about us got something to eat....[3]

"Tell My Wife I Am Shot, but We Fought like Hell"

Barksdale's Mississippians Draw Blood and Shed It Too

As McLaws's attacking Confederate lines were buffeted and staggered by Federal artillery and infantry fire, General Longstreet ordered McLaws's fourth brigade to enter battle. It was composed entirely of soldiers from Mississippi—four regiments of combat veterans described as "almost giants in size and power"—led by Brigadier General William Barksdale. At age forty-one, Barksdale appeared older than his age due to a mane of prematurely white hair worn shoulder length. Born in Tennessee and orphaned as a child in Mississippi, he studied law and opened a practice, but put it aside for the more exciting post of newspaper editor, which enabled him to deliver scathing editorial broadsides aimed at political miscreants, Republicans, and champions of big government. Molded by the frontier mentality and honor code of prewar Mississippi, Barksdale was elected to the U.S. Congress, where his fiery rhetoric once sparked a fistfight on the floor of the House of Representatives.

During the war, he survived a court-martial for drunkenness and earned praise from Lee and others for his decisive leadership. His Mississippi troops matched his zeal for fighting, earning recognition at First Bull Run, the Seven Days, Antietam, and Fredericksburg. At Gettysburg on the second day, Barksdale impatiently awaited orders to follow the rest of McLaws's Brigade into battle. "General, let me go," he pleaded with McLaws. "General, let me charge." Seeing the damage inflicted on McLaws's other brigades by a Federal battery at the Peach Orchard, Barksdale appealed to Longstreet. "I wish you would let me go in, General," he begged. "I will take that battery in five minutes."

When finally given the go-ahead, he jubilantly led his troops in the assault. "Forward, men! Forward!" he shouted. His white mane flowed behind him as he rode forward on horseback, and his face—according to an observer—appeared "radiant with joy." With ease, the screaming Mississippians knocked down the fences that flanked the Emmitsburg Road, and then swarmed the blue-uniformed troops in the Peach Orchard and to the north. It took them less than five minutes to capture two sections of Federal artillery—four guns—shooting down the gun crews before they could limber up the guns and retreat. They also captured almost a thousand Federal infantry. At one point, as Federal troops streamed toward the rear with their line evidently breached, General Sickles—still on two legs—grabbed a retreating Federal officer. "Colonel, for God's sake, can't you hold on?" The officer pointed back toward the piles of his dead soldiers and cried, "Where is my regiment?"

Barksdale's attack was "the grandest charge that was ever made," admitted a Federal officer who witnessed the event. Barksdale and his troops charged on, heading toward Cemetery Ridge—but they never reached it. Meade's chief of artillery, Brigadier General Henry J. Hunt, had skillfully massed forty pieces of field artillery along Cemetery Ridge, and Hunt's guns ripped into the valiant Mississippians—aided by massed fire from the infantry reinforcements that Meade had hurried into line. Now it was Barksdale's men who fell in droves. Among those fatally wounded in the hail of Federal lead and iron was General Barksdale, who was riddled with bullets from dozens of rifles aimed at his conspicuous figure. The men from Mississippi begrudgingly fell back, yielding all that they had gained, and left behind half their numbers lying dead or wounded in the battered Peach Orchard and in the trampled fields north of it. One of those

Brigadier General William Barksdale was known to be zealous and confrontational—as a newspaper editor, a U.S. congressman, and a Confederate commander. On the afternoon of July 2, he pleaded, "General, let me charge."

Rubenstein Rare Book and Manuscripts Library, Duke University

As Lee's attack on July 2 unfolded against the Federal left *en echelon*—in successive waves—it repeatedly fell short of success due to devastating Federal artillery fire and skillful deployment of Federal infantry reinforcements.

Harper's Weekly

left behind was General Barksdale. A Yankee soldier sliced off a piece of gold braid from the dying Rebel general's uniform as a souvenir; otherwise, he was treated respectfully by his Northern captors. As he was dying, he murmured: "Tell my wife I am shot, but we fought like hell."

Captain Fitzgerald Ross, a Scot soldier of fortune and an officer in the Imperial Austrian Army, traveled with Lee's army as a military observer. He observed Longstreet's second day attack on the Federal left from the Confederate lines, and described the event the following year in a Scots magazine:

It was still dusk next morning [July 2] when the sound of cannon aroused me from my sleep. "C'est le sanglant appel de Mars!" I sang out to my tent-mates. I went over to Longstreet's quarters, a few hundred yards off, 'fixed' my saddle and bridle on the horse I was to ride, and then breakfasted with General Longstreet and his Staff. We had to ride some five miles before we got to the front, where we halted at the top of a hill, from which there was a full view of the enemy's position. General Lee was there with his Staff, and we let our horses loose in an enclosed field close by, and lay about for some time looking through our glasses at the Yankees, who were near enough for us to distinguish every individual figure, gun, &c., and who were apparently engaged in the same occupation as ourselves.

As evidently a long time would elapse before Longstreet's corps, which was to do the chief fighting that day, could be placed in position, I determined meanwhile to ride into the town of Gettysburg with the doctors. We crossed the ground which had been fought over yesterday. The Confederate wounded had been removed and their dead buried, but there were still a large number of dead Yankees lying about, and some of their wounded, especially in the cutting of a railroad where some of the fiercest fighting had taken place. I saw one man who had been entirely cut in two, his head and shoulders lying a couple of yards from the rest of his body—a horrible sight. The wounded men, too, who had lain there all night were ghastly to look at; and indeed a battle-field the day after the fight is anything but a pleasant place to come near.

Gettysburg is an insignificant little town, but contains some large buildings—county court-house, colleges, &c.—in and about the town. These have been turned into hospitals. At the end of one or two of the streets some sharp-shooting was going on at the Federal position on the Cemetery Hill behind the town, and the Yankees were returning the fire, but without doing any mischief, as far as I could see. Still we did not take the trouble to go beyond the town in that direction.

We met General Chilton, Lee's Inspector-General, in the town. He was riding about seeking whom he could devour in the shape of a depredator or illegal annexer of private property; but I do not think he found any. Indeed, the good behaviour and discipline of the men of this army is surprising to me, considering the way in which the Northerners have devastated the country and wreaked their wrath on women and children in the South wherever they had an opportunity.

They are as cheerful and good-natured a set of fellows as ever I saw—seem to be full of fun, and are always ready to talk, and joke, and "chaff," but are never pushing or insolent.

We also met General Early, a gruff-looking man, but with a high reputation as a soldier.

On returning to the hill where we had left the generals in command, we found them still there. They had been joined by Generals A. P. Hill and Heth, the latter of whom was wounded in the head yesterday, and several others. General Hill sent for water, and they brought him some dirty stuff in a pail, with an apology that no good water was to be had within a mile, and an inquiry whether he would wait. "Oh no, that will do very well," said the General, and I began to realise that we were actually campaigning.

Wherever an army is stationary for a few days, the wells and pumps are soon drunk dry; and in fact, before we left this neighbourhood, most of the wells had a guard on them, who only permitted water to be fetched for the wounded. For men in health, water brought from the nearest brook or creek is good enough, and sometimes details of men have to be sent a considerable distance for it....

At about three o'clock in the afternoon we were joined by General Longstreet, who, after a long consultation with the Commander-in-Chief, was at this moment riding down with his Staff towards the front. We found his corps already forming for the attack in a wood.

Longstreet rode up the line and down again, occasionally dismounting, and going forward to get a better view of the enemy's position.

The ground just before us was plain and open, but beyond were those hills, since so celebrated, covered with Federal breast-works and rifle-pits, and bristling with cannon. The Federals had also possession of the open ground below in front of their works, and their foremost guns were about a quarter of a mile from the wood we were in.

I especially remarked a battery in a peach orchard, which was blazing away at one of ours not far off.

As we passed Barksdale's Mississippi Brigade the General came up eagerly to Longstreet; "I wish you would let me go in, General; I would take that battery in five minutes." "Wait a little," said Longstreet; "we are all going in presently."

The men were as eager as their leader, and those in the front line began to pull down the fence behind which they were crouching.

"Don't do that, or you will draw the enemy's fire," said Longstreet, who sees and observes everything.

We passed on, and very soon afterwards the General called for his horse, mounted, dashed to the front of the line, gave the word, and led them on himself. We all followed him.

It was a glorious sight. The men who had been lying down sprang to their feet, and went in with a will. There was no lagging behind, no spraining of ankles on the uneven ground, no stopping to help a wounded comrade. Not one fell out of the line unless he was really hurt. On swept the line, breaking out with an occasional yell when they came face to face with the foe, but on the whole silently. The guns in the peach orchard were pounced upon, and half of them taken in a trice, whilst the others limbered up and made off. Hundreds of prisoners were captured, and everything was going so satisfactorily that for a time we hardly doubted that the enemy would be driven from his very strong position on the hills in front.

But at a critical moment General Hood was severely wounded, General Barksdale killed, and their men, at the very moment of apparent victory, when they had overcome almost all the difficulties that lay between them and entire success, hesitated, halted, and at length fell back, losing thereby far more men than they would have done if they had continued their advance. But still we gained decided advantages, taking prisoners and guns, and getting possession of the ground up to the foot of the hill.... The battle ceased at dark. As we rode back from the field, General Longstreet spoke with me about the failure to take the position on the hill, saying, "We have not been so successful as we wished," and attributed it chiefly to the causes before mentioned—Hood's wound and Barksdale's death. Perhaps if the attack had been made a little earlier in the day it might have been more successful....[4]

"My Officers, Men and Horses Were Shot Down"

Federal Artillery Helps Turns the Tide at Great Sacrifice

When the Confederate attack on the Sickles's Salient was finally turned back, it was due in no small part to the Federal artillery. Lieutenant Colonel Freeman McGilvery of the 1st Volunteer Artillery Brigade had cobbled together almost two dozen Federal artillery pieces, and posted them so that they provided concentrated fire from locations near the Peach Orchard. The 1st Volunteer Artillery Brigade—part of the Army of the Potomac's Artillery Reserve—was comprised of artillery crews from Massachusetts, New York, and Pennsylvania. For almost two hours, McGilvery's artillery brigade had traded fire with Confederate artillery and had held its own. As Sickles's line began to break near the Peach Orchard and his Third Corps infantry began to flee to the rear, some of McGilvery's batteries were overwhelmed by the advancing Southerners even as the gun crews frantically tried to withdraw their guns. Instead of taking time to limber up, Captain John Bigelow of the 9th Massachusetts Light Artillery ordered his gun crews to move out immediately, pulling his guns back by ropes—retiring "by prolonge"—even while the guns were still firing.

Northeast of the Peach Orchard, on a farm operated by Abraham and Catherine Trostle, Colonel McGilvery had Bigelow carry out what would be a last stand for many of his artillerymen—holding off the Confederate assault with blasts of canister until the Federal artillery redeployed and infantry reinforcements arrived. Hundreds of Southerners from McLaws's division were felled by McGilvery's guns before the artillerymen retreated. Scores of Bigelow's men were killed or wounded as well. The 21st Mississippi captured four of his guns, and the crossfire killed more than eighty artillery horses. Despite Bigelow's losses, his courageous stand at the Trostle farm stalled the assault by Barksdale's Mississippians until it could be turned back by artillery and infantry reinforcements. Here and elsewhere at Gettysburg, the Federal artillery made a critical difference, but often at a high price. While directing a section of Bigelow's artillery from horseback, for example, Lieutenant Christopher Erickson was wounded repeatedly—seven

Artillerymen of the 9th Massachusetts Light Artillery race their guns into place to defend the Federal left flank in this sketch by bugler and artist Charles W. Reed.

As the Massachusetts artillerymen tried to turn back the charging Confederates of McLaws's division, Lieutenant Christopher Erickson was repeatedly wounded. As sketched by Bugler Reed, he stayed with his guns, vomiting blood, until finally killed.

Library of Congress

times—yet somehow stayed in the saddle, vomiting blood and giving orders, until he finally fell dead.

Bigelow, too, was wounded, shot from his horse as the Mississippi troops swarmed his position. He was rescued under fire by First Bugler Charles W. Reed, who got the bleeding captain onto a horse and braved fire from both sides as he galloped between the lines to safety. Bigelow survived, and more than thirty years later, Reed would be awarded the Congressional Medal of Honor for the rescue—in part due to this letter from Captain Bigelow.

To the Adjutant General, U.S.A.
Washington, D.C. June 19th, 1895
Washington, D.C.

Sir:

I desire to present for your consideration as worthy of the "Medal of honor", for distinguished bravery and faithfulness to duty at the Battle of Gettysburg, the name of

Charles W. Reed

Bugler, 9th Lg't Battery, Mass. Vols.

I was Captain commanding said Battery in said Battle.

After the breaking of the 3rd Corps Lines at the Peach Orchard my command was the last to retire: which it did, pressed by Kershaws skirmishers in front and on the left flank and with Barksdales Brigade marching towards it, 300 yds distant on the right flank, without Infantry support, "firing by prolonge."

When the Angle of the Stone Wall, at the Trostle House was reached, Col McGilvery ordered me to halt and hold the enemy in check, sacrificing my Battery if necessary, until he could get some guns in position in my rear, as the lines were open from the foot of Little Round Top to the left of the Second Corps.

I did so, saving twenty precious minutes for McGilvery to accomplish his purpose before my Officers, men and horses were shot down by the Enemy coming in on my flanks: not one in my front.

Bugler Reed sat by me on his horse, a conspicuous mark, during the trying ordeal. By throwing his horse on his haunches, he saved himself from a volley fired at me by six of Kershaws skirmishers—two of whose bullets struck me; two my horse and two flew wild. He followed me, as my horse turned and when, after going a hundred feet, I fell to the ground, he remained with me, heard the Officers of the 21st Miss. order their men not to fire at me; called my orderly and had him lift me on to his horse; then, taking the reins of both horses in his left hand, with his right hand supporting me in the saddle, took me at a walk into the front of the 6th Maine Battery, which Col McGilvery had placed in position, from 300 to 500

Federal Bugler Charles W. Reed, an art student before the war, sketched numerous events he witnessed at Gettysburg. He also earned the Congressional Medal of Honor for his actions in combat.

Library of Congress

yds in my rear, while it was firing heavily and the shells of the Enemy were breaking all around us.

Before I was halfway back to the 6th Maine Battery Lieut Dow, commanding, sent an Officer to me, urging me to hurry, as he must commence firing on the men, 21st Miss. who had my Battery. I told him to fire away, I could not hurry, so Dow opened with shell, while we were in his front and with Canister after we had entered.

Bugler Reed did not flinch; but steadily supported me: kept the horses at a walk although between the two fires and guided them, so that we entered the Battery between two of the guns that were firing heavily: took me to the Hospital and afterwards, to my own Camp.

While I had many Officers and men worthy of any honor, which the government can bestow upon them, for their gallantry on that and other Battle fields, I present the name of

Charles W. Reed

Shot down in their traces, dead artillery horses litter the grounds of the farm owned by Abraham and Catherine Trostle—where the 9th Massachusetts Light Artillery made its stand.

Library of Congress

address No. 12 West St. Boston, Mass. for the "Medal of honor" for the reasons given and because he was equally gallant and faithful to duty throughout the war.

I remain very respy yrs
John Bigelow.
late Captain Comd'g 9th Light Batty, Mass Vols.[5]

"Advance, Colonel, and Take Those Colors"
The 1st Minnesota Infantry Sacrifices Itself for the Union

A s the Confederate attack on the Federal left flank worked its way northward *en echelon*, starting with Hood's division and followed by McLaws's division, the time came for troops of General A. P. Hill's Third Corps to join the assault. Major General Richard Anderson's division—five brigades of troops from Alabama, Georgia, Florida, Virginia, and Mississippi—was given the task of completing the Confederate attack. This final stage of the attack, also designed to unfold *en echelon* from right to left, would grow in strength as one brigade after another hit the Federal line. There was no delay this time—the assault began at 6:20 p.m., with plenty of daylight left under the summer sun. Brigadier General Cadmus M. Wilcox's Alabama brigade led the assault, followed by Colonel David Lang's brigade of Floridians, with Brigadier General Ambrose R. Wright's Georgians advancing behind Lang. Waiting to go in next were Brigadier William Mahone's Virginia brigade and Brigadier General Carnot Posey's brigade of Mississippians.

It began well. The Third Corps assault targeted the far northern segment of the Federal left flank, which included much of the center of the Federal line on Cemetery Ridge and remained heavily defended by the Army of the Potomac's Second Corps—which was under the command of Major General Winfield S. Hancock. Already, Hancock had made critical contributions to the Federal defense at Gettysburg, rallying the defeated army on the first day of battle, redeploying the rattled troops into line on Cemetery Ridge, setting up a reserve force that plugged the Confederate breakthrough in Sickles's Salient—and now the climax of the Confederate attack on the Federal left was coming his way. General Meade had also put him in charge of the Federal Third Corps when Sickles fell wounded.

Hancock had depleted his Second Corps troops bolstering the Federal left under the assaults by Hood and McLaws. Now he saw his worst fears realized: fresh Confederate troops—scores of them—charged toward the weakened left side of the Federal center. Already, the troops on the far right of Sickles's Salient—a division commanded by Brigadier General Andrew Humphreys—had begun to break and flee toward Cemetery Ridge. Hastily, Hancock summoned Second Corps troops from farther up the Federal line—troops from near Cemetery Hill under the command of Generals John Gibbon and Alexander Hays. But could they arrive in time to shore up Hancock's line on Cemetery Hill? It looked doubtful. As the last of Sickles's men scrambled for the rear just ahead of the oncoming Confederate battle lines, Hancock realized he had no more troops.

Thirty-seven-year-old Ambrose "Ranse" Wright entered Confederate service as a private, and in little over a year rose to brigadier general. On the second day at Gettysburg, his brigade of Georgians pierced the Federal line on Cemetery Ridge.

Library of Congress

If the Southerners continued onward unchecked and pierced the Federal line near its center, they could roll up the entire line and the battle would be over in short order. Hancock believed if he could hold up the enemy assault for just five minutes, he could get his reinforcements into line—but where would he get those five minutes? Just then he saw the first troops he had summoned coming "double quick" down the slope of Cemetery Ridge—eight companies of the 1st Minnesota Volunteer Infantry. "What regiment is this?" he yelled to the officer in front. "First Minnesota," came the reply.

The Minnesota officer was Colonel William Colvill Junior, and that same day he had been released from arrest and returned to command of his regiment. On the march to Gettyburg, the 1st Minnesota had been falsely accused of delaying the Federal march, and in a fit of frustration the Second Corps inspector general had arrested Colvill for insubordination. Tall, stocky, chiseled-faced, and disheveled, Colvill was a former lawyer and newspaper editor from Red Wing, Minnesota, known for his fascination with geology and his friendship with local Indians. When Lincoln called for 75,000 volunteers to invade the South following the firing on Fort Sumter, Colvill was reportedly the first in his county to sign up and helped raise a company of the 1st Minnesota. The regiment had fought well under heavy fire and had suffered serious casualties at First Bull Run and at Antietam.

When confronted by General Hancock, the 1st Minnesota was not at full strength—only eight of ten companies were available, a total of 262 troops. Pointing to the Confederate battle flag at the head of the oncoming mass of troops, Hancock shouted to Colvill: "Advance, Colonel, and take those colors." With one glance, the colonel realized that one small regiment would not last long against several brigades of charging Confederate veterans—but it might buy five minutes for more Federal reinforcements to arrive. "I would have ordered that regiment in," Hancock would later state, "if I had known that every man would be killed." Colvill and his Minnesotans surely understood what fate almost certainly would befall them—and yet they did not hesitate. They allowed a battery of Federal artillery—Battery C of the 4th U.S. Artillery—to unload a deadly cannonade into the enemy ranks. Then they rushed forward, bayonets fixed, and piled into the mass of charging Southerners—smashing into the right side of General Cadmus Wilcox's Alabama brigade.

The regiment was shredded. Of the 262 Minnesotans who made the assault, all but forty-seven were killed or wounded. Colonel Colvill was among them, wounded twice and crippled for life. But the brave men of the 1st Minnesota did not sacrifice themselves in vain—they bought not five minutes, but ten—time enough for the rest of Hancock's reinforcements to reach the threatened Federal line. The far right flank of General Wilcox's brigade was stopped cold—then the entire Southern line came under heavy fire. Savaged by mass volley fire from the Federal infantry reinforcements and simultaneously raked by Federal artillery fire, Wilcox and his Alabamians looked back for help from the Confederate reserves to the rear. So did Colonel Lang and his Florida troops advancing alongside. But there were no reserves. For reasons never fully explained, General Mahone and his brigade of Virginians stayed put and did not advance; while General Posey stopped midway with his Mississippi brigade on his route of attack. Even before reaching the base of Cemetery Ridge, Wilcox and Lang called a retreat.

General Ambrose Wright's Georgians made it farther, pushing up Cemetery Ridge and breaking through the Federal line atop it. General Wright would later state that before him, a flood of blue-uniformed troops broke and ran for the rear, and that it appeared the South had won the day and the battle. But it was a short-lived moment of victory: Federal reinforcements plugged the break in the line, and others surged toward Wright's brigade from both flanks. He, too, realized his Georgians had no support: Major General William D. Pender's division of Georgians and North and South Carolinians lay to the rear, but Pender did not accompany them—he had suffered a slight wound the day before, which would become infected and ultimately kill him. His successor, Brigadier General James H. Lane, had watched the troops of Anderson's division fall to the ground in droves while making the attack, and he, too, decided that his troops would stay put. With no support and on the verge of being overwhelmed by the Federal reinforcements, Wright called retreat and the gray tide that had seemed so unstoppable receded the way it had come. General Robert E. Lee's grand assault on the Federal left flank had failed.

Second Lieutenant William Lochren, a survivor of the 1st Minnesota's sacrificial assault, would later pen a detailed account of his regiment's epic role on Gettysburg's second day.

At a quarter before six on the morning of July 2d we arrived on the battlefield, and the Second Corps was placed in position on the line to the left of the cemetery, being joined on its left by Sickles' Third Corps, which extended that line to the vicinity of the Little Round Top. For some reason the First Minnesota Regiment was not placed *in this line, but apparently in reserve, a short distance to the rear. Early in the morning, just after we reached the battlefield, Col. Colvill was relieved from arrest, and assumed command of the regiment, and Company L (sharpshooters) was detailed to support Kirby's Battery near the cemetery, and did not rejoin us during the battle. While lying here one man was killed, and Sergt. O. M. Knight of Company I was severely wounded by shells from the enemy.*

Some time after noon Sickles advanced the Third Corps half a mile or more, to a slight ridge near the Emmitsburg road, his left extending to Devil's Den, in front of and near the base of Little Round Top, and Company F (Capt. John Ball) was detached as skirmishers, and sent in that direction. Soon after, the remaining eight companies of the regiment, numbering two hundred and sixty-two men (Company C was also absent, being the provost guard of the division), were sent to the centre of the line just vacated by Sickles' advance, to support Battery C of the Fourth United States Artillery. No other troops were then near us, and we stood by this battery, in full view of Sickles' battle in the peach orchard half a mile to the front, and witnessed with eager anxiety the varying fortunes of that sanguinary conflict, until at length, with gravest apprehension, we saw Sickles' men give way before the heavier forces of Longstreet and Hill, and come back, slowly, at first, and rallying at short intervals, but at length broken and in utter disorder, rushing down the slope, by the Trostle House, across the low ground, up the slope on our side, and past our position to the rear, followed by a strong force—the large brigades of Wilcox and Barksdale—in regular lines, moving steadily in the flush

Before the war, Confederate Brigadier General Cadmus Wilcox was a tactics instructor at West Point and author of a rifle training manual used by the U.S. Army. At Gettysburg, his brigade of Alabama troops appeared ready to break the Federal line—until stalled by a single regiment from Minnesota.

Library of Congress

of victory, and firing on the fugitives. They had reached the low ground, and in a few minutes would be at our position, on the rear of the left flank of our line, which they could roll up, as Jackson did the Eleventh Corps at Chancellorsville.

There was no organized force near to oppose them, except our handful of two hundred and sixty-two men. Most soldiers, in the face of the near advance of such an overpowering force, which had just defeated a considerable portion of an army corps, would have caught the panic and joined the retreating masses. But the First Minnesota had never yet deserted any post, had never retired without orders, and desperate as the situation seemed, and as it was, the regiment stood firm against whatever might come. Just then Hancock, with a single aid, rode up at full speed, and for a moment vainly endeavored to rally Sickles' retreating forces. Reserves had been sent for, but were too far away to hope to reach the critical position until it would be occupied by the enemy, unless that enemy were stopped. Quickly leaving the fugitives, Hancock spurred to where we stood, calling out, as he reached us, "What regiment is this?"

Colonel William Colvill, commander of the 1st Minnesota Volunteer Infantry, brought up his regiment just as the Federal line was breaking. "Advance, Colonel," he was ordered, "and take those colors."

Wikimedia Commons Images

"First Minnesota," replied Colvill. "Charge those lines!" commanded Hancock.

Every man realized in an instant what that order meant,—death or wounds to us all; the sacrifice of the regiment to gain a few minutes' time and save the position, and probably the battlefield,—and every man saw and accepted the necessity for the sacrifice, and, responding to Colvill's rapid orders, the regiment, in perfect line, with arms at "right shoulder shift," was in a moment sweeping down the slope directly upon the enemy's centre. No hesitation, no stopping to fire, though the men fell fast at every stride before the

*concentrated fire of the whole Confederate force, directed upon us
as soon as the movement was observed. Silently, without orders,
and, almost from the start, double-quick had changed to utmost
speed; for in utmost speed lay the only hope that any of us would
pass through that storm of lead and strike the enemy.*

*"Charge!" shouted Colvill, as we neared their first line; and with
leveled bayonets, at full speed, we rushed upon it; fortunately, as it
was slightly disordered in crossing a dry brook at the foot of a slope.
The men were never made who will stand against leveled bayonets
coming with such momentum and evident desperation. The first
line broke in our front as we reached it, and rushed back through
the second line, stopping the whole advance. We then poured in our
first fire, and availing ourselves of such shelter as the low banks of
the dry brook afforded, held the entire force at bay for a considerable time, and until our reserves appeared on the ridge we had left.*

*Had the enemy rallied quickly to a counter charge, its great
numbers would have crushed us in a moment, and we would have
made but a slight pause in its advance. But the ferocity of our onset
seemed to paralyze them for the time, and although they poured
upon us a terrible and continuous fire from the front and enveloping flanks, they kept at respectful distance from our bayonets, until,
before the added fire of our fresh reserves, they began to retire, and
we were ordered back.*

*What Hancock had given us to do was done thoroughly. The
regiment had stopped the enemy, and held back its mighty force and
saved the position. But at what sacrifice! Nearly every officer was
dead or lay weltering with bloody wounds, our gallant colonel and
every field officer among them. Of the two hundred and sixty-two
men who made the charge, two hundred and fifteen lay upon the
field, stricken down by rebel bullets, forty-seven were still in line,
and not a man was missing. The annals of war contain no parallel
to this charge.... The wounded were gathered in the darkness by*

their surviving comrades and sent to field hospitals, and the fragment of the regiment lay down for the night....[6]

CHAPTER SEVEN

"It Was a Close and Bloody Struggle"

L ate in the day on July 2, after Lee's army failed to break the left side of the Federal line, the fighting shifted to the Federal right. General Ewell had three divisions posted around the town of Gettysburg: General Jubal Early's division was posted immediately south of town, General Robert Rodes's division to the west, and General Edward Johnson's division on Gettysburg's east side. According to some, General Early was stung by the questions surrounding his decision not to make a follow-up attack on the defeated Federal army the evening before, and was now eager to make a good showing for himself. Yet throughout the day on July 2, he had little opportunity. Lee had ordered Ewell to make a demonstration against the Federal right flank whenever Longstreet launched his attack on the Federal left, in order to keep the Federals from shifting reinforcements from the right side of their line to their left. Again, as he had the day before, Lee gave Ewell discretion—if his demonstration against the Federal right looked promising, he could expand it into a full-scale attack on Culp's Hill and on Cemetery Hill. Ewell decided it *was* promising: he, too, would attack.

He positioned his three divisions to attack the Federal line that was deployed on Culp's Hill and on Cemetery Hill, around which the northern "hook" of the

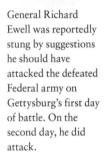

Federal fishhook line curved. All day he waited for the sound of Longstreet's attack, so he could launch his own. Finally, at four o'clock in the afternoon, when he heard Longstreet's cannonade, Ewell ordered his artillery to open fire against the Federal positions on Culp's Hill and Cemetery Hill. He had some eighty pieces of field artillery in his corps, but he could not find suitable locations within range of the Federal targets, and thus posted less than half his guns. Kicking off his attack were six batteries of artillery commanded by Major J. W. Latimer.[1]

General Richard Ewell was reportedly stung by suggestions he should have attacked the defeated Federal army on Gettysburg's first day of battle. On the second day, he did attack.
Library of Congress

"Simply a Hell Infernal"

A Deadly Beginning for the Southern Attack on the Federal Right

Twenty-year-old Major Joseph White Latimer was the seventh son of a Virginia family. He had a baby face and stood small in stature, but nobody laughed at him: he was too good of an artillery commander. At VMI, where he first demonstrated his knack for handling the big guns and their crews, the other cadets called him "Little Latimer," but on the training field they gave him unquestioned respect and obeyed his orders promptly. In Confederate service, he quickly demonstrated his gifts as an artilleryman. In the 1862 Valley Campaign, "Stonewall" Jackson cited him for "coolness, judgment and skill." In the spring of 1863, Latimer, not yet twenty-one, was promoted to the rank of major in Lee's army, quickly becoming known as the "Boy Major."

At Gettysburg, he commanded the artillery attached to Major General Edward Johnson's division in Ewell's Second Corps. As Ewell struggled to find workable locations to post his artillery, Latimer suggested putting his batteries atop Benner's Hill, which lay about a quarter-mile northeast of Cemetery Hill and close to Culp's Hill. Ewell agreed, and General Johnson, Latimer's division commander, ordered the "Boy Major" to put his guns in place on Benner's Hill. Its elevation was lower than both Cemetery Hill and Culp's Hill, where Federal artillery was posted in strength. It had also been timbered, making Latimer's sixteen guns and their crews vulnerable to Federal fire from the higher elevations.

When he opened fire at 4:00 p.m., Latimer delivered his typical precise and remarkably accurate fire, which ripped into the Federal artillery on Cemetery Hill. Latimer's carefully delivered, deadly fire sent "a mighty storm of iron hail" into his Federal targets, according to a Northern officer who was on the receiving end of it. "The shots of the enemy came thick and fast, bursting, crushing and plowing," he would later recall. "One of their shells struck and exploded at our No. 3 gun, killing and wounding every man at that piece...." Latimer inflicted serious damage on the enemy, but he remained severely outgunned and his assignment verged on the suicidal. For unexplained reasons, General Ewell's attack on the Federal right flank was delayed, leaving young Latimer and his men exposed to incessant pounding by Federal artillery.

At a gallop, Confederate field artillery races into position. From Benner's Hill, Confederate artillery opened fire on the Federal extreme right flank—but with dire results.

Battles and Leaders of the Civil War

From Culp's Hill, East Cemetery Hill, and other locations, more than forty Federal cannon blanketed Benner's Hill with hellish incoming fire.

Latimer received permission to withdraw some of his artillery, but when he returned to Benner's Hill to direct its remnants, he, too, fell under the deadly barrage. He and his horse were hit by an exploding Federal shell, which killed the horse and pinned Latimer underneath it with a shattered arm. His surviving soldiers managed to get the horse off of him and helped him leave the field. As he was carried away, he waved his bloody stump at his men, urging them to keep fighting. His arm had to be amputated, and as with many Civil War amputations, he developed complications, contracted gangrene, and died. Cheerful to the end, he told a deathbed visitor that he was ready to go and was hopeful regarding what lay ahead. "Major Latimer," the visitor asked, "on what do you base your hopes for the future?" Replied the young officer: "Not on good works, but on the merits of Jesus Christ alone." A gun crew member from one of Latimer's batteries, the Chesapeake Artillery, would later describe the inferno that consumed Benner's Hill.

Benner's Hill was simply a hell infernal. Our position was well calculated to drive confidence from the stoutest heart. We were directly opposed by some of the finest batteries in the regular service of the enemy, which batteries, moreover, held a position to which ours was but a molehill. Our shells ricochetted over them, whilst theirs plunged into the devoted battalion, carrying death and destruction everywhere.

The Chesapeake received the most deadly evidence of that terrible duel. Our gallant Captain, William D. Brown, was the first to fall. Riding to the front of his battery, he enjoined us, for the honor of our native State, to stand manfully to our guns. The words were still upon his lips when he fell, dreadfully mangled by a solid shot. No braver or more unselfish patriot fell upon that blood-soaked field, and none were more beloved by their commands. There were many deeds of heroism on that field that day, and of these the Chesapeake had its share.

Three of our pieces were silenced, and sadly and with moist eye Sergeant Crowley stood meditatively looking at the wreck around him. Approaching the veteran he pointed, with a trembling voice, to his dead and wounded comrades. There were Doctor Jack Brian, and Daniel Dougherty, and brave little Cusick. They belonged to his detachment. And even while he was deploring their loss, a solid shot struck Thaddeus Parker and literally disemboweled him and killed the two lead horses he was holding.

Twenty-year-old Major Joseph Latimer—the "Boy Major"—commanded the Confederate artillery on Benner's Hill, which Federal return fire quickly transformed into "a hell infernal."

The Long Arm of Lee

The fourth detachment was now all that was service-able of the battery, and it continued to fire. His own piece being disabled, Jacob F. Cook was assigned as No. 2 to Sergeant Phil Brown's detachment, and while inserting a charge in the piece the wheel on the odd number side was hard hit. Sergeant Brown, Smith Warrington, Phil Oldner and Henry Wilson were each severely wounded by this shot. The Sergeant stepped down to Rock Creek, close to our position, bound up his wound, and returned to jack up his gun, put on a spare wheel, and resumed firing. Oldner was suffering at the time from a wound but recently received, and the fresh hurt was more than his system could overcome, and in a short while he was laid in a soldier's grave. And then we lost Lieutenant Ben Roberts and Richard Hardesty, both mortally wounded.

A mounted Confederate staff officer, Robert Stiles, carrying a dispatch for General Johnson, rode through Latimer's artillery position at the height of the Federal artillery bombardment, and would never forget the horrors he witnessed.

*Never, before or after, did I see fifteen or twenty guns in such a
condition of wreck and destruction as this battalion was. It had
been hurled backward, as it were, by the very weight and impact
of metal, from the position it had occupied on the crest of a little
ridge, into a saucer-shaped depression behind it; and such a scene
as it presented—guns dismounted and disabled, carriages splintered and crushed, ammunition chests exploded, limbers upset,
wounded horses plunging and kicking, dashing out the brains of
men tangled in the harness; while cannoneers with pistols were
crawling around through the wreck shooting the struggling horses
to save the lives of the wounded men.*[2]

"The Woods Were Flecked
with Flashes from the Muskets"

Depleted Federal Troops Mount a Mighty Defense Atop Culp's Hill

Despite the Federal show of strength against Benner's Hill, General Ewell
ordered the infantry assaults on Culp's Hill and Cemetery Hill to go forward. All three of Ewell's divisions—Early's, Rodes's, and Johnson's—
might have been shattered like Latimer's gun crews if the Federal line had been
at full strength on its right flank—but it was not. Despite Ewell's demonstration,
General Meade had shifted large numbers of troops from the Federal right flank
to shore up the left side of his line against Longstreet's *en echelon* attack. Left
behind on the northern side of Culp's Hill were some of the battered First Corps
troops of Wadsworth's division. Defending the hill's eastern side was a single
brigade of the Federal Twelfth Corps—five regiments of New Yorkers under
Brigadier General George S. Greene. Meanwhile, Cemetery Hill remained
defended by three divisions of the battle-weary, humiliated Eleventh Corps,
which had been driven through town by Ewell's Confederates the day before.
General Ewell ordered Johnson's division, newly arrived on the field late the day

before, to attack the eastern side of Culp's Hill, while Early's and Rodes's divisions assaulted Cemetery Hill.

Leading the way, Johnson's Brigade began the assault on Culp's Hill at about seven o'clock at night. Known as "Old Clubby" and "Straight Rail" Johnson because of a long, heavy hickory walking stick he preferred to a sword, Johnson had been brevetted twice for bravery while serving in the U.S. Army during the Mexican War. Now he confidently advanced his troops—four brigades of Virginians and Louisianans—who were all known as tough fighters. Their attack encountered problems immediately, however. A force of Federal cavalry appeared and began firing on Johnson's troops from the rear, forcing him to hold one brigade in reserve. It was Jackson's old Stonewall Brigade, which held off the Yankee horse soldiers, and then stood by as reserves if needed. When Johnson finally moved his remaining three brigades forward, sunset was only about a half-hour away. By the time his troops waded through a deep stream—Rock Creek—and began to ascend Culp's Hill, it was almost dark.

It would not have been an easy climb in the best of circumstances: Culp's Hill had two summits—a 150-foot-high main peak and a 50-foot lower peak—and the hill had steep slopes in certain areas, dense forests, and rocks

Appearing deceptively peaceful in this period photograph, Culp's Hill became the site of savage fighting on the evening of July 2.
Library of Congress

and boulders. Johnson's division moved uphill with Brigadier General George H. Steuart's brigade of Virginians, Marylanders, and North Carolinians on the Confederate left, a brigade of Louisiana troops under Colonel J. M. Williams in the center, and Brigadier General John M. Jones's Virginia brigade on the right. They pushed their way up the slopes—the muzzle flashes from their rifles flaring in the growing darkness. The fire cascading from the Federal line above them proved deadly and it dropped many of them, including Brigadier General Jones, who went down early with a serious wound to his thigh. Delivering the sustained fire from above were the New York troops from General Greene's Twelfth Corps brigade. Johnson's Southerners far outnumbered the New Yorkers, three brigades to one, but the Northerners' stout, protective fortifications, erected through the wisdom and leadership of their commander, General Greene, dramatically bolstered their slim numbers.

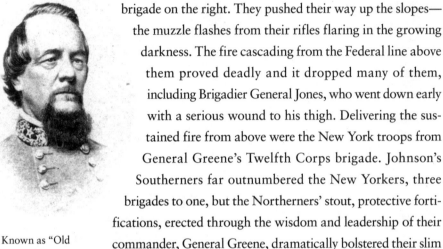

Known as "Old Clubby" because of the hickory walking stick he carried everywhere, Major General Edward Johnson boldly sent three brigades from his division charging up the slopes of Culp's Hill.

Rubenstein Rare Book & Manuscript Library, Duke University

Brigadier General George Sears Greene was the grandson of Revolutionary War hero General Nathanael Greene, who was, by some estimates, George Washington's most capable commander. At age sixty-two, "Pap" Greene, as his troops called him, was far older than the typical commander on the field of battle—on either side. A West Point graduate and instructor, he was a civil engineer when the war began, but he put on his uniform again to serve the Union, and distinguished himself at Antietam and at Chancellorsville. Before the war he had designed New York's Central Park reservoir and the city's water system. He knew how to make men dig ditches and how to teach them the art of construction. At Culp's Hill he had put his troops to work all day, felling trees and piling up rocks into a formidable line of breastworks, taller than five feet in some places. Repeatedly, Johnson's determined Southerners assailed Greene's fortified positions, but each time they failed. Reinforced by troops from Wadsworth's division—who had been posted to the far north side of the hill—and by a detachment of Eleventh Corps troops from Cemetery Hill, Greene's well-protected troops repeatedly repulsed the determined Southern soldiers who came yelling out of the darkness. Finally, after more than three hours of fighting, no more came.

Captain Jesse H. Jones, a company commander in the 60th New York Volunteer Infantry—part of Greene's Brigade—would still remember the dark, grim struggle atop Culp's Hill decades later.

═══════════════

The Second Division of the Twelfth Corps camped on the night of the first day under the shadow of Little Round Top. About 6 o'clock the next morning it was marched over from that point, which was then the extreme left of our line, and posted on Culp's Hill, its left forming a right angle with the right of General Wadsworth's division of the First Corps. Our brigade, commanded by Brigadier-General George S. Greene and comprising five New York regiments, the 60th, 78th, 102d, 137th, and 149th, was on the left of the division, and our regiment, the 60th, was on the left of the brigade. This regiment was largely composed of men accustomed to woodcraft, and they fell to work to construct log breastworks with unaccustomed heartiness. All instinctively felt that a life-and-death struggle was impending, and that every help should be used. Culp's Hill was covered with woods; so all the materials needful were at our disposal. Right and

Rock Creek, which was chest-deep in places, had to be crossed by the Southern soldiers of Johnson's Division before they ever reached Culp's Hill.
Library of Congress

A former New York City civil engineer, sixty-two-year-old Brigadier General George S. Greene understood construction, and put his men to work building breastworks on Culp's Hill.

National Archives

left the men felled the trees, and blocked them up into a close log fence. Piles of cordwood which lay near by were quickly appropriated. The sticks, set slanting on end against the outer face of the logs, made excellent battening. All along the rest of the line of the corps a similar defense was constructed. Fortunate regiments, which had spades and picks, strengthened their work with earth. By 10 o'clock it was finished.

At 6 o'clock in the evening General Meade, finding himself hard pressed on the left, and deeming an attack on the right wing improbable at so late an hour, called for the Twelfth Corps. Our brigade was detailed to remain and hold the lines of the corps. Word was brought from the officer in charge of our pickets that the enemy was advancing in heavy force in line of battle, and, with all possible celerity, such dispositions as the case admitted of were made. The brigade was strung out into a thin line of separate men as far along the breastworks as it would reach. The intention was to place the men an arm's-length apart, but, by the time the left of the brigade had fairly undoubled files, the enemy was too near to allow of further arrangements being made.

In a short time the woods were all flecked with the flashes from the muskets of our skirmishers. Down in the hollow there, at the foot of the slope, you could catch a glimpse now and then, by the blaze of the powder, of our brave boys as they sprang from tree to tree, and sent back defiance to the advancing foe. With desperation they clung to each covering. For half an hour they obstructed the enemy's approach.

The men restrained their nervous fingers; the hostile guns flamed out against us not fifteen yards in front. Our men from the front were tumbling over the breastwork, and for a breathless moment those behind the breastwork waited. Then out into the night like chain-lightning leaped the zigzag line of fire. Now was the value of breastworks apparent, for, protected by these, few of our men were hit, and feeling a sense of security, we worked with corresponding energy. Without breastworks our line would have been swept away in an instant by the hailstorm of bullets and the flood of men. The enemy worked still farther around to our right, entered the breastwork beyond our line, and crumpled up and drove back, a short distance, our extreme right regiment. They advanced a little way, but were checked by the fire of a couple of small regiments borrowed for the emergency from General Wadsworth, and placed in echelon.

General Meade hardly mentioned this affair at the breastworks in his original report of the battle, and those who were there think

Soon after the battle, two civilians examine the rock-and-log breastworks that General Greene's troops erected on Culp's Hill. The formidable works saved the hill—and maybe the battle—for the Federals.
Library of Congress

239

justice has never been done in the case, and that what was there achieved has never been adequately apprehended and stated by any writer.

The left of our brigade was only about eighty rods from the Baltimore turnpike, while the right was somewhat nearer. There were no supports. All the force that there was to stay the onset was that one thin line. Had the breastworks not been built, and had there been only the thin line of our unprotected brigade, that line must have been swept away like leaves before the wind, by the oncoming of so heavy a mass of troops, and the pike would have been reached by the enemy. Once on the pike, the Confederate commander would have been full in the rear of one-third of our army, firmly planted on the middle of the chord of the arc upon which that portion was posted. What the effect must have been it is not needful to describe. The least disaster would have sufficed to force us from the field. During the night our commanders brought back the remainder of the corps....[3]

"It Was a Close and Bloody Struggle"

The 137th New York Fights to Save the Federal Far Right Flank

On the night of July 2, the 137th New York Volunteer Infantry had the responsibility of defending the extreme right flank of the Federal line on Culp's Hill. Recruited from the farms and villages around Binghamton, New York, the troops of the 137th were former farmers, laborers, and tradesmen. Although mustered into the Federal army barely a year earlier, the regiment had shown its mettle at the Battle of Chancellorsville, and its commander—thirty-one-year-old Colonel David Ireland—was a seasoned combat commander. A Scots immigrant who came to New York City with his family as a child, Ireland had seen combat early as a lieutenant with the kilt-clad 79th New

York Infantry—the Cameron Highlanders. At First Bull Run, the Highlanders suffered heavy casualties and their commander was killed. Afterward, Ireland helped rebuild the morale-drained regiment, and as a reward was promoted to captain of the 15th New York Infantry. In the summer of 1862, he took command of the newly-raised 137th New York as its colonel. The regiment saw action at Chancellorsville, but nothing comparable to what awaited them on Culp's Hill.

Just as Colonel Joshua Lawrence Chamberlain and the 20th Maine were responsible for defending the Federal extreme left flank—the end of the line—so, too, were the soldiers of the 137th New York charged with defending the opposite end of the line—the Army of the Potomac's extreme right flank. As with the 20th Maine, if the 137th New York allowed the Confederates to turn the Federal flank, the Baltimore Pike and the rear of the Federal line would have been wide open and vulnerable to attack. If the Federal right flank on Culp's Hill had been

For years to come after the battle, Culp's Hill would retain its rugged nature, marked by bullet-scarred trees that bore witness to the fury of the fighting here.

Library of Congress

Born in Scotland and raised in New York City, thirty-one-year-old Colonel David Ireland commanded the 137th New York Infantry, which defended the crucial far right flank of the Federal line.

Collection of Scott Hilts

successfully breached by the Confederate assault, the Army of the Potomac could have been defeated and even destroyed. To defend it, the 137th New York had 456 men.

Assaulting the Federal far right flank in the darkness of July 2 was Brigadier General George H. Steuart's brigade of Confederate troops, comprised of battle-tested combat veterans from Maryland, North Carolina, and Virginia. "Maryland" Steuart, as he was called, was a Baltimore native who had graduated from West Point at age nineteen. Later, he fought Comanches in Texas in the prewar U.S. Army, saw combat at First Bull Run, and served under "Stonewall" Jackson in the Valley Campaign. Wounded at the Battle of Cross Keys, he returned to the army in time for Lee's march to Pennsylvania. Steuart proved himself an experienced, determined fighter— and so were his troops. They outnumbered the 137th New York many times over, and when they reached the New Yorkers' defensive line, they unleashed a torrent of fire.

The 137th held its own in the darkness, trading fire with the North Carolinians and Marylanders in its front. Some of Steuart's Virginia regiments flanked the 137th and delivered a deadly fire from the side, while in the darkness, the regiment also took accidental fire from other Federal troops. Colonel Ireland and his New Yorkers held fast, however, despite the ferocious fire from far greater numbers. At one point, when Federal troops on their left were driven away, the 137th was raked by enemy fire from three sides. To relieve their desperate situation, Colonel Ireland ordered the regiment to shift position in a complicated tactical movement, which the regiment successfully completed under fire. Then, when low on ammunition, the New Yorkers sortied into the Confederate line with bayonet charges that held back the enemy despite their superior numbers. Finally, after more than two hours of intense fighting, the 137th was reinforced, and Steuart's frustrated Confederates withdrew down the hill in the dead of night. The 137th New York had stubbornly and successfully saved the Federal far right flank. Ironically, when the 137th counted its dead and wounded, the tally totaled 137.

In a letter from camp written just three days later, Lieutenant Samuel Wheelock described that deadly night on Culp's Hill.

━━━━━━━━━━━━━━━━━━━━━━━━━━━━━━

Camp of the 137th Reg't N.Y. Vols.
Littletown, Pa., July 6, 1863

The Army of the Potomac, advancing in three columns, by different roads, began skirmishing with the rebels soon after crossing the Pennsylvania line. The advance, consisting of the First and Eleventh corps, with Bufford's cavalry, came up with Ewell's corps, 30,000 strong, about three miles beyond Gettysburg, on the Chambersburg turnpike, and a heavy engagement took place on the 1st of July. As the rest of the army was not within supporting distance, our forces were compelled to fall back to the heights east of the town. During the battle Gen. Reynolds was killed, and our loss in killed and wounded was heavy. To compensate for this, the First corps captured a large number of prisoners, including General Archer with his whole brigade of ragamuffins.

During the night the balance of the army arrived on the ground, and took position in line of battle. Our corps, the Twelfth, was halting for dinner about five miles from the field of conflict, and immediately hurried to the front, taking position on the left of the line, and slept on our arms during the night. Early the next morning we changed our position to the extreme right of the line; occupying the ridge of a hill [Culp's Hill] overlooking the town of Gettysburg, and commenced throwing up temporary breastworks. These were soon completed, and carefully concealed by branches and leaves to deceive the enemy. At precisely 4 P.M., the thundering of artillery on the left announced the opening of the engagement, which soon spread along the whole length of the line. The enemy came on in their usual style, massing their forces against those portions of the line which they thought to be weakest, and charged upon our batteries and entrenchments with fury of despair. The left was hard pressed, and brigade after brigade was drawn from the right to its assistance, until our brigade alone was left to defend the breastworks previously occupied by the whole division.

Our regiment and the 149th were posted to guard the line of intrenchments thrown up by Kane's brigade, thus scattering our small force over a distance four times greater than that originally occupied by us. Just as this disposition of our troops was made, firing in our front announced the advance of the rebels. The pickets made a gallant stand and then fell back to the trenches. The approach of the enemy was met by a rapid and deliberate fire from our men, who stoutly maintained their position until it became so dark that we could no longer discover the movements of the enemy. Then, taking advantage of our want of support on the right, a body of rebels succeeded in turning our right flank and gained a position behind a stone wall directly in our rear, and not more than a hundred yards distant. A murderous fire was opened upon us, and our regiment was ordered to fall back to the left. Owing to the darkness and the nature of the ground, considerable confusion ensued in executing this movement; but as soon as beyond the reach of the fire in their rear, the men rallied, charged back with a cheer, drove out the rebels, and resumed their position in the trenches, which they held until relieved by Gen. Kane's brigade.

Thus ended, on the right wing, the engagement of the 2d. It was a close and bloody struggle.—Our loss in officers and men was

Brigadier General George H. Steuart had once fought Comanches in Texas, but nothing there equaled the fire coming from Culp's Hill.

Rubenstein Rare Book & Manuscript Library, Duke University

heavy. Capt. Gregg, of Company I, fell mortally wounded while leading his men back to the trenches. He behaved throughout with admirable courage and coolness, and his company feel deeply the loss they have experienced in his death. Capt. Barrager, Lieuts. Hallett, Van Amburg, Beecher and Douglass were wounded—Lieuts. Hallett and Van Amburg mortally.

Early in the morning we were again in the trenches, and the conflict was resumed with additional vigor. The assault of the enemy upon our left having been repulsed, the troops that were withdrawn from our position were returned, the breastworks were fully manned, and for nearly six hours the rattle of musketry was incessant. Not an instant did the firing cease, but as fast as those in the front exhausted their ammunition, fresh regiments would come rushing up, cheering and with flags flying to relieve them. Opposite us was Stonewall Jackson's old corps, commanded by Ewell, who fully maintained their hard-earned reputation for

A musket-bearing, bearded soldier of the 137th New York Infantry—name unknown—proudly displays a kepi bearing his regimental identification.

Library of Congress

fighting, by holding their ground for six hours against a storm of lead that plowed through their ranks, causing every man to bite the dust who had the temerity to show himself from behind the trees and rocks in our front. About 9 A.M., a white flag was seen fluttering from some rocks in front of us. Instantly the firing ceased, and a body of rebels, about fifty in number, sprang forward, threw down their arms, and surrendered themselves to Capt. Silas Pierson, of Co. K. They declared themselves to be conscripts, and unable longer to endure the murderous fire from our men, had determined to throw themselves upon our clemency rather than trust to the mercy of their own commanders, should they be compelled to fall back. This forcibly illustrates the despotism that exists in the rebel army.

A youthful soldier of the 3rd North Carolina Infantry braves the photographer's flash. On July 2, his regiment braved the flashing Federal rifles atop Culp's Hill.

Library of Congress

The firing then became less rapid, and the enemy soon retired, leaving a few sharpshooters to annoy our men. During the day and night occasional shots were exchanged, but on the morning of the 4th of July the battlefield was clear, save of the dead and the dying. The spectacle was hideous. The ground was strewn with the bodies of the dead, and a few from which life had not yet departed. The number of victims bore undisputable testimony to the cool and accurate firing of our men. Over two thousand stand of arms were collected from the field in front of our division.

Of the number of prisoners taken it is difficult to form an estimate. On the left, where the ground was more open than on the right, whole brigades were captured at once while charging on our batteries; some of their best generals were killed, wounded and captured, and thousands of their men blown to pieces by the concentrated fire of our batteries. The official report will probably show the battle of Gettysburg to have been the most destructive to the rebels of any fought since the commencement of the war. Prisoners are constantly being brought in, and our cavalry are in close pursuit. The rebel army of invaders will not return to Richmond with one-half the number of men with which it started.

The behavior of the regiment under fire was creditable to officers and men. Though exposed to fire from three sides of their position, which killed and wounded nearly one-fourth of the whole number of men in the ranks, they refused to quit the trenches until ordered to do so, and then retuaned [sic] with an alacrity that proved them to be the best of soldiers. Col. Ireland and Lieut. Colonel Van Voorhis escaped unhurt, though both carry the marks of bullet-holes through their clothes. Capt. Williams, of Co. G, was killed in the trenches on the 3d of July. The whole number of killed and wounded in the Regiment is 120. A few are still missing, some of whom may be captured, but the majority will probably turn up safe. The aggregate loss in the regiment during the three days' fighting, including the missing, is about 160, or more than one quarter of the whole number engaged. The wounded are doing well, and will probably all recover. They receive the best of attention, both from the Surgeons and the neighboring citizens. The character of the country in which the engagement took place has been heretofore rather copperish, but I think Gen. Lee has worked a reformation.

The enemy are yet strong, and much fighting will take place before complete success is attained. The appointment of Gen. Meade to succeed Hooker, gives general satisfaction. The latter had become very unpopular in the army. We like action better than bombastic words. That this army will fight has been proved on the field of Gettysburg, and when properly led, they will fight as well elsewhere.

Yours Truly, ULYSSES.[4]

"Tell My Father I Died with My Face to the Enemy"

Early's Division Launches a Furious Attack on Cemetery Hill

As ordered by Ewell, General Jubal Early unleashed his attack on the eastern side of Cemetery Hill when he heard the gunfire signaling Johnson's attack on Culp's Hill. An irascible, profane, tobacco-spitting U.S. Army veteran, Early was a brilliant and bold commander—and he sent his troops against Cemetery Hill like a man on a mission. His division would have to do it alone: Rodes's division somehow bogged down moving through Gettysburg's streets, got into place too late, and stayed put in the darkness. Early's division went forward anyway with Brigadier General Harry T. Hays's brigade of Louisiana troops advancing on the Confederate right and Colonel Isaac E. Avery's brigade of North Carolinians on the left. Hays had about 1,200 troops and Avery had about 900. Approximately 1,200 Federal troops from the Federal Eleventh Corps awaited them, defending Cemetery Hill in a series of lines ascending the hill's eastern slopes. The Confederates had moved toward the hill under the cover of a ravine and—to the surprise of the opposing Federal troops—they suddenly rose up and moved forward in battle formation. The surprise was short-lived, however: they had to cross open fields to reach the hill, and enough daylight still remained for Federal forces to savage their ranks with artillery and small-arms fire.

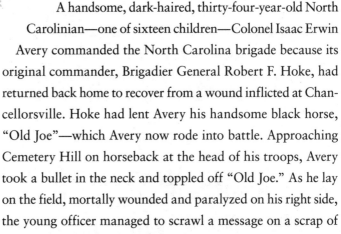

Known as "Old Jubilee" to his troops, Major General Jubal A. Early could be irascible and annoying, but no one doubted his fighting ability.

Rubenstein Rare Book & Manuscript Library, Duke University

A handsome, dark-haired, thirty-four-year-old North Carolinian—one of sixteen children—Colonel Isaac Erwin Avery commanded the North Carolina brigade because its original commander, Brigadier General Robert F. Hoke, had returned back home to recover from a wound inflicted at Chancellorsville. Hoke had lent Avery his handsome black horse, "Old Joe"—which Avery now rode into battle. Approaching Cemetery Hill on horseback at the head of his troops, Avery took a bullet in the neck and toppled off "Old Joe." As he lay on the field, mortally wounded and paralyzed on his right side, the young officer managed to scrawl a message on a scrap of paper with his left hand: "Tell my father I died with my face to the enemy."

Up the hill the North Carolinians charged, losing one color-bearer after another, but not stopping. They came to a stone wall manned by troops of the Eleventh Corps, who had fled their lines north of Gettysburg the day before. Now they fled again, stumbling uphill ahead of their pursuers. In their panic some ran into the fire of their own artillery and were cut down. With the Louisianans of Hays's Brigade charging uphill on their right, the Tarheel soldiers pressed onward. Many made it to the crest, where the guns of Battery F of the 1st Pennsylvania Light Artillery under Captain R. Bruce Ricketts unleashed load after load of canister into their advancing ranks. They took their losses and pressed on, overwhelmed the artillery, killed or drove off the gun crews, and spiked the guns. With that, the dark hill suddenly fell quiet. "We had full possession of East Cemetery Hill, the key to Meade's position," Captain Neill W. Ray of the 6th North Carolina Infantry would recall, "and we held it for several minutes."

For the North Carolinians who survived the charge, that brief time in the darkness on Cemetery Hill would always be the high tide of the Confederacy— the closest point to Southern victory and nationhood. But it was not to last; for a variety of peculiar reasons, the expected Confederate reserves failed to follow Avery's troops up the hill. After only a few minutes of conquest, the North Carolinians came under assault by a brigade of Federal Second Corps soldiers commanded by Colonel Samuel S. Carroll, who had been hurried to Cemetery Hill by General Hancock. Pressed by the enemy reinforcements, the exhausted Tarheel troops retreated back down the hill in the moonlight.

Major James F. Beall of the 21st North Carolina made the charge up Cemetery Hill with Avery's brigade. His account follows.

After lying all day under a July sun, suffering with intense heat, and continually annoyed by the enemy's sharpshooters from the heights, from sheer desperation, we hailed with delight the order to again meet the veteran foe, regardless of his advantage in numbers and position. Really, the enemy's artillery, reopening at the going down of the sun, fell like music upon our ears. At the time the assault was made, the enemy had massed heavily in our front, and placed batteries in the rear of his own lines, which were used with fearful effect against us, firing over the heads of his own men. The ground we had to pass over was ascending, but the troops advanced in double quick time, and with a cheer went over the rifle pits in advance of the enemy's main line of works, killing and capturing a few of them— the greater part taking refuge behind the main line of breastworks.

Newspaper artist Edwin Forbes sketched Cemetery Hill—the site of Gettysburg's Evergreen Cemetery—as it appeared on July 2. General Howard set up Eleventh Corps headquarters in the cemetery gatehouse.

Library of Congress

Here the fighting was desperate, but like an unbroken wave, our maddened column rushed on, facing a continual stream of fire. After charging almost to the enemy's line, we were compelled to fall back, but only a short distance. The column reformed and charged again, but failed to dislodge the enemy. The brigade held it's ground with unyielding determination—ever keeping afloat our flag to battle and breeze.

Four out of five of the color-bearers who dared hold up that flag, went down to a heroic death. As often as the flag went down it was taken up and flaunted in the face of the enemy, holding an impregnable position. The hour was one of horror. Amid the incessant roar of cannon, the din of musketry, and the glare of bursting shells making the darkness intermittent—adding awfulness to the scene—the hoarse shouts of friend and foe, the piteous cries of wounded and dying, one could well imagine, (if it were proper to say it), that "war is hell." Further effort being useless, we were ordered to fall back a short distance under cover. To remain was certain capture, to retreat was almost certain death. Few, except the wounded and dead, were left behind. Here, these brave North Carolinians "stood, few and faint, but fearless still." The enemy did not follow or show any disposition to leave their defenses....

Our loss in officers and men was great. All the field officers of the Twenty-First were killed and wounded except Colonel W. W. Kirkland, who was after this fight, promoted to Briga-dier-General. Here the lamented Colonel Isaac E. Avery, com-manding the brigade, laid down his noble life on the altar of his country's freedom. Lieutenant-Colonel Rankin was badly wounded and left in the hands of the enemy, where he remained a prisoner throughout the war.... The ground was strewn with dead and wounded. Man after man went down, among them Major Alexander Miller, who picked up the flag after the first color-bearer fell. He soon shared the fate of the former. It was soon taken up J. W. Bennett, Company F, who was, also, in quick succession, shot down. The colors were then taken by the writer and very soon after this, we fell back into the works, which we had just passed over a few paces and continued such a terrific fire upon the enemy, that their rifle was completely silenced, the enemy crouching behind their works.

About this time Corporal Eli Wiley, Company M, asked per-mission to take the flag, saying he did not see it when it fell. It was given to him and after the writer had gone a few paces along the line, orders were given to retire at once, which was accomplished under a severe fusillade. We had retreated about twenty-five yards when I saw the flag for the last time. Corporal Wiley was killed, and left, together with the flag, in the lines of the enemy. In the darkness and confusion the flag was not missed until we had rallied under cover about the distance of two hundred yards. The enemy did not follow, or show any disposition to do so, as stated above. Soon all firing ceased....⁵

"Right Foot, Amputated"
A Grim Record of the Cost of War

"The fire was terrific, but our men moved forward quickly," Captain Neill W. Ray of the 6th North Carolina would recall of the night assault on Cemetery Hill. While his regiment helped overrun the Federal artillery on Cemetery Hill, and temporarily planted the 6th's battle flag there, it did so at a high price. Of the 473 troops the regiment took to Gettysburg, 174 were killed, wounded, or missing—and more than half of those casualties occurred at Cemetery Hill. After the battle, the regiment's adjutant meticulously penned a report of the 6th's dead, wounded, and missing—which he entitled "List of Casualties in the 6th N.C. Reg't in the Battles around Gettysburg, Pa." In it, along with listing the dead and wounded, he carefully detailed the types of injuries suffered by the wounded.

List of Casualties in the 6th N.C. Reg't in the Battles around Gettysburg, Pa., on the 2nd July, 1863.

Wounded Civil War soldiers pass time in the shade of a tree. At Gettysburg, the wounded would number more than 20,000 by the time the fighting ended.

Library of Congress

∞ Field & Staff ∞

Col. I. E. Avery, Cmdg brigade   Wounded in neck
                                                  —died July 3, 1863

∞ Co. "A" ∞

Wounded—

Sergt J. M. Curtis	Hip,	severe

Privates—

J. F. Fleming	Arm, slight
J. L. Rich	Shoulder, slight
Chas. W. Burrows	Thigh, slight
Jos. Alston	Head, Slight
J. Chambers	Hand, Slight

Missing—Privates Thomas Keenan, H. Dempsey

∞ Co. "B" ∞

Wounded—

Privates—

A. E. Sauls	Foot, severe
A. Magnum	Slightly
C. P. Couch	Head, severe
N. Duke	Head, severe

Missing—Lt. E. A. Speed, Sergt. H. Tilly, Corpl. J. C. Allison,
Pvt J. M. McGrath

∞ Co. "C" ∞

Killed—

Lt. A. J. Cheek
Private. W. B. Rhodes

Wounded—

Sergt. M. Wilkerson	Thigh, severe

Left armless by battle, an unidentified Civil War amputee faces the photographer— and an uncertain future. Due to medical limitations of the day, few amputees survived the infection that often followed surgery.

Library of Congress

Privates—

T. Redmond	*Arm, severe*
W. Browning	*Thigh, slight*
W. McDaniel	*Arm, slight*
A. Nichols	*Right foot, amputated*
J. Rossin	*Shoulder & neck, very severe*
W. P. Hailey	*Hand, slight*

Missing—*Privates J. S. Leigh, S.G. Proctor, Jas Husky*

∼ Co. "D" ∼

Wounded—

Corpl. T. L. Seabot	*Leg, slight*

Privates—

D. Mull	*Side, severe*
L. S. Bost	*Side, very severe*
A. W. Bunch	*Head, severe*
Wm. Poteet	*Shoulder, severe*
M. L. Snipes	*Slightly*
M. S. Speagle	*Shoulder, slight*

Missing—*Privates J. Pratt, P. Hatchett*

∼ Co. "E" ∼

Killed—

Sergt P. B. Collins

Wounded—

Lt. L. P. Barns	*Groin, slight*

Privates.

J. S. Freeman	*Mortally, since died*
J. A. Smallwood	*Arm, amputated*
W. Matthews	*Foot, severely*
S. Wright	*Knee, slight*

Saml Yough	Thigh, slight
S. C. Vance	Arm, severe

Missing—Sergt N. S. Brunch, Privates R. P. Howell, Louis Rose

≈ Co. "F" ≈

Killed—

Pvt. Thos J. Pettigrew

Wounded—
  Sergts—

J. H. Thompson	Foot, severely
J. M. Durham	Arm, severe

  Privates—

J. S. Albright	Head, severely
J. K. Fowler	Foot, severely
G. W. Moore	Abdomen, mortally, died July 4th 1863
D. M. Sharp	Thigh, severe
S. S. Thompson	Arm, severe
J. B. Thompson	Both legs, severely

≈ Co. "G" ≈

Wounded—

Sergt. H. S. Brown	Head, slightly

  Privates—

A. J. Gullet	Side & hip, severe
J. W. Russell	Leg, severely
L. A. Fessperman	Arm, slight
W. F. Shein	Shoulder, severe
M. M. Miller	Thigh, slight

～ Co. "H" ～

Killed—

    Pvt. Thomas Miles

Wounded—

    Corpl A. J. Thompson   *Thigh, severe*

  Privates—

    R. T. Vaughn   *Thigh, severe*

    W. F. Wells   *Hand, slight*

Missing—Private. M. Miles

～ Co. "I" ～

Killed—

    Corpl. J. C. Castlebury

    Pvt. J. M. Williams

Wounded—

    W. B. Allen   *Foot, very slight*

    Corpl. G. S. Beavers   *Leg, severe*

    J. H. Upchurch   *Breast, slight*

  Privates—

    A. Johnson   *Breast, slight*

    E. Hurndon   *Leg & foot, severe*

    Wm. Lourance   *Thigh, severe*

    W. J. Castlebury   *Groin, slight*

Missing—W. D. Horton, L. Holden, L. Lutes, T. Parish

～ CO. "K" ～

Wounded—

    Coprl. J. T. Vincent   *Shoulder, severe*

  Privates—

    J. Bartow   *Arm, slight*

    J. M. Murray   *Neck, severe*

    E. Jones Slight

Missing—E. M. Allen, L. Allison[6]

Confederate troops from General Jubal Early's division storm the heights of Cemetery Hill on the evening of July 2. For a fleeting moment, they broke the Federal line. It was "the high point," said one Southerner, "of Lee's invasion."

Leslie's Illustrated

"I Captured Several Pieces of Artillery"

The "Louisiana Tigers" Break the Federal Line on Cemetery Hill

A dvancing on the right of Avery's North Carolinians, the brigade of Louisiana troops led by Brigadier General Harry T. Hays hit Cemetery Hill like a human tidal wave, sweeping up the northeast slope and panicking the Federal Eleventh Corps troops at its base. Hays's troops were known as the "Louisiana Tigers"—a name originally given to a zouave regiment of tough New Orleans dock workers raised by Major C. R. Wheat. Hays's regiments had inherited the Tiger name and lived up to its reputation as ferocious fighters. At Second Bull Run the summer before, when the brigade ran out of ammunition the Tigers had turned back a Federal charge by throwing rocks. Now—with General Hays screaming "Forward!" above the roar of battle—they stormed East Cemetery Hill. Farther up its slopes, they bounded over a stone wall as troops of the Federal Eleventh Corps hid in the bottom of their entrenchments.

Up, up they went in the growing darkness, breaking through three Federal lines—until they reached the crest. There, along with the North Carolinians from Avery's brigade, they were blasted by loads of canister from Captain Michael Wiedrich's 1st New York Light Artillery. The panicky Eleventh Corps troops had been rallied by their officers, and finally made a determined stand around Wiedrich's artillery. Both sides savagely struggled over the cannon, fighting hand-to-hand with clubbed muskets, bayonets, and rocks. Finally, the Confederates pried the artillery from their Federal defenders, who fell back to the rear, leaving behind fallen battle flags.

There, atop Cemetery Hill, the winded Tigers looked around the corpse-strewn hill in the moonlight, searching for promised reinforcements from General Ewell—the fresh reserve troops who were expected to rush up from the rear and aid them in turning the Federal right flank. Like the North Carolinians to their left, Hays's Louisianans were at a critical moment—"a high point, perhaps the high point, of Lee's invasion," concluded one Southerner. If Confederate reinforcements could have exploited the breakthrough on Cemetery Hill and poured into the rear of the Federal line, the outcome of the battle and perhaps even the fate of the war might have been decided on the night of July 2, 1863.

Reinforcements *did* arrive—but not the Confederate reserves Hays and his Tigers were expecting. Instead, an explosive flash of volley fire hit them from fresh Federal troops—two regiments of New Yorkers commanded by Colonel Wladimir Krzyzanowski, who had been dispatched from the west side of Cemetery Hill by General Carl Schurz. More savage, deadly close-up combat followed as Hays's Tigers confronted these new blue-clad men, hoping to buy time until Confederate reinforcements arrived. It was not to be: Hays could see his troops were being flanked and finally gave orders to retreat. Like Avery's North Carolinians to their left, the "Louisiana Tigers" backed down the hill in the darkness, giving up the ground they had gained with so much bloodshed. "A madder set of men I never saw," noted an observer.

In his official battle report, excerpted below, General Hays unemotionally described that night of horrors on Cemetery Hill.

HEADQUARTERS HAYS' BRIGADE,
August 3, 1863.

Major: I respectfully submit the following report of the operations of the troops under my command near the city of Gettysburg.... A little before 8 p. m. I was ordered to advance with my own and Hoke's brigade on my left, which had been placed for the time under my command. I immediately moved forward, and had gone but a short distance when my whole line became exposed to a most terrific fire from the enemy's batteries from the entire range of hills in front, and to the right and left; still, both brigades advanced steadily up and over the first hill, and into a bottom at the foot of Cemetery Hill.

Forty-three-year-old Brigadier General Harry Thompson Hays walked away from a New Orleans law practice to lead Louisiana troops in the war. At Gettysburg, he led them in a desperate charge up Cemetery Hill.

Rubenstein Rare Books & Manuscript Library, Duke University

Here we came upon a considerable body of the enemy, and a brisk musketry fire ensued; at the same time his artillery, of which we were now within canister range, opened upon us, but owing to the darkness of the evening, now verging into night, and the deep obscurity afforded by the smoke of the firing, our exact locality could not be discovered by the enemy's gunners, and we thus escaped what in the full light of day could have been nothing else than horrible slaughter.

Taking advantage of this, we continued to move forward until we reached the second line, behind a stone wall at the foot of a fortified hill. We passed such of the enemy who had not fled, and who were still clinging for shelter to the wall, to the rear, as prisoners. Still advancing, we came upon an abatis of fallen timber and the third line, disposed in rifle-pits. This line we broke, and, as before, found many of the enemy who had not fled hiding in the pits for protection. These I ordered to the rear as prisoners, and continued my progress to the crest of the hill.

Arriving at the summit, by a simultaneous rush from my whole line, I captured several pieces of artillery, four stand of colors, and a number of prisoners. At that time every piece of artillery which had been firing upon us was silenced.

A quiet of several minutes now ensued. Their heavy masses of infantry were heard and perfectly discerned through the increasing darkness, advancing in the direction of my position. Approaching within 100 yards, a line was discovered before us, from the whole length of which a simultaneous fire was delivered. I reserved my fire, from the uncertainty of this being a force of the enemy or of our men, as I had been cautioned to expect friends both in front, to the right, and to the left, Lieutenant-General Longstreet, Major-General Rodes, and Major-General Johnson, respectively, having been assigned to these relative positions; but after the delivery of a second and third volley, the flashing of the musketry disclosed the still-advancing line to be one of the enemy.

His name long forgotten, a Louisiana soldier wears a belt buckle adorned with Louisiana's brown pelican state seal. Five regiments of Louisiana troops assaulted Cemetery Hill in Hays's Brigade.

Library of Congress

I then gave the order to fire; the enemy was checked for a time, but discovering another line moving up in rear of this one, and still another force in rear of that, and being beyond the reach of support, I gave the order to retire to the stone wall at the foot of the hill, which was quietly and orderly effected. From this position I subsequently fell back to a fence some 75 yards distant from the wall, and awaited the further movements of the enemy.

Only contemplating, however, to effect an orderly and controlled retreat before a force which I was convinced I could not hope to withstand—at all events, where I then was—I was on the point of retiring to a better position when Captain [John G.] Campbell, the brigade quartermaster, informed me that Brigadier-General Gordon was coming to my support.

I immediately dispatched an officer to hasten General Gordon with all possible speed, but this officer returning without seeing General Gordon, I went back myself, and finding General Gordon *occupying the precise position in the field occupied by me when I received the order to charge the enemy on Cemetery Hill, and not advancing, I concluded that any assistance from him would be too late, and my only course was to withdraw my command. I therefore moved my brigade by the right flank, leading it around the hill, so as to escape the observation of the enemy, and conducted it to the right of my original position, then occupied, as above stated, by Gordon's brigade. This was about 10 o'clock. I remained in this position for the night. About daybreak in the morning, I received an order from Major General Early to withdraw my command from its position....*

I have the honor to be, very respectfully,
your obedient servant,
HARRY T. HAYS,
Brigadier-General, Commanding.[7]

"No, *Dis* Battery is *Unser*"
Federal Reinforcements Save Cemetery Hill

The Federal Eleventh Corps commanders, General O. O. Howard and Carl Schurz, stood atop Cemetery Hill, congratulating each other on the Federal success of July 2, when an "uproar" coming from the slopes below interrupted them: Early's Confederates—the North Carolinians and the Louisianans of Avery's and Hays's brigades—were assaulting the Eleventh Corps line. Soon the scores of blue-uniformed troops came streaming uphill in panic—with Southern forces charging right behind them. Howard quickly sent for reinforcements, while Schurz grabbed Colonel Wladimir Krzyzanowski from nearby, and sent him and two of his New York regiments charging off to support Wiedrich's threatened artillery.

Although battered and rattled, the Federal Eleventh Corps troops *did* rally, fighting stubbornly, desperately in the end. The reinforcements—Second Corps

Prepped for battle, a Federal artillery battery enjoys a brief moment of peace. Atop Cemetery Hill, Wiedrich's Battery fielded three-inch ordnance rifled cannon and Ricketts's Battery was equipped with ten-pounder Parrotts.

troops commanded by Colonel Samuel Carroll—arrived at exactly the right place and at exactly the right time in order to support Ricketts's overrun battery. Along with Culp's Hill, Cemetery Hill and the Federal right flank were saved for the Union. Years later, it was the Eleventh Corps' rally that General Schurz would praise when he recorded his perspective of the savage struggle for Cemetery Hill.

It was already dark when we on Cemetery Hill were suddenly startled by a tremendous turmoil at Wiedrich's and Rickett's [sic] batteries placed on a commanding point on the right of Cemetery Hill. General Howard and I were standing together in conversation when the uproar surprised us. There could be no doubt of its meaning. The enemy was attacking the batteries on our right, and if he gained possession of them he would enfilade a large part of our line toward the south as well as the east, and command the valley between Cemetery Ridge and Culp's Hill, where the ammunition trains were parked. The fate of the battle might hang on the repulse of this attack.

There was no time to wait for superior orders. With the consent of General Howard I took the two regiments nearest to me, ordered them to fix bayonets, and, headed by Colonel Krzyzanowski, they hurried to the threatened point at a double-quick. I accompanied them with my whole staff. Soon we found ourselves surrounded by a rushing crowd of stragglers from the already broken lines. We did our best, sword in hand, to drive them back as we went. Arrived at the batteries, we found an indescribable scene of mêlée. Some rebel infantry had scaled the breastworks and were taking possession of the guns. But the cannoneers defended themselves desperately.

With rammers and fence rails, hand spikes and stones, they knocked down the intruders. In Wiedrich's battery, manned by Germans from Buffalo, a rebel officer, brandishing his sword, cried out: "This battery is ours!" Whereupon a sturdy artillery-man responded: "No, dis battery is unser," and felled him to the ground with a sponge-staff. Our infantry made a vigorous rush upon the invaders, and after a short but very spirited hand-to-hand scuffle tumbled them down the embankment.... Our line to the right, having been reinforced by Carroll's brigade of the Second Corps, which had hurried on in good time, also succeeded in driving back the assailants with a rapid fire, and the dangerous crisis was happily ended. I could say with pride in my official report that during this perilous hour my officers and men behaved splendidly....[8]

"It Was a Strange Sight to See Men Fighting in Elegantly Furnished Rooms"

Civilians Endure Urban Warfare at Gettysburg

Sketched by soldier-artist Charles Reed from eyewitness accounts, Gettysburg civilian "Ginnie" Wade is struck by a stray bullet while kneading dough in her sister's house.

Library of Congress

As soldiers North and South battled each other by the tens of thousands among the fields, forests, ridges, and hills surrounding Gettysburg, warfare came to the town as well. The town's residents found themselves caught up in urban warfare. Some fed troops or tended the wounded from both sides, and many hid in their cellars as the fighting raged on within earshot—and sometimes right before their eyes. Many lost property: fences were dismantled for firewood and breastworks, livestock was confiscated or killed, crops were destroyed, houses and barns were damaged, and dead soldiers were buried in mass graves on private property. At one house, locals counted more than a hundred bullet holes in the structure.

One civilian was accidentally shot and killed. Mary Virginia Wade—known as "Ginnie" to family and friends—had just celebrated her twentieth birthday a few weeks earlier. Her father was ill and institutionalized, and she lived in town with her mother, working as a seamstress. During the battle she went to her sister's home on Baltimore Street, not far from Cemetery Hill, where she helped to care for her sister's newborn. Early on the morning of July 3, as she was kneading dough to bake bread for the family, a stray bullet punched through two doors from the outside, striking young "Ginnie" in the back and killing her instantly. Wrapping her body in quilts and reportedly placing it in a new coffin intended for a Confederate officer, Ginnie was hastily buried in her sister's backyard. By some accounts, she still had dough on her hands.

As the battle continued, Confederate troops barricaded alleys and streets and set up firing posts in town to pick off Federal officers and troops on Cemetery Hill and on Cemetery Ridge. Southern sharpshooters commandeered commercial structures such as John Rupp's tannery and Snider's Wagon Hotel, where they knocked holes in the walls or fired out of the windows from behind piled-up mattresses, furniture, and planking. In a Gettysburg neighborhood close to Cemetery Hill, a battalion of the 5th Alabama Infantry commanded by Major Eugene Blackford assumed firing positions inside a row of houses on July 2. The major's brother, Captain William W. Blackford, also present at Gettysburg, came to check on his sibling. After the war, Captain Blackford would write his memoirs, including this account of the Alabama sharpshooters in action.

I rode through the town of Gettysburg towards our left flank and was delighted to find that my brother Eugene's battalion of skirmishers from Rodes' division was there. They held the range of two- and three-story brick building on Main Street on the side next to Cemetery Ridge, through the back windows of which they were keeping up an incessant firing into the enemy's lines nearby. It was the first time I had seen warfare carried on in this way, and wishing

At Gettysburg, the fighting spilled into town. Confederate marksmen barricaded themselves in houses, and fired out the windows at nearby Federal troops. Artist Alfred Waud sketched this scene of a deserted but dangerous Gettysburg street during the fighting.

Library of Congress

to find my brother, I was glad to have the opportunity of examining into it. Leaving my horse in charge of the courier who accompanied me, at a place in the street somewhat sheltered from the shells which at times came tearing through the houses, I ascended a handsome stairway to the second floor. This floor along the whole block had been used in each house for parlors, sitting rooms and dining rooms, and the floor above for bedrooms, while the lower floor was occupied mostly by stores.

Eugene's men had cut passageways through the partition walls so that they could walk through the houses all the way from one cross street to the other. From the windows of the back rooms, against which were piled beds and mattresses, and through holes punched in the outside back wall, there was kept up a continuous rattle of musketry by men stripped to the waist and blackened with powder. It was a strange sight to see these men fighting in these neatly and sometimes elegantly furnished rooms, while those not on duty reclined on elegant sofas, or stretched themselves out upon handsome carpets.

I was surprised to see in some houses feathers scattered everywhere in every room, upstairs and downstairs, and found it had been done by shells bursting in feather beds on the upper floor. Pools of blood in many places marked the spots where someone had been hit and laid out on the carpets, and here and there a dead body not yet removed, and many great holes in the walls, showed where artillery had been brought to bear upon this hornets' nest when their sting became too severe for endurance.

A native of Great Britain, *Harper's Weekly* combat artist Alfred Waud had been traveling with the Army of the Potomac since the battle of First Bull Run. At Gettysburg, he witnessed much of what he drew.

Library of Congress

I enquired for Major Blackford and was directed to a room in the middle of the block where I found him and some of his officers lolling on the sofas in a handsome parlor. On a marble table were set decanters of wine, around which were spread all sorts of delicacies taken from a sideboard in the adjoining dining room, where they had been left, in their hurry, by the inhabitants when they fled before our advance the day before. Outside could be heard the cannonade and the growl of the musketry around Cemetery Ridge, and echoing through the house the reports from the deadly rifles puffing their little clouds of light blue smoke from the back windows, while the room was pervaded by the smell of powder. After I had partaken with great relish from the refreshments, Eugene showed me over his fortress. From the back windows, by keeping duly out of sight of the watchful men in the rifle pits a short distance behind the houses, I could see all that part of the lines of the enemy....[9]

"He Resolved to Aid in Driving Back the Invading Foe"

An Aged Warrior Takes Up Arms for the Union

The battle made one Gettysburg resident into a national hero in the North. John Burns was a sixty-nine-year-old cobbler, the son of Scots immigrants, and a longtime resident of Gettysburg, where he had once served as a local constable. Said to have been a veteran of the War of 1812, he reportedly tried to join the Federal army when the war began, and may have served the army for awhile as a civilian teamster. He lived in a rambling, white-washed frame house at the corner of West and Chambersburg Streets in Gettysburg, and on July 1 had watched a flood of Federal troops surge by his home to take up positions on the west side of town.

Determined to do his part, Burns pulled on his old uniform coat, shouldered a musket, and hiked out to McPherson's Ridge as the first day's fighting began. An officer allowed him to join the ranks of the 150th Pennsylvania Infantry posted on the ridge near the Chambersburg Road, and later he reportedly fought alongside the 7th Wisconsin of the Iron Brigade. Fearing the aging volunteer might be captured and executed as a bushwhacker, an Iron Brigade officer reportedly had Burns sworn into the Federal army as a volunteer. During the fighting, Burns was wounded several times, and was left behind in the Federal retreat. Confederate troops did capture him, but instead of executing the old man, they treated his wounds and sent him home.

With a flintlock musket propped beside him and his crutches resting behind him, old soldier John Burns mends his wounds at his Gettysburg home.
Library of Congress

After the battle, Northern newspapers printed news of his exploits, and Burns became a celebrated hero. In November of 1863, when President Lincoln came to Gettysburg to help dedicate a Federal soldier's cemetery and make his famous Gettysburg Address, he asked to meet John Burns, and the two attended church together. The U.S. Congress granted Burns a special pension, thousands of dollars in unsolicited donations were mailed to him, and he eventually sold his house to promoters as a tourist attraction. He then moved to a farm far to the east of Gettysburg, where he lived until his death in 1872. Over time, the story of the old man who took up his musket to fight for the Union at Gettysburg became a mixture of history and mythology.

An account of Burns's battlefield adventure was recorded by J. B. Stillson, a Presbyterian layman who came to Gettysburg with the United States Christian Commission to tend to the wounded after the battle. The U.S. Christian Commission, established by the Youth Men's Christian Association in the North early in the war, distributed Bibles, tracts, and songbooks to the army and ministered to soldiers. While in Gettysburg, Stillson apparently befriended Burns and interviewed him. A year later, in his official report to the Commission, Stillson included a dramatic account of what he described as Burns's own story.

Baltimore, August 3d, 1864.
G. S. Griffith, Esq., President Maryland Branch U. S. C. C:

DEAR SIR:—In accordance with your request, permit me to say, the work of the Christian Commission in the hospitals, camps, and forts, and at the docks and rail cars, during the past year, in this city and vicinity, has been steadily pursued by the committees assigned to the several localities, with gratifying results....

The sick, the wounded, and the dying have uniformly been the special objects of attention, and no efforts have been spared to carry out, in the practical detail, the grand central idea of this most blessed agency, in providing for the souls and bodies of men....

Perhaps not a day has passed since the commission began its early labors in this field, but some real-life incident has transpired, to cheer and thrill the heart, and fortify the faith of those engaged in these labors of love.

John C. Burns, a man of temporal habits and of upright and unpretending life, was born in Burlington county, State of New

Jersey, September 5th, 1783, and at the time of the battle [of Gettysburg], was near seventy years old.

Much has been written concerning him since the fight, but very little that has not involved both fiction and error.

As a member of the Christian Commission it was my privilege to know personally of his wounds and deeds. It may not therefore be out of place to record, briefly, some of the facts and incidents that have given rise to a widespread interest in his history....

It will now be my aim to give the old soldier's statements of facts and events substantially as he narrated them to me.

"My heart," said he, "was made sorrowful, when I saw so many of the citizens about the streets on the morning of the battle, who evinced less concern for their country than for their personal effects. I fought for my country in 1812, and then learned to love it, and I have loved and honored it, I believe, with an honest affection to this day. I was sorry for this apathy, and I was sorry also that I had no sons to help fight the Rebels, but I was glad too when I remembered that I was still strong and could help fight them myself.

Without delay I borrowed a rifle and provided myself with powder and ball, as I was accustomed to do when in younger days I hunted the wolf and the deer along these same mountains and valleys so recently swarming with Rebels against our good government—the best government in the world.

I dressed myself for the fight in the same blue coat, and vest, and corderoys I wore in the war of 1812, and which I had sacredly kept as memorials of other days when I had fought and bled in defense of liberty and right.

Thus equipped with as strong a heart and as steady a nerve as I ever possessed, I turned my willing feet to where our troops were forming into line of battle....

Never did I draw a bead with steadier aim on the deer of the mountains than on those Rebel leaders. Vacant saddles attested the *work of the unerring missiles. I had not fought long, however, before a ball from the enemy struck my left side. I did not fall, though at first inclined to, for the shock was severe. It is no time thought I, 'to look at wounds,' I must fight while life and strength remain.*

I resumed my work and continued to fire successfully for sometime, when I was again hit by a minnie ball near the groin, the shock was terrible, but I did not fall.

I now felt the blood running and I expected my end was near....

Another ball penetrated my left arm a few inches below the elbow. Then my work was done, I could no longer hold my gun. I felt that my time was short. The blood was flowing freely from my wounds.

Darkness came stealing over my senses, and fainting, I fell, to remember no more until the first day's battle was closed and I a prisoner within the enemy's lines. When consciousness returned I began to consider my condition as a prisoner, and not being a soldier proper, it occurred to me I would not be entitled to the treatment due prisoners of war, and therefore might be killed without ceremony. With my well hand I succeeded with my pocket knife in burying in the ground my ammunition, and then crept away as far as I could from my gun...."

In view of these wonderful escapes, it may be well to revert briefly to the incidents of this narration, simply for the purpose of tracing in it the hand of the Lord in thus saving from serious injury the old soldier's life and limbs five separate times.

The first ball that struck his side was turned from his body without injury to his person by the intervention of a pair of old fashioned spectacles in his vest pocket. The second struck a truss, worn for an abdominal injury, and glanced off, cutting away the flesh from his thigh about two inches below the top of the hip bone. The third ball passed through his leg between the large and small

*bones without injuring either bones or arteries. The fourth ball
passed through the fleshy part of the left arm below the elbow, also
without breaking or rupturing arteries....*

*Truly the ways of Providence are mysterious and past finding
out.*

Yours, &c.,

J.B. STILLSON.[10]

"If Lee Attacks Tomorrow,
It Will Be on Your Front"

Lee and Meade Make Plans for the Third Day of Battle

At his headquarters in Gettysburg, General Robert E. Lee appeared confident on the night of July 2. He appeared so despite the disappointments of the day: he had repeatedly allowed discretion in the execution of his orders—as he had so often allowed Jackson with great success—but on Gettysburg's second day he had achieved little success. Engaged in battle in unfamiliar territory, his maneuverability had been limited by inadequate reconnaissance and poor position. His commanders had been unable to effectively execute his complex battle plan. Attacks had been made late—far later than he had planned—at times his orders had been ignored or changed, and his chief subordinate, General Longstreet, had questioned his battle plans almost to the point of insubordination. Although untold thousands had been killed, wounded, or captured thus far, neither army was defeated or victorious.

And he was ill. He had been diagnosed earlier with heart problems—what was called "inflammation of the heart-sac"—and he occasionally felt significant pain in his chest, arms, and back. At the time, he also suffered from the common soldier's frequent malady—diarrhea. An officer at Lee's headquarters on the afternoon of July 2 was surprised to see the General walking "as if he were weak or in pain." Nevertheless, the day did bring some good news: Major General

George Pickett's division of Virginia troops—a branch of Longstreet's corps—had reached Gettysburg, fresh and ready
for battle. Furthermore, General Stuart and his cavalry
division had finally arrived. Lee would say nothing of
his meeting with the tardy Stuart that day, although
one of Stuart's aides would state that it seemed "painful beyond description." Lee reportedly greeted Stuart
with a mild reprimand: "Well, General Stuart, you are
here at last."

The Army of Northern Virginia remained strong
despite severe losses, and while the enemy held a fortified
line on what Lee acknowledged as "a high and commanding
ridge," Lee's troops had prevailed against superior odds many
times in the past. Despite the disappointments of the day and
the effects of his poor health, Lee moved through the crowd
of Southern officers congregating around his headquarters
that night, shaking hands. "It is all well, General," he told A.
P. Hill, "everything is well." The Army of Northern Virginia
had won a clear victory on the first day of battle, breaking the
enemy's line and sending thousands of blue-uniformed troops
hurrying away from the battlefield in retreat. And on the
second day, with all its problems and disappointments, his
troops had repeatedly come within a fraction of decisive vic-
tory. "Those partial successes," he would later state, "determined me to continue
the assault the next day." On the next day—Friday, July 3, 1863—he would
attack the Federal line once again and intended to strike the Federal flanks. If
the Federal line could be turned on either flank, the battle could be decided for
the South. If flank attacks failed again, he could then assault the center of the
Federal line, which presumably would be stretched thin meeting the Confederate attacks on the flanks.

Across the battlefield, General George Meade convened a late-night war
council with *his* commanders. Crowded into the cramped quarters of the white-

At Gettysburg,
General Lee
reportedly displayed
symptoms of poor
health, at one point
walking "as if weak
or in pain." Even so,
he remained
confident of his army,
and on July 3 he
planned to attack the
center of the Federal
line.

Library of Congress

washed farmhouse he had commandeered as a headquarters, Meade addressed a critical question to his subordinates: Should the Army of the Potomac withdraw or stay and fight? Gettysburg "was no place to fight a battle in," voiced Major General John Newton, who had taken over the army's First Corps following the death of General Reynolds. Newton remained the sole dissenter. Meade further polled the group, then stated the final decision: the army would stay and fight. As the meeting ended, Meade shared a warning with Brigadier General John Gibbon, whose troops were posted to the center of the Federal line on Cemetery Ridge. Lee had already attacked both Federal flanks, Meade explained, therefore the main Confederate attack tomorrow would likely target the army's center, he believed. "If Lee attacks tomorrow," Meade predicted, "it will be on your front."

In the cramped cottage where he set up his headquarters, General Meade convened a council of his senior commanders on the night of July 2. His key question: Should the Federal army stay and fight another day?

Library of Congress

Soon after all firing had ceased a staff-officer from army headquarters met General Hancock and myself and summoned us both to

General Meade's headquarters, where a council was to be held. We at once proceeded there, and soon after our arrival all the corps commanders were assembled in the little front room of the Liester House—Newton, who had been assigned to the command of the First Corps over Doubleday, his senior; Hancock, Second; Birney, Third; Sykes, Fifth; Sedgwick, who had arrived during the day with the Sixth, after a long march from Manchester; Howard, Eleventh; and Slocum, Twelfth, besides General Meade, General Butterfield, chief of staff; Warren, chief of engineers; A. S. Williams, Twelfth Corps, and myself, Second. It will be seen that two corps were doubly represented, the Second by Hancock and myself, and the Twelfth by Slocum and Williams.

These twelve were all assembled in a little room not more than ten or twelve feet square, with a bed in one corner, a small table on one side, and a chair or two. Of course all could not sit down; some did, some lounged on the bed, and some stood up, while Warren, tired out and suffering from a wound in the neck, where a piece of shell had struck him, lay down in the corner of the room and went sound asleep, and I don't think heard any of the proceedings.

The discussion was at first very informal and in the shape of conversation, during which each one made comments on the fight and told what he knew of the condition of affairs. In the course of this discussion Newton expressed the opinion that "this was no place to fight a battle in." General Newton was an officer of engineers (since chief-engineer of the army), and was rated by me, and I suppose most others, very highly as a soldier. The assertion, therefore, coming from such a source, rather startled me, and I eagerly asked what his objections to the position were. The objections he stated, as I recollect them,

After discussing options with his commanders until midnight, Meade stated the consensus: the Army of the Potomac would stay and fight. And to one officer Meade made a prediction: Lee would next attack the Federal center.

National Archives

related to some minor details of the line, of which I knew nothing except so far as my own front was concerned, and with those I was satisfied; but the prevailing impression seemed to be that the place for the battle had been in a measure selected for us.

Here we are; now what is the best thing to do? It soon became evident that everybody was in favor of remaining where we were and giving battle there. General Meade himself said very little, except now and then to make some comment, but I cannot recall that he expressed any decided opinion upon any point, preferring apparently to listen to the conversation. After the discussion had lasted some time, Butterfield suggested that it would, perhaps, be well to formulate the question to be asked, and, General Meade assenting, he took a piece of paper, on which he had been making some memoranda, and wrote down a question; when he had done he read if off and formally proposed it to the council.

I had never been a member of a council of war before (nor have I been since) and did not feel very confident I was properly a member of this one; but I had engaged in the discussion, and found myself (Warren being asleep) the junior member in it. By the custom of war the junior member votes first, as on court-martial; and when Butterfield read off his question, the substance of which was, "Should the army remain in its present position or take up some other?" he addressed himself first to me for an answer. To say "Stay and fight" was to ignore the objections made by General Newton, and I therefore answered somewhat in this way: "Remain here, and make such correction in our position as may be deemed necessary, but take no step which even looks like retreat."

The question was put to each member and his answer taken down, and when it came to Newton, who was the first in rank, he voted in pretty much the same way as I did, and we had some playful sparring as to whether he agreed with me or I with him; the rest voted to remain.

The next question written by Butterfield was, "Should the army attack or wait the attack of the enemy?" I voted not to attack, and all the others voted substantially the same way; and on the third question, "How long shall we wait?" I voted, "Until Lee moved." The answers to this last question showed the only material variation in the opinion of the members.

When the voting was over General Meade said quietly, but decidedly, "Such then in the decision"; and certainly he said nothing which produced a doubt in my mind as to his being perfectly in accord with the members of the council.... Several times during the sitting of the council reports were brought to General Meade, and now and then we could hear heavy firing going on over on the right of our line. I took occasion before leaving to say to General Meade that his staff officer had regularly summoned me as a corps commander to the council, although I had some doubts about being present. He answered, pleasantly, "That is all right. I wanted you here." Before I left the house Meade made a remark to me which surprised me a good deal, especially when I look back upon the occurrence of the next day. By a reference to the votes in council it will be seen that the majority of the members were in favor of acting on the defensive and awaiting the action of Lee. In referring to the matter, just as the council broke up, Meade said to me, "If Lee attacks tomorrow, it will be in your front." I asked him why he thought so, and he replied, "Because he has made attacks on both our flanks and failed, and if he concludes to try it again it will be on our center." I expressed the hope that he would, and told General Meade, with confidence, that if he did we would defeat him.[11]

CHAPTER EIGHT

"The Whole Rebel Line Was Pouring Out Thunder and Iron"

O n Friday, July 3, 1863, the sun rose over the opposing battle lines at Gettysburg through a white haze of ground fog and campfire smoke. The Army
of the Potomac remained assembled in line, stretching like an upside-down
fishhook from Culp's Hill and Cemetery Hill in the north and along Cemetery
Ridge to Little Round Top in the south. The Army of Northern Virginia roughly
paralleled the Federal line, curving through town and continuing along Seminary Ridge, across the Emmitsburg Road, and through Devil's Den to a point
roughly opposite Big Round Top. As he had decided in his war council the night
before, General Meade waited for the Confederate army to make an attack, but
first he had to reclaim lost ground on the right flank of his line—at Culp's Hill.[1]

"It Is Murder, but It Is the Order"
The Bloody Battle for Culp's Hill Resumes on the Morning of July 3

Confederate troops at the base of Culp's Hill fire at the Federal line above them on the morning of July 3. *Leslie's Illustrated* artist Edwin Forbes studied the fighting with binoculars, then sketched the site in person.

Library of Congress

efore dawn, troops from Major General Henry W. Slocum's Federal Twelfth Corps returned to Culp's Hill from the left side of the Federal line, where they had been shifted as reinforcements the day before. They came down the hill in force this time and attacked the Confederates of Ewell's corps, Johnson's division, who had occupied Federal entrenchments near the base of the hill the previous night. The attack came just as Ewell began to unleash a renewed attack on Culp's Hill. It was a deadly give-and-take for hours, and losses were horrendous on both sides. "Along the slope of Culp's Hill," a Federal officer reported, "the trees were almost literally peeled, from the ground up some fifteen or twenty feet, so thick upon them were the scars the bullets had made. Upon a single tree, in several instances not over a foot and a half in diameter, I counted as many as two hundred and fifty bullet marks. The ground was covered by the little twigs that had been cut off by the hail-storm of lead." By late morning Federal forces reclaimed the lost ground on the Federal far right flank around Culp's Hill. Brigadier General George H. Steuart's brigade of troops from Maryland, Virginia, and North Carolina—which had shed much blood storming Culp's Hill the night before—was shredded by the searing Federal fire in the morning engagement. After the fight, General Steuart was seen weeping, crying aloud, "My poor boys, my poor boys!"

Equally shocking were the losses among some units on the Federal side at Culp's Hill that morning. At the height of the fighting, a questionable order from General Slocum resulted in the near annihilation of two regiments of Twelfth Corps troops. Slocum ordered an assault by his corps' 1st Division on a particularly strong sector of the Confederate line that was occupied by well-armed, well-prepared troops of Johnson's division. Worried about Slocum's order, Brigadier General Thomas H. Ruger requested and received a modification of the order that allowed him to send out skirmishers to determine the Confederate strength before attacking. It was a verbal order, however, and by the time it reached the frontline commander, Colonel Silas Colgrove of the 3rd Brigade, it again called for an immediate assault—which Colgrove realized would be little more than a suicide mission.

Regardless, Colonel Colgrove promptly ordered the assault to be made by two infantry regiments from the 3rd Brigade—the 27th Indiana and the 2nd Massachusetts. When the order reached the 2nd Massachusetts's commander, Lieutenant Colonel Charles R. Mudge, he promptly led his men into a cauldron of Confederate fire—after philosophically observing, "Well, it is murder, but it is the order." It *was* murder: the Confederates drove back his regiment, with half its number killed or wounded—including Mudge, shot dead in the charge. The 27th Indiana incurred casualties that were almost as severe. Lieutenant Edwin E. Bryant of the 2nd Wisconsin Infantry—which supported the assault— would later record the horror on Culp's Hill caused by that bungled order.

━━━━━━━━━━━━━━━━━━━━

When we were awakened it was before the gray of dawn. We were within pistol shot of the enemy, and as soon as the dense mist should rise we should be a fair target to his volleys. So we moved a little to our right and faced north towards Culp's Hill. To our right was the Second Massachusetts, then the Twenty-seventh Indiana. The Thirteenth New Jersey came next, facing, its left wing towards Culp's Hill, its right towards Rock Creek. Between our front and the enemy was the little swampy swale, or meadow.

Throwing out a few skirmishers a few yards to the edge of the swale, they from behind rocks opened fire. The regiments rolled stones together, piled them in little heaps, and thus constructed a slight breastwork; and from this line opened a fire on the Confederates as they showed themselves among the huge rocks upon that slope of the hill. Our position was exposed to the fire of myriads of sharpshooters from our front and our right flank across the creek. The enemy before us were well sheltered by the huge boulders that lie like hundreds of sleeping elephants along the slopes of Culp's Hill just above Spangler's Spring; and as the lines were less than 125 yards apart one was almost certain to be hit whose person was exposed.

Thus we spent an hour or so of the early morning. The enemy had become aware as soon as daylight of the importance of this position. Fresh troops had been thrust in to strengthen Steuart,— Smith's brigade of Early's division, Rhodes' brigade, and Daniels'. These, with the rest of Johnson's division, made seven brigades of closely packed rebels to hold Culp's Hill and push our lines inward toward the Baltimore pike. But they are in a hot place. Our artillery on Power's Hill is dropping shell among them with fearful rapidity.... The musketry is sharp and incessant. A rain of bullets is concentrated on the ground they occupy.

The rebels swarm there, but they are many of them, sheltered. Every tree is riddled with bullets and their dead and wounded lie thick among the rocks. Several times they essay to advance, but reel backward with thinned lines to their fastness among the great boulders. Geary is crowding upon them. A combined movement is, after some consultation, arranged to be made to dislodge them. General Ruger received orders to try the enemy on the right of the line of breastworks to the left of the swale with two regiments, and, if practicable, to dislodge him. He sent Lieut. Snow to Col. Colgrove with an order to advance skirmishers at that point, and if the enemy was not found in too great force, to advance two regiments and drive him out. This order, as Col. Colgrove reports, was to "advance his line immediately." He saw that it was useless to send in skirmishers. It was only possible to carry the hill by storm. His own brave regiment, the Twenty-seventh Indiana and the Second Massachusetts, were at the point on the line from which this assault must be made. They were ordered to go in. The verbal order was given to Col. Mudge. "Are you sure it is the order?" asked he, looking at the frowning rocks behind which the enemy were packed. "Yes." "Well," said this brave gentleman, "it is murder, but it is the order. Up, men, over the works; forward, double-quick!"

In an instant the two regiments rose and with a cheer sprang over their breastworks, ran down the declivity to the swale, and moved at double-quick across the narrow meadow. But as soon as they came in view, the gleam of thousands of gun-barrels were seen among the rocks in their front. Regiments lying in the grass across Rock Creek also rose up and fired into their right flank. They advanced under a perfect hail of balls, men and officers falling at every step, but none save sorely wounded turning back. Colonel Mudge, of the Second, a noble gentleman, fell dead in crossing that fatal meadow. Captain Tom Robeson, a gallant, chivalrous officer of the Second, also fell mortally wounded. He had but a little while before shown the lofty courage of his nature. One of his men had been wounded on the skirmish line, and lay helpless and exposed under a broiling sun. The heroic captain boldly went out with a storm of bullets whistling about him, took the wounded man in his arms and brought him to a place of shelter.

A botched order from Major General Henry Slocum, commander of the Federal Twelfth Corps, led to the near annihilation of two Federal regiments on Culp's Hill.

National Archives

The Twenty-seventh Indiana on the right was terribly exposed, not only from the rocks in front but from the flank, and after losing twenty-three men killed, eight officers and seventy-nine men wounded, the regiment seeing how hopeless was the effort to carry the position fell back under orders. The Second Massachusetts pressed on, but bore a little to the left to find a point to enter between the large rocks in front. As it bore to the left it came in front of the Third Wisconsin, which at the moment the other two regiments advanced, Col. Hawley had moved forward to the edge of the swale to rush in and support the charge. As the Second moved in our front, it prevented the Third regiment firing at the rebels, who were rising up from behind the rocks to rain their fire into the faces of their assailants. There the Second were, a handful of brave men within pistol shot of the enemy, who from higher ground and shelter in front and right were pouring volleys into their ranks.

It was distressing to see and not be able to give them aid. But as they advanced up close to the wall of rocks they became a little less exposed. The rocks and trees gave them shelter, especially from a fire that came from across Rock Creek, on the right. Colonel Morse took command when Mudge fell. Holding the position, though conscious that they were doing but little to effect, he sent to Colgrove for orders and ammunition. Colgrove ordered the Second to fall back. It at once about-faced under a withering fire and passed to the left and rear of our regiment, at double-quick but in as good order as the movement through such swampy ground would permit. . . .

As soon as the Second Massachusetts had cleared the front of the Third Wisconsin, we were able to do good execution upon the Confederates who had risen and exposed themselves to fire on the assaulting regiments. The Confederates had thus had their attention drawn to their left, and changed a large part of their front to resist this danger. . . . Ruger's division advanced simultaneously, and the combined attack finally drove the rebels from their hold on Culp's Hill. As the enemy were driven out of the breastworks on this hill and back to Rock Creek, they were, says Hoke, "mercilessly cut down by repeated and tremendous discharges of grape and canister. Nothing during the war exceeded this engagement in carnage. The slain were lying literally in heaps" In the front of Geary's division and of the division commanded by Ruger were more Confederates dead than the entire list of casualties in the whole Twelfth corps. "The slain were literally lying in heaps." "Human beings, mangled and torn in every manner, from a single shot through the head or body to bodies torn to pieces by exploding shells were everywhere."

It was 10:20 o'clock when the enemy was thus driven from the breastworks, down the slope and thus over Rock Creek....[2]

"I Noticed a Company of Fifty Men Digging Graves"

Two Days of Fighting Yields a Grim Harvest of Dead and Wounded

The fighting on the first two days of battle at Gettysburg had produced a massive, grisly yield of dead and wounded on both sides. Most of the wounded were moved to Federal or Confederate field hospitals, although some lay unattended on the field for hours or overnight until they could be treated. On the morning of the third day of battle, countless numbers of the dead still lay where they had fallen—including many who had perished on the first day of battle. In some cases, fellow officers or friends buried the bodies of officers and of select others in individual graves scattered around the rim of the battlefield in fields, meadows, backyards, and Gettysburg's Evergreen Cemetery.

The body of twenty-one-year-old Colonel Henry K. Burgwyn—the "Boy Colonel" of the 26th North Carolina—was, for instance, cared for by a friend and fellow officer, who wrapped it in a woolen blanket and had it buried in an

Dismembered by an artillery shell, the body of a Federal soldier at Gettysburg awaits burial. Even while the fighting continued, overworked burial details were digging graves.

Library of Congress

ammunition crate beneath a roadside shade tree. Necessity required that others—common soldiers numbering in the thousands—be buried in hastily dug trenches. Numerous corpses received even less dignified attention, being stripped of their footwear by footsore, shoe-less Southern soldiers, or plundered by nighttime grave robbers in a morbid search for valuables

Colonel Charles Weygant of the 124th New York Infantry—the "Orange Blossoms" regiment that had suffered such heavy casualties on July 2—set out in the early morning darkness of July 3 to determine the condition of his regiment's wounded. What he encountered was almost as shocking as the combat he witnessed.

The Third Corps hospital, to which nearly all our wounded were taken, had been established in a grove about half a mile to the left and rear of where we were then lying. Just after dark I decided to walk over to it, and try and find the poor fellows and learn how they were being cared for. When about half way there I fell In with a party of stretcher-bearers with loaded stretchers. They were moving in single file along what appeared to be a beaten path, and said they belonged to the Third Corps. There were but two men to each stretcher; and they all seemed nearly worn out, and were trudging along very slowly with their heavy loads toward the hospital.

As I hurried by one after another I stooped and peered into the faces of the wounded, to see if there were any of the One hundred and twenty-fourth among them, but it was too dark for me to determine positively in that way, and so I asked each one to what regiment he belonged. The first was a member of the Third Michigan; the second was a sergeant of the Sixty-third New York; the third was a Pennsylvanian; the fourth made no answer to my inquiry, though his eyes were wide open and I was sure he was looking at me. Instinctively I placed my hand on his forehead expecting to find it hot and dry, but instead it was cold and clammy—he was dead.

The scene at the hospital was one of the most horrid imaginable. During the afternoon and evening nearly 3,000 wounded men had been brought there, and others were continually arriving. The ground of the entire grove, which was several acres in extent, seemed to be literally covered with them; and such noises filled the air as I had never heard before and trust may never reach my ears again. The wounded of our brigade had been among the first to arrive, and were lying, I had no doubt, near the center of the grove. The thick foliage caused dark shadows to fall upon these acres of mangled, bleeding human forms. Away down through the trees flickering lights could be seen, the reflections of which fell with ghastly effect upon the corps of surgeons who, with coats off and sleeves rolled up, were gathered at, or moving rapidly to and fro about, the amputating tables.

After a moment's hesitation at the edge of the woods I resolved to attempt to pick my way through towards where I hoped to find the objects of my search, but as I moved on among those, for the most part, prostrate men, their groans and piteous appeals for help appalled me. Several in a state of delirium were shouting as if upon the battlefield, and others, believing I was a surgeon, besought me to stop just a moment and bind up their wounds, from which their life-blood was ebbing. Presently a man I was about stepping over, sprang to his feet, shook in front of me a bandage he had just torn from a dreadful, gaping wound in his breast, and uttered a hideous, laughing shriek. This sent the hot blood spurting from his wound into my very face. Then he threw up his arms as if a bullet had just entered his heart, and fell heavily forward across a poor mangled fellow, whose piercing wails of anguish were heart-rending beyond description. I could endure no more, and wheeling about, hurried over the wounded and dying to the open field again.

Several times during the night we were awakened by the thunder of artillery and crash of small arms, and at 4 o'clock, on the morning of the 3^d, the battle opened again with considerable fury and raged without cessation until about 9 a. m. Then an ominous silence prevailed for several hours, during which batteries and columns of troops were hurried hither and thither over the field and toward the front, plainly indicating that the lines were being strengthened in anticipation of another determined onset of the now most desperate foe....

During the quiet hours which preceded this decisive and final struggle, my thoughts very naturally reverted to wounded comrades, and about noon I decided to mount Col. Cummins's "Old

*Bay," ride hurriedly over to the hospital, and make another attempt
to see them.*

*As I dismounted and tied my horse to a shrub at the edge of the
grove, I noticed a short distance beyond me a company of about
fifty men digging graves, and was informed by one of them that
they had been busy since daybreak burying men who had died of
their wounds during the night and morning. On penetrating the
woods I passed by several who were even then in the agonies of
death, and saw two groups of men moving out with dead bodies;
but the chaos of the previous evening had disappeared, and com-
parative order reigned. Nearly all [of the wounded] had received
attention, but the majority of the surgeons had not yet quit their
posts to seek the rest their pale, haggard faces told that they were
much in need of....*[3]

"An Overwhelming Confidence Possessed Us All"

Lee Decides to Attack the Center of the Federal Line

The battle on the Federal right flank at Culp's Hill on the morning of July
3 did not go as General Ewell had hoped—nor as General Lee had
intended. Neither did Lee's plans for a renewed attack by Longstreet's
corps against the Federal left flank. Either Lee did not make his battle plan clear
or Longstreet had plans of his own. Again, for numerous reasons, including
some that would never be clarified, Longstreet's troops were not in place for the
attack Lee had planned for the early morning of July 3. Soon after sunrise, Lee
rode up to check on the progress of Longstreet's preparations for the attack and
discovered that Longstreet's troops were not ready. Realizing that his plans for
coordinated early morning assaults on the Federal flanks had to be discarded,
he immediately made plans to attack the center of the Federal line.

Standing in an open field, binoculars in hand, Lee gestured to a clump of trees towering above the center of the Federal line and outlined his new plan of attack. Major George George E. Pickett's division of Virginia troops, newly arrived and fresh, would attack on the Confederate right, and Major General A. P. Hill's corps, which had not been engaged since the first day, would attack on the left. Lee estimated the combined force would give the assault about 15,000 troops, which he believed would be enough to break the enemy line and win a decisive victory. To organize and execute the grand attack, he again turned to General Longstreet. Longstreet, however, objected. He still favored his own plan to march the army around the enemy line and attack the Federal rear, and he argued with his

From atop Little Round Top, the open fields that lay south of Gettysburg can been seen in the distance. To assault Cemetery Ridge, Lee's troops would have to cross almost three-quarters of a mile of open ground in some places.
Library of Congress

commander, stating flatly that he did not believe that Lee's attack on the Federal center would work. "... I think I can safely say," he reportedly told Lee, "that there was never a body of fifteen thousand men who could make that attack successfully." Lee did not appear offended by Longstreet's forceful remarks, but neither did he change his mind: the Army of Northern Virginia would attack the center of the Federal line.

Colonel Walter H. Taylor, Lee's chief aide-de-camp, would later describe the issues surrounding Lee's July 3 battle plan, including Longstreet's postwar assertion that Lee's attack was a mistake.

Since the date of this correspondence, several communications have appeared in the public prints, from the pen of General Longstreet, in reference to the battle of Gettysburg. He claims that General Lee gave battle there in spite of his remonstrance. Had such been the fact, it would work no discredit to General Lee, though at variance to his usual propensity to defer to such objections on the part of his lieutenants; but I never heard of it before, neither is it consistent with General Longstreet's assertion ... that at the time in question "the Army of Northern Virginia was in condition to undertake anything." In this opinion, he but expressed the opinion of the whole army; an overwhelming confidence possessed us all. Now, in a retrospective view of the results attained, it is easy to conclude that it would have been well not to have attacked the third day. But did we accomplish all that could have been reasonably expected? And if we failed to attain results reasonably to be expected of an army in condition to undertake anything, how did it happen?

General Lee determined to renew the attack upon the enemy's position on the 3d day of July. In his report of the campaign, in speaking of the operations of the second day, he says:

"The result of this day's operations induced the belief that, with proper concert of action, and with the increased support that the positions gained on the right would enable the artillery to render the assaulting columns, we should ultimately succeed; and it was accordingly determined to continue the attack.

The general plan was unchanged. Longstreet, reenforced [sic] by Pickett's three brigades, which arrived near the battle-field during the afternoon of the 2d, was ordered to attack the next morning; and General Ewell was directed to assail the enemy's right at the same time."

General Longstreet's dispositions were not completed as early as was expected; it appears that he was delayed by apprehensions that his troops would be taken in reverse as they advanced. General Ewell, who had orders to cooperate with General Longstreet, and who was, of course, not aware of any impediment to the main attack arranged to be made on the enemy's left, having reenforced General Johnson, whose division was upon our extreme left during the night of the 2d, ordered him forward early the next morning.

In obedience to these instructions, General Johnson became hotly engaged before General Ewell could be informed of the halt which had been called on our right.

After a gallant and prolonged struggle, in which the enemy was forced to abandon part of his intrenchments, General Johnson found himself unable to carry the strongly-fortified crest of the hill. The projected attack on the enemy's left not having been made, he was enabled to hold his right with a force largely superior to that of General Johnson, and finally to threaten his flank and rear, rendering it necessary for him to retire to his original position....

Lee's troops had beaten the Army of the Potomac before and expected to do it again, according to Colonel Walter H. Taylor, who was Lee's chief aide. "An overwhelming confidence possessed us all," Taylor said.

General Lee then had a conference with General Longstreet, and the mode of attack and the troops to make it were thoroughly debated. I was present, and understood the arrangement to be that General Longstreet should endeavor to force the enemy's lines in his front. That front was held by the divisions of Hood and McLaws. To strengthen him for the undertaking, it was decided to reenforce him by such troops as could be drawn from the centre.

Pickett's division, of Longstreet's corps, was then up, fresh and available. Heth's division, of Hill's corps, was also mentioned as available, having in great measure recuperated since its active engagement of the first day; so also were the brigades of Lane and Scales, of Pender's division, Hill's corps; and as our extreme right was comparatively safe, being well posted, and not at all threatened, one of the divisions of Hood and McLaws, and the greater portion of the other, could be moved out of the lines and be made to take part in the attack. Indeed, it was designed originally that the two divisions last named, reenforced by Pickett, should make the attack; and it was only because of the apprehensions of General Longstreet that his corps was not strong enough for the movement, that General Hill was called on to reinforce him.

Orders were sent to General Hill to place Heth's division and two brigades of Pender's at General Longstreet's disposal, and to be prepared to give him further assistance if requested.

The assault was to have been made with a column of not less than two divisions, and the remaining divisions were to have been moved forward in support of those in advance. This was the result of the conference alluded to as understood by me.

Lieutenant-General A. P. Hill appears to have had the same impression, for he says in his report of the operations of his corps at this time: "I was directed to hold my line with Anderson's division and the half of Pender's, now commanded by General Lane, and to order Heth's division, commanded by Pettigrew, and Lane's and Scales's

brigades, of Pender's division, to report to Lieutenant-General Long-
street as a support to his corps, in the assault on the enemy's lines."

General Longstreet proceeded at once to make the dispositions
for attack, and General Lee rode along the portion of the line held
by A. P. Hill's corps, and finally took position about the Confeder-
ate centre, on an elevated point, from which he could survey the
field and watch the result of the movement....[4]

"I Challenge the Annals of Warfare to Produce a More Brilliant Charge"

Confederate and Federal Cavalry Fight
a Bloody Battle behind the Federal Lines

Major General J. E. B. Stuart had returned, eager to do battle—and Lee had a mission for him. As Lee put his army into position to attack the center of the Federal line on Cemetery Ridge, he ordered Stuart and his cavalry to loop around the Federal right and attack the enemy's rear. If Lee's army successfully broke the Federal line and sent Meade's troops flooding to the rear in retreat—as it had done on the first day of battle—Stuart would be in a position to strike the fleeing Federals with his cavalry, increasing the panic and creating chaos that would ensure complete defeat of the Army of the Potomac. At the very least, Stuart's attack would be a useful diversion that would tie up the Federal cavalry and keep them from doing anything to undermine Lee's battle plan.

Stuart took four brigades of cavalry with him—Brigadier General Wade Hampton's brigade, Brigadier General Fitzhugh Lee's brigade, Colonel John R. Chambliss's brigade, and Brigadier General Albert G. Jenkins's brigade. Stuart's brilliance for reconnaissance—the critically important skill that Lee so desperately missed during Stuart's absence—quickly showed itself: Stuart located the Federal cavalry and determined the best way to get behind the Federal army. Almost immediately, however, things went wrong for the Confederate cavalry.

Stuart hoped to keep his movements secret from the enemy, but Federal Signal Corps officers, who were posted on high ground on Culp's Hill, Cemetery Hill, and Power's Hill, spotted his column of cavalry. Stuart himself alerted Federal forces to his location by ordering his horse artillery to fire a series of rounds, which were apparently intended to let Lee know that his cavalry was in place.

Federal cavalry under Brigadier General David Gregg—including troops under Brigadier George Armstrong Custer, Colonel John B. McIntosh and Colonel J. Irvin Gregg—engaged Stuart's cavalry corps in a bloody, tumultuous series of clashes several miles east of Gettysburg at a site that would become known as the East Cavalry Field. Charges and counter-charges unhorsed soldiers from both sides and exhibited the bold courage typical of both Federal and Confederate cavalrymen. Much of the fighting occurred on a farm owned by John and Sarah Rummel, which became the site of vicious, hand-to-hand combat. Facing a battle line of dismounted Confederate cavalry, General Custer—age twenty-three—dramatically drew his saber and ordered his brigade of Michigan troops to charge, shouting, "Come on you Wolverines!" With his shoulder-length blond locks flowing behind him, Custer led the way toward the enemy battle line. The cavalry battle was a tactical draw—although officers from both sides would later claim victory—but it proved to be a strategic defeat for Stuart and Lee because it prevented the Confederate cavalry from weakening the Federal defenses. As one Southern officer put it, it achieved nothing but "the glory of the fighting."

One officer engaged in the battle would later describe it as "a joust or tournament, where the knights, advancing from their respective sides, charge full tilt upon each other in the middle of the field." To farmer John Rummel, whose farmhouse was battered by gunfire and whose fields were left littered with dead

Back from the controversial raid that denied Lee much-needed reconnaissance, Major General J. E. B. Stuart was eager for action at Gettysburg. On July 3, he got plenty.

David M. Rubenstein Rare Book and Manuscript Library, Duke University

men and horses, the battle was anything but romantic. He later reported finding two dead cavalrymen, "one a Virginian, the other a 3rd Pennsylvania man—who fought on horseback with their sabers until they finally clinched and their horses ran from under them. Their heads and shoulders were severely cut, and when found, their fingers, though stiffened in death, were so firmly imbedded in each other's flesh that they could not be removed without the aid of force."

Sitting well in the saddle, a Federal cavalryman blows a bugle call. Federal cavalry under Brigadier General David Gregg fought a tumultuous battle with General J. E. B. Stuart's Confederate cavalry east of Gettysburg.
Library of Congress

Brigadier General George Armstrong Custer filed an official report of his brigade's actions in the July 3 cavalry battle, but it was somehow omitted from the *Official Records of the Union and Confederate Armies*—the Federal government's voluminous official publication of wartime documents. In 1876, Frederick Whitaker, an early Custer biographer, printed the report in part, and it is excerpted below.

At an early hour on the morning of the 3d, I received an order, through a staff-officer of the Brigadier-General commanding the division, to move, at once, my command, and follow the First brigade on the road leading from Two Taverns to Gettysburg. Agreeably to the above instructions, my column was formed and moved out on the road designated, when a staff officer of Brigadier-General Gregg, commanding Second division, ordered me to take my command and place it in position on the pike leading from York to Gettysburg, which position formed the extreme right of our battle on that day. Upon arriving at the point designated, I immediately placed my command in position, facing toward Gettysburg. At the same time I caused reconnoissances to be made on my front, right and rear, but failed to discover any considerable force of the enemy.

Everything remained quiet till ten A. M., when the enemy appeared on my right flank, and opened upon me with a battery of six guns. Leaving two guns and a regiment to hold my first position, and cover the road leading to Gettysburg, I shifted the remaining portion of my command, forming a new line of battle at right angles to my former line. The enemy had obtained correct range of my new position, and were pouring solid shot and shell into my command with great accuracy. Placing two sections of Battery M, Second (regular) Artillery, in position, I ordered them to silence the enemy's battery, which order, notwithstanding the superiority of the enemy's position, was successfully accomplished in a very short space of time. My line, as it then existed, was shaped like the letter L, the shorter branch, formed of the section of battery M, supported by four squadrons of the Sixth Michigan cavalry, faced towards Gettysburg, covering the Gettysburg pike; the long branch, composed of the remaining two sections of battery M, Second artillery, supported by a portion of the Sixth Michigan cavalry, on the right, while the Seventh Michigan cavalry, still further to the right and in advance, was held in readiness to repel any attack the enemy might make coming on the Oxford road. The Fifth Michigan cavalry was dismounted, and ordered to take position in front of my centre and left. The First Michigan cavalry was held in column of squadrons to observe the movements of the enemy.

I ordered fifty men to be sent one mile and a half on the Oxford road, while a detachment of equal size was sent one mile and a half on the road leading from Gettysburg to York, both detachments being under the command of the gallant Major Webber, who from time to time kept me so well informed of the movements of the enemy that I was enabled to make my dispositions with complete success.

At twelve o'clock, an order was transmitted to me from the Brigadier-General commanding the division, by one of his aides, directing me, upon being relieved by a brigade of the Second Division, to move with my command and form a junction with the First brigade, on the extreme left. On the arrival of the brigade of the Second division, commanded by Colonel McIntosh, I prepared to execute the order. Before I had left my position, Brigadier-General Gregg, commanding the Second division, arrived with his entire command. Learning the true condition of affairs on my front, and rightly conjecturing that the enemy was making his dispositions for attacking our position, Brigadier-General Gregg ordered me to remain in the position I then occupied.

The enemy was soon after reported to be advancing on my front. The detachment of fifty men sent on the Oxford road were driven in, and at the same time the enemy's line of skirmishers, consisting of dismounted cavalry, appeared on the crest of the ridge of hills on my front. The line extended beyond my left. To repel their advance, I ordered the Fifth cavalry to a more advanced position, with instructions to maintain their ground at all hazards. Colonel Alger, commanding the Fifth, assisted by Majors Trowbridge and

Ferry, of the same regiment, made such admirable dispo-
sition of their men behind fences and other defences,
as enabled them to successfully repel the repeated
advances of a greatly superior force. I attributed
their success in great measure to the fact that this
regiment is armed with the Spencer repeating rifle,
which, in the hands of brave, determined men, like
those composing the Fifth Michigan cavalry, is, in
my estimation, the most effective fire-arm that our
cavalry can adopt.

Colonel Alger held his ground until his men had
exhausted their ammunition, when he was compelled to
fall back on the main body. The beginning of this move-
ment was the signal for the enemy to charge, which they
did with two regiments, mounted and dismounted. I at
once ordered the Seventh Michigan cavalry, Colonel
Mann, to charge the advancing column of the enemy.
The ground over which we had to pass was very unfa-
vorable for the manoeuvering of cavalry, but despite all
obstacles this regiment advanced boldly to the assault,
which was executed in splendid style, the enemy being
driven from field to field until our advance reached a
high and unbroken fence, behind which the enemy were strongly
posted.

Brigadier General
Wade Hampton III of
South Carolina—the
son and grandson of
American
cavalrymen—
commanded a
brigade of Stuart's
cavalry. His favorite
prewar pastime was
hunting black bear
with a knife.

Library of Congress

Nothing daunted, Colonel Mann, followed by the main body
of his regiment, bravely rode up to the fence and discharged their
revolvers in the very face of the foe. No troops could have main-
tained this position; the Seventh was, therefore, compelled to retire,
followed by twice the number of the enemy. By this time, Colonel
Alger, of the Fifth Michigan cavalry, had succeeded in mounting a
considerable portion of his regiment, and gallantly advanced to the
assistance of the Seventh, whose further pursuit by the enemy he

Freckle-faced
Brigadier General
George Armstrong
Custer, age twenty-
three, favored long,
curly locks and red
neckerchiefs. At
Gettysburg, he boldly
led his Michigan
troops in a charge,
shouting, "Come on,
you Wolverines!"

National Archives

checked. At the same time an entire brigade of the enemy's cavalry, consisting of four regiments, appeared just over the crest in our front. They were formed in column of regiments.

To meet this overwhelming force I had but one available regiment, the First Michigan cavalry, and the fire of Battery M, Second regular artillery. I at once ordered the First to charge, but learned at the same moment that similar orders had been given by Brigadier-General Gregg. As before stated, the First was formed in column of battalions. Upon receiving the order to charge, Colonel Town, placing himself at the head of his command, ordered the "trot" and sabres to be drawn. In this manner this gallant body of men advanced to the attack of a force outnumbering them five to one. In addition to this numerical superiority, the enemy had the advantage of position, and were exultant over the repulse of the Seventh Michigan cavalry.

All these facts considered, would seem to render success on the part of the First impossible. No so, however. Arriving within a few yards of the enemy's column, the charge was ordered, and with a yell that spread terror before them, the First Michigan cavalry, led by Colonel Town, rode upon the front rank of the enemy, sabring all who came within reach. For a moment, but only a moment, that long, heavy column stood its ground, then unable to withstand the impetuosity of our attack, it gave way into a disorderly rout, leaving cast numbers of dead and wounded in our possession, while the First, being masters of the field, had the proud satisfaction of seeing the much vaunted "chivalry," led by their favorite commander, seek safety in head-long flight.

Federal cavalry make a charge at Gettysburg. Although the battle between Stuart's and Gregg's cavalry was a tactical draw; it was a strategic loss for Lee's army because it accomplished nothing but "the glory of fighting."
Battles and Leaders of the Civil War

I cannot find language to express my high appreciation of the gallantry and daring displayed by the officers and men of the First Michigan cavalry. They advanced to the charge of a vastly superior force with as much order and precision as if going upon parade; and I challenge the annals of warfare to produce a more brilliant or successful charge of cavalry than the one just recounted....

Respectfully submitted,
G. A. Custer,
Brigadier-General
Commanding Second Brigade.

An account of the July 3 cavalry battle from the Southern perspective was recorded by Lieutenant G. W. Beale of the 9th Virginia Cavalry, which belonged to Chambliss's brigade. According to Beale, the Southern horse soldiers held their own in the fight, and fought so fiercely that they broke off their saber blades.

We moved forward at a trot, passed Rummel's barn, and engaged the mounted men at close range across a fence. Some of our troops, dismounting, threw down the fence and we entered the field. A short hand to hand fight ensued, but the enemy speedily broke and fled. Whilst pursuing them I observed another body of the enemy approaching rapidly from the right to strike us in the flank and rear. I bore off in company with a portion of our men to meet and check this force.

We soon found ourselves overpowered, and fell back closely pressed on two lines which converged at the barn. I was by General Stuart's side as we approached the barn. My horse fell at this point, placing me in danger of being made a prisoner. At this moment General Hampton dashed up at the head of his brigade. He was holding the colors in his hand, and passed them into the hands of a soldier at his side just as he swept by me. The charge of his brigade, as far as I could judge, was successful in driving the enemy back from that part of the field.

Our brigade reformed on the edge of the woods in which it stood before the charge was made, and this position was held until we were quietly withdrawn at night. Our position commanded an easy view of the barn and of the line our skirmishers assumed at the beginning of the battle. We were so near to the barn that I rode back to where my horse had fallen, to secure if possible the effects strapped on my saddle. Later in the evening I sent two of my men to the same spot to search for the body of Private B. B. Ashton, of my company, who was supposed to have been left dead on the field. These facts warrant me in the conviction that we were not driven from the field, as has been contended.

Among the incidents of this engagement I remember to have seen young Richardson, of company B, 9th Virginia Cavalry, the brother of our sergeant-major, fall on the fence as he was leaping into the field, mortally wounded by a piece of a shell. Corporal

*Caroll and Private Jett, of company C, after the hand to hand fight
in the field, showed me their sabres cut off close to the hilt....*[5]

"Let the Batteries Open"
Lee's Artillery Prepares for a Massive Bombardment

At midday on July 3, Colonel Edward Porter Alexander, age twenty-eight, looked at his pocket-watch, calculating when he would give the signal to launch General Lee's grand assault on the center of the Federal line. The tall, slim, dark-haired Georgian, a West Point graduate, was the acting commander of Longstreet's First Corps artillery. Longstreet's official chief of artillery was Colonel James B. Walton, but Longstreet looked to Alexander—bright, competent, and dependable—for artillery support. He had proven himself repeatedly in the past, especially at Fredericksburg, where the position he selected for Longstreet's artillery—atop Marye's Heights—doomed the Federal attack. He had risen in rank from captain to major to colonel in short order, and earned praise from Longstreet as an officer of "unusual promptness, sagacity and intelligence."

Lee had placed Longstreet in command of his attack on the Federal center, and Longstreet had placed young Alexander in command of a massive Confederate artillery bombardment which would precede the attack. Alexander had been up since three a.m., arranging guns and preparing for the bombardment. More than 170 pieces of Confederate field artillery from Lee's army had been assembled in a line east of Seminary Ridge for the purpose of crippling the Federal artillery and demoralizing the enemy infantry in advance of Lee's grand third day assault. Alexander would oversee the gigantic cannonade—the largest Confederate field artillery barrage of the war.

As planned, Major General George E. Pickett's division of Longstreet's corps would make the assault on the Confederate right. Pickett's division comprised three brigades: Brigadier General Richard B. Garnett's brigade, Brigadier General James L. Kemper's brigade, and Brigadier General Lewis A. Armistead's

brigade, all consisting entirely of Virginia troops. Pickett's division would be supported on its right by two brigades—Florida troops under Colonel David Lang and Alabamians under Brigadier General Cadmus M. Wilcox.

As Confederate artillery bombards Federal positions on Cemetery Ridge, Southern infantry troops await orders to make the Pickett-Pettigrew Charge.

Battles and Leaders of the Civil War

Leading the assault on the Confederate left was General Heth's division of A. P. Hill's corps. General Heth had been wounded on the battle's first day, and his division was now commanded by Brigadier General James J. Pettigrew, who had been promoted from brigade command. Pettigrew's division was composed of four brigades—all of which had suffered heavy losses in the first day's fighting: General Archer's brigade, now commanded by Colonel Birkett D. Fry; Pettigrew's former brigade, now commanded by Colonel James K. Marshall; General Joseph R. Davis's brigade, still commanded by Davis; and Colonel John M. Brockenbrough's brigade, now commanded by Colonel Robert M. Mayo. To support Pettigrew's division, Major General Isaac Trimble had been placed in command of two brigades from the wounded General Pender's division— exclusively North Carolinians—led by Brigadier General James H. Lane and by

Colonel William Lee J. Lowrance. While Pickett's division was composed entirely of Virginians, Pettigrew's division contained troops from Tennessee, Alabama, Mississippi, and Virginia along with its North Carolinians.

Approximately 13,000 troops assembled for the Pickett-Pettigrew Charge, which would become commonly known as "Pickett's Charge" because Longstreet had designated Pickett's division to lead off when the assault began. Colonel Edward Porter Alexander—to his surprise—would decide when the assault would begin. A dispatch from General Longstreet advised Porter of his critical role while he readied his guns for the bombardment. In it, Longstreet ordered the young officer to "let Gen. Pickett know when the moment offers." In other words, Alexander was to call off the assault if he deemed the bombardment ineffective, or he was to order Pickett to go forward when he judged that the time was right. At first, Alexander resisted being placed in the decision-making position, but eventually, obedient to orders, he relented: "When our fire is at its best," he wrote Longstreet, "I will advise General Pickett to advance."

An eerie silence pervaded the field of battle at midday. It was "as silent as a churchyard," in Alexander's words. Finally, at almost one o'clock in the afternoon, Longstreet determined that Pickett's and Pettigrew's troops were in place and that Alexander was ready to open fire. He dispatched a mounted courier to a battery of the Washington Artillery, which would fire a signal gun to begin the bombardment: "Let the batteries open," he ordered. At 1:07 p.m., a signal gun opened fire, followed by a series of shots as signal guns along the line fired in succession—then the mile-long line of Confederate artillery opened an explosive, massive, and sustained fire, which the Federal artillery promptly answered. "The enemy were not slow in coming back at us," Alexander would recall, "and the grand roar of nearly the whole artillery of both armies burst in on the silence, almost as suddenly as the full notes of an organ would fill a church."

In 1907, more than forty years after the event, Edward Porter Alexander would publish his memoirs—modestly entitled *Military Memoirs of a Confederate*—recalling the tense moments preceding the mammoth artillery bombardment he unleashed upon the Federal troops on Cemetery Ridge.

A clump of trees in the enemy's line was pointed out to me as the proposed point of our attack, which I was incorrectly told was the cemetery of the town, and about 9 A.M. I began to revise our line and post it for the cannonade. The enemy very strangely interfered with only an occasional cannon-shot, to none of which did we now reply, for it was easily in their power to drive us to cover or to exhaust our ammunition before our infantry column could be formed. I can only account for their allowing our visible preparations to be completed by supposing that they appreciated in what a trap we would find ourselves. Of Longstreet's 83 guns, 8 were left on our extreme right to cover our flank, and the remaining 75 were posted in an irregular line about 1300 yards long, beginning in the Peach Orchard and ending near the northeast corner of the Spangler wood.

While so engaged, Gen. Pendleton offered me the use of nine 12-Pr. howitzers of Hill's corps, saying that that corps could not use guns of such short range. I gladly accepted and went to receive the guns under command of Maj. Richardson. I placed them under cover close in rear of the forming column with orders to remain until sent for, intending to take them with the column when it advanced.

A few hundred yards to left and rear of my line began the artillery of the 3d corps under Col. Walker. It comprised 60 guns, extending on Seminary Ridge as far as the Hagerstown road, and two Whitworth rifles located nearly a mile farther north on the same ridge. In this interval were located 20 rifle guns of the 2d corps under Col. Carter. Four more rifles of the same corps under Capt. Graham were located about one and a half miles northeast of Cemetery Hill. These 24 guns of the 2d corps were ordered to fire only solid shot as their fuses were unreliable.

There remained unemployed of the 2d corps 25 rifles and 16 Napoleons, and of the 3d corps, fifteen 12-Pr. howitzers. It is notable that of the 84 guns of the 2d and 3d corps to be engaged, 80 were in the same line parallel to the position of the enemy and 56 guns stood idle. It was a phenomenal oversight not to place these guns, and many beside, in and near the town to enfilade the "shank of the fish-hook" and cross fire with the guns from the west.

The Federal guns in position on their lines at the commencement of the cannonade were 166, and during it 10 batteries were brought up from their reserves, raising the number engaged to 220 against 172 used upon our side during the same time.

The formation of our infantry lines consumed a long time, and the formation used was not one suited for such a heavy task. Six brigades, say 10,000 men, were in the first line. Three brigades only were in the second line— very much shorter on the left. It followed about 200 yards in rear of the first. The remaining brigade, Wilcox's, posted in rear of the right of the column, was not put in motion with the column, and being ordered forward 20 minutes or more later, was much too late to be of any assistance whatever. Both flanks of the assaulting column were in the air and the left without any support in the rear. It was sure to crumble away rapidly under fire....

A little before noon there sprung up upon our left a violent cannonade which was prolonged for fully a half-hour, and has often been supposed to be a part of that ordered to precede Pickett's charge. It began between skirmishers in front of Hill's corps over the occupation of a house. Hill's artillery first took part in it, it was said, by his order. It was most unwise, as it consumed uselessly a

Colonel Edward Porter Alexander, age twenty-eight, directed the massive artillery bombardment that preceded the Pickett-Pettigrew Charge. He had attended West Point while Robert E. Lee was superintendent. Now Lee's greatest assault would depend on Alexander's artillery.

Photographic History of the Civil War

large amount of his ammunition, the lack of which was much felt in the subsequent fighting. Not a single gun of our corps fired a shot, nor did the enemy in our front.

When the firing died out, entire quiet settled upon the field, extending even to the skirmishers in front, and also to the enemy's rear; whence behind their lines opposing us we had heard all the morning the noise of Johnson's combats.

My 75 guns had all been carefully located and made ready for an hour, while the infantry brigades were still not yet in their proper positions, and I was waiting for the signal to come from Longstreet, when it occurred to me to send for the nine howitzers under Richardson, that they might lead in the advance for a few hundred yards before coming into action. Only after the cannonade had opened did I learn that the guns had been removed and could not be found. It afterward appeared that Pendleton had withdrawn four of the guns, and that Richardson with the other five, finding himself in the line of the Federal fire during Hill's cannonade, had moved off to find cover. I made no complaint, believing that had these guns gone forward with the infantry they must have been left upon the field and perhaps have attracted a counter-stroke after the repulse of Pickett's charge.

Meanwhile, some half-hour or more before the cannonade began, I was startled by the receipt of a note from Longstreet as follows:—"Colonel: If the artillery fire does not have the effect to drive off the enemy or greatly demoralize him, so as to make our effort pretty certain, I would prefer that you should not advise Pickett to make the charge. I shall rely a great deal upon your judgment to

Arms confidently folded and his kepi placed squarely on his head, a determined-looking Southern artilleryman strikes a pose for his photograph. On July 3, such troops unleashed the largest field artillery bombardment of the war.

Library of Congress

determine the matter and shall expect you to let Gen. Pickett know when the moment offers."

Until that moment, though I fully recognized the strength of the enemy's position, I had not doubted that we would carry it, in my confidence that Lee was ordering it. But here was a proposition that I should decide the question. Overwhelming reasons against the assault at once seemed to stare me in the face. Gen. Wright of Anderson's division was standing with me. I showed him the letter and expressed my views. He advised me to write them to Long-street, which I did as follows:—"General: I will only be able to judge of the effect of our fire on the enemy by his return fire, as his infantry is little exposed to view and the smoke will obscure the field. If, as I infer from your note, there is any alternative to this attack, it should be carefully considered before opening our fire, for it will take all the artillery ammunition we have left to test this one, and if the result is unfavorable we will have none left for another effort. And even if this is entirely successful, it can only be so at a very bloody cost."

To this note, Longstreet soon replied as follows:—"Colonel: The intention is to advance the infantry if the artillery has the desired effect of driving the enemy's off, or having other effect such as to warrant us in making the attack. When that moment arrives advise Gen. Pickett and of course advance such artillery as you can use in aiding the attack."

Evidently the cannonade was to be allowed to begin. Then the responsibility would be upon me to decide whether or not Pickett should charge. If not, we must return to Va. to replenish ammunition, and the campaign would be a failure. I knew that our guns could not drive off the enemy, but I had a vague hope that with Ewell's and Hill's cooperation something might happen, though I knew little either of their positions, their opportunities, or their orders. I asked Wright: "What do you think of it? Is it as hard to get there as it looks?" He answered: "The trouble is not in going there. I went there with my brigade yesterday. There is a place where you can get breath and re-form. The trouble is to stay there after you get there, for the whole Yankee army is there in a bunch."

I failed to fully appreciate all that this might mean. The question seemed merely one of support, which was peculiarly the province of Gen. Lee. I had seen several of Hill's brigades forming to support Pickett, and had heard a rumor that Lee had spoken of a united attack by the whole army. I determined to see Pickett and get an idea of his feelings. I did so, and finding him both cheerful and sanguine, I felt that if the artillery fire opened, Pickett must make the charge; but that Longstreet should know my views, so I wrote him as follows:—"General: When our fire is at its best, I will advise Gen. Pickett to advance."

It must have been with bitter disappointment that Longstreet saw the failure of his hope to avert a useless slaughter, for he was fully convinced of its hopelessness. Yet even he could have scarcely realized, until the event showed, how entirely unprepared were Hill and Ewell to render aid to his assault and to take prompt advantage of even temporary success. None of their guns had been posted with a view to cooperative fire, nor to follow the charge, and much of their ammunition had been prematurely wasted. And although Pickett's assault, when made, actually carried the enemy's guns, nowhere was there the slightest preparation to come to his assistance. The burden of the whole task fell upon the 10 brigades employed. The other 27 brigades and 56 fresh guns were but widely scattered spectators.

It was just 1 P.M. by my watch when the signal guns were fired and the cannonade opened....[6]

As sketched by Edwin Forbes, entire teams of Federal artillery horses lie unmoving, victims of the Confederate artillery bombardment. Noted Forbes: "The whole slope was massed with dead horses—sixty-two lying in one battery."

Library of Congress

"The Whole Rebel Line Was Pouring Out Thunder and Iron"

A Storm of Fire Hurtles toward Federal Forces on Cemetery Ridge

O n Cemetery Ridge, opposite Alexander's line of artillery, Federal troops waited behind a stone wall fortified with piled-up fence posts and took advantage of the lull to doze in the summer warmth. "The silence and the heat were oppressive," a Northern officer would later recall. "The troops stretched upon the ground with the hot July sun pouring upon them.... Some sat with haversacks on the knee, pencil in hand, writing to the dear ones at home."

General Meade, who had been riding his lines during the morning, sat in the shade of a tree near his headquarters, sharing a chicken stew made from "an old and tough rooster" with some of his commanders. Meade had reconsidered his prediction about Lee's attack, concluding that it might again hit the Federal flanks instead of the center. Accordingly, he had shifted troops from the center to the flanks, leaving less than 6,000 troops to defend the center of his line. The chicken stew dinner party ended, and Meade and his commanders dispersed—

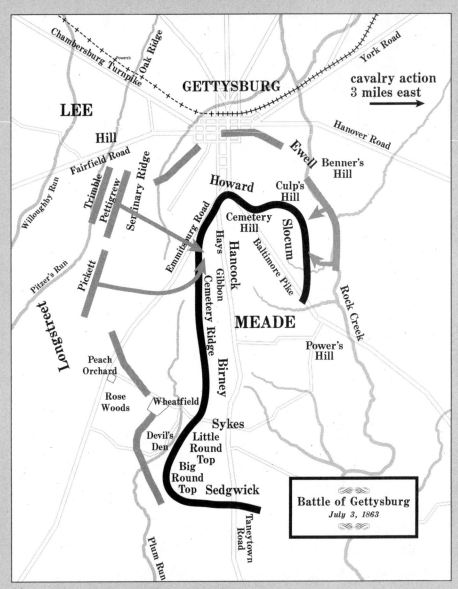

Chambersburg Turnpike

Oak Ridge

Powers's

York Road

GETTYSBURG

cavalry action
3 miles east →

LEE

Hanover Road

Hill

Ewell

Benner's
Hill

Fairfield Road

Culp's
Hill

Trimble

Pettigrew

Seminary Ridge

Howard

Cemetery
Hill

Slocum

Willoughby Run

Emmitsburg Road

Hays

Hancock

Baltimore Pike

Pitzer's Run

Pickett

Gibbon

Cemetery Ridge

MEADE

Rock Creek

Longstreet

Birney

Power's
Hill

Peach
Orchard

Rose
Woods

Wheatfield

Sykes

Devil's
Den

Little
Round
Top

Big
Round
Top

Sedgwick

Taneytown Road

Plum Run

Battle of Gettysburg
July 3, 1863

Based on a map by Hal Jespersen, www.CWmaps.com

the commanders back to their commands and Meade to resume riding his lines. Then, just after one o'clock, the distant line of Confederate artillery belched smoke, followed by a heavy roar, and—as Brigadier General John Gibbon would recall—"the air was all murderous iron," especially at the center of the Federal line.

Forced to endure it alongside General Gibbon stood his staff aide, thirty-four-year-old Lieutenant Frank Haskell of Vermont. A prewar lawyer and the former adjutant of the 6th Wisconsin Infantry, Haskell would later describe the unprecedented Confederate artillery bombardment in a long letter to his brother.

———————————————

We dozed in the heat, and lolled upon the ground, with half open eyes. Our horses were hitched to the trees munching some oats. A great lull rests upon all the field. Time was heavy, and for want of something better to do, I yawned, and looked at my watch. It was five minutes before one o'clock. I returned my watch to its pocket, and thought possibly that I might go to sleep, and stretched myself upon the ground accordingly. My attitude and purpose were those of the General and the rest of the staff.

What sound was that? There was no mistaking it! The distinct, sharp sound of one of the enemy's guns, square over to the front, caused us to open our eyes and turn them in that direction, when we saw directly above the crest the smoke of the bursting shell, and heard its noise. In an instant, before a word was spoken, as if that was the signal gun for general work, loud, startling, booming, the report of gun after gun, in rapid succession, smote our ears, and their shells plunged down and exploded all around us. We sprang to our feet. In briefest time the whole rebel line to the west was pouring out its thunder and its iron upon our devoted crest.

The wildest confusion for a few moments obtained sway among us. The shells came bursting all about. The servants ran terror-stricken for dear life, and disappeared. The horses hitched to

Brigadier General John Gibbon lived in the South as a child, but he was a firm Union man. He had plenty of combat experience, and he would need it: his division's sector of the Federal line was the target of the Pickett-Pettigrew Charge.

Library of Congress

the trees, or held by the slack hands of orderlies, neighed out in fright, and broke away and plunged riderless through the fields. The general at the first had snatched his sword, and started on foot for the front. I called for my horse; nobody responded. I found him tied to a tree, near by, eating oats, with an air of the greatest composure, which, under the circumstances, even then struck me as exceedingly ridiculous. He alone, of all beasts or men near, was cool. I am not sure but that I learned a lesson then from a horse. Anxious alone for his oats, while I put on the bridle and adjusted the halter, he delayed me by keeping his head down, so I had time to see one of the horses of our mess wagon struck and torn by a shell. The pair plunge—the driver has lost the rein; horses, driver, and wagon go into a heap by a tree. Two mules close at hand, packed with boxes of ammunition, are knocked all to pieces by a shell.

General Gibbon's groom has just mounted his horse, and is starting to take the general's horse to him, when the flying iron meets him and tears open his breast; he drops dead, and the horses gallop away. No more than a minute since the first shot was fired, and I am mounted and riding after the General. The mighty din that now rises to heaven and shakes the earth is not all of it the voice of the rebellion; for our guns, the guardian lions of the crest, quick to awake when danger comes, have opened their fiery jaws and begun to roar,—the great hoarse roar of battle. I overtook the general half way up to the line. Before we reach the crest his horse is brought by an orderly. Leaving our horses just behind a sharp declivity of the ridge, on foot we go up among the batteries. How the long streams of fire spout from the guns! how the rifled shells hiss! how the smoke deepens and rolls! But where is the infantry? Has it vanished in smoke? Is this a nightmare or a juggler's devilish trick? All too real.

The men of the infantry have seized their arms, and behind their works, behind every rock, in every ditch, wherever there is any shelter, they hug the ground, silent, quiet, unterrified, little harmed. The enemy's guns, now in action, are in position at their front of the woods along the second ridge that I have before mentioned, and towards their right, behind a small crest in the open field, where we saw the flags this morning. Their line is some two miles long, concave on the side towards us, and their range is from one thousand to eighteen hundred yards. A hundred and twenty-five rebel guns, we estimate, are now active, firing twenty-four pound, twenty, twelve, and ten-pound projectiles, solid shot and shells, spherical, conical, spiral....

From the Cemetery to Round Top, with over a hundred guns, and to all parts of the enemy's line, our batteries reply, of twenty and ten-pound Parrotts, ten-pound rifled ordnance, and twelve-pound Napoleons, using projectiles as various in shape and name as those of the enemy. Captain Hazard, commanding the Artillery Brigade of the Second Corps, was vigilant among the batteries of his command, and they were all doing well. All was going on satisfactorily. We had nothing to do, therefore, but to be observers of the grand spectacle of battle. Captain Wessels, Judge Advocate of the division, now joined us, and we sat down behind the crest, close to the left of Cushing's Battery, to bide our time, to see, to be ready to act when the time should come, which might be at any moment.

Who can describe such a conflict as is raging around us? To say that it was like a summer storm, with the crash of thunder, the glare of lightning, the shrieking of the wind, and the clatter of hailstones, would be weak. The thunder and lightning of these two hundred and fifty guns, and their shells, whose smoke darkens the sky, are incessant, all-pervading, in the air above our heads, on the ground

at our feet, remote, near, deafening, ear-piercing, astounding; and these hailstones are massy iron, charged with exploding fire. And there is little of human interest in a storm; it is an absorbing element of this. You may see flame and smoke, and hurrying men, and human passion at a great conflagration; but they are all earthly, and nothing more. These guns are great infuriate demons, not of the earth, whose mouths blaze with smoky tongues of living fire, and whose murky breath, sulphur-laden, rolls around them and along the ground, the smoke of Hades. These grimy men, rushing, shouting, their souls in frenzy, plying the dusky globes and the igniting spark, are in their league, and but their willing ministers.

We thought that at the second Bull Run, at the Antietam, and at Fredericksburg on the 11th of December, we had heard heavy

A battery of Federal field artillery assembles for drill a year before Gettysburg. As they returned the Confederate artillery fire on July 3, Federal gun crews were described as "grimy men, rushing, shouting, their souls in frenzy...."

Library of Congress

cannonading; they were but holiday salutes compared with this. Besides the great ceaseless roar of the guns, which was but the background of the others, a million various minor sounds engaged the ear. The projectiles shriek long and sharp. They hiss, they scream, they growl, they sputter,—all sounds of life and rage; and each has its different note, and all are discordant. Was ever such a chorus of sound before? We note the effect of the enemy's fire among the batteries and along the crest. We see the solid shot strike axle, or pole, or wheel, and the tough iron and heart of oak snap and fly like straws. The great oaks there by Woodruff's guns heave down their massy branches with a crash, as if the lightning smote them. The shells swoop down among the battery horses standing there apart.

A half dozen horses start, they tumble, their legs stiffen, their vitals and blood smear the ground. And these shot and shells have no respect for men either. We see the poor fellows hobbling back from the crest, or unable to do so, pale and weak, lying on the ground, with the mangled stump of an arm or leg dripping their life-blood away, or with a cheek torn open or a shoulder mashed. And many, alas! hear not the roar as they stretch upon the ground with upturned faces and open eyes, though a shell should burst at their very ears. Their ears and their bodies this instant are only mud. We saw them but a moment since, there among the flame, with brawny arms and muscles of iron, wielding the rammer and pushing home the cannon's plethoric load.

Strange freaks these round shot play! We saw a man coming up from the rear with his full knapsack on, and some canteens of water held by the straps in his hands. He was walking slowly, and with apparent unconcern, though the iron hailed around him. A shot struck the knapsack, and it and its contents flew thirty yards in every direction; the knapsack disappearing like an egg thrown spitefully against a rock. The soldier stopped, and turned about in puzzled surprise, put up one hand to his back to assure himself that the knapsack was not there, and then walked slowly on again unharmed, with not even his coat torn. Near us was a man crouching behind a small disintegrated stone, which was about the size of a common water-bucket. He was bent up, with his face to the ground, in the attitude of a pagan worshipper before his idol. It looked so absurd to see him thus, that I went and said to him, "Do not lie there like a toad,—why not go to your regiment and be a man?" He turned up his face with a stupid, terrified look upon me, and then without a word turned his nose again to the ground. An orderly that was with me at the time told me a few moments later, that a shot struck the stone, smashing it in a thousand fragments, but did not touch the man, though his head was not six inches from the stone.

All the projectiles that came near us were not so harmless. Not ten yards away from us a shell burst among some small bushes, where sat three or four orderlies holding horses. Two of the men and one horse were killed. Only a few yards off a shell exploded over an open limber box in Cushing's battery, and at the same instant, another shell over a neighboring box. In both the boxes the ammunition blew up with an explosion that shook the ground, throwing fire and splinters and shells far into the air and all around, and destroying several men. We watched the shells bursting in the air, as they came hissing in all directions. Their flash was a bright gleam of lightning radiating from a point, giving place in the thousandth part of a second to a small, white, puffy cloud, like a fleece of the lightest, whitest wool. These clouds were very numerous. We could not often see the shell before it burst, but sometimes, as we faced towards the enemy, and looked above our heads, the approach would be heralded by a prolonged hiss, which always seemed to me to be a line of something tangible, terminating in a black globe, distinct to the eye, as the sound had been to the ear. The shell would seem to stop, and hang suspended in the air an instant, and then vanish in fire and smoke and noise.

We saw the missiles tear and plow the ground. All in rear of the crest for a thousand yards, as well as among the batteries, was the field of their blind fury. Ambulances passing down the Taneytown road with wounded men were struck. The hospitals near this road were riddled. The house which was General Meade's headquarters was shot through several times, and a great many horses of officers and orderlies were lying dead around it. Riderless horses, galloping madly through the fields, were brought up, or down rather, by these invisible horse-tamers, and they would not run any more. Mules with ammunition, pigs wallowing about, cows in the pastures, whatever was animate or inanimate, in all this broad range, were no exception to their blind havoc. The percussion shells would strike and thunder, and scatter the earth, and their whistling fragments, the Whitworth bolts, would pound and ricochet, and bowl far away sputtering, with the sound of a mass of hot iron plunged in water; and the great solid shot would smite the unresisting ground with a sounding "thud," as the strong boxer crashes his iron fist into the jaws of his unguarded adversary. Such were some of the sights and sounds of this great iron battle of missiles....[7]

"The Enemy Was under the Mistaken Impression That He Had Silenced Our Guns"

The Federal Artillery Prepares a Killing Field

Brigadier General Henry J. Hunt, chief of artillery for the Army of the Potomac, had just completed a three-hour inspection of his artillery when the Confederate bombardment opened. A middle-aged, bewhiskered West Pointer from Michigan, Hunt was a third generation army officer. Thoroughly professional in bearing and conduct, he had been decorated for bravery in the Mexican War, and, as a major at First Bull Run, he had organized cover fire from his artillery to protect the inexperienced, panicky Federal troops as they retreated. At the Battle of Malvern Hill, his placement and direction of the Federal artillery had shredded the Confederate ranks assaulting his batteries, proving crucial to the Federal victory. Afterward General McClellan had promoted him to chief of artillery as a brigadier general. Later, McClellan's replacement, General Hooker, had demoted Hunt to a desk job, but after the Federal loss at Chancellorsville, he was restored as the army's chief of artillery.

Brigadier General Henry J. Hunt, commander of the Federal artillery at Gettysburg, was co-author of *Instructions for Field Artillery*—the field manual used by artillery officers on both sides. At Gettysburg, his expertise would prove invaluable.

Library of Congress

At Gettysburg, Hunt's artillery was greatly responsible for turning back the Confederate attacks on both ends of the Federal line on July 2. That night Hunt stayed up half the night getting his guns in place, so his artillery would be ready if the Confederates attacked the center of the Federal line on July 3. He watched the incoming Confederate artillery fire with the eye of an expert, and concluded that while the barrage was grimly spectacular, it did not do the job the enemy had expected. It killed many soldiers, blew up artillery caissons, knocked horses dead in their tracks, and was frightfully unnerving to endure, but it did not destroy or demoralize the Federal army. For some reason, most of the unprecedented bombardment fell in the rear of the Federal lines, and did little harm to the rows of blue-uniformed infantrymen hunched down behind their stone and fence-rail breastworks.

Hunt expected much more from his own artillery. He had placed thirty-six artillery batteries—a total of 163 guns—at key positions to defend Cemetery Ridge, and at least seventy-four of them directly supported the center of the Federal line. Hunt ordered his artillery to return the Confederate fire, and his skillfully placed line of Federal artillery poured forth a torrent of shot and shell toward the distant line of Confederate cannon—for a while. Hunt watched the Federal fire carefully, measuring it moment by moment. He wanted to be sure his guns had ample ammunition for the Confederate infantry assault that he believed would soon strike the center of the Federal line. After about a half-hour of furious return fire, he ordered the Federal artillery to cease firing to conserve ammunition. Hunt trusted his forces could handle whatever the Confederates sent across the sprawling open fields that lay in front of Cemetery Ridge: his guns had transformed the Southern route of assault into a killing field.

Decades later, General Hunt would describe in detail the careful way he had positioned the Army of the Potomac's artillery to defend Cemetery Ridge on July 3.

On the Federal side Hancock's corps held Cemetery Ridge with Robinson's division, First Corps, on Hays's right in support, and Doubleday's at the angle between Gibbon and Caldwell. General Newton, having been assigned to the command of the First Corps, vice Reynolds, was now in charge of the ridge held by Caldwell. Compactly arranged on its crest was McGilvery's artillery, forty-one guns, consisting of his own batteries, reenforced by others from the Artillery Reserve. Well to the right, in front of Hays and Gibbon, was the artillery of the Second Corps under its chief, Captain Hazard. Woodruff's battery was in front of Ziegler's Grove; on his left, in succession, Arnold's Rhode Island, Cushing's United States, Brown's Rhode Island, and Rorty's New York.

In the fight of the preceding day the two last-named batteries had been to the front and suffered severely. Lieutenant T. Fred Brown was severely wounded, and his command devolved on Lieutenant Perrin. So great had been the loss in men and horses that they were now of four guns each, reducing the total number in the corps to twenty-six. Daniels's battery of horse artillery, four guns, was at the angle.

With the U.S. Artillery's crossed-cannon insignia affixed to his kepi, a Federal artilleryman strikes a jaunty pose. On July 3, Federal gun crews composed of such men would inflict huge casualties on Lee's army.

Library of Congress

In addition, some of the guns on Cemetery Hill, and Rittenhouse's on Little Round Top, could be brought to bear, but these were offset by batteries similarly placed on the flanks of the enemy, so that on the Second Corps line, within the space of a mile, were seventy-one guns to oppose nearly one hundred and fifty. They were on an open crest plainly visible from all parts of the opposite line. Between ten and eleven A. M., everything looking favorable at Culp's Hill, I crossed over to Cemetery Ridge, to see what might be going on at other points. Here a magnificent display greeted my eyes. Our whole front for two miles was covered by [Confederate] batteries already in line or going into position. They stretched— apparently in one unbroken mass—from opposite the town to the Peach Orchard, which bounded the view to the left, the ridges of which were planted thick with cannon.

Never before had such a sight been witnessed on this continent, and rarely, if ever, abroad. What did it mean? It might possibly be to hold that line while its infantry was sent to aid Ewell, or to guard against a counter-stroke from us, but it most probably meant an assault on our center, to be preceded by a cannonade in order to crush our batteries and shake our infantry; at least to cause us to exhaust our ammunition in reply, so that the assaulting troops might pass in good condition over the half mile of open ground which was beyond our effective musketry fire. With such an object the cannonade would be long and followed immediately by the assault, their whole army being held in readiness to follow up a success. From the great extent of ground occupied by the enemy's batteries, it was evident that all the artillery on our west front, whether of the army corps or the reserve, must concur as a unit, under the chief of artillery, in the defense....

It was of the first importance to subject the enemy's infantry, from the first moment of their advance, to such a cross-fire of our artillery as would break their formation, check their impulse, and drive them back, or at least bring them to our lines in such condition as to make them an easy prey. There was neither time nor necessity for reporting this to General Meade, and beginning on the right, I instructed the chiefs of artillery and battery commanders to with-hold their fire for fifteen or twenty minutes after the cannonade commenced, then to concentrate their fire with all possible accuracy on those batteries which were most destructive to us—but slowly, so that when the enemy's ammunition was exhausted, we should have sufficient left to meet the assault.

I had just given these orders to the last battery on Little Round Top, when the signal gun was fired, and the enemy opened with all his guns. From that point the scene was indescribably grand. All their batteries were soon covered with smoke, through which the flashes were incessant, whilst the air seemed filled with shells, whose sharp explosions, with the hurtling of their fragments, formed a running accompaniment to the deep roar of the guns. Thence I rode to the Artillery Reserve to order fresh batteries and ammunition to be sent up to the ridge as soon as the cannonade ceased; but both the reserve and the train were gone to a safer place. Messengers, however, had been left to receive and convey orders, which I sent by them, then I returned to the ridge. Turning into the Taneytown pike, I saw evidence of the necessity under which the reserve had "decamped," in the remains of a dozen exploded caissons, which had been placed under cover of a hill, but which the shells had managed to search out. In fact, the fire was more dangerous behind the ridge than on its crest, which I soon reached at the position occupied by General Newton behind McGilvery's batteries, from which we had a fine view as all our own guns were now in action.

Most of the enemy's projectiles passed overhead, the effect being to sweep all the open ground in our rear, which was of little benefit to the Confederates—a mere waste of ammunition, for everything here could seek shelter. And just here an incident already published may be repeated, as it illustrates a peculiar feature of civil war. Colonel Long, who was at the time on General Lee's staff, had a few years before served in my mounted battery expressly to receive a course of instruction in the use of field artillery. At Appomattox, we spent several hours together, and in the course of conversation I told him I was not satisfied with the conduct of this cannonade which I had heard was under his direction, inasmuch as he had not done justice to his instruction; that his fire, instead of being concentrated on the point of attack, as it ought to have been, and as I expected it would be, was scattered over the whole field. He was amused at the criticism and said: "I remembered my lessons at the time, and when the fire became so scattered, wondered what you would think about it!"

I now rode along the ridge to inspect the batteries. The infantry were lying down on its reverse slope, near the crest, in open ranks, waiting events. As I passed along, a bolt from a rifle-gun struck the ground just in front of a man of the front rank, penetrated the surface and passed under him, throwing him "over and over." He fell behind the rear rank, apparently dead, and a ridge of earth where he had been lying reminded me of the backwoods practice of "barking" squirrels.

Our fire was deliberate, but on inspecting the chests I found that the ammunition was running low, and hastened to General Meade to advise its immediate cessation and preparation for the assault which would certainly follow. The headquarters building, immediately behind the ridge, had been abandoned, and many of the horses of the staff lay dead. Being told that the general had gone to the cemetery, I proceeded thither. He was not there, and on telling General Howard my object, he concurred in its propriety, and I rode back along the ridge, ordering the fire to cease. This was followed by a cessation of that of the enemy, under the mistaken impression that he had silenced our guns, and almost immediately his infantry came out of the woods and formed for the assault.

On my way to the Taneytown road to meet the fresh batteries which I had ordered up, I met Major Bingham, of Hancock's staff, who informed me that General Meade's aides were seeking me with orders to "cease firing"; so I had only anticipated his wishes. The batteries were found and brought up, and Fitzhugh's, Cowan's and Parsons's were put in near the clump of trees. Meantime the enemy advanced....[8]

"For God's Sake, Come on Quick"

The Pickett-Pettigrew Charge Gets Underway

Colonel Edward Porter Alexander stood near one of his artillery batteries, which was firing away at Cemetery Ridge, and surveyed the distant Federal line by telescope. He was trying to measure the effect of the Confederate artillery bombardment, but the clouds of whitish smoke produced by his guns and the Federal return fire made it almost impossible to see anything. Meanwhile, incoming rounds peppered Alexander's line of artillery and landed in the woods to the rear, where Pickett's and Pettigrew's infantry lay on the ground waiting for the order to advance. Much of the Federal artillery return fire also overshot its target—the Confederate artillery—and hit far to the rear, but many rounds landed amidst the Southern artillery batteries and the massed troops waiting in the woods.

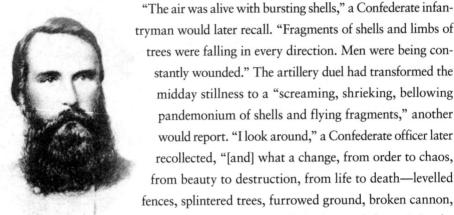

Perched on a snake rail fence behind the Confederate artillery, General James Longstreet reluctantly obeyed Lee's orders and sent the Pickett-Pettigrew Charge forward. "I do not want to make this attack…," he told a subordinate.

DeGolyer Library, Southern Methodist University

"The air was alive with bursting shells," a Confederate infantryman would later recall. "Fragments of shells and limbs of trees were falling in every direction. Men were being constantly wounded." The artillery duel had transformed the midday stillness to a "screaming, shrieking, bellowing pandemonium of shells and flying fragments," another would report. "I look around," a Confederate officer later recollected, "[and] what a change, from order to chaos, from beauty to destruction, from life to death—levelled fences, splintered trees, furrowed ground, broken cannon, exploded caissons, slaughtered horses, mangled men." On the far left flank of the Confederate line—on Pettigrew's side of the assault force—the Federal shelling triggered a panic in Colonel Robert Mayo's brigade of Virginians. Formerly Brockenbrough's Brigade, the Virginians had survived the first day's fighting, where their brigade had been badly shot up on McPherson's Ridge. Now scores of them fled under the shelling—they "shamefully ran away," in the words of an officer. They proved, however, to be the exception among the Southern troops waiting to make their assault: instead of fleeing, most flattened themselves on the ground and weathered the barrage of falling iron.

Propped against a tree to steady his telescope, Colonel Alexander finally spotted what he had been looking for—through the smoke of battle he could see Federal gun crews limbering up their artillery and heading for the rear—and the Federal artillery fire slackened. "At first, I thought it was only crippled guns," he would later explain, "but, with my large glass, I discovered entire batteries limbering up & leaving their positions." The Confederate artillery bombardment had done its work, he believed: the Federal artillery was being forced from the field. Surely the Federal infantry was also unnerved, demoralized, and ready to break. By Alexander's reckoning, the Confederate artillery bombardment had been underway for more than forty gruelling minutes. His ammunition was running low, leaving little to support the infantry assault, and—to his dismay—he realized that his reserve ammunition was nowhere close by. For all these reasons, he believed it was time to cease fire and to notify Pickett to advance. Pulling out a scrap of paper, he hastily scribbled a note to General Pickett: "For God's sake," it read, "come on quick...."

General Pickett received Alexander's dispatch and took it to General Longstreet, who had picked a spot of ground from which to watch the assault. "General, shall I advance?" he asked. Longstreet, still opposed to Lee's battle plan, looked away, nodded grimly, and said nothing. "I am going to move forward, sir," Pickett stated, then saluted and raced away on horseback to begin the charge. Decades later, Longstreet would publish his memoirs—*From Manassas to Appomattox*—recalling his version of the events leading up to the Pickett-Pettigrew Charge.

===========

I rode to a woodland hard by, to lie down and study for some new thought that might aid the assaulting column. In a few minutes report came from Alexander that he would only be able to judge of the effect of his fire by the return of that of the enemy, as his infantry was not exposed to view, and the smoke of the batteries would soon cover the field. He asked, if there was an alternative, that it be carefully considered before the batteries opened, as there was not enough artillery ammunition for this and another trial if this should not prove favorable.

He was informed that there was no alternative; that I could find no way out of it; that General Lee had considered and would listen to nothing else; that orders had gone for the guns to give signal for the batteries; that he should call the troops at the first opportunity or lull in the enemy's fire.

The signal-guns broke the silence, the blaze of the second gun mingling in the smoke of the first, and salvoes rolled to the left and

Southern gun crews put a section of artillery to work against distant Federal positions. On Gettysburg's third day, the Confederate artillery bombardment was terrifying in its intensity, but it did far less damage than expected.

Battles and Leaders of the Civil War

repeated themselves, the enemy's fine metal spreading its fire to the converging lines, plowing the trembling ground, plunging through the line of batteries, and clouding the heavy air. The two or three hundred guns seemed proud of their undivided honors and organized confusion. The Confederates had the benefit of converging fire into the enemy's massed position, but the superior metal of the enemy neutralized the advantage of position. The brave and steady work progressed.

Before this the Confederates of the left were driven from their captured trenches, and hope of their effective co-operation with the battle of the right was lost, but no notice of it was sent to the right of the battle. They made some further demonstrations, but they were of little effect. Merritt's cavalry was in rear of my right, threatening on the Emmitsburg road. Farnsworth's brigade took position between Merritt's and close on my right rear. Infantry regiments and batteries were broken off from my front line and posted to guard on that flank and rear.

Not informed of the failure of the Confederates on the left and the loss of their vantage-ground, we looked with confidence for them to follow the orders of battle.

General Pickett rode to confer with Alexander, then to the ground upon which I was resting, where he was soon handed a slip of paper. After reading it he handed it to me. It read:

"If you are coming at all, come at once, or I cannot give you proper support, but the enemy's fire has not slackened at all. At least eighteen guns are still firing from the cemetery itself."

ALEXANDER.

Pickett said, "General, shall I advance?" The effort to speak the order failed, and I could only indicate it by an affirmative bow. He accepted the duty with seeming confidence of success, leaped on his horse, and rode gayly [sic] to his command. I mounted and spurred for Alexander's post. He reported that the batteries he had reserved for the charge with the infantry had been spirited away by General Lee's chief of artillery; that the ammunition of the batteries of position was so reduced that he could not use them in proper support of the infantry. He was ordered to stop the march at once and fill up his ammunition-chests. But, alas! there was no more ammunition to be had.

The order was imperative. The Confederate commander had fixed his heart upon the work. Just then a number of the enemy's batteries hitched up and hauled off, which gave a glimpse of unexpected hope. Encouraging messages were sent for the columns to hurry on,—and they were then on elastic springing step. General Pickett, a graceful horseman, sat lightly in the saddle, his brown locks flowing quite over his shoulders. Pettigrew's division spread their steps and quickly rectified the alignment, and the grand march moved bravely on. General Trimble mounted, adjusting his seat and reins as if setting out on a pleasant afternoon ride. When aligned to their places, a solid march was made down the slope and past our batteries of position....[9]

CHAPTER NINE

"Up, Men, and to Your Posts!"

A s the Confederate bombardment rained shells on the center of the Federal line, Major General Winfield S. Hancock mounted his horse and rode back and forth along his line, trailed by an orderly bearing the corps flag. His troops cheered wildly and appeared heartened by the demonstration, which was Hancock's intent. When urged to dismount—a corps commander should not risk his life, he was told—he replied: "There are times when a corps commander's life does not count." Soon, his life—and the lives of his troops—would be in even greater jeopardy. The target of the impending Confederate assault—the center of the Federal line on Cemetery Ridge—was defended by Hancock and the soldiers of his Second Corps.

Dead center was a sector of the line defended by Brigadier General John Gibbon's division. To Gibbon's right was Brigadier General Alexander Hays's division and to his left Brigadier General John C. Caldwell's division. Waiting in support just to the rear was a detachment of troops from Major General Abner Doubleday's First Corps division. In total, the troops under Hancock's command at the center of the line numbered fewer than 6,000—facing Lee's advancing battle line of approximately 13,000.

To steady his troops, General Winfield S. Hancock braved the Confederate bombardment on horseback, as recorded by artist Alfred Waud in this battlefield sketch. "There are times," stated Hancock, "when a corps commander's life does not count."

Library of Congress

Throughout the bombardment, Hancock, Gibbon, and the other commanders at the center of the line studied the Confederate positions in the distance, but the smoke obscured their vision. Then the Federal artillery ceased fire, and afterward, the Confederate bombardment slackened and stopped. As the smoke drifted away, General Gibbon stared at the faraway tree line to the west and saw movement: it was a sight he would always remember: "The enemy in a long grey line was marching towards us over the rolling ground in our front," he would recall, "their flags fluttering in the air and serving as guides to their line of battle."[1]

"Up, Men, and to Your Posts!"
The Pickett-Pettigrew Charge Goes Forward

Mounted on a handsome dark warhorse named "Old Black," Major General George Edward Pickett galloped up to the troops of his division. They were sprawled near the edge of the woods behind the Confederate artillery, and were awaiting orders. At thirty-eight, Pickett was given to fancy uniforms and perfumed locks, which he wore shoulder-length in ringlets. Raised in the antebellum Virginia aristocracy, he waved away his family's attempts to make him into a lawyer and instead gained admittance to West Point. There, he amassed scores of demerits, mainly for trivial offenses such as trying to trip a line of cadets marching to supper, and graduated last in his class. He demonstrated courage in combat in the Mexican War, and was sobered by the deaths of his first two wives and a newborn child while posted to the American West in the 1850s. At a military outpost on the coast of Washington Territory near Canada, he triumphed over British naval forces in a border dispute over a pig. In Confederate service he quickly rose from colonel to major general, leading troops in battle during the Seven Days Battles, where he was seriously wounded.

Despite his reputation as a dandy, Pickett was viewed as an aggressive combat officer, and after months of recovering from his wound, he was eager for battle at Gettysburg. Riding up to his troops on the afternoon of July 3, drawn sword in hand, he shouted, "Up, men, and to your posts! Don't forget today that you are from Old Virginia!" The effect of his words was "electrical," said one officer, as the soldiers sprang to their feet, formed their lines, and advanced. They marched forward under billowing national colors and battle-flags, passing General Longstreet, who exchanged salutes with Pickett, and moved through the now-silent line of Confederate artillery, heading resolutely toward the distant enemy line on Cemetery Ridge. Pickett would advance only midway, stopping with his staff somewhere near the Emmitsburg Road, at or near a farm owned by Nicholas Cordori. From there, in accordance with accepted military practice, he would direct his division from the rear.

Garnett's Brigade was on the left, Kemper's Brigade was on the right, and Armistead's Brigade followed Garnett's—with Wilcox's Brigade advancing to the right and the rear of Armistead's. Down the field to the left, General Pettigrew's division was also preparing to move forward. When the assault began, the wild, high-pitched "Rebel Yell" echoed across the fields between the opposing lines. Colonel Alexander's artillery ceased fire as Pickett's men moved through the line of guns, then, when the Southerners were safely ahead, the guns reopened a cover fire for as long as their ammunition would last. In their front lay a sprawling, open range of fields and fences—three-quarters of a mile wide in places—which ended at the Emmitsburg Road. Beyond the road sprawled more fields, which sloped upward to the stone wall atop Cemetery Ridge where Federal troops watched and waited. At the approximate center of the Federal line on Cemetery Ridge was a clump of leafy trees—"the copse of trees," some called it—the target of the Pickett-Pettigrew Charge. On that point all the troops planned to converge, Pickett's division maneuvering toward it from the right and Pettigrew's division from the left.

Major General
George Pickett did
not command Lee's
July 3 grand assault
against the center of
the Federal line—
General Longstreet
did—but the attack
would become
known to generations
of Americans as
"Pickett's Charge."

Library of Congress

As the mile-wide formation of Southern troops advanced—some 13,000 strong—the ranks of Federal soldiers atop Cemetery Ridge watched with a mixture of dread and awe. A mild westerly breeze dispersed the smoke of the Confederate artillery barrage, and the advancing mass of men in gray and butternut moved steadily forward in the sunlight. "Here they come!" soldiers began shouting. "They are coming!" Even as an enemy, a New Jersey private could not help but admit it was "the grandest sight" he had ever seen. "Their lines looking to be as straight as a line could be," he would recall, "their bayonets glistening in the sun, from right to left as far as the eye could see...." A Connecticut soldier agreed, reporting that the distant Confederate line advanced "like a victorious giant, confident of power and victory."

Soon the straight, neat lines—marked by scattered red and blue "Starry Cross" battle-flags—began to come under a torrent of Federal artillery fire from the many cannon expertly placed by General Hunt, the Federal chief of artillery. Due to his decision to cut short the Federal artillery barrage, Hunt's guns had ample ammunition, both long-range and close-up—solid shot, grapeshot, explosive shell, case shot, and canister. Case shot, when exploded, would spray deadly marble-sized lead balls in all directions. Explosive shell would break up into killer iron fragments when exploded. Solid shot would plow through rank after rank of marching troops. Grapeshot—large iron balls packed in a cluster like grapes—and canister—tin cans packed with lead balls—were used at close range to transform cannon into monster shotguns.

Twenty-five years later, a New York officer—Captain Winfield Scott—would record how the Pickett-Pettigrew Charge appeared to the Federal troops atop Cemetery Ridge—before the "magnificent line of battle" was raked by searing Federal fire.

———————————

From our position we could overlook the whole valley between the two lines.... All at once, over their works and through the bushes that skirted them, came a heavy skirmish line. The skirmishers were about two paces apart, covering about three quarters of a mile of our front. Behind them about 20 rods came another heavy skirmish line. Behind them, about the same distance, came out the first line of battle. As they first emerged, had they continued straight to the front, their charge would have been centered upon the troops to our left.

It was a magnificent line of battle, over three-quarters of a mile long. The men carried their guns, with bayonets fixed, at right shoulder. The regimental flags and guidons were plainly visible along the whole line. The guns and bayonets in the sunlight shone like silver. The whole line of battle looked like a stream or river of silver moving towards us. Behind this came the regimental officers; while behind them, mounted and followed by their aids, came the brigade and division commanders, with their orderlies carrying their guidons and headquarters flags.

Then came the second line of infantry, in the same form and order as the first, followed by their commanders on horses. Behind this still, in heavy massed columns on the center and wings, were the supports and reserves. Two streaming lines of silver led off, decorated and enlivened by their battle flags. Their order was magnificent. The movement of such a force over such a field, in such perfect order, to such a destiny, was grand beyond expression. After moving forward about a quarter of a mile, a change was made in the direction of the line. A left half wheel was executed and they came straight for us, so that their left would just strike the right of our brigade....

The whole line, to us who were in front, seemed straight as an arrow— the whole force like a perfect and magnificent parade.

My own heart was thrilled at the sight. I was so absorbed with the beauty and grandeur of the scene that I became oblivious to the shells that were bursting about us. This passage of scripture came to my mind, and I repeated it aloud: "Fair as the moon, bright as the sun, and terrible as an army with banners."

Shortly their skirmishers came within range. Ours reserved their fire until the enemy came close to them. Our fire was then so accurate and severe, that their first line was held in check and could not force ours back. Their second line of skirmishers re-enforced the first, and ours then began to yield, falling back slowly. Our batteries from Cemetery Hill fired over our heads and threw shells, which went through the lines, bursting among them. Gaps were opened and quickly closed again. The shells kept flying, gaps opened and closed, and the silver lines in perfect order came on. Skirmishers fired sharply; the horsemen galloped to and fro behind the lines as the goal was approached. The half-wheel of the enemy exposed their flank to the fire of McGilvray's and Hazlitt's guns from near Round Top. But there was no flinching. Gaps opened and closed, but the lines came forward.

As the lines neared us, the enemy's batteries slackened. Our batteries in the front line opened with grape and canister. Greater gaps were opened, and quickly closed, and still on in sublime order came the silver lines. It was then cannon, and gaps, and closing of ranks, and on, on, on, in magnificent and unflinching valor, came the lines of silvery steel.... The commands and the tramp of the on-coming hosts could now be heard. There was a moment's quiet of skirmishers and musketry. Orders of the enemy, a little clearer and sharper, ran out upon the air. Another crash of canister—other and terrifying gaps, and still heroic closing of ranks. Our first line by the stone wall was held by troops of Webb's Brigade. They clutched their muskets and fixed their bayonets. The order was given to hold their fire until the enemy was close upon them.

From the tree line visible in the distance, 13,000 Confederate troops emerged to launch the Pickett-Pettigrew Charge. The Southern bayonets were "glistening in the sun," said a Northern soldier, "as far as the eye could see..."

Adams County Historical Society

Men peered through the crevices of the fence with anxious but determined looks. The conflict of thought, and purpose, and will was now upon both armies. Moments seemed ages. The shock to heart and nerve was awful. The enemy, as if anticipating the deadly reception, brought down their gleaming muskets from the shoulder to charge bayonets. Our line was neared. One more crash of grape and canister, another fearful rending of ranks, another determined closing, and on they came....[2]

"Round Shots Tore through Their Ranks"

The Troops of Pickett's Division Are Swept by a Storm of Fire

Forty-five-year-old Brigadier General Richard B. Garnett made the Pickett-Pettigrew Charge on horseback. A West Pointer who had fought Indians in Florida and in the West before the war, Garnett was handsome, affable, and fun-loving—his favorite tune was "Willie Brewed a Peck of Malt." Before the charge, he had been kicked by a horse but had climbed out of an army ambulance to lead his brigade into battle. Despite the sultry heat of the day,

Garnett—"Dick" to his friends—was so ill that he wore a heavy overcoat. Seeing Garnett on horseback and knowing he likely intended to ride all the way to the enemy line, General Pickett reportedly gave him a good-natured but serious warning: "Dick, old fellow … you are going to catch hell." Garnett dismissed the advice.

An experienced, capable officer, Garnett had risen in the Confederate ranks from major to brigadier general in less than six months. When General "Stonewall" Jackson had been promoted to a higher command, it was Garnett who was selected to command Jackson's famed Stonewall Brigade. However, at the Battle of Kernstown in March of 1862, Garnett had ordered his troops to withdraw without Jackson's permission, and Jackson subsequently had him relieved from command. Lee had given him a brigade command in Pickett's division, but Garnett remained determined to clear his name. "He was therefore anxious to expose himself," observed a fellow officer.

Expose himself he did: on horseback Garnett made an obvious target as the five regiments of his brigade advanced on the front left of Pickett's division. They and the other Confederate troops in the assault were heading toward the slope that led to the clump of trees and the center of the Federal line. He would never return. When last seen, Garnett, still mounted, was waving his hat and cheering on his troops—until he disappeared in a blast of swirling white smoke. His wounded horse came galloping back, drenched in blood, but "Dick" Garnett was never found.

Decades later, Captain Henry T. Owen, a company commander in the 18th Virginia Infantry, would describe the bloody route followed by Garnett and his men.

━━━━━━━━━━━━━━━

Then came the command in a strong, clear voice: "Forward! Guide center! March!" and the column, with a front of more than half a mile, moved grandly up the slope. Meade's guns opened upon the column as it appeared above the crest of the ridge, but it neither paused nor faltered. Round shot, bounding along the plain, tore through their ranks and ricochetted [sic] around them; shells exploded incessantly in blinding, dazzling flashes before them, behind them, overhead and among them. Frightful gaps were made from center to flank, yet on swept the column, and as it advanced the men steadily closed up the wide rents made along the line in a hundred places at every discharge of the murderous batteries in front. A long line of skirmishers, prostrate in the tall grass, firing at the column since it came within view, rose up within fifty yards, fired a volley into its front, then trotted on before it, turning and firing back as fast as they could reload.

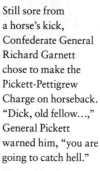

Still sore from a horse's kick, Confederate General Richard Garnett chose to make the Pickett-Pettigrew Charge on horseback. "Dick, old fellow…," General Pickett warned him, "you are going to catch hell."
Library of Congress

The column moved on at a quick step with shouldered arms, and the fire of the skirmish line was not returned. Half way over the field an order ran down the line, "Left oblique," which was promptly obeyed, and the direction is changed forty-five degrees from the front to the left. Men looking away, far off toward the left flank, saw that the supporting columns there were crumbling and melting rapidly away…. The command now came along the line, "Front, forward!" and the column resumed its direction straight down upon the center of the enemy's position…. The destruction of life in the ranks of that advancing host was fearful beyond precedent, officers going down by dozens and the men by scores and fifties….

We were now four hundred yards from the foot of Cemetery Hill, when away off to the right, nearly half a mile, there appeared in the open field a line of men at right angles with our own, a long, dark mass, dressed in blue, and coming down at a "double quick" upon the unprotected right flank of Pickett's men, with their muskets upon "the right shoulder shift," their battle flags dancing and fluttering in the breeze created by their own rapid motion, and their

As the Confederate troops advanced, their neat battle lines resembled "a perfect and magnificent parade," a Northern officer would recall. The impressive "parade" was quickly marred by Federal artillery fire.

Library of Congress

burnished bayonets glistening above their heads like forest twigs covered with sheets of sparkling ice when shaken by a blast....

The enemy were now seen strengthening their lines, where the blow was expected to strike, by hurrying up reserves from the right and left, the columns from opposite directions passing each other double along our front like the fingers of a man's two hands locking together. The distance had again shortened and officers in the enemy's lines could be distinguished by their uniforms from the privates. Then was heard that heavy thud of a muffled tread of armed men that roar and rush of tramping feet as Armistead's column from the rear closed up behind the front line and he (the last brigadier) took command, stepped out in front with his hat uplifted on the point of his sword and led the division, now four ranks deep, rapidly and grandly across that valley of death, covered with clover as soft as a Turkish carpet.

There it was again! and again! A sound filling the air above, below, around us, like the blast through the top of a dry cedar, or the whirring sound made by the sudden flight of a flock of quail. It was grape and canister, and the column broke forward into a double-quick and rushed toward the stone wall where forty cannon were belching forth grape and canister twice and thrice a minute. A hundred yards from the stone wall the flanking party on the right, coming down on a heavy run, halted suddenly within fifty yards and poured a deadly storm of musket balls into Pickett's men, double-quicking across their front, and under this terrible cross-fire the men reeled and staggered between falling comrades and the right came pressing down upon the center, crowding the companies into confusion. We all knew the purpose to carry the heights in front, and the mingled mass, from fifteen to thirty feet deep, rushed toward the stone wall, while a few hundred men, without orders, faced to the right and fought the flanking party there, although fifty to one, and for a time held them at bay.

Muskets were seen crossed as some fired to the right and others to the front, and the fighting was terrific,—far beyond all other experience even of Pickett's men, who for once raised no cheer, while the welkin rang around them with the "Union triple huzza." The old veterans saw the fearful odds against them, and other hosts gathering darker and deeper still. The time was too precious, too serious for a cheer; they buckled down to the heavy task in silence, and fought with a feeling like despair.... On swept the column over ground covered with dead and dying men, where the earth seemed to be on fire, the smoke dense and suffocating, the sun shut out, flames blazing on every side, friend could hardly be distinguished from foe, but the division, in the shape of an inverted V, with the point flattened, pushed forward....[3]

"For the Honor of the Good Old North State, Forward"

Pettigrew's Division Moves Forward on the Confederate Left

Brigadier General James Johnson Pettigrew trotted his horse up to the center of his assembled troops. On either side, soldiers in gray and butternut spread out for hundreds of yards. Pettigrew was a dashing figure—dark-haired, dark-eyed, with a long, neatly groomed goatee—and at age thirty-four, he was also a genuine intellectual. He had grown up on a prosperous North Carolina plantation, where he immersed himself in his father's 3,000-volume library. To overcome a childhood illness, he became an accomplished boxer and fencer. A mathematics genius, he entered the University of North Carolina at age fourteen, and received an illustrious astronomy professorship at the National Observatory upon graduating. Soon bored, he became a lawyer in Charleston, South Carolina, but left that to tour Europe, mastering six languages, including Hebrew. Upon returning home, he authored a book on Spanish culture, became colonel of a militia company, served in the state legislature, and provoked controversy by opposing reopening of the slave trade—all by the age of thirty.

In Confederate service, he quickly rose to brigadier general, although he was wounded and captured at the Battle of Seven Pines. Recovered and released in a prisoner exchange, he was given command of the brigade he led to Gettysburg, where he took over Heth's division when Heth was wounded. He too planned to ride into battle on horseback, and intended to go all the way to the enemy's line. In front of him now, at the head of his brigade and at the center of Pettigrew's assembled division, was Colonel James K. "Jimmie" Marshall, who at age twenty-four was the youngest front-line brigade commander in the assault force. The grandson of U.S. Supreme Court chief justice John Marshall, young Jimmie had been promoted from commander of the 52nd North Carolina Infantry to head Pettigrew's former brigade—a Virginian leading North Carolinians. Now, as Pickett's division advanced to their right, the troops of Pettigrew's division were ready to go. Pettigrew looked at Marshall and stated: "Now Colonel for the Honor of the Good Old North State Forward."

Pettigrew led his division to within yards of the Federal line on Cemetery Ridge, "guiding right" to maneuver the assault toward the clump of trees at the center of the Federal line just as Pickett's division likewise shifted to the left. Despite displays of valor and determination aplenty, Pettigrew's division was driven back after momentarily reaching the Federal line. Pettigrew reportedly had three horses shot from under him and suffered a wounded arm before retreating with his troops. Young Colonel "Jimmie" Marshall was shot dead off his horse with a bullet in the forehead. Raked by Federal artillery fire, struck by flanking fire from their left, and savaged by volley fire from the Federal infantry, thousands of Pettigrew's troops fell dead or wounded. "A storm of grape and canister tore its way from man to man," a Federal artilleryman would later recollect, "and marked its track with corpses straight down their line." With Cemetery Ridge looming just ahead, Pettigrew's troops were forced to retreat.

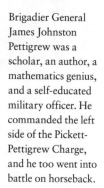

Brigadier General James Johnston Pettigrew was a scholar, an author, a mathematics genius, and a self-educated military officer. He commanded the left side of the Pickett-Pettigrew Charge, and he too went into battle on horseback.

Southern Historical Collection, University of North Carolina

A skeleton of troops from the 26th North Carolina Infantry marched at the center of Pettigrew's division in Marshall's Brigade. Of the 800 men who had come to Gettysburg with the huge regiment, a mere 230 had survived the first day's near-annihilation on McPherson's Ridge in any condition to join the Pickett-Pettigrew Charge. Even so, troops from the 26th made it all the way to the center of the Federal line on Cemetery Ridge, despite enduring a longer assault route than other regiments. Less than a hundred returned from the charge unharmed, leaving the 26th North Carolina Infantry with the grim, unique legacy of suffering "the severest regimental loss during the war." Two soldiers from the 26th, advancing beneath their regimental battle flag, somehow reached the stone wall near the clump of trees on

Like Pickett's troops, Pettigrew's division had to cross a wide-open killing field to reach the center of the Federal line. Federal artillery fire, noted a Northern soldier, "marked its track with corpses straight down their line." Artist and bugler Charles W. Reed, who was engaged at Gettysburg, sketched the action.

Library of Congress

Cemetery Ridge. "Come over on this side of the Lord," a Yankee soldier called to them, and pulled them over to safety as prisoners.

Captain Thomas J. Cureton, a company commander in the 26th, was one of the few officers in the regiment who survived the first day's fighting unharmed. Of nine captains, only Cureton and two others had escaped unscathed. Cureton would be one of a handful of officers in the regiment who would survive the first day's fight on McPherson's Ridge and the Pickett-Pettigrew Charge. In 1890, on the eve of the twenty-seventh anniversary of Gettysburg, he would write to his former regimental commander, Colonel John R. Lane, sharing his recollections of the Pickett-Pettigrew Charge.

Charlotte, N.C., June 22, 1890
Col J.R. Lane

Dear Sir

I rec'd a letter from Col W.H.S. Burgwyn stating you were to make a speech at Pittsboro about 7ᵗʰ August—on the 26ᵗʰ Regiment at Gettysburg and as I am the only living officer (I know of) that went through both days' engagements and Falling Waters etc from the 26ᵗʰ Regiment N.C.T., I decided to write you again and be more explicit, as I only wrote of the first day's engagement and the charge of 1ˢᵗ July 1863, and said nothing of the Charge 3ʳᵈ July. Hope you will have the speech published and send me a copy....

It was early in the morning July 3ʳᵈ 1863—the writer and Capt Wagg, Company A 26ᵗʰ, walked forward to view the position occupied by the enemy. We saw a ridge about a mile to a mile and a half from us, a High and elevated position with a Beautiful Valley covered with grass and a long fence stretching through rather diagonally across. No trees or anything, not even a hill, to protect a charging line from artillery etc—only the long fences. The ridge we occupied was splendid for defense. "Pickett's Division" was on our right, Pettigrew's Brigade rested on Pickett's left. Joe Davis' Mississippi Brigade was on our left and (I think) Archer's Tennessee Brigade was on Davis' left—and Brockenbrough's Va. on Archer's left, but am not certain about Archer and Brockenbrough. 100 pieces of artillery lined the ridge in our front and right, which was known to our men was to open fire at 12 o'clock.

Two lines were formed in our rear which was understood was to be for our support. It was known as soon as our artillery ceased firing we were to charge. The 26ᵗʰ Regiment was the left Regiment of Pettigrew's Brigade. Maj John Jones (afterwards Lt Col) commanded the 26ᵗʰ. Col Marshall, 52ⁿᵈ N.C.T. commanded the Brigade Genl Pettigrew commanded (Heth's Division). Every precaution was taken, showing something desperate was to be done. The chaplains of "Pickett's Division" held services—alas—ours were at the Hospital nursing the wounded and consoling the dying—from the first day's engagement—and we had no religious consolations, only from what we could hear from Pickett's chaplains and the singing Hymns etc. It reminded me of Bruce at Bannockburn etc.

Promptly at 12 o'clock, Genl Pendelton, Genl Lee's chief of artillery, fired the signal gun and then 100 guns opened fire— promptly replied to by the enemy—not once can have an idea of this artillery duel. The very ground trembled under it as if an Earthquake. Tis said that it broke window glass three miles in the rear, but the guns did our line very little injury as we were protected by the Hill, etc.

As soon as the artillery ceased, Genl Pettigrew rode up to Col Marshal in front of the Brigade with the Bright Look he (Pettigrew) always wore in the Hour of danger, and said, "Now Colonel for the Honor of the Good Old North State forward." Colonel Marshall promptly repeated the command, which was repeated by regimental commanders etc. We marched pass the valley down the Hill into the valley between the lines (with the Confederate Yell). As we marched forward our artillery would occasionally fire a shot over our heads as if to let us know we had friends in the rear. The enemy's artillery did not open on us till we got within about a Half mile of the works.

After we got in the valley out from the trees etc, the writer looked to the right and left and as far as the eye could see on either side saw that splendid sight of a perfect line of battle. But the enemy's artillery opened on up with Grape, Canister and such. Our lines crossed the lane in splendid order. When about two hundred yards from their works, the musketry opened on us but nothing daunted our brave men. We pressed quickly forward and when we had reached within about Forty yards of the works our regiment had been reduced to a skirmish line by the constant falling of the men at every step. But still they kept closing to the colors.

We were still pressing quickly forward when a cry came from the left and I looked and saw the right regiment of Davis' Mississippi Brigade, our left regiment, driven from the field as chaff before a "Whirl Wind"—the entire left of the line was gone. We were then exposed to a front and enfiladed fire. What could we do. Nothing. Only retire as quickly as possible which we did. The writer and some other officers tried to form our men in the Lane where they were somewhat protected by the Road and would have succeeded but a line of the enemy had moved outside of the works to the left, and were quickly advancing down the fences, capturing every man they could find. We called the men's attention to it and left in a hurry. Despite the warning many remained and were captured.

The writer made his way back to the artillery, selecting as the course the best and safest route, but before he reached the artillery or starting point he run up to a solitary man in front. When he looked at him it was Genl J. Johnston Pettigrew. Three (3) horses had been killed under him in the charge that day and now wounded in the arm he was making his way out on foot. I promptly asked him if I could assist him. He thanked me, offered me his unwounded arm and I assisted him up the steep little hill to the artillery. Just then two privates of Archer's Brigade, seeing Genl Pettigrew and recognizing him as the Division Commander, Genl Pettigrew ordered me to station them (separated) in rear of the guns and tell every man of Heth's Division to rally and form there. Our Brigade promptly rallied and formed when told where to go, but we could do nothing with "Pickett's Men" though we appealed to them to stay and help us protect the artillery—as it had not supports—they went on to the rear.

By night we had a pretty good skirmish line and the Gallant old 26th Regiment had sixty seven muskets and three (3) officers present—on the night of July 3rd 1863—of the eight hundred and fifty carried into the fight July 1st 1863. My tale is about told. We lay

behind our artillery all night and all day July 4ᵗʰ 1863. The enemy's
pickets communicated it to ours, or it got out some way, that Pem-
berton had surrendered Vicksburg Miss that day. I have never liked
the 4ᵗʰ July since. About dark that night we commenced slowly
falling back through the mountains to Hagerstown, Md.

Yours Truly

T.J. Cureton[4]

"Arms, Heads, Blankets, Guns
and Knapsacks Were Tossed into the Air"

Federal Troops Unleash a Deadly Flank Fire
against Pettigrew's Division

From atop Cemetery Ridge, Brigadier General Alexander Hays watched the dense ranks of Pettigrew's troops advance toward his position. Hays's division manned the right side of the Federal center, just to the right of General Gibbon's division. It was composed of troops from New York, Delaware, Connecticut, Ohio, Rhode Island, and New Jersey—and most of Pettigrew's assault force was headed straight for them. Their commander, General Hays—known as "Sandy" to those close to him—had five days until his forty-fourth birthday. A burly, towering Pennsylvanian—a U.S. Congressman's son—Hays had graduated from West Point in the same class as General Hancock, and came to be known for a personality that was alternately cheerful, affectionate, opinionated, and brash. Robust and athletic, he was a superb horseman, an expert marksman with a pistol, and he also cherished poetry, classic literature, and flowers. He was a combat veteran of the Mexican War, where he had been wounded in action and promoted for gallantry.

After a stint as a "Forty-Niner" in the California gold fields, he had worked as a civil engineer until the war led him back into the army. In less than a year and a half, he had risen from captain to brigadier general. Wounded at Second Bull Run, he had only recently taken command of his division—the 3rd Division

of Hancock's Second Corps—which he had affectionately dubbed his "Blue Birds" in recognition of
their blue insignia. As Pettigrew's troops steadily
marched his way, Hays rode up and down his line,
encouraging his troops. "Now, boys," he shouted,
"you will see some fun!" He finally dismounted and
paced his line, ordering his troops to hold their fire
until Pettigrew's crowded ranks were well in range.
Then, when the Southerners were no more than 200
yards away, he shouted the order: "Fire!" Many of
the men in gray were hit as they were scaling the rail
fences that flanked the Emmitsburg Road. The hail
of volley fire sounded like "large rain drops pattering
on the roof" to some of Pettigrew's men. Recalled
one North Carolinian, "The time it took to climb to
the top of the fence seemed, to me, an age of suspense."

Commanding the
sector of the Federal
line in the path of
Pettigrew's division
was Brigadier
General Alexander
Hays. Bold and
brash, he treated
combat like a sport.
"Now, boys," he
yelled to his troops,
"you'll see some fun."
National Archives

As his "Blue Birds" poured fire into the staggering Confederate line, General Hays looked above the struggle in his front to see
another thin line of Confederates approaching on his far right
flank. It was the remnants of Brockenbrough's former brigade—
the Virginia troops commanded by Colonel Robert Mayo.
Reduced in strength when the troops of the 22nd Virginia ran
away during the Federal artillery barrage, Mayo's Virginians had
started late. Their route of attack took them within easy range of
the 8th Ohio Infantry, which was posted far in front of Hays's
extreme right flank. The Ohioans, commanded by Lieutenant Colonel Franklin
Sawyer, savaged Mayo's troops with a ferocious flank fire followed by a bayonet
charge, which sent the Virginians reeling in retreat.

Sawyer then ordered his regiment to shift its fire toward the next closest
Confederate troops, and was joined by about seventy-five marksmen from the
First Massachusetts sharpshooters. Hays saw the effect of the 8th Ohio's fire on
Mayo's men and rushed two New York regiments—the 108th and the 126th—

An officer of the 39th New York Infantry practices his aim. The fire from the 39th and other Northern regiments on the Federal right was so fierce that one of Pettigrew's Confederates compared its effect to hog-butchering.

over to his far right flank to increase the fire. Together, they unleashed a staggering flank fire against the left side of Pettigrew's division, taking down and driving away Davis's Brigade just as its thin line was heading up the slope toward Cemetery Ridge. As the Federal flank fire cleared out Davis's troops, it tore into the surviving troops of Marshall's Brigade and then struck the support troops coming in from behind—General James H. Lane's brigade of Trimble's division. Slammed with searing infantry fire from the front and side, and blasted by Federal artillery just as they approached the crest of Cemetery Ridge, the entire left side of Pettigrew's assault force fell back in retreat.

In 1881, Lieutenant Colonel Sawyer, commander of the 8th Ohio Infantry, would publish a history of his regiment, in it recounting in gruesome detail the critically important flanking fire his regiment unleashed against Pettigrew's troops.

Finally the artillery ceased firing, and all knew that an assault was the next movement. Soon we saw the long line of rebel infantry emerge from the woods along the rebel front, that had hitherto concealed them.

These troops were the division of PICKETT, followed by that of PETTIGREW. They moved up splendidly, deploying into column as they crossed the long, sloping interval between the Second Corps and their base. At first it looked as if their line of march would sweep our position, but as they advanced their direction lay considerably to our left, but soon a strong line, with flags, directed its march immediately upon us.

I formed the few remaining braves in a single line, and as the rebels came within short range of our skirmish line, charged them. Some fell, some run back, most of them, however, threw down their arms and were made prisoners. In this maneuver among the killed was Lieut. HAYDEN, Co. H. We changed our front, and taking position by a fence, facing the left flank of the advancing column of rebels, the men were ordered to fire into their flank at will. Hardly a musket had been fired at this time. The front of the column was nearly up the slope, and within a few yards of the line of the Second Corps' front and its batteries, when suddenly a terrific fire from every available gun, from the Cemetery to Round Top Mountain, burst upon them. The distinct, graceful lines of the rebels underwent an instantaneous transformation.

They were at once enveloped in a dense cloud of smoke and dust. Arms, heads, blankets, guns and knapsacks were thrown and tossed into the clear air. Their track, as they advanced, was strewn with dead and wounded. A moan went up from the field, distinctly to be heard amid the storm of battle, but on they went, too much enveloped in smoke and dust now to permit us to distinguish their lines or movements, for the mass appeared more like a cloud of moving smoke and dust than a column of troops. Still it advanced amid the now deafening roar of artillery and storm of battle.

Suddenly the column gave way, the sloping landscape appeared covered, all at once, with the scattered and retreating foe. A withering sheet of missiles swept after them, and they were torn and tossed and prostrated as they ran. It seemed as if not one would escape. Of the mounted officers who rode so grandly in the advance not one was to be seen on the field, all had gone down.

The Eighth advanced and cut off three regiments, or remnants of regiments, as they passed us, taking their colors, and capturing many prisoners. The colors captured were those of the Thirty-fourth North Carolina, Thirty-eighth Virginia, and one that was taken from the captor, Sergt. MILLER, Co. G, by a staff officer, the number of the regiment not being remembered.

The battle was now over. The field was covered with the slain and wounded, and everywhere were to be seen white handkerchiefs held up asking for quarter. The rebel loss had been terrible, the victory to the Union army complete....[5]

"It Was a Slaughter-Pen"

Federal Infantry and Artillery Shatter Pettigrew's Ranks

Pettigrew's shredded ranks did not quit easily. As they were shot down in droves climbing the fences flanking the Emmitsburg Road, more followed, leaving the bloody roadway carpeted with bodies. Those who made it over the fence and surged up the slope toward Cemetery Ridge were shot down, swept away by artillery fire, or taken prisoner. As Pettigrew's troops made their climactic surge toward the stone wall, a gun crew from Captain William A. Arnold's battery of the 1st Rhode Island Light Artillery unleashed a blast of canister almost in the faces of the Southerners leading the charge. "The number four obeyed orders," a Federal artilleryman would recall, "and the gap made in that North Carolina regiment was simply terrible."

Advancing on the far right flank of Pettigrew's division were the survivors of Archer's brigade from the first day's fighting—now commanded by Colonel Birkett Fry. As they converged on the center of the Federal line near the clump of trees, they merged with the troops of Pickett's division, and Tennesseans charged up the slope toward the stone wall alongside Virginians. As his troops neared their objective, Colonel Fry felt certain they were going to break the Federal line and achieve victory, when suddenly he went down with a serious

leg wound. When some of his men stopped to help him, he waved them forward. "Go on," he shouted, "it will not last five minutes longer." Smoke obscured his vision as he heard the roar of rifle fire increase. Then the firing subsided and he heard rousing cheers—enemy cheers. He knew then that the charge had been repulsed. "All of the five regimental colors of my command reached the line of the enemy's works, and many of my men and officers were killed or wounded after passing over it," he would later report. "I believe the same was true of other brigades in General Pettigrew's command."

Southern troops had to scale the fences flanking the Emmitsburg Road in order to assault the center of the Federal line. As they climbed the rails, they were pummeled with searing volley fire from the Federal defenders.

National Archives

As Pettigrew's front-line brigades faltered and fell back from the crest of Cemetery Ridge, troops from General Trimble's two support brigades—under General Lane and under Colonel Lee J. William Lowrance—piled up in the body-littered Emmitsburg Road and in the fields west of it and took to the ground. Lane tried to get his troops up and moving again—until he was frantically admonished by one of his officers. "My God!" the officer cried over the racket of battle. "General, do you intend sending your men into such a place

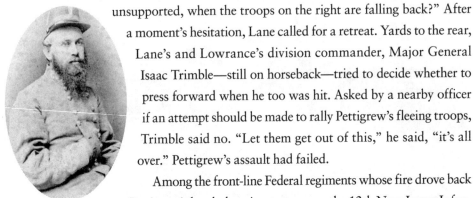

unsupported, when the troops on the right are falling back?" After a moment's hesitation, Lane called for a retreat. Yards to the rear, Lane's and Lowrance's division commander, Major General Isaac Trimble—still on horseback—tried to decide whether to press forward when he too was hit. Asked by a nearby officer if an attempt should be made to rally Pettigrew's fleeing troops, Trimble said no. "Let them get out of this," he said, "it's all over." Pettigrew's assault had failed.

Among the front-line Federal regiments whose fire drove back Pettigrew's hard-charging troops was the 12th New Jersey Infantry. Posted with other regiments of Hays's division behind the stone wall near the clump of trees, the Jersey men had armed themselves with buck-and-ball ammunition—cartridges loaded with a 69-caliber musket ball and three or more buckshot slugs. When Pettigrew's men surged up the slope toward them, the troops of the 12th New Jersey delivered "a sheet of flame." Lieutenant Richard S. Thompson, an officer of the 12th New Jersey, would later chronicle the fight that unfolded before his eyes.

Brigadier General James H. Lane saw the Federal fire stall his support troops at the Emmitsburg Road. "My God!" exclaimed one of his officers, "General, do you intend sending your men into such a place....?"

Wikimedia Commons Images

From their cover, on the wooded slope of Seminary Ridge, emerged the assaulting column of the enemy. It advanced in double line of battle, with a strong force of skirmishers in front. The right of their line consisted of three brigades of Pickett's division, with Wilcox's brigade in support of their right flank; the left of their column consisted of the four brigades of Heth's division, then under command of General Pettigrew, closely supported by the brigades of Scales and Lane of Pender's division, under the command of General Trimble. Two batteries of artillery also advanced in support of the assaulting column. On they came, a column seventeen thousand strong, with flags flying, bands playing, and arms at right shoulder shift. All in open sight of friend and foe, over the green valley they marched in "battle's magnificently stern array...."

Commencing at the right of Hays's division, which rested on Zeigler's Grove, the front line was occupied as follows: Thirty-ninth New York; One Hundred and Twenty-sixth New York, of Willard's brigade; then followed the Twelfth New Jersey, First Delaware, and Fourteenth Connecticut, of Smyth's brigade, in the order named. In rear of the right regiment at Zeigler's Grove was stationed Woodruff's Battery I, First U.S. Artillery, supported by the One Hundred and Eighth New York, of Smyth's brigade. While in rear of the Twelfth New Jersey and the First Delaware were the One Hundred and Eleventh New York and One Hundred and Twenty-fifth New York, of Willard's brigade.

At the left of Hays's division the low wall, made of loose stones and fence rails, turned at a right angle to the front for about fifty feet, and then at a right angle resumed the general southerly direction toward Round Top. On the left of Smyth's brigade of Hays's division, and with their right resting in the advance angle of this wall, were the brigades of Webb, Hall, and Harrow, of Gibbon's division, in the order named, with Stannard's brigade of the Third division of the First corps thrown out in front on the left. Gibbon's division, in order from right to left, in the front line, was as follows: Seventy-first Pennsylvania; Sixty-ninth Pennsylvania, of Webb's brigade; Fifty-ninth New York; Seventh Michigan; Twentieth Massachusetts, of Hall's brigade; Nineteenth Maine; Fifteenth Massachusetts; First Minnesota; and Eighty-second New York, of Harrow's brigade. In rear of Webb's brigade was Cushing's Battery A, Fourth U.S. Artillery, supported by the Seventy-second Pennsylvania, of Webb's brigade. In rear of Hall's front were Brown's Battery B, First Rhode Island Artillery, and Rorty's Battery B, First New York Artillery, supported by the Forty-second New York and the Nineteenth Massachusetts, of Hall's brigade, while Arnold's Battery A, First Rhode Island Artillery, was stationed in rear of the junction of these two divisions.

The distance between the lines of the two armies at the point in question was between 1,300 and 1,400 yards. The charging column advanced for some time without interruption, the enemy's artillery continuing its fire upon the divisions of Hays and Gibbon. When about a third of the distance had been covered by the advancing column, the Union artillery stationed on the left, toward Round Top, opened fire. The bands of the enemy then retired. As the assaulting column neared our line, the artillery of the enemy ceased its fire on the divisions of Hays and Gibbon, and turned its attention to the batteries in the other portions of the line....

Relieved from the cannonade, we immediately unfurled and raised our colors. The batteries in the divisions of Hays and Gibbon had nothing but canister left. As the enemy came within canister range, these batteries opened. Hundreds fell, but from the fact that their lines were somewhat converging, the tendency was to thicken, rather than leave the gaps open.

Our infantry held their fire until the enemy were within about 250 yards, when a sheet of flame flashed along our front and the rifle regiments were in action. For a moment the enemy hesitated, in the next they returned the fire, which they continued as the advance progressed.

The Twelfth New Jersey regiment had about four hundred men in line. They were armed, as already stated, with smoothbore Springfield muskets. The regulation cartridge contained a ball and three buckshot; but the men always provided themselves with extra buckshot, and on occasions like this, when close work was to be done, added a generous supply of buckshot to the regulation charge. General Hays ordered that this regiment be kept down until the enemy were within forty yards. Hence, on its immediate front seemed the safest road to our line.

As the alignment of the advance became more and more broken, there was a very decided thickening and doubling up in the position of apparent least resistance. It was with the greatest difficulty that the men were kept down, and when the mass in that front was less than fifty yards away, and the men could be restrained no longer, the caution was given, "Aim low." The order that followed was neither needed nor heard; it was drowned in the roar of musketry, and the position of least resistance was to be looked for somewhere else.

The front of the column opposite Smyth's brigade went down. The brigades of Scales and Lane of Pender's division, being immediately in rear of Heth's right, were staggered for a moment, but, recovering, advanced over the fallen double line of Heth's division in the face of a fire that had settled into that continuous character where firing is at will instead of by volley. Soon all semblance of the enemy's line of battle was abandoned; yet still they advanced until the foremost reached a position about twelve to fifteen yards from our line, when the entire force in front of Hays's division gave way, not in sullen retreat, but in disordered flight. Many threw themselves upon the ground to escape the deadly fire. Large numbers of Hays's division rushed to the front to capture battle-flags and secure prisoners.

As the firing on Hays's front ceased, we discovered the enemy's flags flying in the angle to the front on our left, where Pickett's division had broken through the line held by Webb's brigade of Gibbon's division. Instantly Smyth's brigade opened an oblique fire on the left of this mass of Pickett's division occupying the angle. Stannard's brigade was pouring upon them a destructive fire from their right rear, while Gibbon's division, on their front and right,

was bravely closing in on them. It was a slaughter-pen. Pickett's
temporary success was soon over and the remnant of his division
in flight....[6]

"You Can Never Know What
This Has Cost Me"

General Lewis A. Armistead and His Friend the Enemy

On the Confederate right, Federal artillery raked the troops of Pickett's division as they crossed more than a half-mile of open fields. For much of the way they were somewhat protected by a swale—low ground—but when they emerged near the Emmitsburg Road, they were scoured with deadly artillery fire from General Hunt's well-placed guns. On they came, absorbing their losses, and moving forward. When huge gaps were torn in the ranks by incoming rounds, they "closed ranks"—sliding toward each other to fill the open spaces—and kept going. Garnett's front-line brigade shifted to the left as it advanced, aiming for the distant clump of trees. Its ranks had been thinned by the Federal artillery fire, and as the troops neared the fences lining the Emmitsburg Road, they slowed their pace—which allowed the troops of General Armistead's Brigade to catch up with them and join their ranks as they pressed forward.

Forty-six-year-old Brigadier General Lewis A. Armistead led his troops toward the enemy line on Cemetery Hill with a unique burden: the Second Corps Federal troops posted there were commanded by his dear friend, General Winfield Scott Hancock. Armistead, a North Carolinian, came from a prominent family with a tradition of American military service and a parade of American presidents in its lineage, including James Monroe and John Tyler. He had entered West Point, but was dismissed after two years for allegedly breaking a plate on the head of another cadet—the future Confederate general Jubal Early. Armistead saw combat in the Seminole War and in the Mexican War, where he was decorated for valor three times. Highly disciplined but soft-spoken and attentive, he developed close friendships with his fellow officers, especially Hancock. He and Hancock had served in the Mexican War, and Armistead—who had been widowed twice—developed a deep friendship with Hancock and his wife Almira. Posted to California before the war, he was often a guest in the Hancock home. When Virginia seceded, his loyalties were torn between his state and his nation. He finally chose Virginia, which led to a heart-wrenching farewell with his friend Hancock, a Pennsylvanian who decided to side with the North.

The final parting of Armistead, Hancock, and other officers occurred at Hancock's home in Los Angeles, where the group of officers was posted. Almira Russell Hancock would later describe the last meeting between Armistead and Hancock before they went their separate ways to become "enemies" at war.

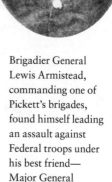

Brigadier General Lewis Armistead, commanding one of Pickett's brigades, found himself leading an assault against Federal troops under his best friend— Major General Winfield S. Hancock.

Reminiscences of the Civil War

A never-to-be-forgotten evening was the one spent at our home by the officers who were to start upon their overland trip to the South at 12 o'clock that night. General and Mrs. Johnston were of the party. Before leaving, the General said to his wife, "Come, sing me one or two of the old songs you used to sing, 'Mary of Argyle' and 'Kathleen Mavourneen.'" She complied reluctantly in the presence of such an audience, saying, with deep emotion, that she felt as though her music days were over. Those songs will ever be remembered by the survivors of that mournful gathering. All were endeavoring to conceal, under smiling exteriors, hearts that were filled with sadness over the sundering of life-long ties, and doubts as to the result of their sacrifice.

The most crushed of the party was Major Armistead, who, with tears, which were contagious, streaming down his face, and hands upon Mr. Hancock's shoulders, while looking him steadily in the eye, said, "Hancock, good-by; you can never know what this has cost me, and I hope God will strike me dead if I am ever induced to leave my native soil, should worse come to worst." Turning to me, he placed a small satchel in my hand, requesting that it should not be opened except in the event of his death, in which case the souvenirs it contained, with the exception of a little prayer-book, intended for me, and which I still possess, should be sent to his family. On the fly-leaf of this book is the following: "Lewis A. Armistead. Trust in God and fear nothing." At the same time he presented Mr. Hancock with a new major's uniform, saying that "he might sometime need it...."[7]

"At Every Volley, the Gray Uniforms Fall Thick and Fast"

Timely Flanking Fire by a Vermont Brigade Shatters Pickett's Right

On Armistead's right, Brigadier General James Lawson Kemper advanced his brigade through the swale and up toward the fences flanking the Emmitsburg Road. At forty, Kemper was a burly, dark-haired Virginian who sported a bushy, black, chest-length beard. Before the war, he had been the Speaker of the House in the Virginia legislature and had raised his own regiment for Confederate service. His courage in battle had quickly vaulted him from colonel to brigadier general. Now he rushed his troops through the hail of artillery fire toward the ridge ahead, ordering the "guide left" that shifted their approach to converge on the clump of trees at the center of the Federal line. Meanwhile, a calamity unraveled for Kemper's troops: the support troops that were supposed to be following his brigade—Wilcox's and Lang's two brigades—had started late for some reason and were nowhere near. Kemper's Brigade, now completely exposed on its right flank, with no other Southern troops alongside or coming up in support.

Up ahead to the right, meanwhile, a brigade of Federal troops from Vermont was posted out in front of the Federal far left flank, positioned there due to the

In the distance, the Pickett-Pettigrew Charge approaches Cemetery Ridge and the targeted clump of trees at its center. Artist Edwin Forbes watched the attack from Federal lines, then sketched it from the Southern perspective.

Library of Congress

lay of the land. They had been put there by Major General Abner Doubleday, who was supporting Hancock's line with some of his First Corps troops. Doubleday thought the brigade of Vermonters might be useful on the far left flank of Hancock's line—and he was right. The brigade commander was Brigadier General George J. Stannard. A balding, bearded, unpretentious, and no-nonsense leader, Stannard was a merchant-turned-commander who had banished drunkards and shirkers from his ranks and had shaped his brigade of nine-month volunteers into a dependable fighting force. Stannard took a look at Kemper's advancing Confederates—completely unprotected on their right flank—and realized his troops were in a position to advance and deliver a potentially damaging flank fire into the Rebels as they charged past.

Stannard was not alone in his thinking: when the detached force from Hays's division opened the flank fire on General Pettigrew's left flank, General Hancock, viewing the battle from horseback, saw Pettigrew's Confederates falling like a row of dominoes under the devastating flank fire delivered by the troops General Hays had deployed in front of his far right flank. Hancock wheeled his horse and galloped for the other side of his line, where he knew the Vermont troops were posted to the front and might be advanced to provide flanking fire. On the way, he was waved down by a frantic-looking officer, Colonel Arthur Devereux, commander of the 19th Massachusetts Infantry, one of the regiments being held in reserve to support Hancock's line. Devereux pointed to the center of the line around the clump of trees and yelled, "They have broken through! Shall I get in there!" At the center of the line, in a swirl of smoke and movement, Hancock could see a forward surge of bodies, topped by Confederate battle flags, that was driving his troops backward. "Go at it!" he yelled, along with a blast of profanity, and raced his horse down his line toward the Vermonters.

When Hancock reached Stannard's troops, the general already had them moving. Troops from two regiments—the 13th and the 16th Vermont Infantry—advanced out of the swale where they had been posted and moved forward, staying low. Kemper's Brigade of Confederates had crossed the Emmitsburg Road and was heading up the slope of Cemetery Ridge. As Kemper's men rushed past just yards away, the Vermonters suddenly rose up and delivered a murderous fire into the Confederate right flank. "At this short range," a Vermont officer would later recollect, "the Thirteenth fired 10 or 12 rounds, and the Sixteenth perhaps half that number, into a mass of men on which every bullet took effect, and many doubtless found two or three victims. The effect upon the Confederate mass was instantaneous. Its progress ceased." As it had done on the other side of the Federal line, the fierce flanking fire toppled great ranks of men in gray and butternut like a row of falling bricks. Many of the survivors, shocked by the surprise flank fire, threw down their weapons and raised their hands.

Other troops swerved away from the deadly blast on their right, leaving a mass of dead and wounded on the field, and merged with Garnett's surviving troops heading still for the center of the Federal line on Cemetery Hill. Their advance was slowed by the deadly shock wave from their right, however, and then they were further mauled by sustained infantry fire coming from the front. Reduced to a mere few hundred in number and still led by Kemper, they breached the low stone wall south of the clump of trees and in front of field artillery manned by troops from Battery B of the 1st New York Light Artillery. "There are the guns, boys," Kemper yelled, "Go for them!" Boldly, the Virginians surged toward the Federal cannon—and took a blast of canister directly into their ranks. With their numbers already reduced by Stannard's Vermonters, Kemper's troops were now too few in number to overwhelm the Federal defenders behind the wall. Kemper went down as well, shot in the spine and crippled for life. His men fell back, many of them surrendering, and Kemper's assault was spent. As Kemper's troops were falling back, the two tardy brigades of Confederates under Wilcox and Lang finally came up—but Stannard's Vermonters opened fire on them and turned them back. Later, General Doubleday would say that the Vermont troops had "saved the day, and with it, the whole North...."

A half-century after Gettysburg, Private Ralph O. Sturtevant of the 13th Vermont Infantry would recount his regiment's dramatic role in repulsing the Pickett-Pettigrew Charge.

The left flank of General Stannard's brigade was well down on the low flat ground of Plum Run behind thick copse that lined its banks and mostly out of sight of the enemy, and therefore suffered but little from Longstreet's artillery. The troops of the First, Second and Third corps were closely massed on and about this central position with the Eleventh and Twelfth corps on the right and the Fifth and Sixth corps with Kilpatrick's cavalry on the left and artillery planted over the whole field where it would be best in hand for most effective use. And all arranged and placed to make our position impregnable and secure, against the Rebel host....

It was summer, the day was perfect and all nature about seemed dressed in its richest color for the slaughter of precious lives and passage of thousands of immortal souls from that field of glory to realms beyond. Everything had been determined and nothing could prevent the carnage soon to follow. The artillery opened, concentrating its fire against the left center the salient point of which, was occupied and held by the Vermonters of General Stannard's brigade. The tremendous roar of cannon, the crack and crash of shell, the exploding caissons here and there, the horrid whiz of shrapnel, the consternation and anxiety, all this held us prostrate and fast to the ground anxiously watching and waiting for the guns to cease firing.

We of the 13th now realized the value of the low breastworks of rails that protected us during the deadly storm.... Suddenly the cannon ceased on Cemetery Hill and from battery to battery all along our lines until every Federal gun was silent followed in a few moments with complete suspension of Confederate cannonading. We knew the time had come for the final charge and eagerly gazed and watched the crest of Seminary Ridge across the valley expecting each moment to see the long lines of gray with tilted bayonets glistening in the sunshine rapidly approaching....

We saw them first as they reached the crest of Seminary Ridge a full half mile away, at first horse and rider, then glistening bayonets and then flags and banners waving and fluttering in the sultry air could be seen. Suddenly a battery opened on Cemetery Hill with deafening roar, and sent hurling across the valley into the approaching columns the first complimentary salute that warned them that all of our guns had not been silenced by their hundred and fifty guns during the early hours of the afternoon, but on they come regardless of exploding shells hurled against them, turning not to the right or left climbing the fences and walls, quickly reached the Emmitsburg Road, passed on both sides of the Cadora House and other buildings in that locality making momentary openings in their lines as they [passed]....

They crossed the road, reached the open field before them, moved rapidly forward in solid columns the first and second divisions in advance, and then the third in support in short echelon as they moved down the slope into the valley from the Emmitsburg Road. The charging columns were now in plain sight and range of our guns from Round Top to Ziegler's Grove which with an infilading [sic] fire made

numerous gaps in their lines which were quickly closed, but on they came as if impelled by some unresistless force, paying no attention to the grape and canister that made gory swaths through their battle lines....

On they came regardless of the carnage among them, nearer and nearer until horse and rider, officer and private, standards and banners waving in the lead were plainly seen, and almost within musket range, the right wing now face to face with the right wing of Stannard's brigade. Down the line of the 13th regiment comes the order from company to company, "Steady boys, hold your position, don't fire until the word is given, keep cool, lie low till order is given to fire, make ready, take good aim, fire low." Then like an electric flash came down the line the order from Colonel Randall quickly repeated by every officer in the line: "Fire."

The Southern breakthrough on Cemetery Ridge is marked by furious hand-to-hand combat in this work by period artist Peter F. Rothermel, who interviewed veterans for authenticity—then, for dramatic effect, depicted most troops fighting bareheaded.

Library of Congress

Up rose the Green Mountain Boys, 3,000 strong, as if by magic with forms erect took deliberate aim and with a simultaneous flash and roar, fired into the compact ranks of the desperate foe and again and again in quick succession until a dozen or more volleys had been discharged with deadly effect. We saw at every volley the gray uniforms fall quick and fast and the front line hesitated, moved slowly and melted away, could not advance against such a curious and steady storm of bullets in their faces and the raking fire of McGilvery's batteries against their flank and midst this, unexpected fusillade of bullets, grape and canister they halted and quickly in good order massed in columns to our right uncovering the immediate front of Stannard's brigade and with an awful menacing yell dashed forward with the evident purpose of carrying the crest of Cemetery Ridge at our right and rear.

Pickett's massing of columns and verging to his left and our right opened a clear field in front of Stannard's brigade, furnishing a golden opportunity for a flank advance attack against General Pickett's advancing battle lines.

General Stannard ordered the 13th and 16th regiments of his brigade to move forward (the 14th to remain in position in support) toward the enemy, and these two regiments, the 13th and 16th, advanced about one hundred yards in quick time.... As General Stannard looked over the field his quick eye discovered the salient angle, and like a flash of lightning came the inspired thought that evolved the famous and now historic order (unique in maneuvering in the midst of battle) "Change front forward on first company." Colonel Randall repeated this order to Captain Lonergan of Company A and sent it along the line. Captain Lonergan on receiving the order halted his [company] which was the right of the line placed First Sergeant James B. Scully in position and quickly swung his company around into position and thus each company was brought into line facing the right flank of General Pickett's advancing heroes and each company as it faced into line saw in their immediate front not sixty yards away General Pickett's command charging forward up the slope and at once opened a deadly fire on their flank which surprised and disconcerted officers and rank and file alike some turned about and returned our fire but knowing their objective point moved on.

This was at short range and the concentrated fire of the 13th into the moving flank before them thickly covered the ground with the dead and wounded.... Not until then did they realize their awful situation, and then they waved handkerchiefs, and threw up their hands as evidence of surrender. It was at this juncture that Colonel Randall at risk of his own life from the muskets of his own regiment passed rapidly down the line and shouted "Stop firing." Then we advanced....

As the 13th charged forward from its last position, some of the more revengeful and desperate continued to fire in our faces as we advanced. We opened fire again and then rushed up against them with bayonets, revengefully determined to slay the very last man unless they would heed our offer of surrender. Bayonets were crossed and the desperate thrusts exchanged, and the hand to hand struggle followed. Many fell wounded and bleeding pierced with bayonet, sword and pistol and musket balls. This was the final struggle and was soon over. We were now in their front and rear and escape was impossible. The crouching rose up and all the living including the slightly wounded hurriedly and anxiously passed through our ranks to the rear, turning over their guns, pistols and sabres as they passed on.

If there was any spot on that great field of battle that approximated more nearly than any other the maelstrom of destruction this was the place. They lay one upon the other clutched in death side by side. The dead dying and horribly wounded some had on the blue but nearly all wore the gray for on a few square rods one could *hardly step so thickly lay the dead. A thousand could have been counted on less than two acres of ground. This was indeed the great slaughter pen on the field of Gettysburg and in it lay hundreds of the brave heroes who an hour before buoyed up with hope and ambition were being led ... as they fully believed, to victory....*[8]

"The Two Lines Come with a Shock"

The Pickett-Pettigrew Charge Reaches a Bloody Climax on Cemetery Ridge

Even as the right flank of Pickett's division began collapsing, General Armistead kept going. He had placed his hat on the tip of his sword—a model 1850 U.S. foot officer's sword—and he held it high so his troops could see him at the front. It was here near the Emmitsburg Road that Garnett—while riding back and forth on horseback and urging his troops forward—disappeared into the smoke, never to be seen again. Armistead and his men crossed the Emmitsburg Road, scaling or ducking through the fences that bordered it, and pushed forward up the slope toward the stone wall on Cemetery Ridge. In the final rush toward their target, Pickett's advancing battle lines compressed: Armistead's troops became mixed with Garnett's and even some of Pettigrew's troops coming up from the left. Up ahead, close now, loomed the clump of trees.

There—near what would become known as Gettysburg's "Bloody Angle"—the mass of Confederates were slammed with crushing fire—point-blank blasts of canister from the Federal artillery and torrents of volley fire from the Federal infantry behind the stone wall. The spearhead of the assault came in along the wall where it was defended by three brigades of General Gibbon's division—Brigadier General Alexander S. Webb's brigade of Pennsylvanians, troops from Massachusetts, Maine, New York, and Minnesota under Brigadier General William Harrow, and Colonel Norman J. Hall's brigade of troops from New York, Massachusetts, and Michigan. The Federal infantry there was supported by a battery of the 4th U.S. Artillery, which was commanded by twenty-two-year-old Lieutenant Alonzo H. Cushing. Horribly wounded in the stomach, holding in his intestines with his hand, Cushing insisted on staying with his guns. As he discharged his final blast of canister, he was killed by a bullet to the face. General Hunt, the army's Chief of Artillery, was shouting encouragement to his artillery crews when he too went down, dumped from the saddle when his horse was hit. Unhurt but furious, Hunt jumped to his feet and opened fire on the advancing Southerners with his revolver.

Pickett's soldiers fell in droves in front of the stone wall, but the survivors pressed on, spilling over the wall on both sides of the clump of trees and fighting hand-to-hand with the men in blue. Troops in General Webb's brigade—the Philadelphia Brigade—began to break and run for the rear. Many stood firm, however, refusing to yield, frantically firing and fighting up close. Webb desperately tried to hold his troops in place, then ran to the rear under fire and ordered up a nearby regiment. When those troops refused to go forward, he sprinted to a regiment on his left, the 69th Pennsylvania Infantry, and ordered them to turn and fire into enemy troops who were pouring over the wall. Another regiment, the 106th Pennsylvania, added its firepower, and so did two more regiments—the 19th Massachusetts and the 42nd New York—which were rushed over

When his brigade of Pennsylvanians began crumbling under the Confederate assault, Brigadier General Alexander Webb frantically collared reinforcements and rushed them forward to plug the gap.

National Archives

from the left by Colonel Devereux. It was a frenzied, ferocious standoff. For perhaps as long as twenty minutes, the two sides struggled face-to-face on Cemetery Ridge around the clump of trees. Even in the desperation of the moment, men on both sides knew the outcome of the battle would be decided in that small deadly space.

Long afterward, Ernest L. Waitt, a soldier in the 19th Massachusetts Infantry—one of the regiments rushed to reinforce the Federal line—would try to describe the desperate struggle around the "copse of trees" on Cemetery Ridge.

369

Based on eyewitness accounts and his own observations, combat artist Edwin Forbes re-recreated the moment Federal reinforcements drove back the Confederate breakthrough on Cemetery Ridge and repulsed the Pickett-Pettigrew Charge.

Library of Congress

After Pickett's division crosses the Emmitsburg Road and comes sweeping up the slope, they still bear everything before them, as if carried forward by an all-ruling fate. Their right flank just touches the Cordora house. The left, a hundred and fifty rods away, is slightly in advance. Three lines of battle are moving up…. As they cross the road only 800 yards away, huge gaps begin to show in their lines as a result of the effective fire of the Union artillery, but they are quickly closed up in magnificent style, and the line still advances. At 300 yards canister takes the place of shell and their men fall like leaves in the Autumn gale, but the great mass silently, swiftly moves forward.

They are approaching the "little oak grove" in front of which, behind a stone-wall, lies Webb's brigade of Pennsylvanians. The advancing columns close in on the infantry. With a yell they rush forward. A sheet of flame welcomes them and in its warm grasp their line melts like ice. Being obliged to cross a fence oblique to their line of advance, the rebels are crowded and closed in mass in the endeavor to regain their formation.

It is seen that Webb cannot firmly hold his men against the shock of that fierce charge, although he throws himself, with reckless courage, in front of them to face the storm and beg, threaten and command. They are obliged to fall back upon the second line.

Hall's right, overlapped, has to sag back, swaying to the rear because of the pressure, but swaying forward again as the ocean surges against a rock. Regimental organization is lost, ranks are eight or ten deep—pushing struggling, refusing to yield, but almost impotent for good.

A gap opens between Webb and Hall for a brief instant, at the time when there was a sudden lull in the firing of the cannon. Woodruff, Brown, Cushing, Rorty and every other commissioned officer, almost without exception, of their respective batteries is dead or disabled. Gen. Gibbon, commanding the division is also wounded.... "Mallon! We must move!" shouts Col. Devereux to his friend, the commander of the Forty-Second New York....

The Nineteenth Massachusetts, trained from its inception in a discipline as stern as that of Cromwell's "Ironsides," is material upon which reliance in such an emergency can be placed. With it is the Forty-Second New York, which has served by its side in the same brigade, in the camp, on the march and on the battle field from Ball's Bluff to the present moment.

Like a bolt of flame the little line is launched upon the enemy on the south side of the "Clump of Trees." The first line is struck and broken through.

The heroic regiment pauses an instant to gather breath and then, with a furious bound, goes on to the second line. As the men break through the first line, Maj. Rice is in front. With a cry "Follow me, boys!" he dashes forward and is the first man to come into contact

Lieutenant Alonzo Cushing, a twenty-two-year-old Federal artillery officer, commanded field artillery at the center of the Federal line. Although desperately wounded, he struggled to fire one last round.

Wisconsin Historical Society

with the second line. He is severely wounded through the thigh and falls inside the enemy's lines.

The two lines come together with a shock which stops them both and causes a slight rebound. For several minutes they face and fired into each other at a distance of fifteen paces, (as measured after the battle). Everything seems trembling in the balance. The side that can get in forward motion first will surely win.

The men in blue are jammed in, five and six deep. Sometimes there are groups which are even deeper and every time a man stoops to load, others crowd in ahead of him so that he will have to elbow his way through in order to get another chance to fire.

All can not be in the front rank, and the men in the rear are dodging around, firing through openings made by the changing crowd, no matter how small. There is little doubt that many are wounded in this manner, because of the rapid changes being made as the entire mass forges ahead. Muskets are exploding all around, flashing their fire almost in one's face and so close to the head as to make the ears ring—and so the battle rages.

A battery had followed the Nineteenth Massachusetts and Forty-Second New York, and, in an instant more, from rear, right and left, at pistol range, these guns poured in an iron shower. Webb's brigade came charging down. The remainder of Hall's brigade rushed down upon the left. It cleared its front. Downward to the wall they forced the rebels back and for another twenty minutes, with ball and steel and rifles clubbed, hand to hand, they plied the awful work.

A rebel color bearer came out between the trees in front of Webb and placed his battle flag upon one of Cushing's guns,—and fell dead beside it. Another ran out to get it, but before reaching the gun he too fell dead. Then several rushed out together. They all fell about

the piece and the rebel flag still waved on the Union cannon. Sub-
sequently two more flags were placed upon the gun, all of which
were captured, one of them by Corporal Joseph DeCastro, of the
Nineteenth Massachusetts, who had become separated from his
command and had joined the 72nd Pennsylvania regiment in the
tumult. He turned, broke through the line, and thrust the captured
flag into hands of Col. Devereux....

The opposing lines were standing as if rooted, dealing death
into each other. There they stood and would not move. Foot to foot,
body to body and man to man they struggled, pushed, and strived
and killed. Each had rather die than yield. The mass of wounded
and heaps of dead entangled the feet of the contestants, and, under-
neath the trampling mass, wounded men who could no longer
stand, struggled, fought, shouted and killed—hatless, coatless,
drowned in sweat, black with powder, red with blood, stifling in
the horrid heat, parched with smoke and blind with dust, with
fiendish yells and strange oaths they blindly plied the work of
slaughter....[9]

"Boys, Give Them Cold Steel!"
Victorious Northern Forces Turn back the Pickett-Pettigrew Charge

With his hat still held high on his sword point, General Armistead led the Virginians over the stone wall at "Bloody Angle" and into the ranks of the desperate Federal defenders. Before them, the men in blue began to fall away toward the rear. "Rise men!" he had told his soldiers back at their assembly point, before their long and bloody trek to the clump of trees. "Men, remember what you are fighting for—your homes, your firesides, and your sweethearts. Follow me!" Despite his forty-six years, he had led them the entire way—hustling across the deadly fields of fire yards in advance—and continued to lead once they crossed the stone wall. He had been that kind of leader in the

Southern army, promoted from colonel to brigadier general in less than a year. He and his brigade had earned a reputation as fighters on fields of fire such as Malvern Hill, Fredericksburg, and Chancellorsville. Now, as he climbed over the stone wall near the clump of trees and headed for Lieutenant Cushing's abandoned artillery, his troops were still following him—although their bloodied ranks were reduced to probably less than 200. "Boys," he shouted, "give them the cold steel."

Federal troops in greater numbers now began to stumble toward the rear—like rabbits, one soldier said—and General Lee's hope for victory once again seemed possible. But it was a fleeting moment. Yards away, General Alexander Webb was frantically pushing reinforcements forward to fill the gap in the Federal line. A veteran combat officer at age twenty-eight, Webb was a native New Yorker, the son of an American diplomat, and the grandson of one of George Washington's staff officers from the Revolutionary War. Praised by his superiors and respected by his troops, he had been engaged in many of the same battles as Armistead—Malvern Hill, Fredericksburg, and Chancellorsville—but his rank had remained stalled at lieutenant colonel. In frustration, he had been ready to quit the army, but three days before Gettysburg he received his promotion to brigadier general. He was new to command of the Philadelphia Brigade— assigned the post only days before the battle—but he proved his worth on Cemetery Ridge. He rushed troops forward to seal the break in the Federal line, directed the fire of others, and at one point even threatened to shoot a wavering color-bearer. "General Webb was everywhere," one of his men would report.

Others also rushed troops to the gap or hurried to the fight there themselves. Among them were the survivors of the 1st Minnesota Infantry, whose regiment had almost been wiped out the day before while holding the line farther to the south. Now the regiment was again responsible for helping hold the line, although its ranks were drastically reduced in numbers. Even compared to the frenzied bloodletting the 1st Minnesota had experienced on Gettysburg's second day, the fighting atop Cemetery Ridge was savage. "We were crazy with the excitement of the fight," a Minnesota officer would recall. "We just rushed in like wild beasts. Men swore and cursed and struggled and fought, grappled in hand-to-hand fights, threw stones, clubbed their muskets, kicked, yelled, and hurrahed. But it was over in no time." All but two members of Webb's 72nd Pennsylvania's color guard were shot down. In Armistead's 53rd Virginia, eight of the nine members of the color guard were killed, and the sole survivor was wounded. General Webb suffered a leg wound. General Gibbon was shot in the shoulder. General Hancock also went down, seriously wounded when a Confederate bullet sent splinters and a nail from his saddle into his upper thigh.

General Armistead was shot down, too, and his wound *was* mortal. He led his troops across the stone wall and all the way to one of Lieutenant Cushing's cannon, but as he reached his hand toward its muzzle, he was hit. When a Federal officer stooped to help him after the storm of battle, Armistead's chief concern was the welfare of his friend Hancock. The rush of Federal reinforcements proved too much for Pickett's men, who were overwhelmed after their breakthrough, and were shot down, driven back, or captured. The Confederate surge through the Federal line at "Bloody Angle," with Armistead reaching for the muzzle of a Federal cannon, would become known as the "High Water Mark of the Confederacy." As the defeated Confederates from the Pickett-Pettigrew Charge retreated, the Federal troops atop Cemetery Ridge broke into rousing cheers.

Thirty-four years after Gettysburg, Lieutenant Colonel Rawley W. Martin—an officer in Armistead's Brigade—responded to a request from a Northern veteran to record his memories of the Pickett-Pettigrew Charge—when he went all the way to Cemetery Ridge with General Armistead.

LYNCHBURG, VA., August 11, 1897.
Commander SYLVESTER CHAMBERLAIN, Buffalo, N.Y.

My dear Sir, —
In the effort to comply with your request to describe Pickett's charge at Gettysburg, I may unavoidably repeat what has often been told before, as the position of troops, the cannonade, the advance, and

the final disaster are familiar to all who have the interest or the curiosity to read. My story will be short, for I shall only attempt to describe what fell under my own observation.

You ask for a description of the "feelings of the brave Virginians who passed through that hell of fire in their heroic charge on Cemetery Ridge." The esprit du corps could not have been better; the men were in good physical condition, self reliant and determined. They felt the gravity of the situation, for they knew well the metal of the foe in their front; they were serious and resolute, but not disheartened. None of the usual jokes, common on the eve of battle, were indulged in, for every man felt his individual responsibility, and realized that he had the most stupendous work of his life before him; officers and men knew at what cost and at what risk the advance was to be made, but they had deliberately made up their minds to attempt it. I believe the general sentiment of the division was that they would succeed in driving the Federal line from what was their objective point; they knew that many, very many, would go down under the storm of shot and shell which would greet them when their gray ranks were spread out to view, but it never occurred to them that disaster would come after they once placed their tattered banners upon the crest of Seminary Ridge.

I believe if those men had been told: "This day your lives will pay the penalty of your attack upon the Federal lines," they would have made the charge just as it was made. There was no straggling, no feigned sickness, no pretence of being overcome by the intense heat; every man felt that it was his duty to make that fight; that he was his own commander, and they would have made the charge without an officer of any description; they only needed to be told what they were expected to do. This is as near the feeling of the men of Pickett's Division on the morning of the battle as I can give, and with this feeling they went to their work. Many of them were veteran soldiers, who had followed the little cross of stars from Big Bethel to Gettysburg; they knew their own power, and they knew the temper of their adversary; they had often met before, and they knew the meeting before them would be desperate and deadly.

Pickett's three little Virginia brigades were drawn up in two lines, Kemper on the right (1st, 3d, 7th, 11th and 24), Garnett on the left (8th, 18th, 19th, 28th and 56th), and Armistead in the rear and center (9th, 14th, 38th, 53d and 57th) Virginia Regiments, covering the space between Kemper's left and Garnett's right flanks. This position was assigned Armistead, I suppose, that he might at the critical moment rush to the assistance of the two leading brigades, and if possible, put the capstone upon their work. We will see presently how he succeeded. The Confederate artillery was on the crest of Seminary Ridge, nearly in front of Pickett; only a part of the division had the friendly shelter of the woods; the rest endured the scorching rays of the July sun until the opening of the cannonade, when the dangers from the Federal batteries were added to their discomfort. About 1 o'clock two signal guns were fired by the Washington Artillery, and instantly a terrific cannonade was commenced, which lasted for more than an hour, when suddenly everything was silent. Every man knew what that silence portended. The grim blue battle line on Seminary Ridge began at once to prepare for the advance of its antagonists; both sides felt that the tug of war was about to come, and that Greek must meet Greek as they had never met before.

From this point, I shall confine my description to events connected with Armistead's brigade, with which I served. Soon after the cannonade ceased, a courier dashed up to General Armistead, who was pacing up and down in front of the 53d Virginia Regiment, his battalion of direction (which I commanded in the charge and at the head of which Armistead marched), and gave him the order from General Pickett to prepare for the advance. At once the command "Attention, battalion!" rang out clear and distinct. Instantly every man was on his feet and in his place; the alignment was made with as much coolness and precision as if preparing for dress parade.

Then Armistead went up to the color sergeant of the 53d Virginia Regiment and said: "Sergeant, are you going to put those colors on the enemy's works to-day?" The gallant fellow replied: "I will try, sir, and if mortal man can do it, it shall be done." It was done, but not until this brave man, and many others like him, had fallen with their faces to the foe; but never once did that banner trail in the dust, for some brave fellow invariably caught it as it was going down, and again bore it aloft, until Armistead saw its tattered folds unfurled on the very crest of Seminary Ridge.

After this exchange of confidence between the general and the color-bearer, Armistead commanded: "Right shoulder, shift arms. Forward, march." They stepped out at quick time, in perfect order and alignment tramp, tramp, up to the Emmitsburg road; then the advancing Confederates saw the long line of blue, nearly a mile distant, ready and awaiting their coming. The scene was grand and terrible, and well calculated to demoralize the stoutest heart; but not a step faltered, not an elbow lost the touch of its neighbor, not a face blanched, for these men had determined to do their whole duty, and reckoned not the cost. On they go; at about 1,100 yards the Federal batteries opened fire; the advancing Confederates encounter and sweep before them the Federal skirmish line. Still forward they go; hissing, screaming shells break in their front, rear, on their flanks, all about them, but the devoted band, with the blue line in their front as their objective point, press forward, keeping step to the music of the battle. The distance between the opposing forces grows less and less, until suddenly the infantry behind the rock fence poured volley after volley into the advancing ranks. The men fell like stalks of grain before the reaper, but still they closed the gaps and pressed forward through that pitiless storm. The two advance brigades have thus far done the fighting. Armistead has endured the terrible ordeal without firing a gun; his brave followers have not changed their guns from the right shoulder. Great gaps have been torn in their ranks; their field and company officers have fallen; color-bearer after color-bearer has been shot down, but still they never faltered.

At the critical moment, in response to a request from Kemper, Armistead, bracing himself to the desperate blow, rushed forward to Kemper's and Garnett's line, delivered his fire, and with one supreme effort planted his colors on the famous rock fence. Armistead himself, with his hat on the point of his sword, that his men might see it through the smoke of battle, rushed forward, scaled the wall, and cried: "Boys, give them the cold steel!" By this time, the Federal hosts lapped around both flanks and made a counter advance in their front, and the remnant of those three little brigades melted away. Armistead himself had fallen, mortally wounded, under the guns he had captured, while the few who followed him over the fence were either dead or wounded. The charge was over, the sacrifice had been made, but, in the words of a Federal officer: "Banks of heroes they were; they fled not, but amidst that still continuous and terrible fire they slowly, sullenly recrossed the plain—all that was left of them—but few of the five thousand."

When the advance commenced General Pickett rode up and down in rear of Kemper and Garnett, and in this position he continued as long as there was opportunity of observing him. When the assault became so fierce that he had to superintend the whole line, I am sure he was in his proper place. A few years ago Pickett's staff held a meeting in the city of Richmond, Va., and after comparing recollections, they published a statement to the effect that he was with the division throughout the charge; that he made an effort to secure reinforcements when he saw his flanks were being turned, and one of General Garnett's couriers testified that he carried orders from him almost to the rock fence. From my knowledge of General Pickett I am sure he was where his duty called him throughout the engagement. He was too fine a soldier, and had fought too many battles not to be where he was most needed on that supreme occasion of his military life.

The ground over which the charge was made was an open terrene, with slight depressions and elevations, but insufficient to be serviceable to the advancing column. At the Emmettsburg road, where the parallel fences impeded the onward march, large numbers were shot down on account of the crowding at the openings where the fences had been thrown down, and on account of the halt in order to climb the fences. After passing these obstacles, the advancing column deliberately rearranged its lines and moved forward. Great gaps were made in their ranks as they moved on, but they were closed up as deliberately and promptly as if on the parade ground; the touch of elbows was always to the centre, the men keeping constantly in view the little emblem which was their beacon light to guide them to glory and to death.

I will mention a few instances of individual coolness and bravery exhibited in the charge. In the 53d Virginia Regiment, I saw every man of Company F (Captain Henry Edmunds, now a distinguished member of the Virginia bar) thrown flat to the earth by the explosion of a shell from Round Top, but every man who was not killed or desperately wounded sprang to his feet, collected himself and moved forward to close the gap made in the regimental front. A soldier from the same regiment was shot on the shin; he stopped in the midst of that terrific fire, rolled up his trousers leg, examined his wound, and went forward even to the rock fence. He escaped further injury, and was one of the few who returned to his friends, but so bad was his wound that it was nearly a year before he was fit for duty. When Kemper was riding off, after asking Armistead to move up to his support, Armistead called him, and, pointing to his brigade, said: "Did you ever see a more perfect line than that on dress parade?" It was, indeed, a lance head of steel, whose metal had been tempered in the furnace of conflict. As they were about to enter upon their work, Armistead, as was invariably his custom

on going into battle, said: "Men, remember your wives, your mothers, your sisters and your sweethearts." Such an appeal would have made those men assault the ramparts of the infernal regions.

You asked me to tell how the field looked after the charge, and how the men went back. This I am unable to do, as I was disabled at Armistead's side a moment after he had fallen, and left on the Federal side of the stone fence. I was picked up by the Union forces after their lines were reformed, and I take this occasion to express my grateful recollection of the attention I received on the field, particularly from Colonel Hess, of the 72d Pennsylvania (I think). If he still lives, I hope yet to have the pleasure of grasping his hand and expressing to him my gratitude for his kindness to me. Only the brave know how to treat a fallen foe.

I cannot close this letter without reference to the Confederate chief, General R. E. Lee. Somebody blundered at Gettysburg but not Lee. He was too great a master of the art of war to have hurled a handful of men against an army. It has been abundantly shown

His hat held high on his sword-tip, General Lewis Armistead leads the men of Pickett's division over the stone wall at the Center of the Federal line—at what would become known as the "High Water Mark" of the Confederacy.

Library of Congress

that the fault lay not with him, but with others, who failed to exe-cute his orders.

This has been written amid interruptions, and is an imperfect attempt to describe the great charge, but I have made the effort to comply with your request because of your very kind and friendly letter, and because there is no reason why those who once were foes should not now be friends. The quarrel was not personal, but sec-tional, and although we tried to destroy each other thirty-odd years ago, there is no reason why we should cherish resentment against each other now.

I should be very glad to meet you in Lynchburg if your business or pleasure should ever bring you to Virginia.

With great respect,
Yours most truly,
RAWLEY W. MARTIN[10]

CHAPTER TEN

"Only the Flag of the Union Greets the Sky"

A s the Confederate survivors of the Pickett-Pettigrew Charge fled back to their lines in retreat, General George Meade sat mounted on horseback on the crest of Cemetery Ridge. A look of disbelief crossed his face. "Have they turned?" he asked a nearby officer. When assured the enemy was really retreating, Meade simply muttered, "Thank God." Nearby, a Federal band recognized the commander of the now victorious Army of the Potomac, and broke into "Hail to the Chief." All along Cemetery Ridge, the Federal troops who had repulsed Lee's legions whooped and shouted and threw their caps in the air. Some, mindful of the similar slaughter they had suffered months earlier at Fredericksburg, began chanting "Fredericksburg! Fredericksburg!" toward the backs of the retreating Southerners.

General Hancock, who had applied a makeshift tourniquet to his wounded thigh during the fighting, now allowed himself to be carried to the rear so his wound could be treated. General Hays, who had two horses shot while under him during the fighting, now mounted another, jumped it over the stone wall, and rode up and down before his line, trailing a fallen Confederate battle flag

After the Pickett-Pettigrew Charge collapsed, General George Meade—heroically depicted in this period art—was saluted with "Hail to the Chief" by a regimental band. "Thank God," Meade said, when assured his army had won.

Library of Congress

while his troops cheered triumphantly. Meanwhile, exultant Federal soldiers raced each other over the copse-cluttered front between Cemetery Ridge and the Emmitsburg Road, hurrying to gather fallen Confederate battle flags.[1]

"The Plain in Our Front Was Strewn with Dead Men and Dead Horses"

In the Wake of Battle, the Horrors of War Shock the Survivors

The sobering reality of war soon muted the Federal celebration atop Cemetery Ridge. Federal troops moved forward among the fallen Confederates, rousting hundreds to their feet as prisoners of war, marching them to the rear to captivity, or, if they were wounded, to Federal field hospitals. As the field slowly emptied of the living, the sight of so many dead—even enemy dead—shocked many Federal soldiers. "There were literally acres of dead lying in front of our line, a New York soldier would report. "I counted 16 dead bodies on one rod square, and the dead in every direction lay upon the field in heaps and scattered as far as the eye could reach." A New Jersey soldier was horrified to find a young Southerner, partially paralyzed by two wounds to his head, still using his one working arm to stuff grass in the bullet holes.

Forty years after surveying the harvest of horror left by the Pickett-Pettigrew Charge, Private Henry Meyer of the 148th Pennsylvania Infantry still remembered it in vivid detail.

One of the Confederate prisoners with both eyes shot out was led into our lines, crying bitterly. A Confederate officer related that the most pitiful spectacle he ever beheld was that presented by some officer in [Pickett's] division, sitting with his back to the fence along the Emmitsburg road, having his lower jaw shot clean away; sitting there with staring eye watching the men as they passed by to the charge....

Federal troops atop Cemetery Ridge watch Lee's defeated ranks retreat back toward the Confederate line.

Battles and Leaders of the Civil War

A heavy thunderstorm burst over the field in the evening, adding to the discomforts of the situation. From frequent rains and copious perspiration produced by toilsome marches, the boys' clothes never got dry from the time they left Thoroughfare Gap, June 25th, until several days after the battle at Gettysburg....

The plain in our front was strewn with dead soldiers and dead horses. Hats, haversacks, canteens, accoutrements, shells, solid shot, and muskets, wrecked gun carriages, and all the debris of a great battle were scattered in promiscuous confusion over field and in the woods. The ground was torn up in deep furrows by the enemy's solid shot and shell. I noticed one point where three such furrows had crossed each other, one having been made by a ball coming from the northwest, one from the west, and one from the southwest, showing how the fire was concentrated on that part of our line.

I pitied the poor wounded horses dragging themselves about the field, trying to nibble a tuft of grass here and there not trampled into the ground. I noticed the day before with what patience, almost human, the battery horses hitched to the caissons, endured the storm of iron missiles hurled over and amongst them. One after another the dumb brutes dropped to the ground, but none attempted to break away. Corporal S. M. Spangler of our company was put in command of a detail to shoot the wounded horses in that part of the field.

Every house, barn, shed or building whatsoever, was crowded with wounded and dying soldiers. In one of these crowded sheds near General Doubleday's headquarters, I noticed a young boy, who was badly wounded, trying, in his delirium, to creep through an opening in the side of the shed, moaning and crying in piteous tones. The first few days, the wounded suffered greatly for want of food, water, nursing and proper medical attendance, for sufficient supplies and assistance could not be brought to the field in a moment. Several

Federal troops march Confederate prisoners of war away from Gettysburg on the first leg to Northern prison camps. Each side captured more than 5,000 prisoners.
Library of Congress

hundred steps to the rear of our Regiment was a small dwelling house with some outbuildings. These were crowded with wounded soldiers.

A small orchard of about an acre in extent, near by, was literally covered with the dead; they presented a ghastly sight, some being covered with rubber blankets, or parts of shelter tents, lying there in the rain and mud. Close by was a small spring in a swampy place where the boys used to get their water while occupying their position in that part of the field. During the rain, surface water carried blood from the field into the spring, but water being scarce in the locality, the boys were obliged to fill their canteens with the tainted liquid....[2]

"All This Has Been My Fault"

Lee Meets the Survivors of the Pickett-Pettigrew Charge

As the troops from Pickett's, Pettigrew's, and Trimble's brigades streamed back to the Confederate main line, General Lee rode among them on horseback, trying to give them encouragement. He also took full responsibility for the defeat. "All this has been my fault," he repeatedly told his soldiers. "The fault is mine, but it will be all right in the end." Many of the troops wanted to attack again, or hoped that the Federals would follow-up the repulse with an assault on the Confederate line. "Not withstanding the failure of its efforts," a Southern officer would recall, "the army was still unconquered in spirit, and had Meade followed us back to Seminary Ridge, he would have found our troops ready to mete out to him what he had given to us." When soldiers shouted for him to let them make a second assault, Lee would not hear of it—although he did immediately deploy his troops to receive a Federal assault if Meade made one. Meade did not—his losses had been too costly.

General Pickett approached Lee on foot, almost dazed by his losses, and when Lee directed him to put his division back in line, Pickett responded, "General Lee, I have no division now...." Lee also directed Pettigrew to prepare his division to repel a possible Federal assault, until he noticed Pettigrew's bloody arm. "General," he said, "I am sorry to see you wounded," and ordered Pettigrew to the rear for treatment. General Wilcox came up to Lee, near tears, and tried to explain his losses. "Never mind, General Wilcox," Lee told him, "it is all my fault—it is I who have lost this fight, and you must help me out of it the best way you can."

Lieutenant Colonel Arthur Fremantle, the British military observer who had been traveling throughout the Confederacy prior to the battle, spoke to Lee as he rode through the ranks of his bloodied troops. After Gettysburg, Fremantle made his way through Federal lines and returned to Great Britain, where he published an account of his experiences, including the moments following the defeat of the Pickett-Pettigrew Charge.

When I got close up to General Longstreet, I saw one of his regiments advancing through the woods in good order; so, thinking I was just in time to see the attack, I remarked to the General that "I wouldn't have missed this for any thing." Longstreet was seated at the top of a snake fence at the edge of the wood, and looking perfectly calm and unperturbed. He replied, laughing, "The devil you wouldn't! I would like to have missed it very much; we've attacked and been repulsed: look there!"

For the first time I then had a view of the open space between the two positions, and saw it covered with Confederates slowly and sulkily returning towards us in small broken parties, under a heavy fire of artillery. But the fire where we were was not so bad as further to the rear; for although the air seemed alive with shell, yet the greater number burst behind us.

The General told me that Pickett's division had succeeded in carrying the enemy's position and capturing his guns, but after remaining there twenty minutes, it had been forced to retire, on the retreat of Heth and Pettigrew on its left.

No person could have been more calm or self-possessed than General Longstreet, under these trying circumstances, aggravated as they now were by the movements of the enemy, who began to show a strong disposition to advance. I could now thoroughly appreciate the term bulldog, which I had heard applied to him by the soldiers. Difficulties seem to make no other impression upon him than to make him a little more savage.

Major Walton was the only officer with him when I came up— all the rest had been put into the charge. In a few minutes Major Latrobe arrived on foot, carrying his saddle, having just had his horse killed. Colonel Sorrell was also in the same predicament, and Captain Goree's horse was wounded in the mouth.

As the survivors of the Pickett-Pettigrew Charge streamed back to Confederate lines, Lee rode among them on horseback. "All this has been my fault," he stated repeatedly.

Wikimedia Commons Images

The General was making the best arrangements in his power to resist the threatened advance, by advancing some artillery, rallying the stragglers, &c. I remember seeing a General (Pettigrew, I think it was) come up to him, and report that "he was unable to bring his men up again." Longstreet turned upon him and replied, with some sarcasm: "Very well; never mind, then, General; just let them remain where they are: the enemy's going to advance, and will spare you the trouble."

He asked for something to drink: I gave him some rum out of my silver flask, which I begged he would keep in remembrance of the occasion;—he smiled, and, to my great satisfaction, accepted the memorial. He then went off to give some orders to McLaws's division.

Soon afterwards I joined General Lee, who had in the meanwhile come to the front on becoming aware of the disaster. If Longstreet's conduct was admirable, that of General Lee was perfectly sublime. He was engaged in rallying and in encouraging the broken troops, and was riding about a little in front of the wood, quite alone—the whole of his Staff being engaged in a similar manner further to the rear. His face, which is always placid and cheerful, did not show signs of the slightest disappointment, care, or annoyance; and he was addressing to every soldier he met a few words of encouragement, such as, "All this will come right in the end: we'll talk it over afterwards; but, in the mean time, all good men must rally. We want all good and true men just now," &c. He spoke to all the wounded men that passed him, and the slightly wounded he exhorted "to bind up their hurts and take up a musket" in this emergency.

Very few failed to answer his appeal, and I saw many badly wounded men take off their hats and cheer him.

He said to me, "This has been a sad day for us, Colonel—a sad day; but we can't expect always to gain victories." He was also kind enough to advise me to get into some more sheltered position.

Notwithstanding the misfortune which had so suddenly befallen him, General Lee seemed to observe every thing, however trivial. When a mounted officer began licking his horse for shying at the bursting of a shell, he called out. "Don't whip him, Captain; don't whip him. I've got just such another foolish horse myself, and whipping does no good."

I happened to see a man lying flat on his face in a small ditch, and I remarked that I didn't think he seemed dead; this drew General Lee's attention to the man, who commenced groaning dismally. Finding appeals to his patriotism of no avail, General Lee had him ignominiously set on his legs by some neighboring gunners.

I saw General Wilcox (an officer who wears a short round jacket and a battered straw hat) come up to him, and explain, almost crying, the state of his brigade. General Lee immediately shook hands with him and said cheerfully, "Never mind, General, all this has been MY fault—it is I that have lost this fight, and you must help me out of it in the best way you can."

In this manner I saw General Lee encourage and reanimate his somewhat dispirited troops, and magnanimously take upon his own shoulders the whole weight of the repulse. It was impossible to look at him or to listen to him without feeling the strongest admiration, and I never saw any man fail him except the man in the ditch.

It is difficult to exaggerate the critical state of affairs as they appeared about this time. If the enemy or their general had shown any enterprise, there is no saying what might have happened. General Lee and his officers were evidently fully impressed with a sense of the situation; yet there was much less noise, fuss, or confusion of orders than at an ordinary field-day: the men, as they were rallied in the wood, were brought up in detachments, and lay down quietly and coolly in the positions assigned to them.

We heard that Generals Garnett and Armistead were killed, and General Kemper mortally wounded; also, that Pickett's division had only one field-officer unhurt. Nearly all this slaughter took place in an open space about one mile square, and within one hour.

At 6 P.M. we heard a long and continuous Yankee cheer, which we at first imagined was an indication of an advance, but it turned out to be their reception of a general officer, whom we saw riding down the line, followed by about thirty horsemen.

Soon afterwards I rode to the extreme front, where there were four pieces of rifled cannon almost without any infantry support. To the non-withdrawal of these guns is to be attributed the otherwise surprising inactivity of the enemy.

I was immediately surrounded by a sergeant and about half-a-dozen gunners, who seemed in excellent spirits and full of confidence, in spite of their exposed situation. The sergeant expressed his ardent hope that the Yankees might have spirit enough to advance and receive the dose he had in readiness for them. They spoke in admiration of the advance of Pickett's division, and of the manner in which Pickett himself had led it. When they observed General Lee they said, "We've not lost confidence in the old man: this day's work won't do him no harm. 'Uncle Robert' will get us into Washington yet; you bet he will," &c.

Whilst we were talking, the enemy's skirmishers began to advance slowly, and several ominous sounds in quick succession told us that we were attracting their attention, and that it was necessary to break up the conclave. I therefore turned round and took leave of these cheery and plucky gunners....[3]

"It Has Been a Sad, Sad Day"
Lee Decides to Fight No More

L ate on the night of July 3, Brigadier General John D. Imboden, a cavalry officer who had spent the battle protecting Lee's long line of ammunition and supply wagons, was fetched by a courier to come to Lee's headquarters. Imboden left the wagon park west of Gettysburg and followed the courier through the darkness into town. There, at Lee's headquarters, he found himself in the unique situation of listening to General Lee as he shared his personal feelings about the Southern defeat at Gettysburg.

Seven years later, Imboden would share his story of that memorable encounter with the readers of *The Galaxy* magazine.

Horses are tied outside General Robert E. Lee's headquarters site in this sketch by soldier-artist Charles W. Reed. Here, on the night of July 3, Lee made plans to move his army back to Virginia.

Library of Congress

When night closed upon the grand scene our army was repulsed. Silence and gloom pervaded our camps. We knew that the day had gone against us, but the extent of the disaster was not known except in high quarters. The carnage of the day was reported to have been frightful, but our army was not in retreat, and we all surmised that with to-morrow's dawn would come a renewal of the struggle; and we knew that if such was the case those who had not been in the fight would have their full share in the honors and the dangers of the next day. All felt and appreciated the momentous consequences of final defeat or victory on that great field. These considerations made that, to us, one of those solemn and awful nights that every one who fought through our long war sometimes experienced before a great battle.

Few camp fires enlivened the scene. It was a warm summer's night, and the weary soldiers were lying in groups on the luxuriant grass of the meadows we occupied, discussing the events of the day

*or watching that their horses did not straggle off in brows-
ing around. About eleven o'clock a horseman
approached and delivered a message from General
Lee, that he wished to see me immediately. I
mounted at once, and, accompanied by Lieutenant McPhail of my staff, and guided by the
courier, rode about two miles toward Gettysburg, where half a dozen small tents on the
roadside were pointed out as General Lee's
headquarters for the night. He was not there, but
I was informed that I would find him with General A. P. Hill half a mile further on. On reaching
the place indicated, a flickering, solitary candle, visible
through the open front of a common tent, showed
where Generals Lee and Hill were seated on camp
stools, with a county map spread upon their knees, and
engaged in a low and earnest conversation. They
ceased speaking as I approached, and after the ordinary salutations General Lee directed me to go to his
headquarters and wait for him. He did not return until
about one o'clock, when he came riding alone at a slow
walk and evidently wrapped in profound thought.*

Summoned to Lee's headquarters late at night, Brigadier General John Imboden witnessed a rare comment from Lee about his defeat at Gettysburg. "It has been a sad, sad day," said Lee.

Library of Congress

*There was not even a sentinel on duty, and no one of his staff was
about. The moon was high in the heavens, shedding a flood of soft
silvery light, almost as bright as day, upon the scene. When he
approached and saw us, he spoke, reined up his horse, and essayed to
dismount. The effort to do so betrayed so much physical exhaustion
that I stepped forward to assist him, but before I reached him he had
alighted. He threw his arm across his saddle to rest himself, and fixing
his eyes upon the ground leaned in silence upon his equally weary
horse; the two forming a striking group, as motionless as a statue. The
moon shone full upon his massive features, and revealed an expression*

of sadness I had never seen upon that fine countenance before, in any of the vicissitudes of the war through which he had passed. I waited for him to speak until the silence became painful and embarrassing, when to break it, and change the current of his thoughts, I remarked in a sympathetic tone, and in allusion to his great fatigue: "General, this has been a hard day on you."

This attracted his attention. He looked up and replied mournfully: "Yes, it has been a sad, sad day to us," and immediately relapsed into his thoughtful mood and attitude. Being unwilling again to intrude upon his reflections, I said no more. After a minute or two he suddenly straightened up to his full height, and turning to me with more animation, energy, and excitement of manner than I had ever seen in him before, he addressed me in a voice tremulous with emotion, and said:

"General, I never saw troops behave more magnificently than Pickett's division of Virginians did to-day in their grand charge upon the enemy. And if they had been supported, as they were to have been—but, for some reason not yet fully explained to me, they were not—we would have held the position they so gloriously won at such a fearful loss of noble lives, and the day would have been ours." After a moment he added in a tone almost of agony: "Too bad! Too bad!! OH! TOO BAD!!!"

I never shall forget, as long as I live, his language, and his manner, and his appearance and expression of mental suffering. Altogether it was a scene that a historical painter might well immortalize had one been fortunately present to witness it.

In a little while he called up a servant from his sleep to take his horse; spoke mournfully, by name, of several of his friends who had fallen during the day; and when a candle had been lighted invited me alone into his tent, where, as soon as we were seated, he remarked:

"We must return to Virginia. As many of our poor wounded as possible must be taken home. I have sent for you because your men are fresh, to guard the trains back to Virginia. The duty will be arduous, responsible, and dangerous, for I am afraid you will be harassed by the enemy's cavalry. I can spare you as much artillery as you require, but no other troops, as I shall need all I have to return to the Potomac by a different route from yours. All the transportation and all the care of the wounded will be intrusted [sic] to you. You will recross the mountain by the Chambersburg road, and then proceed to Williamsport by any route you deem best, without halting. There rest and feed your animals, then ford the river, and make no halt....[4]

"The Sights and Smells That Assailed Us Were Indescribable"

The Two Armies Remain in Place on a Field of Dead

Dawn arrived on Saturday, July 4, with drizzling rain, which steadily increased into a downpour. The two armies remained in place all day, exhausted, like spent boxers glowering at one another after a match. The torrents of rain added to the misery of the wounded still left on the field—mostly Confederates—soaked the uniforms of the dead, both blue and gray, and turned Gettysburg's many roads into muddy quagmires. There had been some quick follow-up clashes after the Pickett-Pettigrew Charge as well as some sporadic skirmishing on the fringes of the armies' lines, but the charge marked the end of the battle. Neither Meade nor Lee attempted to resume combat, and at nightfall on July 4, Lee's army began pulling back from its lines and heading southward toward Virginia. Alerted to Lee's retreat, General Meade would move in his army in pursuit—but not immediately.

A dead Confederate soldier lies beside a breastwork of piled stones in Devil's Den—one of many bodies that awaited burial for days. "We were all sickened," a Southern officer would recall.

Major Robert Stiles, an artillery officer in Lee's army, surveyed the battlefield before the Confederate army retreated southward, and felt sickened by what he observed.

On the 4th of July, in readjusting and straightening our lines, the guns of Hilary Jones' battalion were put in position on a part of the field which Hill's corps had fought over on the 1st, and upon which the pioneer corps and burying parties had not been able to complete their work; so that the dead bodies of men and horses had lain there putrefying under the summer sun for three days. The sights and smells that assailed us were simply indescribable—corpses swollen to twice their original size, some of them actually burst asunder with the pressure of foul gases and vapors. I recall one feature never before noted, the shocking distension and protrusion of the eyeballs of dead men and dead horses. Several human or unhuman corpses sat upright against a fence, with arms extended in the air and faces hideous with something very like a fixed leer, as if taking a fiendish pleasure in showing us what we essentially were and might at any moment become.

The odors were nauseating, and so deadly that in a short time we all sickened and were lying with our mouths close to the ground, most of us vomiting profusely. We protested against the cruelty and folly of keeping men in such a position. Of course to fight in it was utterly out of the question, and we were soon moved away; but for the rest of that day and late into the night, the fearful odors I had inhaled remained with me and made me loathe myself as if an already rotting corpse.[5]

"The Real Nature of War Appeared in All Its Repulsiveness"

Volunteers Are Shocked by the Aftermath of Battle

A week after the battle, a Methodist pastor from New York, the Reverend William G. Browning, joined a group ministers who arrived by train at Gettysburg. Their mission was to assist the thousands of wounded troops from both sides who were still being treated in field hospitals with limited attention and medical supplies. The amount of wounded troops proved too numerous for efficient treatment.

Pastor Browning and his fellow pastors worked in the army hospitals as volunteers, doing whatever needed to be done at the given moment. Afterward, he would record a candid account of ministering to the wounded on what he called Gettysburg's "field of gore."

Volunteer staff of the U.S. Christian Commission pause momentarily from their work at the Gettysburg General Hospital, which was established on the battlefield soon after the fighting ended. Comprised of pastors and YMCA volunteers, the Commission ministered to the wounded on both sides.

Library of Congress

With many delays, caused mainly by the difficulties of continued travel, occasioned by the necessities of the war and the transportation of the hundreds and thousands of suffering men being moved to Northern hospitals, we reached Gettysburg on Friday, July 10th.... I was specially favored in having a note of introduction to one of the principal residents, who furnished me a place to sleep in her open house, where were sheltered all that could be accommodated in rooms and halls and stoops.

The whole place was turned into a hospital for the victims of the bloody strife; the evidences of which were everywhere. Dwellings, churches, and other buildings were all appropriated to the sufferers, and in some of these places no distinction was recognized between Union men and Confederates. Soldiers from both armies lay side by side as brothers, receiving the ministrations of the "Angels of mercy." A sickening odor filled the air, and the real nature of war appeared in all its repulsiveness. A tour of the battlefield was enough to fill the mind and heart with the deepest aversion to everything that could result in such a conflict as was then raging. The

armies had left, one in retreat, and the other in pursuit, but the distant firing gave evidence that more deadly work was being performed.

Among the least visible results of the fiery contest that had so recently swept over all this section, were the shattered houses, prostrate fences, and numerous trees destroyed, intentionally, and by being cut off with flying missiles. Horses in multitudes lay stretched in death and, worse than that, in some cases in dying groans and struggles. I saw one group of dead horses, perhaps numbering eight or ten, and remarked to one accompanying me: "That it was strange that these animals should be left exposed to be shot down one after another." His answer was: "That probably they had all been slain by a single shell." The destructive nature of these flying engines of death I never conceived until told by eye-witnesses of the wholesale execution sometimes accomplished, when just one of them would do its work along the line of soldiers it was sent to kill.

A Federal surgeon performs an amputation on a wounded soldier in a field hospital. Untold numbers of Gettysburg's wounded died from lack of medical treatment—or because of it.

Library of Congress

The "field hospitals" contained the most dreadfully mangled, who had not been removed because of the severe nature of their injuries, demanding immediate attention. Armless and legless men were there found in scores, bearing their pangs as it would seem impossible that they could, if the evidence were not so positive as to be undoubted. In the hospital tents containing the wounded Union men, the joys of victory mounted above the groans of anguish. Songs and shouts were the expressions of their delight that they had been successful.

The rebel field hospitals, as the places were called, where lay the Confederate officers and soldiers that had been severely wounded

A Southern physician holds the tools of his trade—his doctor's kit and a medicine bottle. After crossing the Mason-Dixon Line, some of Lee's seriously wounded troops were left in private homes to be tended by civilian doctors like this one.

Southern Communications

and left behind, beggars all description. One of these was a barnyard. Its surroundings contained more human misery than I ever expected to see; and I pray most earnestly that I may never witness the like again. The dead and dying lay intermingled. Nearby, in an open field, were the dead who had been separated from the dying. And in the midst of the unattended sufferers on the ground outside and on the barn floor, were those who had breathed their last, but no hand had been found as yet to lift the mangled corpse away from those still living. Wretchedness was stamped on the countenances of both the dead and the living.

A stack of arms and legs were thrown on a heap where they had been left when they had been roughly severed from their bodies, with only a board for the surgeon's table. Among this pity-demanding brotherhood I picked my way carefully and rendered such assistance as I could, changing the position of some shattered limb, when requested by its owner, and administering of what I had. When I asked in kindly words how these men came to enlist in this unnatural war, there was a moment or two of silence, when one said, "Led into it, sir!" and another responded, "Yes, led into it, sir!" Poor fellows, they were undoubtedly led into it; and many of them were, without doubt, as sincere in their devotion to their cause, as was any Union soldier to his. They thought they had been wronged, and that they were only acting upon the defensive against oppressors. As a further illustration of this I heard a prisoner, who had just been brought into Gettysburg, asked: "Were you one who thought for yourself, with reference to the cause which originated this war, or did you just believe what others told you?" I listened for the answer, and it was: "Of course I believed what I was told, or I would not have been here."

There was something strangely fascinating in wandering over this battlefield. Dead men were buried (as soldiers are buried in haste) all about the plains, and even along the roadsides. Buried, at best, so as just to be fairly covered, and often not even so much as that. Many bodies had not yet been discovered among the knolls and dells, where they lay bloating in the sunshine and rain.

One of my Kingston parishioners, with whom I had held a close correspondence, was reported among the wounded in the accounts first received. I ascertained that he died on the field, and I succeeded in finding the grave where his body had been buried, and his name marked on a board. The best I could do was to make a sketch of the spot so that it could be found by his friends. They, with this aid, soon afterward removed his remains. By invitation, I preached a memorial service in the church in Kingston, from which he had gone forth to do battle for the salvation of the nation. The service was on Sabbath afternoon, August 2, 1863, and the text, II Samuel, first chapter, nineteenth verse: "The beauty of Israel is slain upon thy high places; how are the mighty fallen!"

The lesser calamities accompanying the carrying on of this war for the Union were partially shown by the hundreds and thousands of broken guns, hats, coats, cartridge boxes, bayonets, and other implements, as well as wasted provisions, that strewed the ground. The temptation to gather some of these things as relics was very strong, and not always resisted. The military regulations, however, were against so doing, and many a visitor found himself in the guard-house for presuming to disobey.

I spent one night in camp, and slept with Chaplain Gilder in his tent. Brother Gilder went to the seat of war with a regiment from

Yonkers, and afterward died from disease contracted in the army. With some messages to friends of the soldiers I had met, and having in charge for bereaved ones some tokens that the departed had left to be conveyed to those who would never witness the return of the givers, I turned my face homeward again.[6]

The discovery of this photograph in the hands of an unidentified dead Federal soldier at Gettysburg sparked a nationwide clamor in the North to identify the soldier and locate his family.

Library of Congress

"The Children of the Battlefield"
A Photograph of a Dead Soldier's Children Grips the Hearts of Millions

After Lee's army withdrew on its march southward, Federal troops rounded up Confederate stragglers and continued to bury the dead, which was a staggering task. "The corpses are brought into rows and counted," a Federal soldier noted in his journal, "the Confederates and Federals being separated into different rows. At the foot of each row of fifty or a hundred dead, a trench is dug about seven or eight feet wide and about three feet deep—for there is no time for normal grave depth. Then the bodies … are placed in the shallow ditch and quickly covered with dirt." As Federal burial details moved through the town of Gettysburg, removing one corpse after another, they found a dead Northern soldier lying in an out-of-the-way spot near the intersection of the York and Stratton Streets. In his hand he clutched an ambrotype photograph of three small children—two boys and a girl. The soldier had apparently been mortally wounded, likely in the first day's fighting, and had retreated into town, where he died—most likely looking at the photograph, probably of his children, in his dying moments.

After the unidentified soldier's body was buried, the photograph of the children eventually came into the possession of Dr. Francis J. Bourns, a Philadelphia physician who was volunteering at Gettysburg. When he returned home to Philadelphia, Dr. Bourns took the poignant story and the ambrotype photograph to the *Philadelphia Inquirer* newspaper, which reported the story under the headline "Whose Father Was He?" The limited technology of the day prevented the newspaper from publishing the photograph, but the brief story described the children and their clothing. Other newspapers picked up the story, and it rapidly circulated throughout the North. With so many families grieving for loved ones lost in the war, the story of the "Children of the Battlefield" touched the hearts of newspaper readers throughout the North, and it became a national sensation. Dr. Bourns made inexpensive *carte de visite* copies of the photograph, which he distributed and mailed to soldiers' families who contacted him in hopes of learning the fate of a missing husband and father.

In November of 1863, a neighbor brought a copy of *The American Presbyterian* newspaper to Philinda Humiston, a thirty-two-year-old soldier's wife and mother of three children, who was living in the southwestern New York town of Portville. Philinda had married a former harness-maker who was serving in the Army of the Potomac but had not heard from her husband since before the battle of Gettysburg. When she read the description of the children and their apparel, she feared the dead soldier to be her husband, to whom she had mailed an ambrotype photograph of their children. The postmaster in Portville helped her contact Dr. Bourns, who mailed her a *carte de visite* copy of the ambrotype.

It *was* the photograph she had mailed her husband, Sergeant Amos Humiston of the 154th New York Infantry, and it depicted their three children: eight-year-old Frank, four-year-old Frederick, and six-year-old Alice. Sergeant Humiston had left his harness-making work to fight for the Union, despite the misgivings of his wife, who had been widowed once before as a young woman. In a letter home before Gettysburg, Humiston had written Philinda about his pleasure at receiving the photograph she had mailed him: "... I got the likeness of the children and it pleased me more than anything that you could have sent me. How I want to see them and their mother is more than I can tell. I hope that we may all live to see each other again...." On Gettysburg's first day of battle, Southern troops of Early's division overwhelmed Humiston's regiment northeast of town. Mortally wounded, he somehow made it into town, where he died with the photograph of his children clutched in his hands.

News of the discovery of Humiston's identity as well as the story of his family sent another wave of emotion throughout the North, resulting in the production of a popular song, "The Children of the Battlefield," and brisk sales of sheet music—with donations from it sent to the Humiston family. Funds were also raised in order to establish an orphanage for soldiers' children in Gettysburg, and the institution hired Philinda to be the headmistress. After a few years, she remarried and moved with her children to New England—far from the battlefield that had so affected her family. Below is the *Philadelphia Inquirer* story that launched the search for the father of the "Children of the Battlefield."

Whose Father Was He?

After the battle of Gettysburg, a Union soldier was found in a secluded spot on the field, where, wounded, he had laid himself down to die. In his hands, tightly clasped, was an ambrotype containing the portraits of three small children, and upon this picture his eyes, set in death, rested. The last object upon which the dying father looked was the image of his children, and as he silently gazed upon them his soul passed away. How touching! how solemn! What pen can describe the emotions of this patriot-father as he gazed upon these children, so soon to be made orphans! Wounded and alone, the din of battle still sounding in his ears, he lies down to die. His last thoughts and prayers are for his family. He has finished his work on earth; his last battle has been fought; he has freely given his life to his country; and now, while his life's blood is ebbing, he clasps in his hands the image of his children, and, commending them to the God of the fatherless, rests his last lingering look upon them.

When, after the battle, the dead were being buried, this soldier was thus found. The ambrotype was taken from his embrace, and has since been sent to this city for recognition. Nothing else was found upon his person by which he might be identified. His grave has been marked, however, so that if by any means this ambrotype will lead to his recognition he can be disinterred. This picture is now in the possession of Dr. BOURNS, No. 1104 Spring Garden street, of this city, who can be called upon or addressed in reference to it.

The children, two boys and a girl, are, apparently, nine, seven and five years of age, the boys being respectively the oldest and youngest of the three. The youngest boy is sitting in a high chair, and on each side of him are his brother and sister. The eldest boy's jacket is made from the same material as his sister's dress. These are the most prominent features of the group. It is earnestly desired that all the papers in the country will draw attention to the discovery of this picture and its attendant circumstances, so that, if possible, the family of the dead hero may come into possession of it. Of what inestimable value it will be to these children, proving, as it does, that the last thoughts of their dying father was for them, and them only.[7]

"This Distressing Casualty"
The Decisive Battle of the Civil War Comes at a Great Price

The Army of Northern Virginia moved southward in long, slow columns, heading for the fords across the Potomac River. Moving the thousands of Southern wounded required a seventeen-mile-long wagon train, and for those inside the wagons, bumping along over the muddy roads, the journey caused excruciating pain. "Very few of the wagons even had straw in them," General Imboden, who oversaw the column, would later recall. "As the horses trotted on, while the winds howled through the driving rain, there arose from

On the night of July 4, as heavy rains turned the roads to mud bogs, Lee put his defeated army on the road southward back to Virginia.

Battles and Leaders of the Civil War

that awful procession of the dying, oaths and curses, sobs and prayers, moans and shrieks that pierced the darkness and made the storm seem gentle."

At the Potomac, Lee found that the rains had brought the river to near flood stage, making the fords impassable, and the pontoon bridge he had used to cross the river on his way north had been destroyed by Federal raiders. Lee's army was trapped on the north side of the Potomac River. His troops deployed into battle lines, expecting Meade's army to arrive and attack at any moment.

General Meade and his army, however, still remained at Gettysburg. Keenly aware of his losses, Meade acknowledged that his army was in no condition to immediately pursue Lee. Not until July 7 did he get the army on the move, urged on by General in Chief Henry Halleck, and—behind him, President Lincoln— who resolved that Meade should overtake Lee's defeated army and destroy it. "Do not let the enemy escape," Halleck telegraphed Meade. But Lee did escape— barely. On July 13, eight days after leaving Gettysburg, Lee's army managed to cross the Potomac on a rigged-up pontoon bridge—just as the forward elements

of Meade's army arrived on the opposite bank. A skirmish ensued between Lee's rear guard and Federal cavalry at a riverside village called Falling Waters, and General James Johnston Pettigrew—who had survived the Pickett-Pettigrew Charge—was mortally wounded. Despite that blow, the Army of Northern Virginia made it across to safety, cutting loose the pontoon bridge after crossing. Much to President Lincoln's chagrin, Lee and his army made it back to Virginia to fight again.

Aware of Lincoln's dismay that Lee's army had escaped, General George Gordon Meade offered to resign as commander of the Army of the Potomac. However, Meade was now the victor who had turned back Lee's

Concerned that his exhausted troops were in no condition for a forced march, Meade was slow to pursue Lee's army. When he finally did take up the chase, Federal forces were hampered by rain and bad roads. Artist and eyewitness Edwin Forbes sketched the soggy, lumbering pursuit.

Library of Congress

invasion of the North, and his resignation was not accepted. Almost three months after the battle, Meade wrote a lengthy official report of the combat, outlining the main actions of the campaign and concluding with praise for his victorious troops. "I will only add my tribute to the heroic bravery of the whole army, officers and men," he wrote, "which, under the blessing of Divine Providence, enabled a crowning victory to be obtained, which I feel confident the country will never cease to bear in grateful remembrance." In his official report, he summarized the results of the Federal victory at Gettysburg in tally form: "the defeat of the enemy at Gettysburg, his compulsory evacuation of Pennsylvania and

When both armies moved on, left behind at Gettysburg was a huge source of heartbreak—an estimated 8,000 sons, husbands, and fathers buried beneath a thin layer of Pennsylvania soil. Countless others later died of wounds.

Library of Congress

Maryland, and withdrawal from the upper valley of the Shenandoah, and in the capture of 3 guns, 41 standards, and 13,021 prisoners; 24,978 small-arms were collected on the battle-field."

General Lee also tendered his resignation. In typical fashion, Lee blamed no one but himself for the defeat at Gettysburg, and in his official statement, he, too, heralded his soldiers, proclaiming "their courage in battle entitles them to rank with the soldiers of any army at any time." His resignation was also declined. At first, many Southerners hailed the Gettysburg campaign as a success, based on the much-needed supplies that were obtained and the fear instilled in the North. "I believe that the battle of Gettysburg has done more to strike terror in them than anything else," observed a Southern soldier soon after the battle. Eventually, however, the Southern press, the Southern people, and even Lee's veterans would come to view Gettysburg as an incomparable loss that proved disastrous for the South. As a Confederate private wounded at Gettysburg put it: "It was a trip that didn't pay."

Gettysburg would also prove to be the bloodiest battle of the American Civil War. Combined casualties—dead, wounded, and missing—totaled 51,112. Northern casualties amounted to 23,049, while Southern losses numbered 28,063. The bare statistics belie the human suffering they represent. Throughout America, in both the North and South, a tidal wave of mourning followed the Battle of Gettysburg, leaving untold numbers of communities and families awash in grief for the husbands, sons, and fathers who were no more.

Two weeks after Gettysburg, Colonel C. M. Avery of the 33rd North Carolina Infantry wrote the father of one of his young officers—Second Lieutenant

John Caldwell—to report the death of his son. Lieutenant Caldwell—"Jonny" to family and friends—who made the Pickett-Pettigrew Charge in Lane's Brigade of Trimble's division, and was shot down at the foot of Cemetery Ridge. "To console a Father for an only son is a difficult task," Avery concluded—a sentiment that undoubtedly reflected the hearts of countless Americans, North and South alike.

Hd. Qrs. 33d Rgt. N.C.S.
Bunker Hill 18th July /63

Dear Sir,
I delayed until this time in writing you with the fond hope that I could write you certainly with regard to the fate of your gallant son in the late fight at Gettysburg.

My Regiment was engaged in the fight on the 1st July and although greatly exposed suffered very little on the 2d. We were under shelling all day. On the 3d day we were ordered forward to storm the heights.

We advanced to within forty yards of the Enemys work and it was here that my little friend Jonny fell. I saw him but a few moments before we were ordered to fall back discharging his whole duty. You cannot imagine my feelings after reforming my Rgt to find him absent and upon being told that he was seen to fall forward on his face. As soon as we fell back the Enemy occupied the ground and hence it is I am forced to write so unsatisfactorily to a fond and doting father.

I have used every exertion to obtain all the information I could in regard to Jonny and Candor compels me to say that there is very little hope but that he was killed or mortally wounded.

The loss of my little friend is to me one of the most distressing incidents of the war. His noble nature in a short time had won from my bosom the warmest affection. He had made in the Rgt many friends and his death is regretted by officers and men.

To console a Father for an only son is a difficult task. You may have the satisfaction to know that he fell where we would all wish to fall (if it be God's will) with his face to the enemy.

He was in Command of his Company but by this he was not more exposed than he would otherwise have been. The other Sgt. of his Company fell about the same time and is supposed to have been killed.

A wounded Lt who was near Jonny (but was able to walk off the field) thinks he was shot in the breast. I will write you again in few days more especially if I can find any information on which to predicate a hope that Jonny is alive.

Accept for yourself and Mrs. Caldwell my warmest sympathy in account of this distressing casualty.

Very truly yours
C. M. Avery[8]

"Only the Flag of
the Union Greets the Sky"

Gettysburg Veterans End the Civil War with a Mutual Salute

For almost two years after Gettysburg, the war would continue to grind out its bloody numbers until more than 620,000 Americans in blue and gray would lie in the grave. By spring of 1865, however, Federal forces had effectively divided and conquered most of the South and had captured its last operational seaport, shutting down imported weapons of war. Despite a masterful defense against the Army of the Potomac—by then under the command of Lieutenant General Ulysses S. Grant—Lee's army had been forced into trench warfare to defend Richmond. At Petersburg, Lee's thin defensive line finally broke. Richmond fell. The Army of Northern Virginia was trapped, and Lee surrendered at Appomattox, Virginia, on April 9, 1865. After Lee surrendered, the other Southern armies, one by one, did likewise, and the war ended in a Union victory.

In many ways, it was a victory that began at Gettysburg. The three-day battle, the largest battle ever fought in North America, would prove to be the turning point of the American Civil War. In ages to come, some would argue with good reason that the turning point was the capture of Vicksburg—which occurred the day after Lee's defeat at Gettysburg—placing the Mississippi River under Federal control. Others would cite the Battle of Antietam or the fall of Atlanta as the turning point. It was General Robert E. Lee, however, who had kept the Confederacy alive with his brilliant victories in the East, while Federal forces steadily prevailed in the war's Western Theater and slowly strangled the South with a naval blockade. After Gettysburg, Lee continuously remained on the defensive. Meade's army would quickly replace the losses it had suffered at Gettysburg, but it was not so with the Army of Northern Virginia. The depleted ranks of Southern manhood would be slow to fill the great gaps in Lee's army. By wearing down the Northern people's will to fight, it was perhaps still possible for the South to win the war after Gettysburg—but the attempt was made to no avail. Gettysburg proved to be *the* decisive battle of the Civil War.

At Appomattox, Lee's depleted army, whittled down to less than 25,000 troops, was largely manned by Gettysburg veterans. Just as some of his troops had urged him to allow them to assault Cemetery Ridge one more time, many of his soldiers mobbed him as he left the McLean House at Appomattox, where he signed surrender terms. "I saw the old ragged veterans crying," one Gettysburg

At an ending that began in many ways at Gettysburg, General Robert E. Lee surrendered his depleted Army of Northern Virginia to Lieutenant General Ulysses S. Grant in the McLean house at Appomattox, Virginia, on April 9, 1865.

Library of Congress

Three days after Lee signed the surrender terms, his troops stacked their arms and furled their flags before the victorious Army of the Potomac. In the ranks of both armies were countless veterans of Gettysburg.

survivor recalled, "as if their hearts would break." The next day, when Lee issued his farewell address to the Army of Northern Virginia, did he have the bloody fields of Gettysburg on his mind? "You will take with you the satisfaction that proceeds from the consciousness of duty faithfully performed," he told his troops, "and I earnestly pray that a merciful God will extend to you his blessing and protection."

Four days later on April 12, 1865, the Army of the Potomac received the official surrender of Lee's troops. The Federal ranks at Appomattox, also filled with veterans of Gettysburg, lined a road leading into the village of Appomattox. Lee's defeated army would march between the rows of men in blue to the surrender site. There, they would stack arms and furl their flags. Given the honor of presiding over the Confederate surrender was Brigadier General Joshua Lawrence Chamberlain, the former commander of the 20th Maine Infantry, credited by many with saving the Battle of Gettysburg—and the Union—through his desperate defense of the Federal far left flank on Little Round Top. Chamberlain's actions at Little Round Top would later earn him the Congressional Medal of Honor, but following Gettysburg, he had been repeatedly passed over for promotion even while holding brigade command. After successfully overseeing the Confederate defeat in the

Western Theater, General Grant had been promoted to General in Chief of the U.S. Army. While he retained General Meade as official army commander, Grant had taken personal command of the Army of the Potomac. It was he—at a bloody price—who had successfully driven Lee to surrender at Appomattox.

Joshua Lawrence Chamberlain had missed much of the bloody fighting between Grant and Lee due to court-martial duty, but at the siege of Petersburg, he suffered a grievous wound leading his brigade in an assault. Army surgeons deemed his wound mortal, and Chamberlain scribbled a farewell to his wife. His corps commander, Major General Gouverneur Warren—who had first rushed Federal troops to Little Round Top at Gettysburg—recommended that Grant honor Chamberlain's heroic actions by promoting him to brigadier general on his deathbed. Grant did so—then Chamberlain surprised everyone by not dying. He recovered, and his brigade was instrumental in the actions that drove Lee to Appomattox. Grant decided that Chamberlain—eventually viewed as one of Gettysburg's preeminent heroes—was the appropriate choice to oversee the surrender of Lee's army.

As Lee's ragged ranks marched smartly to the surrender point on April 12, Chamberlain forbade the Federal troops from any demonstrations that would offend the surrendering Southerners—no jeers, no cheers, no drums, no bugles. Grant had done the same when announcing Lee's surrender to the Federal troops, and had shown an attitude of respect and reconciliation by offering generous surrender terms to Lee and issuing rations to Lee's army. Instead of lording over the defeated Southerners as fallen foes, Grant and Chamberlain intended to treat them as former enemies now welcomed back into the national fold. Their actions reflected the heart of reconciliation that President Lincoln had called for in the words of his second inaugural address—"with malice toward none"—and which General Lee demonstrated when he refused to let his army devolve into a guerilla force.

A devout Christian, Chamberlain displayed that same spirit of reconciliation at the formal surrender ceremony. His Federal troops lined the road entering Appomattox. When the leading ranks of the Confederate Army of Northern Virginia appeared alongside, the Federal troops—as Chamberlain had ordered—

shifted from the position of "order arms" to "carry arms"—a salute of respect: "honor answering honor." At the head of the Confederate column rode another Gettysburg veteran, Major General John Brown Gordon, whose troops had helped send the Federal army fleeing through town on Gettysburg's first day. When Gordon saw the Federal troops snap to their salute, he immediately raised his sword in respect and ordered the Southern ranks to salute the Federal army in response. And so, Gettysburg veterans Joshua Lawrence Chamberlain and John Brown Gordon oversaw what amounted to the end of the war—a war that claimed 620,000 Northern and Southern lives—by leading the former foes in an extraordinary display of mutual respect and reconciliation—as Americans all.

In the early twentieth century, an elderly Joshua Lawrence Chamberlain would record the remarkable moment in his memoir *The Passing of the Armies.*

It was now the morning of the 12th of April. I had been ordered to have my lines formed for the ceremony at sunrise. It was a chill gray morning, depressing to the senses. But our hearts made warmth. Great memories uprose; great thoughts went forward. We formed along the principal street, from the bluff bank of the stream to near the Court House on the left,—to face the last line of battle, and receive the last remnant of the arms and colors of that great army which ours had been created to confront for all that death can do for life. We were remnants also: Massachusetts, Maine, Michigan, Maryland, Pennsylvania, New York; veterans, and replaced veterans; cut to pieces, cut down, consolidated, divisions into brigades, regiments into one, gathered by State origin; this little line, quintessence or metempsychosis of Porter's old corps of Gaines' Mill and Malvern Hill; men of near blood born, made nearer by blood shed. Those facing us—now, thank God! the same.

As for me, I was once more with my old command. But this was not all I needed. I had taken leave of my little First Brigade so endeared to me, and the end of the fighting had released the Second from all orders from me. But these deserved to share with me now as they had so faithfully done in the sterner passages of the campaign. I got permission from General Griffin to have them also in the parade. I placed the First Brigade in line a little to our rear, and the Second on the opposite side of the street facing us and leaving ample space for the movements of the coming ceremony. Thus the whole division was out, and under my direction for the occasion, although I was not the division commander. I thought this troubled General Bartlett a little, but he was a manly and soldierly man and made no comment. He contented himself by mounting his whole staff and with the division flag riding around our lines and conversing as he found opportunity with the Confederate officers. This in no manner disturbed me; my place and part were definite and clear.

Our earnest eyes scan the busy groups on the opposite slopes, breaking camp for the last time, taking down their little shelter-tents and folding them carefully as precious things, then slowly forming ranks as for unwelcome duty. And now they move. The dusky swarms forge forward into gray columns of march. On they come, with the old swinging route step and swaying battle-flags. In the van, the proud Confederate ensign— the great field of white with canton of star-strewn cross of blue on a field of red, the regimental battle-flags with the same escutcheon following on, crowded so thick, by thinning out of men, that the whole column seemed crowned with red. At the right of our line our little group mounted beneath our flags, the red Maltese cross on a field of white, erewhile so bravely borne through many a field more crimson than itself, its mystic meaning now ruling all.

Presiding over the surrender was Brigadier General Joshua Lawrence Chamberlain, who— as colonel of the 20th Maine—had successfully defended the extreme left flank of the Federal army at Gettysburg. On Chamberlain's orders at Appomattox—in an act of reconciliation—the Northern army saluted its former foes—and received a salute of honor in return.

Library of Congress

The momentous meaning of this occasion impressed me deeply. I resolved to mark it by some token of recognition, which could be no other than a salute of arms. Well aware of the responsibility assumed, and of the criticisms that would follow, as the sequel proved, nothing of that kind could move me in the least. The act could be defended, if needful, by the suggestion that such a salute was not to the cause for which the flag of the Confederacy stood, but to its going down before the flag of the Union. My main reason, however, was one for which I sought no authority nor asked forgiveness. Before us in proud humiliation stood the embodiment of manhood: men whom neither toils and sufferings, nor the fact of death, nor disaster, nor hopelessness could bend from their resolve; standing before us now, thin, worn, and famished, but erect, and with eyes looking level into ours, waking memories that bound us together as no other bond;—was not such manhood to be welcomed back into a Union so tested and assured?

Americans all, old soldiers of the Blue and the Gray pose beneath their battleflags at Gettysburg on the fiftieth anniversary of battle.

Instructions had been given; and when the head of each division column comes opposite our group, our bugle sounds the signal and instantly our whole line from right to left, regiment by regiment in succession, gives the soldiers salutation, from the "order arms" to the old "carry"—the marching salute. Gordon at the

head of the column, riding with heavy spirit and downcast face, catches the sound of shifting arms, looks up, and, taking the meaning, wheels superbly, making with himself and his horse one uplifted figure, with profound salutation as he drops the point of his sword to the boot toe; then facing to his own command, gives word for his successive brigades to pass us with the same position of the manual,—honor answering honor. On our part not a sound of trumpet more, nor roll of drum; not a cheer, nor word nor whisper of vain-glorying, nor motion of man standing again at the order, but an awed stillness rather, and breath-holding, as if it were the passing of the dead!

As each successive division masks our own, it halts, the men face inward towards us across the road, twelve feet away; then carefully "dress" their line, each captain taking pains for the good appearance of his company, worn and half starved as they were. The field and staff take their positions in the intervals of regiments; generals in rear of their commands. They fix bayonets, stack arms; then, hesitatingly, remove cartridge-boxes and lay them down. Lastly,—reluctantly, with agony of expression,—they tenderly fold their flags, battle-worn and torn, blood-stained, heart-holding colors, and lay them down; some frenziedly rushing from the ranks, kneeling over them, clinging to them, pressing them to their lips with burning tears. And only the Flag of the Union greets the sky![9]

APPENDIX 1

Official After-Action Report of Major General George Meade

HEADQUARTERS ARMY OF THE POTOMAC,
October 1, 1863.

GENERAL: I have the honor to submit herewith a report of the operations of this army during the month of July last, including the details of the battle of Gettysburg, delayed by the failure to receive until now the reports of several corps and division commanders, who were severely wounded in the battle.

On June 28, I received the orders of the President of the United States placing me in command of the Army of the Potomac. The situation of affairs at that time was briefly as follows:

The Confederate army, commanded by General R. E. Lee, estimated at over 100,000 strong, of all arms, had crossed the Potomac River and advanced up the Cumberland Valley. Reliable intelligence placed his advance (Ewell's corps) on the Susquehanna, at Harrisburg and Columbia; Longstreet's corps at Chambersburg, and Hill's corps between that place and Cashtown. My own army, of which the most recent return showed an aggregate of a little over

100,000, was situated in and around Frederick, Md., extending from Harper's Ferry to the mouth of the Monocacy, and from Middletown to Frederick.

June 28 was spent in ascertaining the position and strength of the different corps of the army, but principally in bringing up the cavalry, which had been covering the rear of the army in its passage over the Potomac, and to which a large increase had just been made from the forces previously attached to the Defenses of Washington. Orders were given on that day to Major-General French, commanding at Harper's Ferry, to move with 7,000 men of his command to occupy Frederick and the line of the Baltimore and Ohio Railroad, and, with the balance of his force, estimated at 4,000, to remove and escort, the public property to Washington.

On the 29th, the army was put in motion, and on the evening of that day was in position, the left at Emmitsburg and the right at New Windsor. Buford's division of cavalry was on the left flank, with the advance at Gettysburg. Kilpatrick's division was in the front at Hanover, where he encountered this day General Stuart's Confederate cavalry, which had crossed the Potomac at Seneca Creek, and, passing our right flank, was making its way toward Carlisle, having escaped Gregg's division, delayed in taking position on the right flank by the occupation of the roads by columns of infantry.

On the 30th, the right flank of the army was moved up to Manchester, the left still being at Emmitsburg, in the vicinity of which place three corps (the First, Eleventh, and Third) were collected, under the orders of Major-General Reynolds. General Buford having reported from Gettysburg the appearance of the enemy on the Cashtown road in some force, General Reynolds was directed to occupy Gettysburg.

On reaching that place on July 1, General Reynolds found Buford's cavalry warmly engaged with the enemy, who had debouched his infantry through the mountains on the Cashtown road, but was being held in check in the most gallant manner by Buford's cavalry. Major General Reynolds immediately moved around the town of Gettysburg, and advanced on the Cashtown road, and without a moment's hesitation deployed his advanced division and attacked the enemy, at the same time sending orders for the Eleventh Corps (General

Howard) to advance as promptly as possible. Soon after making his dispositions for the attack, Major-General Reynolds fell, mortally wounded, the command of the First Corps devolving on Major-General Doubleday, and the command of the field on Major-General Howard, who arrived about this time, 11.30 a. m., with the Eleventh Corps, then commanded by Major-General Schurz. Major-General Howard pushed forward two divisions of the Eleventh Corps to the support of the First Corps, now warmly engaged with the enemy on the ridge to the north of the town, and posted his 3rd Division, with three batteries of artillery, on the Cemetery Ridge, on the south side of the town.

Up to this time the battle had been with the forces of the enemy debouching from the mountains on the Cashtown road, known to be Hill's corps. In the early part of the action, success was on our side, Wadsworth's division, of the First Corps, having driven the enemy back some distance, capturing numerous prisoners, among them General Archer, of the Confederate army. The arrival of re-enforcements for the enemy on the Cashtown road, and the junction of Ewell's corps, coming on the York and Harrisburg roads, which occurred between 1 and 2 p. m., enabled the enemy to bring vastly superior forces against both the First and Eleventh Corps, outflanking our line of battle, and pressing it so severely that about 4 p. m. Major-General Howard deemed it prudent to withdraw these two corps to the Cemetery Ridge, on the south side of the town, which operation was successfully accomplished; not, however, without considerable loss in prisoners, arising from the confusion incident to portions of both corps passing through the town, and the men getting confused in the streets.

About the time of this withdrawal, Major-General Hancock arrived, whom I had dispatched to represent me on the field, on hearing of the death of General Reynolds. In conjunction with Major-General Howard, General Hancock proceeded to post the troops on the Cemetery Ridge, and to repel an attack that the enemy made on our right flank. This attack was not, however, very vigorous, and the enemy, seeing the strength of the position occupied, seemed to be satisfied with the success he had accomplished, desisting from any further attack this day.

About 7 p. m., Major-Generals Slocum and Sickles, with the Twelfth Corps and part of the Third, reached the ground, and took post on the right and left of the troops previously posted. Being satisfied from the reports received from the field that it was the intention of the enemy to support with his whole army the attack already made, and the reports from Major-Generals Hancock and Howard on the character of the position being favorable, I determined to give battle at this point; and, early in the evening of the 1st, issued orders to all the corps to concentrate at Gettysburg, directing all trains to be sent to the rear, at Westminster.

At 10 p. m. of the 1st, I broke up my headquarters, which until then had been at Taneytown, and proceeded to the field, arriving there at 1 a. m. of the 2d. So soon as it was light, I proceeded to inspect the position occupied, and to make arrangements for posting the several corps as they should reach the ground.

By 7 a. m. the Second and Fifth Corps, with the rest of the Third, had reached the ground, and were posted as follows: The Eleventh Corps retained its position on the Cemetery Ridge, just opposite the town; the First Corps was posted on the right of the Eleventh, on an elevated knoll, connecting with a ridge extending to the south and east, on which the Twelfth Corps was placed, the right of the Twelfth Corps resting on a small stream at a point where it crossed the Baltimore pike, and which formed, on the right flank of the Twelfth, something of an obstacle. The Cemetery Ridge extended in a westerly and southerly direction, gradually diminishing in elevation until it came to a very prominent ridge called Round Top, running east and west. The Second and Third Corps were directed to occupy the continuation of the Cemetery Ridge on the left of the Eleventh Corps. The Fifth Corps, pending the arrival of the Sixth, was held in reserve.

While these dispositions were being made, the enemy was massing his troops on an exterior ridge, distant from the line occupied by us from 1 mile to 1 ½ miles.

At 2 p. m. the Sixth Corps arrived, after a march of 32 miles, accomplished from 9 p. m. the day previous. On its arrival being reported, I immediately directed the Fifth Corps to move over to our extreme left, and the Sixth to occupy its place as a reserve for the right.

About 3 p. m. I rode out to the extreme left, to await the arrival of the Fifth Corps and to post it, when I found that Major-General Sickles, commanding the Third Corps, not fully apprehending the instructions in regard to the position to be occupied, had advanced, or rather was in the act of advancing, his corps some half a mile or three-quarters of a mile in front of the line of the Second Corps, on the prolongation of which it was designed his corps should rest. Having found Major-General Sickles, I was explaining to him that he was too far in advance, and discussing with him the propriety of withdrawing, when the enemy opened on him with several batteries in his front and on his flank, and immediately brought forward columns of infantry and made a most vigorous assault. The Third Corps sustained the shock most heroically. Troops from the Second Corps were immediately sent by Major-General Hancock to cover the right flank of the Third Corps, and soon after the assault commenced the Fifth Corps most fortunately arrived and took position on the left of the Third, Major-General Sykes, commanding, immediately sending a force to occupy the Round Top Ridge, where a most furious contest was maintained, the enemy making desperate but unsuccessful efforts to secure it.

Notwithstanding the stubborn resistance of the Third Corps, under Major-General Birney (Major-General Sickles having been wounded early in the action), the superiority of numbers of the enemy enabling him to outflank the corps in its advanced position, General Birney was compelled to fall back and reform behind the line originally designed to be held.

In the meantime, perceiving the great exertions of the enemy, the Sixth Corps, Major-General Sedgwick, and part of the First Corps (to the command of which I had assigned Major-General Newton), particularly Lockwood's Maryland brigade, together with detachments from the Second Corps, were all brought up at different periods, and succeeded, together with the gallant resistance of the Fifth Corps, in checking and finally repulsing the assault of the enemy, who retired in confusion and disorder about sunset, and ceased any further efforts on the extreme left. An assault was, however, made about 8 p. m. on the

Eleventh Corps from the left of the town, which was repelled, with assistance of troops from the Second and First Corps.

During the heavy assault upon our extreme left, portions of the Twelfth Corps were sent as re-enforcements. During their absence, the line on the extreme right was held by a very much reduced force. This was taken advantage of by the enemy, who, during the absence of Geary's division of the Twelfth Corps, advanced and occupied a part of his line.

On the morning of the 3d, General Geary (having returned during the night) attacked at early dawn the enemy, and succeeded in driving him back and reoccupying his former position. A spirited contest was, however, maintained all the morning along this part of the line, General Geary, re-enforced by Wheaton's brigade, Sixth Corps, maintaining his position, and inflicting very severe losses on the enemy.

With this exception, the quiet of the lines remained undisturbed till 1 p. m. on the 3d, when the enemy opened from over one hundred and twenty-five guns, playing upon our center and left. This cannonade continued for over two hours, when our guns, in obedience to my orders, failing to make any reply, the enemy ceased firing, and soon his masses of infantry became visible, forming for an assault on our left and left center. The assault was made with great firmness, directed principally against the point occupied by the Second Corps, and was repelled with equal firmness by the troops of that corps, supported by Doubleday's division and Stannard's brigade of the First Corps. During the assault, both Major-General Hancock, commanding the left center, and Brigadier-General Gibbon, commanding Second Corps, were severely wounded. This terminated the battle, the enemy retiring to his lines, leaving the field strewn with his dead and wounded, and numerous prisoners in our hands.

Buford's division of cavalry, after its arduous service at Gettysburg on the 1st, was on the 2d sent to Westminster to refit and guard our trains. Kilpatrick's division, that on the 29th, 30th, and 1st had been successfully engaging the enemy's cavalry, was on the 3d sent on our extreme left, on the Emmitsburg road, where good service was rendered in assaulting the enemy's line and occupying his attention. At the same time, General Gregg was engaged with the enemy on our extreme right, having passed across the Baltimore pike and Bonaughtown road, and boldly attacked the enemy's left and rear.

On the morning of the 4th, reconnaissances developed that the enemy had drawn back his left flank, but maintained his position in front of our left, apparently assuming a new line parallel to the mountains.

On the morning of the 5th, it was ascertained the enemy was in full retreat by the Fairfield and Cashtown roads. The Sixth Corps was immediately sent in pursuit on the Fairfield road, and the cavalry on the Cashtown road and by the Emmitsburg and Monterey Passes.

July 5 and 6 were employed in succoring the wounded and burying the dead. Major-General Sedgwick, commanding the Sixth Corps, having pushed the pursuit of the enemy as far as the Fairfield Pass, in the mountains, and reporting that the pass was a very strong one, in which a small force of the enemy could hold in check and delay for a considerable time any pursuing force, I determined to follow the enemy by a flank movement, and, accordingly, leaving McIntosh's brigade of cavalry and Neill's brigade of infantry to continue harassing the enemy, put the army in motion for Middletown, Md. Orders were immediately sent to Major-General French at Frederick to reoccupy Harper's Ferry and send a force to occupy Turner's Pass, in South Mountain. I subsequently ascertained Major-General French had not only anticipated these orders in part, but had pushed a cavalry force to Williamsport and Falling Waters, where they destroyed the enemy's pontoon bridge and captured its guard. Buford was at the same time sent to Williamsport and Hagerstown.

The duty above assigned to the cavalry was most successfully accomplished, the enemy being greatly harassed, his trains destroyed, and many captures of guns and prisoners made.

After halting a day at Middletown to procure necessary supplies and bring up the trains, the army moved through the South Mountain, and by July 12 was in front of the enemy, who occupied a strong position on the heights of Marsh Run, in advance of Williamsport. In taking this position, several skirmishes and affairs had been had with the enemy, principally by the cavalry and the Eleventh and Sixth Corps.

The 13th was occupied in reconnaissances of the enemy's position and preparations for attack, but, on advancing on the morning of the 14th, it was ascertained he had retired the night previous by a bridge at Falling Waters and the ford at Williamsport. The cavalry in pursuit overtook the rear guard at Falling Waters, capturing two guns and numerous prisoners.

Previous to the retreat of the enemy, Gregg's division of cavalry was crossed at Harper's Ferry, and, coming up with the rear of the enemy at Charlestown and Shepherdstown, had a spirited contest, in which the enemy was driven to Martinsburg and Winchester and pressed and harassed in his retreat.

The pursuit was resumed by a flank movement, the army crossing the Potomac at Berlin and moving down the Loudoun Valley. The cavalry were immediately pushed into the several passes of the Blue Ridge, and, having learned from scouts the withdrawal of the Confederate army from the lower valley of the Shenandoah, the army, the Third Corps, Major-General French, in advance, was moved into the Manassas Gap, in the hope of being able to intercept a portion of the enemy.

The possession of the gap was disputed so successfully as to enable the rear guard to withdraw by way of Strasburg, the Confederate army retiring to the Rapidan. A position was taken with this army on the line of the Rappahannock, and the campaign terminated about the close of July.

The result of the campaign may be briefly stated in the defeat of the enemy at Gettysburg, his compulsory evacuation of Pennsylvania and Maryland, and withdrawal from the upper valley of the Shenandoah, and in the capture of 3 guns, 41 standards, and 13,621 prisoners; 24,978 small-arms were collected on the battle-field.

Our own losses were very severe, amounting, as will be seen by the accompanying return, to 2,834 killed, 13,709 [13,713] wounded, and 6,643 missing; in all, 23,180 [23,190].

It is impossible in a report of this nature to enumerate all the instances of gallantry and good conduct which distinguished such a hard-fought field as Gettysburg. The reports of corps commanders and their subordinates, herewith submitted, will furnish all information upon this subject. I will only add my tribute to the heroic bravery of the whole army, officers and men, which, under the blessing of Divine Providence, enabled a crowning victory to be obtained, which I feel confident the country will never cease to bear in grateful remembrance.

It is my duty, as well as my pleasure, to call attention to the earnest efforts of co-operation on the part of Maj. Gen. D. N. Couch, commanding Department of the Susquehanna, and particularly to his advance, 4,000 men, under Brig. Gen. W. F. Smith, who joined me at Boonsborough just prior to the withdrawal of the Confederate army.

In conclusion, I desire to return my thanks to my staff, general and personal, to each and all of whom I was indebted for unremitting activity and most efficient assistance.

Very respectfully, your obedient servant,
GEO. G. MEADE, Major-General, Commanding.[1]

APPENDIX 2

Official After-Action Report of General Robert E. Lee

General S. COOPER,
Adjt. and Insp. Gen.,
C. S. Army, Richmond, Va.
HEADQUARTERS ARMY OF NORTHERN VIRGINIA,
January 20, 1864.

GENERAL: I forward to-day my report of the late campaign of this army in Maryland and Pennsylvania, together with those of the corps and other commanders, as far as they have been received. General Longstreet's list of casualties, and the reports of his subordinate officers, shall be sent as soon as they can be obtained from him.

I also forward the report of the medical director, and some other documents mentioned in the accompanying schedule. With reference to the former, I would remark that it is necessarily imperfect, for reasons stated in my report. The actual casualties and the number of missing can only be learned from the reports of the commanding officers, and it should be borne in mind that they usually embrace all the slightly wounded, even such as remain on duty, under the impression, commonly entertained, that the loss sustained is a measure of the service performed and the danger incurred.

I also inclose a map of the routes of the army, and one of the lines at Hagerstown and Williamsport. That of the battle-field of Gettysburg shall be forwarded as soon as completed.

Very respectfully, your obedient servant,

R. E. LEE,

General.

HEADQUARTERS ARMY OF NORTHERN VIRGINIA,
January —, 1864.

GENERAL: I have the honor to submit a detailed report of the operations of this army from the time it left the vicinity of Fredericksburg, early in June, to its occupation of the line of the Rapidan, in August.

Upon the retreat of the Federal Army, commanded by Major-General Hooker, from Chancellorsville, it reoccupied the ground north of the Rappahannock, opposite Fredericksburg, where it could not be attacked excepting at a disadvantage. It was determined to draw it from this position, and, if practicable, to transfer the scene of hostilities beyond the Potomac. The execution of this purpose also embraced the expulsion of the force under General Milroy, which had infested the lower Shenandoah Valley during the preceding winter and spring. If unable to attain the valuable results which might be expected to follow a decided advantage gained over the enemy in Maryland or Pennsylvania, it was hoped that we should at least so far disturb his plan for the summer campaign as to prevent its execution during the season of active operations.

The commands of Longstreet and Ewell were put in motion, and encamped around Culpeper Court-House June 7. As soon as their march was discovered by the enemy, he threw a force across the Rappahannock, about 2 miles below Fredericksburg, apparently for the purpose of observation. Hill's corps was left to watch these troops, with instructions to follow the movements of the army as soon as they should retire.

The cavalry, under General Stuart, which had been concentrated near Culpeper Court-House, was attacked on June 9 by a large force of Federal cavalry, supported by infantry, which crossed the Rappahannock at Beverly and Kelly's Fords. After a severe engagement, which continued from early in the morning until late in the afternoon, the enemy was compelled to recross the river with heavy loss, leaving about 500 prisoners, 3 pieces of artillery, and several colors in our hands.

General Imboden and General Jenkins had been ordered to cooperate in the projected expedition into the Valley, General Imboden by moving toward Romney with his command, to prevent the troops guarding the Baltimore and Ohio Railroad from re-enforcing those at Winchester, while General Jenkins advanced directly toward the latter place with his cavalry brigade, supported by a battalion of infantry and a battery of the Maryland Line.

General Ewell left Culpeper Court-House on June 10. He crossed the branches of the Shenandoah near Front Royal, and reached Cedarville on the 12th, where he was joined by General Jenkins. Detaching General Rodes with his division, and the greater part of Jenkins' brigade, to dislodge a force of the enemy stationed at Berryville, General Ewell, with the rest of his command, moved upon Winchester, Johnson's division advancing by the Front Royal road, Early's by the Valley turnpike, which it entered at Newtown, where it was joined by the Maryland troops.

BATTLE OF WINCHESTER.

The enemy was driven in on both roads, and our troops halted in line of battle near the town on the evening of the 13th. The same day the force which had occupied Berryville retreated to Winchester on the approach of General Rodes. The following morning, General Ewell ordered General Early to carry an intrenched position northwest of Winchester, near the Pughtown road, which the latter officer, upon examining the ground, discovered would command the principal fortifications.

To cover the movement of General Early, General Johnson took position between the road to Millwood and that to Berryille, and advanced his skirmishers toward the town. General Early, leaving a portion of his command to engage the enemy's attention, with the remainder gained a favorable position without being perceived, and, about 5 p. m., twenty pieces of artillery, under Lieut. Col. H. P. Jones, opened suddenly upon the intrenchments. The enemy's guns were soon silenced. Hays' brigade then advanced to the assault, and carried the works by storm, capturing six rifled pieces, two of which were turned upon and dispersed a column which was forming to retake the position. The enemy immediately abandoned the works on the left of those taken by Hays, and retired into his main fortifications, which General Early prepared to assail in the morning. The loss of the advanced works, however, rendered the others untenable, and the enemy retreated in the night, abandoning his sick and wounded, together with his artillery, wagons, and stores. Anticipating such a movement, as soon as he heard of Early's success, General Ewell directed General Johnson to occupy, with part of his command, a point on the Martinsburg road, about 2 ½ miles from Winchester, where he could either intercept the enemy's retreat, or aid in an attack should further resistance be offered in the morning. General Johnson marched with Nicholls' and part of Steuart's brigades, accompanied by Lieutenant-Colonel [R. S.] Andrews with a detachment of his artillery, the Stonewall Brigade being ordered to follow. Finding the road to the place indicated by General Ewell difficult of passage in the darkness, General Johnson pursued that leading by Jordan Springs to Stephenson's Depot, where he took a favorable position on the Martinsburg road, about 5 miles from Winchester. Just as his line was formed, the retreating column, consisting of the main body of General Milroy's army, arrived, and immediately attacked him. The enemy, though in superior force, consisting of both infantry and cavalry, was gallantly repulsed, and, finding all efforts to cut his way unavailing, he sent strong flanking parties simultaneously to the right and left, still keeping up a heavy fire in front. The party on the right was driven back and pursued by the Stonewall Brigade, which opportunely arrived. That on the left was broken and dispersed by the Second and Tenth Louisiana Regiments, aided by the artillery, and in a short time nearly the whole infantry force, amounting to more than 2,300 men, with eleven stand of colors, surrendered, the cavalry alone escaping. General Milroy, with a small party of fugitives, fled to Harper's Ferry. The number of prisoners taken in this action exceeded the force engaged under General Johnson, who speaks in terms of well-deserved praise of the conduct of the officers and men of his command.

In the meantime, General Rodes marched from Berryville to Martinsburg, reaching the latter place in the afternoon of the 14th. The enemy made a show of resistance, but soon gave way, the cavalry and artillery retreating toward Williamsport, the infantry toward Shepherdstown, under cover of night. The route taken by the latter was not known until it was too late to follow; but the former were pursued so rapidly, Jenkins' troops leading, that they were forced to abandon five of their six pieces of artillery. About 200 prisoners were taken, but the enemy destroyed most of his stores.

These operations resulted in the expulsion of the enemy from the Valley; the capture of 4,000 prisoners, with a corresponding number of small-arms; 28 pieces of superior artillery, including those taken by Generals Rodes and Hays; about 300 wagons and as many horses, together with a considerable quantity of ordnance, commissary, and quartermaster's stores.

Our entire loss was 47 killed, 219 wounded, and 3 missing.

MARCH INTO PENNSYLVANIA.

On the night of Ewell's appearance at Winchester, the enemy in front of A. P. Hill, at Fredericksburg, recrossed the Rappahannock, and the whole army of General Hooker withdrew from the north side of the river. In order to mislead him as to our intentions, and at the same time protect Hill's corps in its march up the Rappahannock, Longstreet left Culpeper Court-House on the 15th, and, advancing along the eastern side of the Blue Ridge, occupied Ashby's and Snicker's Gaps. He had been joined, while at Culpeper, by General Pickett, with three brigades of his division. General Stuart, with three brigades of cavalry, moved on Longstreet's right, and took position in front of the Gaps. Hampton's and [W. E.] Jones' brigades remained along the Rappahannock and Hazel

Rivers, in front of Culpeper Court-House, with instructions to follow the main body as soon as Hill's corps had passed that point.

On the 17th, Fitz. Lee's brigade, under Colonel Munford, which was on the road to Snicker's Gap, was attacked near Aldie by the Federal cavalry. The attack was repulsed with loss, and the brigade held its ground until ordered to fall back, its right being threatened by another body, coming from Hopewell toward Middleburg. The latter force was driven from Middleburg, and pursued toward Hopewell by Robertson's brigade, which arrived about dark. Its retreat was intercepted by W. H. F. Lee's brigade, under Colonel Chambliss, jr., and the greater part of a regiment captured.

During the three succeeding days there was much skirmishing, General Stuart taking a position west of Middleburg, where he awaited the rest of his command.

General Jones arrived on the 19th, and General Hampton in the afternoon of the following day, having repulsed, on his march, a cavalry force sent to reconnoiter in the direction of Warrenton.

On the 21st, the enemy attacked with infantry and cavalry, and obliged General Stuart, after a brave resistance, to fall back to the gaps of the mountains. The enemy retired the next day, having advanced only a short distance beyond Upperville.

In these engagements, the cavalry sustained a loss of 510 killed, wounded, and missing. Among them were several valuable officers, whose names are mentioned in General Stuart's report. One piece of artillery was disabled and left on the field. The enemy's loss was heavy. About 400 prisoners were taken and several stand of colors.

The Federal Army was apparently guarding the approaches to Washington, and manifested no disposition to assume the offensive.

In the meantime, the progress of Ewell, who was already in Maryland, with Jenkins' cavalry advanced into Pennsylvania as far as Chambersburg, rendered it necessary that the rest of the army should be within supporting distance, and Hill having reached the Valley, Longstreet was withdrawn to the west side of the Shenandoah, and the two corps encamped near Berryville.

General Stuart was directed to hold the mountain passes with part of his command as long as the enemy remained south of the Potomac, and, with the remainder, to cross into Maryland, and place himself on the right of General Ewell. Upon the suggestion of the former officer that he could damage the enemy and delay his passage of the river by getting in his rear, he was authorized to do so, and it was left to his discretion whether to enter Maryland east or west of the Blue Ridge; but he was instructed to lose no time in placing his command on the right of our column as soon as he should perceive the enemy moving northward.

On the 22d, General Ewell marched into Pennsylvania with Rodes' and Johnson's divisions, preceded by Jenkins' cavalry, taking the road from Hagerstown, through Chambersburg, to Carlisle, where he arrived on the 27th. Early's division, which had occupied Boonsborough, moved by a parallel road to Greenwood, and, in pursuance of instructions previously given to General Ewell, marched toward York.

On the 24th, Longstreet and Hill were put in motion to follow Ewell, and, on the 27th, encamped near Chambersburg.

General Imboden, under the orders before referred to, had been operating on Ewell's left while the latter was advancing into Maryland. He drove off the troops guarding the Baltimore and Ohio Railroad, and destroyed all the important bridges on that route from Martinsburg to Cumberland, besides inflicting serious damage upon the Chesapeake and Ohio Canal. He was at Hancock when Longstreet and Hill reached Chambersburg, and was directed to proceed to the latter place by way of McConnellsburg, collecting supplies for the army on his route.

The cavalry force at this time with the army, consisting of Jenkins' brigade and [E. V.] White's battalion, was not greater than was required to accompany the advance of General Ewell and General Early, with whom it performed valuable service, as appears from their reports. It was expected that as soon as the Federal Army should cross the Potomac, General Stuart would give notice of its movements, and nothing having been heard from him since our entrance into Maryland, it was inferred that the enemy had not yet left Virginia. Orders were, therefore, issued to move upon Harrisburg. The expedition of General Early to York was designed in part to prepare for this undertaking by breaking the railroad between Baltimore and Harrisburg, and seizing the bridge over the Susquehanna at Wrightsville. General Early succeeded in the first object, destroying a number of bridges above and below York, but on the approach of the troops sent by him to Wrightsville, a body of militia stationed at that place fled across the river and burned the bridge in their retreat. General Early then marched to rejoin his corps.

The advance against Harrisburg was arrested by intelligence received from a scout on the night of the 28th, to the effect that the army of General Hooker had crossed the Potomac, and was approaching the South Mountain. In the absence of the cavalry, it was impossible to ascertain his intentions; but to deter him from advancing farther west, and intercepting our communication with Virginia, it was determined to concentrate the army east of the mountains.

BATTLE OF GETTYSBURG.

Hill's corps was accordingly ordered to move toward Cashtown on the 29th, and Longstreet to follow the next day, leaving Pickett's division at Chambersburg to guard the rear until relieved by Imboden. General Ewell was recalled from Carlisle, and directed to join the army at Cashtown or Gettysburg, as circumstances might require. The advance of the enemy to the latter place was unknown, and the weather being inclement, the march was conducted with a view to the comfort of the troops. Heth's division reached Cashtown on the 29th, and the following morning Pettigrew's brigade, sent by General Heth to procure supplies at Gettysburg, found it occupied by the enemy. Being ignorant of the extent of his force, General Pettigrew was unwilling to hazard an attack with his single brigade, and returned to Cashtown.

General Hill arrived with Pender's division in the evening, and the following morning (July 1) advanced with these two divisions, accompanied by Pegram's and McIntosh's battalions of artillery, to ascertain the strength of the enemy, whose force was supposed to consist chiefly of cavalry. The leading division, under General Heth, found the enemy's vedettes about 3 miles west of Gettysburg, and continued to advance until within a mile of the town, when two brigades were sent forward to reconnoiter. They drove in the advance of the enemy very gallantly, but subsequently encountered largely superior numbers, and were compelled to retire with loss, Brigadier-General Archer, commanding one of the brigades, being taken prisoner. General Heth then prepared for action, and as soon as Pender arrived to support him, was ordered by General Hill to advance. The artillery was placed in position, and the engagement opened with vigor. General Heth pressed the enemy steadily back, breaking his first and second lines, and attacking his third with great resolution. About 2.30 p. m. the advance of Ewell's corps, consisting of Rodes' division, with Carter's battalion of artillery, arrived by the Middletown road, and, forming on Heth's left, nearly at right angles with his line, became warmly engaged with fresh numbers of the enemy. Heth's troops, having suffered heavily in their protracted contest with a superior force, were relieved by Pender's, and Early, coming up by the Heidlersburg road soon afterward, took position on the left of Rodes, when a general advance was made.

The enemy gave way on all sides, and was driven through Gettysburg with great loss. Major-General Reynolds, who was in command, was killed. More than 5,000 prisoners, exclusive of a large number of wounded, three pieces of artillery, and several colors were captured. Among the prisoners were two brigadier-generals, one of whom was badly wounded. Our own loss was heavy, including a number of officers, among whom were Major-General Heth, slightly, and Brigadier-General Scales, of Pender's division, severely, wounded. The enemy retired to a range of hills south of Gettysburg, where he displayed a strong force of infantry and artillery.

It was ascertained from the prisoners that we had been engaged with two corps of the army formerly commanded by General Hooker, and that the remainder of that army, under General Meade, was approaching Gettysburg. Without information as to its proximity, the strong position which the enemy had assumed could not be attacked without danger of exposing the four divisions present, already weakened and exhausted by a long and bloody struggle, to overwhelming numbers of fresh troops. General Ewell was, therefore, instructed to carry the hill occupied by the enemy, if he found it practicable, but to avoid a general engagement until the arrival of the other divisions of the army, which were ordered to hasten forward. He decided to await Johnson's division, which had marched from Carlisle by the road west of the mountains to guard the trains of his corps, and consequently did not reach Gettysburg until a late hour.

In the meantime the enemy occupied the point which General Ewell designed to seize, but in what force could not be ascertained, owing to the darkness. An intercepted dispatch showed that another corps had halted that afternoon 4 miles from Gettysburg. Under these circumstances, it was decided not to attack until the arrival of Longstreet, two of whose divisions (those of Hood and McLaws) encamped about 4 miles in the rear during the night. Anderson's division of Hill's corps came up after the engagement.

It had not been intended to deliver a general battle so far from our base unless attacked, but coming unexpectedly upon the whole Federal Army, to withdraw through the mountains with our extensive trains would have been difficult and dangerous. At the same time we were unable to await an attack, as the country was unfavorable for collecting supplies in the presence of the enemy, who could restrain our foraging parties by holding the mountain passes with local and other troops. A battle had, therefore, become in a measure unavoidable, and the success already gained gave hope of a favorable issue.

The enemy occupied a strong position, with his right upon two commanding elevations adjacent to each other, one southeast and the other, known as Cemetery Hill, immediately south of the town, which lay at its base. His line extended thence upon the high ground along the Emmitsburg road, with a steep ridge in rear, which was also occupied. This ridge was difficult of ascent, particularly the two hills above mentioned as forming its northern extremity, and a third at the other end, on which the enemy's left rested. Numerous stone and rail fences along the slope served to afford protection to his troops and impede our advance. In his front, the ground was undulating and generally open for about three-quarters of a mile.

General Ewell's corps constituted our left, Johnson's division being opposite the height adjoining Cemetery Hill, Early's in the center, in front of the north race of the latter, and Rodes upon his right. Hill's corps faced the west side of Cemetery Hill, and extended nearly parallel to the Emmitsburg road, making an angle with Ewell's, Pender's division formed his left, Anderson's his right, Heth's, under Brigadier-General Pettigrew, being in reserve. His artillery, under Colonel [R. L.] Walker, was posted in eligible positions along his line.

It was determined to make the principal attack upon the enemy's left, and endeavor to gain a position from which it was thought that our artillery could be brought to bear with effect. Longstreet was directed to place the divisions of McLaws and Hood on the right of Hill, partially enveloping the enemy's left, which he was to drive in.

General Hill was ordered to threaten the enemy's center, to prevent re-enforcements being drawn to either wing, and co-operate with his right division in Longstreet's attack.

General Ewell was instructed to make a simultaneous demonstration upon the enemy's right, to be converted into a real attack should opportunity offer.

About 4 p. m. Longstreet's batteries opened, and soon afterward Hood's division, on the extreme right, moved to the attack. McLaws followed somewhat later, four of Anderson's brigades, those of Wilcox, Perry, [A. R.] Wright, and Posey supporting him on the left, in the order named. The enemy was soon driven from his position on the Emmitsburg road to the cover of a ravine and a line of stone fences at the foot of the ridge in his rear. He was dislodged from these after a severe struggle, and retired up the ridge, leaving a number of his batteries in our possession. Wilcox's and Wright's brigades advanced with great gallantry, breaking successive lines of the enemy's infantry, and compelling him to abandon much of his artillery. Wilcox readied the foot and Wright gained the crest of the ridge itself, driving the enemy down the opposite side; but having become separated from McLaws and gone beyond the other two brigades of the division, they were attacked in front and on both flanks, and compelled to retire, being unable to bring off any of the captured artillery. McLaws' left also fell back, and, it being now nearly dark, General Longstreet determined to await the arrival of General Pickett. He disposed his command to hold the ground gained on the right, withdrawing his left to the first position from which the enemy had been driven.

Four pieces of artillery, several hundred prisoners, and two regimental flags were taken. As soon as the engagement began on our right, General Johnson opened with his artillery, and about two hours later advanced up the hill next to Cemetery Hill with three brigades, the fourth being detained by a demonstration on his left. Soon afterward, General Early attacked Cemetery Hill with two brigades, supported by a third, the fourth having been previously detached. The enemy had greatly increased by earthworks the strength of the positions assailed by Johnson and Early.

The troops of the former moved steadily up the steep and rugged ascent, under a heavy fire, driving the enemy into his intrenchments, part of which was carried by Steuart's brigade, and a number of prisoners taken. The contest was continued to a late hour, but without further advantage. On Cemetery Hill, the attack by Early's leading brigades—those of Hays and Hoke, under Colonel Avery—was made with vigor. Two lines of the enemy's infantry were dislodged from the cover of some stone and board fences on the side of the ascent, and driven back into the works on the crest, into which our troops forced their way, and seized several pieces of artillery.

A heavy force advanced against their right, which was without support, and they were compelled to retire, bringing with them about 100 prisoners and four stand of colors. General Ewell had directed General Rodes to attack in concert with Early, covering his right, and had requested Brigadier-General Lane, then commanding Pender's division, to co-operate on the right of Rodes. When the time to attack arrived. General Rodes, not having his troops in position, was unprepared to co-operate with General Early, and before he could get in readiness the latter had been obliged to retire for want of the expected support on his right. General Lane was prepared to give the assistance required of him, and so informed General Rodes, but the latter deemed it useless to advance after the failure of Early's attack.

In this engagement our loss in men and officers was large. Major-Generals Hood and Pender, Brigadier-Generals [J. M.] Jones, Semmes, G. T. Anderson, and Barksdale, and Colonel Avery, commanding Hoke's brigade, were wounded, the last two mortally. Generals Pender and Semmes died after their removal to Virginia.

The result of this day's operations induced the belief that, with proper concert of action, and with the increased support that the positions gained on the right would enable the artillery to render the assaulting columns, we should ultimately succeed, and it was accordingly determined to continue the attack. The general plan was unchanged. Longstreet, re-enforced by Pickett's three brigades, which arrived near the battle-field during the afternoon of the 2d, was ordered to attack the next morning, and General Ewell was directed to assail the enemy's right at the same time. The latter, during the night, re-enforced General Johnson with two brigades from Rodes' and one from Early's division.

General Longstreet's dispositions were not completed as early as was expected, but before notice could be sent to General Ewell, General Johnson had already become engaged, and it was too late to recall him. The enemy attempted to recover the works taken the preceding evening, but was repulsed, and General Johnson attacked in turn.

After a gallant and prolonged struggle, in which the enemy was forced to abandon part of his intrenchments, General Johnson found himself unable to carry the strongly fortified crest of the hill. The projected attack on the enemy's left not having been made, he was enabled to hold his right with a force largely superior to that of General Johnson, and finally to threaten his flank and rear, rendering it necessary for him to retire to his original position about 1 p. m.

General Longstreet was delayed by a force occupying the high, rocky hills on the enemy's extreme left, from which his troops could be attacked in reverse as they advanced. His operations had been embarrassed the day previous by the same cause, and he now deemed it necessary to defend his flank and rear with the divisions of Hood and McLaws. He was, therefore, re-enforced by Heth's division and two brigades of Pender's, to the command of which Major-General Trimble was assigned. General Hill was directed to hold his line with the rest of his command, afford General Longstreet further assistance, if required, and avail himself of any success that might be gained.

A careful examination was made of the ground secured by Longstreet, and his batteries placed in positions, which, it was believed, would enable them to silence those of the enemy. Hill's artillery and part of Ewell's was ordered to open simultaneously, and the assaulting column to advance under cover of the combined fire of the three. The batteries were directed to be pushed forward as the infantry progressed, protect their flanks, and support their attacks closely.

About 1 p. m., at a given signal, a heavy cannonade was opened, and continued for about two hours with marked effect upon the enemy. His batteries replied vigorously at first, but toward the close their fire slackened perceptibly, and General Longstreet ordered forward the column of attack, consisting of Pickett's and Heth's divisions, in two lines, Pickett on the right. Wilcox's brigade marched in rear of Pickett's right, to guard that flank, and Heth's was supported by Lane's and Scales' brigades, under General Trimble.

The troops moved steadily on, under a heavy fire of musketry and artillery, the main attack being directed against the enemy's left center.

His batteries reopened as soon as they appeared. Our own having nearly exhausted their ammunition in the protracted cannonade that preceded the advance of the infantry, were unable to reply, or render the necessary support to the attacking party. Owing to this fact, which was unknown to me when the assault took place, the enemy was enabled to throw a strong force of infantry against our left, already wavering under a concentrated fire of artillery from the ridge in front, and from Cemetery Hill, on the left. It finally gave way, and the right, after penetrating the enemy's lines, entering his advance works, and capturing some of his artillery, was attacked simultaneously in front and on both flanks, and driven back with heavy loss.

The troops were rallied and reformed, but the enemy did not pursue.

A large number of brave officers and men fell or were captured on this occasion. Of Pickett's three brigade commanders, Generals Armistead and [R. B.] Garnett were killed, and General Kemper dangerously wounded.

Major-General Trimble and Brigadier-General Pettigrew were also wounded, the former severely.

The movements of the army preceding the battle of Gettysburg had been much embarrassed by the absence of the cavalry. As soon as it was known that the enemy had crossed into Maryland, orders were sent to the brigades of [B. H.] Robertson and [William E.] Jones, which had been left to guard the passes of the Blue Ridge, to rejoin the army without delay, and it was expected that General Stuart, with the remainder of his command, would soon arrive. In the exercise of the discretion given him when Longstreet and Hill marched into Maryland, General Stuart determined to pass around the rear of the Federal Army with three brigades and cross the Potomac between it and Washington, believing that he would be able, by that route, to place himself on our right flank in time to keep us properly advised of the enemy's movements. He marched from Salem on the night of June 24, intending to pass west of Centreville, but found the enemy's forces so distributed as to render that route impracticable. Adhering to his original plan, he was forced to make a wide detour through Buckland and Brentsville, and crossed the Occoquan at Wolf Run Shoals on the morning of the 27th. Continuing his march through Fairfax Court-House and Dranesville, he arrived at the Potomac, below the mouth of Seneca Creek, in the evening.

He found the river much swollen by the recent rains, but, after great exertion, gained the Maryland shore before midnight with his whole command.

He now ascertained that the Federal Army, which he had discovered to be drawing toward the Potomac, had crossed the day before, and was moving toward Frederick, thus interposing itself between him and our forces.

He accordingly marched northward, through Rockville and Westminster, to Hanover, Pa., where he arrived on the 30th; but the enemy advanced with equal rapidity on his left, and continued to obstruct communication with our main body.

Supposing, from such information as he could obtain, that part of the army was at Carlisle, he left Hanover that night, and proceeded thither by way of Dover.

He reached Carlisle on July 1, where he received orders to proceed to Gettysburg.

He arrived in the afternoon of the following day, and took position on General Ewell's left. His leading brigade, under General Hampton, encountered and repulsed a body of the enemy's cavalry at Hunterstown, endeavoring to reach our rear.

General Stuart had several skirmishes during his march, and at Hanover quite a severe engagement took place with a strong force of cavalry, which was finally compelled to withdraw from the town.

The prisoners taken by the cavalry and paroled at various places amounted to about 800, and at Rockville a large train of wagons coming from Washington was intercepted and captured. Many of them were destroyed, but 125, with all the animals of the train, were secured.

The ranks of the cavalry were much reduced by its long and arduous march, repeated conflicts, and insufficient supplies of food and forage, but the day after its arrival at Gettysburg it engaged the enemy's cavalry with unabated spirit, and effectually protected our left.

In this action, Brigadier-General Hampton was seriously wounded, while acting with his accustomed gallantry.

Robertson's and Jones' brigades arrived on July 3, and were stationed upon our right flank. The severe loss sustained by the army and the reduction of its ammunition, rendered another attempt to dislodge the enemy inadvisable, and it was, therefore, determined to withdraw.

The trains, with such of the wounded as could bear removal, were ordered to Williamsport on July 4, part moving through Cashtown and Greencastle, escorted by General Imboden, and the remainder by the Fairfield road.

The army retained its position until dark, when it was put in motion for the Potomac by the last-named route.

A heavy rain continued throughout the night, and so much impeded its progress that Ewell's corps, which brought up the rear, did not leave Gettysburg until late in the forenoon of the following day. The enemy offered no serious interruption, and, after an arduous march, we arrived at Hagerstown in the afternoon of the 6th and morning of July 7.

The great length of our trains made it difficult to guard them effectually in passing through the mountains, and a number of wagons and ambulances were captured. They succeeded in reaching Williamsport on the 6th, but were unable to cross the Potomac on account of the high stage of water. Here they were attacked by a strong force of cavalry and artillery, which was gallantly repulsed by General Imboden, whose command had been strengthened by several batteries and by two regiments of infantry, which had been detached at Winchester to guard prisoners, and were returning to the army.

While the enemy was being held in check, General Stuart arrived with the cavalry, which had performed valuable service in guarding the flanks of the army during the retrograde movement, and, after a short engagement, drove him from the field. The rains that had prevailed almost without intermission since our entrance into Maryland, and greatly interfered with our movements, had made the Potomac unfordable, and the pontoon bridge left at Falling Waters had been partially destroyed by the enemy. The wounded and prisoners were sent over the river as rapidly as possible in a few ferry-boats, while the trains awaited the subsiding of the waters and the construction of a new pontoon bridge.

On July 8, the enemy's cavalry advanced toward Hagerstown, but was repulsed by General Stuart, and pursued as far as Boonsborough.

With this exception, nothing but occasional skirmishing occurred until the 12th, when the main body of the enemy arrived. The army then took a position previously selected, covering the Potomac from Williamsport to Falling Waters, where it remained for two days, with the enemy immediately in front, manifesting no disposition to attack, but throwing up intrenchments along his whole line.

By the 13th, the river at Williamsport, though still deep, was fordable, and a good bridge was completed at Falling Waters, new boats having being constructed and some of the old recovered. As further delay would enable the enemy to obtain re-enforcements, and as it was found difficult to procure a sufficient supply of flour for the troops, the working of the mills being interrupted by high water, it was determined to await an attack no longer.

Orders were accordingly given to cross the Potomac that night, Ewell's corps by the ford at Williamsport, and those of Longstreet and Hill on the bridge.

The cavalry was directed to relieve the infantry skirmishers, and bring up the rear.

The movement was much retarded by a severe rain storm and the darkness of the night. Ewell's corps, having the advantage of a turnpike road, marched with less difficulty, and crossed the river by 8 o'clock the following morning. The condition of the road to the bridge and the time consumed in the passage of the artillery, ammunition wagons, and ambulances, which could not ford the river, so much delayed the progress of Longstreet and Hill, that it was daylight before their troops began to cross. Heth's division was halted about a mile and a half from the bridge, to protect the passage of the column. No interruption was offered by the enemy until about 11 a. m., when his cavalry, supported by artillery, appeared in front of General Heth.

A small number in advance of the main body was mistaken for our own cavalry retiring, no notice having been given of the withdrawal of the latter, and was suffered to approach our lines. They were immediately destroyed or captured, with the exception of two or three, but Brigadier-General Pettigrew, an officer of great merit and promise, was mortally wounded in the encounter. He survived his removal to Virginia only a few days.

The bridge being clear, General Heth began to withdraw. The enemy advanced, but his efforts to break our lines were repulsed, and the passage of the river was completed by 1 p. m. Owing to the extent of General Heth's line, some of his men most remote from the bridge were cut off before they could reach it, but the greater part of those taken by the enemy during the movement (supposed to amount in all to about 500) consisted of men from various commands who lingered behind, overcome by previous labors and hardships, and the fatigue of a most trying night march. There was no loss of materiel excepting a few broken wagons and two pieces of artillery, which the horses were unable to draw through the deep mud. Other horses were sent back for them, but the rear of the column had passed before their arrival.

The army proceeded to the vicinity of Bunker Hill and Darkesville, where it halted to afford the troops repose.

The enemy made no effort to follow excepting with his cavalry, which crossed the Potomac at Harper's Ferry, and advanced toward Martinsburg on July 16.

They were attacked by General Fitz. Lee, with his own and Chambliss' brigades, and driven back with loss.

When the army returned to Virginia, it was intended to move into Loudoun, but the Shenandoah was found to be impassable. While waiting for it to subside, the enemy crossed the Potomac east of the Blue Ridge, and seized the passes we designed to use. As he continued to advance along the eastern slope, apparently with the purpose of cutting us off from the railroad to Richmond, General Longstreet was ordered, on July 19, to proceed to Culpeper Court-House, by way of Front Royal. He succeeded in passing part of his command over the Shenandoah in time to prevent the occupation of Manassas and Chester Gaps by the enemy, whose cavalry had already made its appearance.

As soon as a pontoon bridge could be laid down, the rest of his corps crossed the river, and marched through Chester Gap to Culpeper Court-House, where it arrived on the 24th. He was followed without serious opposition by General A. P. Hill.

General Ewell having been detained in the Valley by an effort to capture a force of the enemy guarding the Baltimore and Ohio Railroad west of Martinsburg, Wright's brigade was left to hold Manassas Gap until his arrival. He reached Front Royal on the 23d, with Johnson's and Rodes' divisions, Early's being near Winchester, and found General Wright skirmishing with the enemy's infantry, which had already appeared in Manassas Gap. General Ewell supported Wright with Rodes' division and some artillery, and the enemy was held in check.

Finding that the Federal force greatly exceeded his own, General Ewell marched through Thornton's Gap, and ordered Early to move up the Valley by Strasburg and New Market. He encamped near Madison Court-House on July 29.

The enemy massed his army in the vicinity of Warrenton, and, on the night of July 31 his cavalry, with a large supporting force of infantry, crossed the Rappahannock at Rappahannock Station and Kelly's Ford.

The next day they advanced toward Brandy Station, their progress being gallantly resisted by General Stuart with Hampton's brigade, commanded by Colonel [L. S.] Baker, who fell back gradually to our lines, about 2 miles south of Brandy. Our infantry skirmishers advanced, and drove the enemy beyond Brandy Station. It was now determined to place the army in a position to enable it more readily to oppose the enemy should he attempt to move southward, that near Culpeper Court-House being one that he could easily avoid. Longstreet and Hill were put in motion August 3, leaving the cavalry at Culpeper. Ewell had been previously ordered from Madison, and, by the 4th, the army occupied the line of the Rapidan.

The highest praise is due to both officers and men for their conduct during the campaign. The privations and hardships of the march and camp were cheerfully encountered, and borne with a fortitude unsurpassed by our ancestors in their struggle for independence, while their courage in battle entitles them to rank with the soldiers of any army and of any time. Their forbearance and discipline, under strong provocation to retaliate for the cruelty of the enemy to our own citizens, is not their least claim to the respect and admiration of their countrymen and of the world.

I forward returns of our loss in killed, wounded, and missing. Many of the latter were killed or wounded in the several assaults at Gettysburg, and necessarily left in the hands of the enemy. I cannot speak of these brave men as their merits and exploits deserve. Some of them are appropriately mentioned in the accompanying reports, and the memory or all will be gratefully and affectionately cherished by the people in whose defense they fell.

The loss of Major-General Pender is severely felt by the army and the country. He served with this army from the beginning of the war, and took a distinguished part in all its engagements. Wounded on several occasions, he never left his command in action until he received the injury that resulted in his death. His promise and usefulness as an officer were only equaled by the purity and excellence of his private life.

Brigadier-Generals Armistead, Barksdale, Garnett, and Semmes died as they had lived, discharging the highest duty of patriots with devotion that never faltered and courage that shrank from no danger.

I earnestly commend to the attention of the Government those gallant officers and men whose conduct merited the special commendation of their superiors, but whose names I am unable to mention in this report.

The officers of the general staff of the army were unremittingly engaged in the duties of their respective departments. Much depended on their management and exertion. The labors of the quartermaster's, commissary, and medical departments were more than usually severe. The inspectors-general were also laboriously occupied in their attention to the troops, both on the march and in camp, and the officers of engineers showed skill and judgment in expediting the passage of rivers and streams, the swollen condition of which, by almost continuous rains, called for extraordinary exertion.

The chief of ordnance and his assistants are entitled to praise for the care and watchfulness given to the ordnance trains and ammunition of the army, which, in a long march and in many conflicts, were always at hand and accessible to the troops.

My thanks are due to my personal staff for their constant aid afforded me at all times, on the march and in the field, and their willing discharge of every duty.

There were captured at Gettysburg nearly 7,000 prisoners, of whom about 1,500 were paroled, and the remainder brought to Virginia. Seven pieces of artillery were also secured.

I forward herewith the reports of the corps, division, and other commanders mentioned in the accompanying schedule, together with maps of the scene of operations, and one showing the routes pursued by the army.

Respectfully submitted.

R. E. LEE,

General.[1]

Acknowledgments

No one writes a book alone—especially a work of history. Many people contributed to this one. My thanks to associate publisher Alex Novak of Regnery History for his direction in developing this title, and to Regnery executive editor and fellow historian Harry Crocker. Maria Ruhl, Amber Colleran, Amanda Larsen, Lindsey Reinstrom, and others on the Regnery team were consistently professional and pleasant, and I appreciate their valuable assistance. Many thanks are due as well to Joel Kneedler, my literary agent, and the other great folks at Alive Communications. I'm grateful to Coastal Carolina University and the Center for Military and Veterans Studies at CCU for the opportunity to research and publish in the field of military history. I'm also grateful to Center chairman George H. Goldfinch Jr. and the Center's board of directors.

Numerous research and archival institutions graciously assisted in the research for this work, including the Manuscripts Division and the Prints and Photographs Division at the Library of Congress, the National Archives, Musselman Library at Gettysburg College, the Minnesota Historical Society, the David M. Rubenstein Rare Book and Manuscript Library at Duke University, the U.S. Military Academy Library at West Point, the Southern Historical

Collection at the University of North Carolina-Chapel Hill, the Adams County Historical Society in Gettysburg, the Eleanor Brockenbrough Library at the Museum of the Confederacy, the Civil War Library and Museum of Philadelphia, the North Carolina Department of Archives and History, the U.S. Army Historical Center at Carlisle Barracks, the Moravian Musical Foundation, the Bentley Historical Library at the University of Michigan, DeGolyer Library at Southern Methodist University, Alderman Library at the University of Virginia, and Kimbel Library at Coastal Carolina University.

I'm also grateful to historians Edward Bonekemper, H. W. Crocker III, David Cleutz, Robert Hancock, Edward Longacre, Phillip Tucker, Clyde Wilson, and Stephen E. Woodworth. Many thanks also to Scott Hilts, Dennis Reed, J. R. Gorrell, Mark Roach, and the Wednesday Bible study group; Jerry Curkendal and the men's group at Carolina Forest Community Church; Stoval Witte, David Frost, the Rev. Rick Atkins, the Rev. John R. Riddle, Dr. Harry Reeder, and many others. I owe a unique debt to my parents, Skip and Elizabeth Gragg, who sparked my lifelong love of history with many books and trips, including my first visit to Gettysburg as a small boy in 1959. I'm very grateful to my brother Ted, my cousins Bob, Charles, and Tony, and "Aunty" Delores, who helped fuel the fires of history—and for Connie, Sandra, and Martha for their good-natured patience. I'm also thankful for Deborah, Margaret, Joe, Jackie, Doug, Tina, John, Gail, Jimmy, Newt, and Mama-O—and for the next generations of history-lovers: Wendy, John, Eddie, Vaughn, Holly, Shelley, Meagan, Chris, Emerson, Caroline, William, Mary Catherine, Rachel Grace, Clayte, Will, Danielle, Christi, Tommy, Abbey, Shannon, Joseph, Margaret, Sam, and Caleb. Special thanks for the love and encouragement I consistently receive from by beloved brigade of "troops"—Faith, Troy, Rachel, Jay, Elizabeth, Jon, Joni, Penny, Ryan, Skip, Matt, and Miranda—and my future campers and trekkers: Kylah, Sophia, Jaxon, Gracie, Cody, Ashlyn, and Jate. Always, my deepest love and gratitude to my wife Cindy, who has patiently worn the title of "Civil War widow" throughout our marriage. Finally, I'm eternally grateful for the abiding truth of John 3:16.

Rod Gragg
Conway, SC

Notes

Chapter 1
"Advance into Pennsylvania"

1. Ralston W. Balch, *The Battle of Gettysburg: An Historical Account* (Harrisburg: Gettysburg & Harrisburg Railroad, 1885), 33–37; Edwin B. Coddington, *The Gettysburg Campaign: A Study in Command* (New York: Charles Scribner's Sons, 1963), 265.

2. *War of the Rebellion: The Official Records of the Union and Confederate Armies* (Washington, D.C.: Official Government Printing Office, 1880–1901), 27:2:305 (hereafter cited as OR); Coddington, *Gettysburg Campaign*, 73–52; Hermann Schuricht, "Jenkins' Brigade in the Gettysburg Campaign: Extracts from the Diary of Lieutenant Hermann Schuricht, of the Fourteenth Virginia Cavalry," *Southern Historical Society Papers* 24:339.

3. Douglas Southall Freeman, *R. E. Lee: A Biography* (Charles Scribner's Sons, 1947), 1:92–93, 371, 421, 436, 440–41, 2:92; J. William Jones, *Christ in the Camp: Or, Religion in Lee's Army* (Richmond: B. F. Johnson, 1888), 50; Mark Mayo Boatner III, *The Civil War Dictionary* (New York: David McKay, 1959); David S. Heidler and Jeanne T. Heidler, eds., *Encyclopedia of the American Civil War: A Political, Social, and Military History* (New York: W. W. Norton, 2000): 1153–63; Arthur Lyon Fremantle, *Three Months in the Southern States: April–June 1863* (Mobile: S. H. Goetzel, 1864), 248–49.

4.	Freeman, *R. E. Lee*, 3:18–28; Coddington, *Gettysburg Campaign*, 4–14; OR, 1:27:3:881, 887.

5.	John Bell Hood, *Advance and Retreat: Personal Experiences in the United States and Confederate States Armies* (New Orleans: G. T. Beauregard, 1880), 137; Henry K. Burgwyn to father, May 21, 1863, Burgwyn Family Papers, Southern Historical Collection (University of North Carolina at Chapel Hill); Coddington, *Gettysburg Campaign*, 11–15; Freeman, *R. E. Lee*, 3:13–16; James Bradshaw to wife, June 18, 1863, Samuel S. Biddle Papers (Special Collections Library, Duke University); Fremantle, *Three Months in the Southern States*, 205; Bell I. Wiley, *The Life of Johnny Reb* (Baton Rouge: LSU Press, 1970), 291; Boatner, *Civil War Dictionary*, 768; Alexander Hunter, "A High Private's Account of the Battle of Sharpsburg," *Southern Historical Society Papers* (October–November 1882) 10:508–9.

6.	*Encyclopedia of the Civil War*, 999–1002; Walter H. Hebert, *Fighting Joe Hooker* (Indianapolis: Bobbs-Merrill, 1944), 49; OR, 1:24:2:4; Edward G. Longacre, *The Commanders of Chancellorsville* (Nashville: Rutledge Hill Press, 2005), 100, 273; Theodore Lyman, *Meade's Headquarters, 1863–1865: Letters from Colonel Theodore Lyman from the Wilderness to Appomattox*, ed. George R. Aggasiz (Boston: Atlantic Monthly Press, 1922), 230.

7.	Hebert, *Fighting Joe Hooker*, 183; *Encyclopedia of the Civil War*, 98–101; Coddington, *Gettysburg Campaign*, 34–36; Stephen Minot Weld, *War Diary and Letters* (Boston: Riverside Press, 1912), 213; J. E. Ryder to father, June 24, 1863, Ryder Family Papers (Bentley Historical Library, University of Michigan); John P. Sheahan to father, March 2, 1863 (John Parris Sheahan Collection, Collection # 184 1/5, Maine Historical Society).

Chapter 2
"Look at Pharoah's Army Going to the Red Sea"

1.	Henry Steele Commager, ed., *The Blue and the Gray: The Story of the Civil War as Told by Participants* (New York: Fairfax Press, 1982), 591–92; Coddington, *Gettysburg Campaign*, 8–11.

2.	Coddington, *Gettysburg Campaign*, 54–60; *Encyclopedia of the Civil War*, 1531; George M. Neese, *Three Years in the Confederate Horse Artillery* (New York: Neale Pubishing, 1911), 175–79.

3.	Coddington, *Gettysburg Campaign*, 73–77; Henry K. Burgwyn to father, May 21, 1863, Burgwyn Family Papers; David H. McGee, ed., "The James Wright Letters," *Company Front* (1992) 1:69; Bradshaw to wife, June, 18, 1863,

Samuel S. Biddle Papers; George S. Bernard, "The Gettysburg Campaign," *Petersburg Enterprise*, March 3, 1894.

4. *Encyclopedia of the Civil War*, 827–28; Coddington, *Gettysburg Campaign*, 104–8; Julius Lineback, "Extracts from a Civil War Diary," *Twin Cities Daily Sentinel*, June 14, 1914–April 3, 1915; Julius Lineback Journal, June 15, 1863, Julius Lineback Papers, Southern Historical Collection, University of North Carolina at Chapel Hill; Thomas Perrett, "A Trip That Didn't Pay," Thomas Perrett Papers, North Carolina Department of Archives and History.

5. Coddington, *Gettysburg Campaign*, 150–53, 170–78; Fremantle, *Three Months in the Southern States*, 191; "Rebel Letter," Newspaper File, Edward McPherson Papers, Library of Congress; Bernard, "Gettysburg Campaign," *Petersburg Enterprise*; J. A. Strikeleather, "Recollections of the Late War," *Company Front* (October 1993), 17; W. W. Blackford, *War Years with Jeb Stuart* (New York: Charles Scribner's Sons, 1945), 223; Worsham, *Jackson's Foot Cavalry*, 150; Hoke, *Invasion of 1863*, 208, 176; OR, 1:27:3:942–943.

6. Hebert, *Fighting Joe Hooker*, 243–45; George C. Gorham, *Life and Public Services of Edwin M. Stanton* (Boston: Houghton Mifflin, 1899) 2:98–99; Coddington, *Gettysburg Campaign*, 129, 133; Journal of Marsena R. Patrick, June 17–19, 1863, Manuscripts Collection, Library of Congress; OR, 1:27:1:53, 60.

7. Gorham, *Life and Public Services of Edwin M. Stanton*, 2:99; Morris Schaff, *Battle of the Wilderness* (Boston: Houghton Mifflin, 1910), 40; Gamaliel Bradford (Boston: Houghton Mifflin, 1916), 87–88; Freeman Cleaves, *Meade of Gettysburg* (Norman: University of Oklahoma, 1960), viii–ix; Robert Underwood Johnson and Clarence Clough Buel, eds., *Battles and Leaders of the Civil War* (New York: Thomas Yoseloff, 1956), 3:242–43; OR, 1:27:3:374.

8. *Encyclopedia of the Civil War*, 827, 1295; *Boston Morning Journal*, July 4, 1863 in Coddington, *Gettysburg Campaign*, 224; *Battles and Leaders of the Civil War*, 3: 256; Rufus Dawes, *Service With The Sixth Wisconsin Volunteers* (Marietta: Alderman & Sons, 1890), 152–53; Charles W. Reed, *A Grand Terrible Drama: The Civil War Letters of Charles Wellington Reed*, ed. Eric Campbell (New York: Fordham University Press), 107–8; Charles Wellington Reed Papers, Manuscripts Collection, Library of Congress; Samuel W. Fiske, *Mr. Dunn Browne's Experiences in the Army* (Boston: Nichols and Noyes, 1866), 175–76.

9. Bell I. Wiley, *The Life of Billy Yank: The Common Soldier of the Union* (Baton Rouge: LSU Press, 1978), 36, 69; Julius Lineback Journal, July 1, 1863, Julius

Lineback Papers; John P. Sullivan, *An Irishman in the Iron Brigade: The Civil War Memoirs of James P. Sullivan*, William J. K. Beaudot and Lance J. Herdegen, (New York: Forham University Press, 1993), 93; J. Michael Miller, "Perrin's Brigade on July 1, 1863," *Gettysburg Magazine* 13:22; Matthew Marvin Diary, Matthew Marvin Papers, Minnesota Historical Society.

Chapter 3
"Into the Jaws of the Enemy"

1. Coddington, *Gettysburg Campaign*, 244–50; Charles Carlton Coffin, *Four Years of Fighting: A Volume of Personal Observations with the Army and the Navy* (Boston: Ticknor and Fields, 1866), 259.

2. Richard N. Current, ed., *Encyclopedia of the Confederacy* (New York: Simon & Schuster, 1993), 4:1551–1553; Douglas Southall Freeman, *Lee's Lieutenants: A Study in Command* (New York: Charles Scribner's Sons, 1944), 3:58–72; George Cary Eggleston, *A Rebel's Recollections* (New York: G. P. Putnam, 1878), 169; Coffin, *Four Years of Fighting*, 259; Boatner, *Civil War Dictionary*, 333; G. Moxley Sorrell, *Recollections of a Confederate Staff Officer* (New York: Neale Publishing, 1905), 61–62; John Esten Cooke, *Wearing of the Grey: Being Personal Portraits, Scenes and Adventrues of the War* (New York: E. B. Treat, 1867), 242–57.

3. Freeman, *Lee's Lieutenants*, 3:76–78; Coddington, *Gettysburg Campaign*, 260–61; Rod Gragg, *Covered With Glory: The 26th North Carolina Infantry at Gettysburg* (New York: HarperCollins, 2000), 83–86; Louis G. Young, "Pettigrew's Brigade at Gettysburg," *Histories of Several Regiments and Battalions from North Carolina in the Great War 1861–65*, Walter Clark, ed. (Goldsboro: Nash Brothers, 1901), 5:115–17.

4. Coddington, *Gettysburg Campaign*, 260–62; Boatner, *Civil War Dictionary*, 334; Willard Glazier, *Three Years in the Federal Cavalry* (New York: R. H. Fergeson), 1970: 37; Tillie Pierce Alleman, *At Gettysburg: Or, What a Girl Heard and Saw at the Battle* (New York: Lake Borland, 1889), 28–29.

5. Edward G. Longacre, *General John Buford: A Military Biography* (Cambridge: De Capo, 1995), 191; J. Willard Brown, *The Signal Corps, USA, in the War of the Rebellion* (Boston: U.S. Veterans Signal Corps Association, 1896), 193; Aaron B. Jerome to Winfield S. Hancock, October 18, 1865, *The Bachelder Papers: Gettysburg in Their Own Words*, David and Audrey Ladd, eds. (Dayton: Morningside, 1994–1995), 1:200–2; Charles S. Wainwright, *A Diary of Battle: The Personal Journals of Col. Charles S. Wainwright*, Allan Nevins, ed.

(New York: Harcourt, Brace and World, 1961), 258; John W. Busey and David G. Martin, *Regimental Strengths and Losses at Gettysburg* (Hightstown: Longstreet House, 1994), 101; OR, 27:1:368; Erick J. Wittenberg, "An Analysis of the Buford Manuscripts." *Gettysburg Magazine* 15: 9–11.

6. Henry Heth, *The Memoir of Henry Heth*, James L. Morrison, Jr., ed. (Westport: Greenwood Press, 1974), 173–74; Busey and Martin, *Regimental Strengths and Losses at Gettysburg*, 174; Coddington, *Gettysburg Campaign*, 266–67; OR, 1:27:2:637–639.

7. Coddington, *Gettysburg Campaign*, 266–67; OR, 1:27:1:927; John H. Calef, "Gettysburg: The Opening Guns," *Journal of the Military Service Institution of the United States* (January–May, 1907), 40:46–52.

8. Coddington, *Gettysburg Campaign*, 268–69; OR, 1:27:1:922–924; Ezra J. Warner, *Generals in Blue: Lives of Union Commanders* (Baton Rouge: LSU Press, 1964), 269–70); Charles H. Veil to David McConaughy, April 7, 1864, David McConaughy Papers, Special Collections, Musselman Library, Gettysburg College.

9. *Battles and Leaders of the Civil War*, 3:274–78; Coddington, *Gettysburg Campaign*, 269–71; E. P. Halstead, "The First Day of the Battle of Gettysburg," *Papers of the Military Order of the Loyal Legion, District of Columbia Commandery* (March 2, 1887) 1:3–10; W. H. Moon, "Beginning the Battle of Gettysburg," *Confederate Veteran* (December 1925), 33:449–450.

10. Coddington, *Gettysburg Campaign*, 269–73; James Henry Stine, *A History of the Army of the Potomac* (Washington: Gibson Brothers, 1893), 463–65.

Chapter 4
"We Must Fight a Battle Here"

1. Freeman, *Lee's Lieutenants*, 3:80–81; O. O. Howard to M. Jacobs, March 23, 1864, in Coddington, *Gettysburg Campaign*, 277; *Civil War Encyclopedia*, 1008–1010; James I. Robertson Jr., *A. P. Hill: The Story of a Confederate Warrior* (New York: Random House, 1987), 11, 205; Fremantle, *Three Months in the Southern States*, 254; *Encyclopedia of the Confederacy*, 2:770–71.

2. John A. Patterson, "The Death of Iverson's Brigade," *Gettysburg Magazine* (July 1991) 5:10–15; *Encyclopedia of the Civil War*, 1054, 1668; Coddington, *Gettysburg Campaign*, 290; *Histories of the Several Regiments and Battalions from North Carolina in the Great War 1861–1864*, Walter Clark, ed. (Goldsboro: Nash Brothers), 2:234–37; Isaac Hall, "Iverson's Brigade and the Part the 97th New York Played in its Capture," *National Tribune*, June 26, 1884. H. C.

Wall, "Twenty-Third Regiment," *Histories of the Several Regiments and Battalions from North Carolina in the Great War 1861–1864*, Walter Clark, ed. (Goldsboro: Nash Brothers), 2:234–37.

3. *Battles and Leaders of the Civil War*, 3:281; Tom J. Edwards, *Raising the Banner of Freedom: The 25th Ohio in the War for the Union* (Bloomington, iUniverse, 2009), 85; Charles Carlton Coffin, *Marching to Victory* (New York: Harper & Brothers, 1888), 216–18; Frank Moore, *The Civil War in Song and Story, 1861–1865* (New York: P. F. Collier, 1889), 334.

4. Coddington, *Gettysburg Campaign*, 304–5; *Encyclopedia of the Civil War*, 1713–14; *Battles and Leaders of the Civil War*, 3:281; Gary W. Gallagher, *Chancellorsville: The Battle and Its Aftermath* (Chapel Hill: University of North Carolina Press, 1996), 24–25; Francis C. Barlow, *"Fear Was Not in Him": The Civil War Letters of Francis C. Barlow,* Christian G. Samito, ed. (New York: Fordham University Press, 2004), xxi, xxxv; Alfred Lee, "Reminiscences of the Gettysburg Battle," *Lippincott's Magazine of Popular Literature and Science* (July 1883) 32:54–63.

5. *Encyclopedia of the Confederacy*, 696–97; *Encyclopedia of the Civil War*, 178–79; 853–54; Coddington, *Gettysburg Campaign*, 296–304; John B. Gordon, *Reminiscences of the Civil War* (New York: Charles Scribner's Sons, 1903), 150–55.

6. Gragg, *Covered With Glory*, 113–36; Roger L. Rosentreter, "Those Damned Black Hats: The Twenty-fourth Michigan at Gettysburg," *Michigan History Magazine* (July–August 1991) 25–31; Henry E. Marsh, "The Nineteenth Indiana at Gettysburg," Civil War Collection, U.S. Army Military History Institute; "Anniversary of Gettysburg: Forty Years After the Battle," *Charlotte Daily Observer*, July 4, 1903.

7. Henry K. Burgwyn Journal, August 27, 1861, Burgwyn Family Papers, Southern Historical Collection, University of North Carolina; William S. Powell, ed., *Dictionary of North Carolina Biography* (Chapel Hill: University of North Carolina Press, 1991), 1:276; Archie K. Davis, *Boy Colonel of the Confederacy: The Life and Times of Henry King Burgwyn Jr.* (Chapel Hill: University of North Carolina Press, 1985), 9–19; Wilbur Dorsett, "The Fourteenth Color-Bearer," *The Carolina Magazine* (1932) 8; Fred A. Olds, "Brave Carolinian Fell at Gettysburg," *Southern Historical Society Papers* 35:320.

8. Rosentreter, "Those Damned Black Hats," 25–31; Alan T. Nolan, *The Iron Brigade: A Military History* (New York: Macmillan, 1961), 359–66; Alan D. Gaff, "Here was Made Our Last and Hopeless Stand: The 'Lost' Gettysburg

Reports of the 19th Indiana," *Gettysburg Magazine* 2:30–31; "From the Twenty-Fourth," *Detroit Free Press*, July 17, 1863; OR, 1:27:1:267–73.

9.   Coddington, *Gettysburg Campaign*, 295–98; OR, 1:27:1:925; *Encyclopedia of the Civil War*, 922–23; Warner, *Generals in Blue*, 202–3; "How an Eyewitness Watched the Great Battle," *Baltimore American*, June 29, 1913; Rufus Robinson Dawes, *Service with the Sixth Wisconsin Volunteers* (Marietta: Alderman & Sons, 1890), 177–79.

10.   Freeman, *Lee's Lieutenants*, 3:91–96; *Encyclopedia of the Confederacy*, 2:549; *Encylopedia of the Civil War*, 664–65; Coddington, *Gettysburg Campaign*, 319; James I. Robertson Jr., *Stonewall Jackson: The Man, the Soldier, the Legend* (New York: Macmillan: 1997), 589; Walter H. Taylor, *Four Years with General Lee* (New York: D. Appleton, 1878), 95–96; James Power Smith, "General Lee at Gettysburg," *Southern Historical Society Papers*, 33:144–45.

Chapter 5
"He Is There and I Am Going to Attack Him"

1.   George Gordon Meade, *The Life and Letters of George Gordon Meade*, George Meade, ed. (New York; Scribner's, 1913), 2:62; *Battles and Leaders of the Civil War*, 3:336; Alexander Gardner, *Photographic Sketchbook of the War* (Mineola: Dover, 1959), 2:86.

2.   Meade, *Life and Letters of George Meade*, 2:68–72; *Battles and Leaders of the Civil War*, 3:336; OR, 1:27:1:72.

3.   Freeman, *Lee's Lieutenants*, 2:108–10; Henry Moyer, *General Lee's Headquarters at Gettysburg, Penna* (Allentown, n.p.: 1911), 1–3; *Battles and Leaders of the Civil War*, 3:245–48; James Longstreet, *From Manassas to Appomattox: Memoirs of the Civil War in America* (Philadelphia: J. B. Lippincott, 1908), 329–31; Alexander K. McClure, ed., *The Annals of the War: Written by Leading Participants North and South* (Philadelphia: Times Publishing, 1879), 421–23.

4.   *Encyclopedia of the Civil War*, 1785–1786; Glen Tucker, *High Tide at Gettysburg* (Gettysburg: Stan Clark Mililtary Books), 241; Meade, *Life and Letters*, 75–78; *Report of the Joint Committee of the Conduct of the War* (Washington: U.S. Government Printing Office, 1865), 3–15; OR, 1:27:1:126–37.

5.   Harry W. Pfanz, *Gettysburg: The Second Day* (Chapel Hill: University of North Carolina Press, 1987), 170–73; *Encyclopedia of the Civil War*, 195–96; Hood, *Advance and Retreat*, 55–56.

6. OR, 1:27:1:495–98; *Civil War Encyclopedia*, 1145–46; Coddington, *Gettysburg Campaign*, 391; Val Gile, *Rags and Hope: The Recollections of Val C. Giles, Four Years with Hood's Brigade, Fourth Texas Regiment, 1861–1864* (New York: Cowan-McCann, 1961), 180–86; Val Giles, "Four Years with Hood's Brigade, Fourth Texas Infantry," Annie B. Giles Papers, John Barker Texas History Center, University of Texas at Austin.

7. Samuel L. Webb and Margaret England Armbrester, *Alabama Governors: A Political History of the State* (University: University of Alabama Press, 2001), 121–26; William C. Oates, "Gettysburg: The Battle on the Right," *Southern Historical Society Papers* (1878) 6:172–80.

8. Edward Longacre, *Joshua Chamberlain: The Man and the Soldier* (Cambridge: Da Capo, 2003), 18–24, 27–28, 134–45; Warner, *General in Blue*, 76–77; Alice Rains Trulock, *In the Hands of Providence: Joshua Chamberlain and the American Civil War* (Chapel Hill: University of North Carolina Press, 1992), 52, 131–34; Joshua Lawrence Chamberlain, "Through Blood and Fire at Gettysburg," *Hearst's Magazine* (June 1913) 23:894–909.

Chapter 6
"Advance, Colonel, and Take Those Colors"

1. Coddington, *Gettysburg Campaign*, 411; Freeman, *Lee's Lieutenants*, 3:580; Richard Moe, *The Last Full Measure: The Life and Death of the the First MinnesotaVolunteers* (New York: Henry Holt, 1993), 268–75.

2. Pfanz, *Gettysburg*, 170–78; Carl Smith, *Gettysburg, 1863: High Tide of the Confederacy* (Oxford: Osprey, 1998), 73; Frederick H. Dyer, *A Compendium of the War of the Rebelllion* (New York: Thomas Yoseloff, 1959), 3:1425; Coddington, *Gettysburg Campaign*, 391; Frederick Phisterer, ed., *New York in the War of the Rebellion, 1861 to 1865* (Albany: D. B. Lyon, 1912), 691; Charles Weygant, *History of the One Hundred Twenty-Fourth Regiment, New York State Volunteers* (Newburgh: Journal Printing House, 1877), 180–85.

3. *Battles and Leaders of the Civil War*, 3:36; Lafayette McLaws, "Gettysburg," *Southern Historical Society Papers*, 7:70–72; Coddington, *Gettysburg Campaign*, 381; *Encyclopedia of the Civil War*, 578, 859; J. B. Polley, *Hood's Texas Brigade* (Dayton: Morningside, 1976), 177; John Coxe, "The Battle of Gettysburg," *Confederate Veteran* (1913), 21: 433–36.

4. Freeman, *Lee's Lieutenants*, 3:121–23; Levi W. Baker, *History of the Ninth Massachusetts Battery* (South Framington: Lakeview Press, 1888), 69; J. W. Muffly, ed., *A History of the 148th Pennsylvania Volunteeers* (Des Moines:

Kenyon Printing, 1904), 543; *Encyclopedia of the Confederacy*, 1:131–32; Noah Andre Trudeau, *Gettysburg: A Testing of Courage* (New York: HarperCollins, 2002), 133; Fitzgerald Ross, "A Visit to the Cities and Camps of the Confederate States, 1863-1864," *Blackwood's Edinburgh Magazine* (December 1864) 96:658–61.

5. OR, I:27:1:809,883; John Bigelow, *The Peach Orchard* (Minneapolis, MN: Kimball-Storer, 1910), 52–55; Charles Wellington Reed, *"A Grand Terrible Dramma": From Gettsyburg to Petersburg, the Civil War Letters of Charles Wellington Reed*, Eric A. Campbell, ed. (New York: Forham University Press, 2000), 345.

6. Coddington, *Gettysburg Campaign*, 422–24; Burt Feeler, "Reminscences of Col. Colvill," Paper Presented to North Shore Historical Assembly, August 22, 1936, North Shore Historical Assembly; Moe, *Last Full Measure*, 268–75; Franklyn Curtiss-Wedge, ed., *History of Goodhue County, Minnesota* (Chicago: H. C. Cooper, 1909), 520; William Lochren, "Narrative of the First Regiment," *Minnesota in the Civil and Indian Wars, 1861–1865*, C. C. Andrews, ed. (St. Paul: Pioneer Press, 1891), 34–38.

Chapter 7
"It Was a Close and Bloody Struggle"

1. *Battles and Leaders*, 312–13; Jennings Cooper Wise, *The Long Arm of Lee: The History of the Artillery of the Army of Northern Virginia* (Lincoln: University of Nebraska Press, 1991), 2: 652–53; Coddington, *Gettysburg Campaign*, 428–30.

2. Jennings Cooper Wise, *The Long Arm of Lee: The History of the Artillery of the Army of Northern Virginia* (Lincoln: University of Nebraska Press, 1991), 2: 652–53; Charles D. Walker, *Memorial Virginia Military Institute: Biographical*, 328–34; Robert Stiles, *Four Years Under Marse Robert* (New York: Neale Publishing, 1910), 217–18; John P. Nicholson, ed., *Pennsylvania at Gettysburg: Ceremonies at the Dedication of the Monuments Erected by the Commonwealth of Pennsylvania* (Harrisburg: E. K. Meyers, 1893), 2:881–82. William Worthington Goldsborough, *The Maryland Line in the Confederate Army, 1861–1865* (Baltimore: Guggenheimer, Weil, 1900), 324–25.

3. OR, 1:27:1:775, 780, 827, 856, 866; *Encyclopedia of the Confederacy*, 2:850, 866; Stephen W. Sears, *Gettysburg* (New York: Houghton Mifflin, 2003), 325–31; William F. Fox, ed., *New York at Gettysburg* (Albany: State of New

York, 1900), 2:213; *Civil War Encyclopedia*, 880–81; *Battles and Leaders*, 3:316.

4.   OR, 1:27:2:510; Coddington, *Gettysburg Campaign*, 425–27; Warner, *Generals in Gray*, 290; *Encyclopedia of the Civil War*, 1859–1860; David Cleutz, *Fields of Fame and Glory: Col. David Ireland and the 137th New York State Volunteers* (Bloomington: Xlibris: 2010), 16, 25–26, 156–61, 168; John W. Moore, ed., *Roster of North Carolina Troops in the War Between the States* (Raleigh: Ashe and Gatling, 1892), 102–4; *Ithaca Journal*, July 15, 1863.

5.   Terry Jones, *Cemetery Hill: The Struggle for the High Ground, July 1–3, 1863* (Cambridge: DaCapo, 2003), 86–89; "General Howard's Best Supper," *Daily Free Press*, September 25, 1902; Warner, *Generals in Gray*, 140; "Isaac Avery's Message to His Father, July 1863," Digital Collections, North Carolina Department of Achives and History; Daniel F. Barefoot, *General Robert F. Hoke: Lee's Modest Warrior* (Winston-Salem: J. F. Blair), 91–92; *Histories of the Several Regiments and Battalions from North Carolina*, 1:313, 2:136–138.

6.   *Histories of the Several Regiments and Battalions from North Carolina*, 1:313; Sixth North Carolina Regiment Casualties Report, *Confederate States Army Casualties: Lists and Narrative Reports*, 1861–1865, Record Group 109, War Department Collection of Confederate Records, National Archives.

7.   Terry L. Jones, *Lee's Tigers: The Louisiana Infantry in the Army of Northern Virginia* (Baton Rouge: LSU Press, 1987), 173–75; Carl Schurz, *The Reminiscences of Carl Schurz* (Garden City: Doubleday and Page: 1917), 3:24–25; OR, 1:27:2:479–82.

8.   Coddington, *Gettysburg Campaign*, 427; Bradley M. Gottfried, *The Brigades of Gettysburg: The Union and Confederate Brigades at the Battle of Gettysburg* (Campbridge: DaCapo Press, 2003), 505–6; Schurz, *Reminiscences of Carl Schurz*, 3:24–25.

9.   Jeffry D. Wert, *Gettysburg Day Three* (New York: Touchstone, 1993), 158–59; John White Johnston, *The True Story of "Jennie" Wade* (Rochester: Johnston, 1917), 15–27; William Willis Blackford, *War Years with Jeb Stuart* (Baton Rouge: LSU Press, 2001), 232–33.

10.   *Encylopedia of the Civil War*, 326–327; Daniel J. Hosington, *Gettysburg and the Christian Commission* (Brunswick: Edinborough Press, 2002), 3–5; J. B. Stillson, "Report of J.B. Stillson," *Christian Commission: Report of the Committee of Maryland* (Baltimore: James Young, 1864), 255–65.

11.   OR, 1:27:2:308; Jeffry D. Wert, *Cavalryman of the Lost Cause: A Biography of J.E.B. Stuart* (New York: Simon and Schuster, 2003), 282; Freeman, *R.E.*

Lee, 4:521; Freeman, *Lee's Lieutenants*, 2:144–148; Robertson, *A.P. Hill*, 220; Blackford, *War Years with Jeb Stuart*, 230; *Battles and Leaders*, 3:313.

Chapter 8
"The Whole Rebel Line Was Pouring Out Thunder and Iron"

1. OR, 1:27:2:319–21; Coddington, *Gettysburg Campaign*, 458–61, 473–75; Steven E. Woodworth, *Beneath a Northern Sky: A Short History of the Gettysburg Campaign* (Lanham: Rowman & Littlefield, 2008), 161.

2. Coddington, *Gettysburg Campaign*, 473–75; Woodworth, *Beneath a Northern Sky*, 161; Frank Aretas Haskell, *The Battle of Gettysburg* (Madison: Democrat Printing, 1908), 59; Edwin E. Bryant, *A History of the 3rd Wisconsin Veteran Volunteers* (Madison: Veterans Association, 1890), 393–96.

3. Fremantle, *Three Months in the Southern States*, 209–10; Richard Thompson, "A Scrap of Gettysburg," *Gettysburg Papers*, 2:101–2; Charles Weygant, "Officer Gives View of the Battlefield After the Second Day's Fighting," *New York Sun*, June 29, 1913.

4. OR, 1:27:2:319–21; Coddington, *Gettysburg Campaign*, 458–61, 473–75; Woodworth, *Beneath a Northern Sky*, 161; Longstreet, *From Manassas to Appomattox*, 385–89; Walter H. Taylor, *Four Years with General Lee* (New York: Appleton, 1878), 101–4.

5. Coddington, *Gettysburg Campaign*, 520–24; James Harvey Kidd, *Personal Recollections of a Cavalryman with Custer's Michigan Cavalry Brigade in the Civil War* (Ionia: Sentinel, 1908), 148; Eric J. Wittenberg, ed., *At Custer's Side: The Civil War Writings of James Harvy Kidd* (Kent: Kent State University Press, 2001), 129–30; James Harvey Kidd, "Address of James H. Kidd, at the Dedication of Michigan Monuments on the Battlefield at Gettysburg, June 12, 1889," *Journal of the United States Cavalry Association* (March 1891) 4:56; Frederick Whitaker, *A Complete Life of General George A. Custer* (New York: Sheldon, 1876), 2:540–43; Henry B. McClellan, *The Life and Campaigns of Major General J.E.B. Stuart* (Boston: Houghton Mifflin, 1885), 343–44.

6. OR, 1:27:1:158–59; 417–18, 464–66, 470–71; *Battles and Leaders of the Civil War*, 3:357–66; Edward Porter Alexander, *Fighting for the Confederacy: The Personal Recollections of General Edward Porter Alexander*, edited by Gary W. Gallagher (Chapel Hill: University of North Carolina Press, 1989), 253–56; Edward Porter Alexander, *Military Memoirs of a Confederate: A Critical Narrative* (New York: Charles Scribner's Sons, 1907), 418–23.

7. OR, 1:27:1:238–39; Winfield Scott, "Pickett's Charge as Seen from the Front Lines," *The Gettysburg Papers*, compiled by Ken Bandy and Florence Freeland (Dayton: Morningside, 1978), 2:904; John Gibbon, *Personal Recollections of the Civil War* (New York: G. P. Putnam's Sons, 1928), 146; Haskell, *Battle of Gettysburg*, 33–35.

8. OR, 1:27:1:228–43; Warner, *Generals in Blue*, 242; *Encyclopedia of the Civil War*, 1018; *Battles and Leaders of the Civil War*, 3:372–374.

9. OR, 1:27:1:239; *Battles and Leaders of the Civil War*, 3:364–65; Alexander, *Fighting for the Confederacy*, 258–59; Gabor S. Boritt, ed., *The Gettysburg Nobody Knows* (New York: Oxford University Press, 1997), 125; E. P. Alexander to G. Pickett, July 3, 1863, Edward Porter Alexander Papers, Manuscripts Collection, Library of Congress; Longstreet, *From Manassas to Appomattox*, 393–94.

Chapter 9
"Up, Men, and to Your Posts!"

1. OR, 1:27:1:428–35; Sears, *Gettysburg*, 400; Coddington, *Gettysburg*, 511; Gibbon, *Personal Recollections*, 150.

2. G. Moxley Sorrell, *Recollections of a Confederate Staff Officer* (New York: Neale Publishing, 1905), 54; Earl J. Hess, *Pickett's Charge: The Last Attack at Gettysburg* (Chapel Hill: University of North Carolina Press, 2001), 166; *Encyclopedia of the Civil War*, 1518; Freeman, *Lee's Lieutenants*, 3:157; George Edward Pickett and La Salle Corbell Pickett, *The Heart of a Soldier: As Revealed in the Intimate Letters of George E. Pickett* (New York: Seth Moye, 1913), 51–59; Winfield Scott, "Pickett's Charge as Seen From the Front Line," *War Papers* (Military Order of the Loyal Legion: California Commandary, 1888), 1:1–16.

3. *Encyclopedia of the Confederacy*, 664; Sorrell, *Recollections of a Confederate Staff Officer*, 172; Alexander, *Fighting for the Confederacy*, 261; Derek Smith, *The Gallant Dead: Union and Confederate Generals Killed in the Civil War* (Mechanicsburg: Stackpole), 172; Jacob Hoke, *The Great Invasion* (Dayton: W. J. Shuey, 1887), 383–87; Henry T. Owen, "Pickett at Gettysburg," *Philadelphia Weekly Times*, March 26, 1881.

4. Clyde N. Wilson, *Carolina Cavalier: The Life and Mind of James Johnston Pettigrew* (Athens: University of Georgia Press, 1990), 13–17, 41–44, 98–106, 109–14; William S. Powell, ed., *Dictionary of North Carolina Biography* (Chapel Hill: University of North Carolina Press, 1991), 5:77–79; "Pettigrew's

Old Brigade," Southern Commanders and Staff Officers File, Robert L. Brake Collection, U.S. Army Military History Institute; Michael W. Taylor, "Col. James Keith Marshall: One of Three Brigade Commanders Killed in the Pickett-Pettigrew-Trimble Charge," *Gettysburg Magazine*, 15: 78–80, 84; William F. Fox, *Regimental Losses in the American Civil War, 1861–1865* (Albany: Randow, 1889), 555–56; T. J. Cureton to Colonel J. R. Lane, June 22, 1890, John R. Lane Papers, Southern Historical Collection, University of North Carolina at Chapel Hill.

5. George T. Fleming, *The Life and Letters of Alexander Hays* (Pittsburgh: n.p., 1919), 3–4, 14–15, 28–29, 474–75; Warner, *Generals in Blue*, 223–24; *Encyclopedia of the Civil War*, 958; OR, 1:27:2:644; Gragg, *Covered With Glory*, 191–96; Franklin Sawyer, *A Military History of the 8th Ohio Volunteer Infantry* (Cleveland: Fairbanks, 1881), 130–31.

6. OR, 1:27:2:467–69, 644, 879–80; June Kimble, "Tennesseeans at Gettysburg," *Confederate Veteran* (September 1910) 18:451; Shulz, *"Double Canister at Ten Yards": The Federal Artillery and the Repulse of Pickett's Charge* (Redondo Beach: Rank and File, 1995), 55–57; Thomas M. Aldrich, *The History of Battery A, First Regiment Rhode Island Light Artillery* (Providence: Snow and Farnham, 1904), 216; James H. Lane, "Letter From General Lane," *Raleigh Observer*, November 29, 1877; "Maj. Gen. Isaac R. Trimble," *The Bachelder Papers: Gettysburg in Their Own Words*, David L. and Audrey J. Ladd, editors (Dayton: Morningside House, 1994), 2:934, 1199; Birkett D. Fry, "Pettigrew's Charge at Gettysburg," *Southern Historical Society Papers* (January–December 1879), 7: 92–93; Richard S. Thompson, "A Scrap of Gettysburg," *Military Essays and Recollections Read Before the Illinois Commandery of the Military Order of the Loyal Legion* (Chicago: Dial, 1897), 3: 104–7.

7. Freeman, *Lee's Lieutenants*, 3:191; *Encyclopedia of the Civil War*, 78–79; Almira Russell Hancock, *Reminiscences of Winfield Scott Hancock by His Wife* (New York: Charles L. Webster, 1887), 69–71.

8. Howard Coffin, *Nine Months to Gettysburg: Stanard's Vermonters and the Repulse of Pickett's Charge* (Woodstock: Countryman, 1997), 47, 232; *Encyclopedia of the Civil War*, 1112; *Proceedings of the Vermont Historical Society* (Montpelier: n.p. 1871), 73; Ralph O. Sturtevant, *Pictorial History of the 13th Regiment, Vermont Volunteers, in the War of 1861–1865* (Burlington, n.p.: 1910), 301–9.

9. Jasper Newton Searles and Matthew F. Taylor, *History of the First Regiment, Minnesota Volunteer Infantry, 1861–1865* (Stillwater: Easton & Masterman,

1916), 364–65; *Encyclopedia of the Civil War*, 2080; Wert, *Gettysburg Day Three*, 224–26; Adin Underwood, *The Three Years Service of the Thirty-Third Massachusetts Infantry Regiment, 1862–1865* (Boston: A. Williams, 1882), 135–43; Ernest Linden Waitt, *History of the Nineteenth Regiment, Massachusetts Volunteer Infantry, 1861–1865* (Salem: Salem Printing, 1906), 230–39.

10.   Charles H. Bane, *History of the Philadelphia Brigade* (Philadelphia: J. P. Lippincott, 1876), 129–35; *Encylopedia of the Civil War*, 2080, 837; *American Heroism: As Told by the Medal Winners and Roll of Honor Men* (Springfield, J. W. Jones, 1897), 313; Searles and Taylor, *History of the First Minnesota*, 366; Gabor S. Boritt, ed., *The Gettysburg Nobody Knows* (Oxford: 1997), 125, 133; Wert, *Gettysburg Day Three*, 224–26; Rawley Martin and John H. Smith, "The Battle of Gettysburg and the Charge of Pickett's Division," *Southern Historical Society Papers* (January–December 1904) 32:31–33.

Chapter 10
"Only the Flag of the Union Greets the Sky"

1.   OR, 1:27:1:467, 469; Herman Hattaway, *Shades of Blue and Gray* (Columbia: University of Missouri Press, 1997), 149; Fleming, *Life of Alexander Hays*, 409, 421, 433; Shulz, *Double Canister*, 64–65; David L. Ladd and Audrey J. Ladd, eds., "Letter of Lt. Egan to George Meade Jr.," *The Bachelder Papers: Gettysburg in Their Own Words* (Dayton: Morningside House, 1994), 1: 389.

2.   David L. Ladd and Audrey J. Ladd, eds., "The First Delaware Regiment," *The Bachelder Papers: Gettysburg in Their Own Words* (Dayton: Morningside House, 1994), 3:1399; John R. Foster, *New Jersey and the Rebellion: A History of the Services of the Troops and People of New Jersey in Aid of the Union Cause* (Newark: Martin R. Dennis, 1868), 38; William P. Haines, *History of the Men of Co. F of the 12th New Jersey Vols.* (Mickleton: n.p. 1897), 137; J. W. Muffly, ed., *The Story of Our Regiment: A History of the 148th Pennsylvania Vols.* (Des Moines: Kenyon, 1904), 541–42.

3.   OR, 1:27:1:94; J. H. Moore, "Heth's Division at Gettysburg," *Southern Bivouac* (May 1885) 3:392–93; Young, "Pettigrew's Brigade," 128; Coddington, *Gettysburg Campaign*, 555–57; Freeman, *R. E. Lee*, 3:130; Fremantle, *Three Months in the Southern States*, 269.

4.   J. D. Imboden, "The Confederate Retreat from Gettysburg," *Battles and Leaders of the Civil War*, Robert U. Johnson and Clarence C. Buell, eds. (New York: Century Company, 1884), 4:424; J. D. Imboden, "Lee at Gettysburg," *The Galaxy* (April 1871) 11:4: 501–13.

5. William C. Byrnes Diary, July 4, 1863, William C. Byrnes Papers, Special Collections Library, Duke University; Stiles, *Four Years Under Marse Robert*, 219–21.

6. Ralston W. Balch, *The Battle of Gettysburg: An Historical Accounts* (Harrisburg, Gettysburg and Harrisburg Railroad, 1885), 107–8; Thomas F. Galwey, *The Valiant Hours*, W. S. Nye, ed. (Harrisburg: Stockpole, 1961), 121; "William G. Browning," *New York Observer*, May 12, 1910; William Garritson Browning, *Grace Magnified: Incidents in the Life, Ministry, Experiences and Travel of William Garritson Browning* (New York: Palmer & Hughes, 1887), 231–33.

7. Mark H. Dunkelman, *Gettysburg's Unknown Soldier: The Life, Death and Celebrity of Amos Humiston* (Westport: Praeger Publishing, 1999), 131–36; Mark Roth, "Gettysburg: Profiles in Courage," *Pittsburgh Post-Gazette*, July 6, 2003; "Whose Father Was He?" *Philadelphia Inquirer*, October 19, 1863.

8. OR, 1:27:1:92, 119; OR, 1:27:2:312-326; Imboden, "Retreat from Gettysburg," 4:424; Coddington, *Gettysburg Campaign*, 555–57; Clyde N. Wilson, *Carolina Cavalier: The Life and Mind of James Johnston Pettigrew* (Athens: University of Georgia Press, 1990), 204–5; C. M. Avery to John Caldwell, July 18, 1863, Tod Robinson Caldwell Papers, Southern Historical Collection, Wilson Library, University of North Carolina at Chapel Hill.

9. E. B. Long, *The Civil War Day by Day: An Almanac 1861–1865* (Garden City: Doubleday, 1971), 709–11; Freeman, *Lee's Lieutenants*, 3:752, 767–68; Patricia Faust, ed., *Historical Times Illustrated History of the Civil War* (New York: Harper & Row, 1986), 20–21; OR, 1:46:3:774; Thomas Devereux Memoir, Family Correspondence 1885–1936, Devereux Family Papers, Special Collections Library, Duke University; Gordon, *Reminiscences of the Civil War*, 444–45; Joshua Lawrence Chamberlain, *The Passing of the Armies: An Account of the Final Campaign of the Army of the Potomac* (New York: G. P. Putnam, 1915), 260–65.

Appendix 1
Official After-Action Report of Major General George Meade

1. Reports. Series 1, vol. 27, part 1, *The War of the Rebellion: A Compilation of the Official Records of the Union and Confederate Armies* (Washington: U.S. Government Printing Office, 1889), 114–19.

Appendix 2
Official After-Action Report of General Robert E. Lee

1. Report. Series 1, vol. 27, part 2, *The War of the Rebellion: A Compilation of the Official Records of the Union and Confederate Armies* (Washington: U.S. Government Printing Office, 1889), 312–25.

Bibliography

Akerman, Robert K. *Wade Hampton III*. Columbia: University of South Carolina Press, 2007.

Aldrich, Thomas M. *The History of Battery A, First Regiment Rhode Island Light Artillery*. Providence: Snow and Farnham, 1904.

Alexander, Edward Porter. *Fighting for the Confederacy: The Personal Recollections of General Edward Porter Alexander*. Edited by Gary W. Gallagher. Chapel Hill: University of North Carolina Press, 1989.

———. *Military Memoirs of a Confederate: A Critical Narrative*. New York: Charles Scribner's Sons, 1907.

Alexander (Edward Porter) Papers. Manuscripts Collection. Library of Congress, Washington, D.C.

Alleman, Tillie Pierce. *At Gettysburg: Or, What a Girl Heard and Saw at the Battle*. New York: Lake Borland, 1889.

American Heroism: As Told by the Medal Winners and Roll of Honor Men. Springfield: J. W. Jones, 1897.

"Anniversary of Gettysburg: Forty Years After the Battle." *Charlotte Daily Observer*, July 4, 1903.

Baker, Levi W. *History of the Ninth Massachusetts Battery*. South Framingham: Lakeview Press, 1888.

Balch, Ralston W. *The Battle of Gettysburg: An Historical Account*. Harrisburg: Gettysburg & Harrisburg Railroad, 1885.

Bane, Charles H. *History of the Philadelphia Brigade*. Philadelphia: J.P. Lippincott, 1876.

Barefoot, Daniel F. *General Robert F. Hoke: Lee's Modest Warrior*. Winston-Salem: J. F. Blair, 1995.

Barlow, Francis C. *"Fear Was Not in Him": The Civil War Letters of Francis C. Barlow*. Edited by Christian G. Samito. New York: Fordham University Press, 2004.

Bernard, George S. "The Gettysburg Campaign." *Petersburg Enterprise*, March 3, 1894.

Biddle (Samuel S.) Papers, Special Collections Library, Duke University, Durham.

Bigelow, John. *The Peach Orchard*. Minneapolis: Kimball-Storer, 1910.

Blackford, W. W. *War Years with Jeb Stuart*. New York: Charles Scribner's Sons, 1945.

Boatner, Mark Mayo, III. *The Civil War Dictionary*. New York: David McKay, 1959.

Boritt, Gabor S., ed. *The Gettysburg Nobody Knows*. Oxford: Oxford University Press, 1997.

Bradford, Gamaliel. Boston: Houghton Mifflin, 1916.

Browning, William Garritson. *Grace Magnified: Incidents in the Life, Ministry, Experiences and Travel of William Garritson Browning*. New York: Palmer & Hughes, 1887.

Brown, J. Willard. *The Signal Corps, USA, in the War of the Rebellion*. Boston: U.S. Veterans Signal Corps Association, 1896.

Bryant, Edwin E. *A History of the 3rd Wisconsin Veteran Volunteers*. Madison: Veterans Association, 1890.

Burgwyn Family Papers, Southern Historical Collection, University of North Carolina at Chapel Hill.

Busey, John W. and David G. Martin. *Regimental Strengths and Losses at Gettysburg*. Hightstown: Longstreet House, 1994.

Byrnes (William C.) Diary. William C. Byrnes Papers. Special Collections Library. Duke University, Durham.

Caldwell (Tod Robinson) Papers. Southern Historical Collection. Wilson Library, University of North Carolina at Chapel Hill.

Calef, John H. "Gettysburg: The Opening Guns." *Journal of the Military Service Institution of the United States* 40 (January–May, 1907).

Chamberlain, Joshua Lawrence. *The Passing of the Armies: An Account of the Final Campaign of the Army of the Potomac.* New York: G. P. Putnam, 1915.

———. "Through Blood and Fire at Gettysburg." *Hearst's Magazine* 23 (June 1913).

Cleaves, Freeman. *Meade of Gettysburg.* Norman: University of Oklahoma, 1960.

Cleutz, David. *Fields of Fame and Glory: Col. David Ireland and the 137th New York State Volunteers.* Bloomington: Xlibris, 2010.

Coddington, Edwin B. *The Gettysburg Campaign: A Study in Command.* New York: Charles Scribner's Sons, 1963.

Coffin, Charles Carlton. *Four Years of Fighting: A Volume of Personal Observations with the Army and the Navy.* Boston: Ticknor and Fields, 1866.

———. *Marching to Victory.* New York: Haper & Brothers, 1888.

Coffin, Howard. *Nine Months to Gettysburg: Stannard's Vermonters and the Repulse of Pickett's Charge.* Woodstock: Countryman, 1997.

Commager, Henry Steele, ed. *The Blue and the Gray: The Story of the Civil War as Told by Participants.* New York: Fairfax Press, 1982.

Cooke, John Esten. *Wearing of the Grey: Being Personal Portraits, Scenes and Adventrues of the War.* New York: E. B. Treat, 1867.

Coxe, John. "The Battle of Gettysburg." *Confederate Veteran* 21 (1913).

Current, Richard N., ed. *Encyclopedia of the Confederacy.* New York: Simon & Schuster, 1993.Davis, Archie K. *Boy Colonel of the Confederacy: The Life and Times of Henry King Burgwyn Jr.* Chapel Hill: University of North Carolina Press, 1985.

Dawes, Rufus. *Service With The Sixth Wisconsin Volunteers.* Marietta: Alderman & Sons, 1890.

Devereux (Thomas) Memoir. Family Correspondence 1885–1936. Devereux Family Papers. Special Collections Library. Duke University, Durham.

Dorsett, Wilbur. "The Fourteenth Color-Bearer." *The Carolina Magazine* 8 (1932).

Dunkelman, Mark H. *Gettysburg's Unknown Soldier: The Life, Death and Celebrity of Amos Humiston.* Westport: Prager Publishing, 1999.

Dyer, Frederick H. *A Compendium of the War of the Rebelllion.* New York: Thomas Yoseloff, 1959.

Edwards, Tom J. *Raising the Banner of Freedom: The 25th Ohio in the War for the Union,* Bloomington: iUniverse, 2009.

Eggleston, George Cary. *A Rebel's Recollections.* New York: G. P. Putnam, 1878.

Faust, Patricia, ed. *Historical Times Illustrated History of the Civil War.* New York: Harper & Row, 1986.

Feeler, Burt, "Reminscences of Col. Colvill." Paper Presented to North Shore Historical Assembly, August 22, 1936. North Shore Historical Assembly.

Fiske, Samuel W. *Mr. Dunn Browne's Experiences in the Army.* Boston: Nichols and Noyes, 1866.

Fleming, George T. *The Life and Letters of Alexander Hays.* Pittsburgh, 1919.

Forbes, Edwin. *Thirty Years After: An Artist's Memoir of the Civil War.* New York: Fords, Howard & Hulbert, 1890.

Foster, John R. *New Jersey and the Rebellion: A History of the Services of the Troops and People of New Jersey in Aid of the Union Cause.* Newark: Martin R. Dennis, 1868.

Fox, William F., ed. *New York at Gettysburg.* Albany, 1902.

Fox, William F. *Regimental Losses in the American Civil War, 1861–1865.* Albany: Randow, 1889.

Freeman, Douglas Southall. *Lee's Lieutenants: A Study in Command.* New York: Charles Scribner's Sons, 1944.

———. *R. E. Lee: A Biography.* New York: Charles Scribner's Sons, 1947.

Fremantle, Arthur Lyon. *Three Months in the Southern States.* Mobile: S. H. Goetzel, 1864.

"From the Twenty-Fourth." *Detroit Free Press.* July 17, 1863.

Fry, Birkett D. "Pettigrew's Charge at Gettysburg." *Southern Historical Society Papers* 7 (January–December 1879).

Gaff, Alan D. "Here was Made Our Last and Hopeless Stand: The 'Lost' Gettysburg Reports of the 19th Indiana." *Gettysburg Magazine 2.*

Gallagher, Gary W. *Chancellorsville: The Battle and Its Aftermath.* Chapel Hill: University of North Carolina Press, 1996.

Galwey, Thomas F. *The Valiant Hours.* Edited by W. S. Nye. Harrisburg: Stockpole, 1961.

Gardner, Alexander. *Photographic Sketchbook of the War.* Mineola: Dover, 1959.

"General Howard's Best Supper." *Daily Free Press.* September 25, 1902.

Gibbon, John. *Personal Recollections of the Civil War.* New York: G. P. Putnam's Sons, 1928.

Giles (Annie B.) Papers. John Barker Texas History Center. University of Texas at Austin.

Giles, Val. *Rags and Hope: The Recollections of Val C. Giles, Four Years with Hood's Brigade, Fourth Texas Regiment, 1861–1864.* New York: Cowan-McCann, 1961.

Glazier, Willard. *Three Years in the Federal Cavalry.* New York: R. H. Fergeson, 1970.

Goldsborough, William Worthington. *The Maryland Line in the Confederate Army, 1861–1865.* Baltimore: Guggenheimer, Weil, 1900.

Gordon, John B. *Reminiscences of the Civil War.* New York: Charles Scribner's Sons, 1903.

Gorhan, George C. *Life and Public Services of Edwin M. Stanton.* Boston: Houghton Mifflin, 1899.

Gottfried, Bradley M. *The Brigades of Gettysburg: The Union and Confederate Brigades at the Battle of Gettysburg.* Campbridge: DaCapo Press, 2003.

Gragg, Rod. *Covered With Glory: The 26th North Carolina Infantry at Gettysburg.* New York: HarperCollins, 2000.

Haines, William P. *History of the Men of Co. F, with description of Marches and Battles of the 12th New Jersey Vols.* Mickleton, 1897.

Hall, Isaac. "Iverson's Brigade and the Part the 97th New York Played in its Capture." *National Tribune.* June 26, 1884.

Halstead, E. P. "The First Day of the Battle of Gettysburg." *Papers of the Military Order of the Loyal Legion, District of Columbia Commandery* 1 (March 2, 1887).

Hancock, Almira Russell. *Reminiscences of Winfield Scott Hancock by His Wife.* New York: Charles L. Webster, 1887.

Haskell, Frank Aretas. *The Battle of Gettysburg.* Edited by Bruce Catton. Boston: Houghton Mifflin, 1958.

Hattaway, Herman. *Shades of Blue and Gray.* Columbia: University of Missouri Press, 1997.

Hebert, Walter H. *Fighting Joe Hooker.* Indianapolis: Bobbs-Merrill, 1944.

Heidler, David S., and Jeanne T. Heidler, eds. *Encyclopedia of the Civil War: A Political, Social, and Military History.* New York: W. W. Norton, 2000.

Hess, Earl J. *Pickett's Charge: The Last Attack at Gettysburg.* Chapel Hill: University of North Carolina Press, 2001.

Heth, Henry. *The Memoir of Henry Heth.* Edited by James L. Morrison Jr. Westport: Greenwood Press, 1974.

History of Goodhue County, Minnesota. Edited by Franklyn Curtiss-Wedge. Chicago: H. C. Cooper, 1909.

Hoke, Jacob. *The Great Invasion of 1863.* Dayton: W. J. Shuey, 1887.

Hood, John Bell. *Advance and Retreat: Personal Experiences in the United States and Confederate States Armies.* New Orleans: G. T. Beauregard, 1880.

Hosington, Daniel J. *Gettysburg and the Christian Commission,* Brunswick: Edinborough Press, 2002.

"How an Eyewitness Watched the Great Battle." *Baltimore American.* June 29, 1913.

Hunter, Alexander. "A High Private's Account of the Battle of Sharpsburg," *Southern Historical Society Papers* 10 (October–November 1882).

"Isaac Avery's Message to His Father, July 1863," Digital Collections. North Carolina Department of Achives and History.

Imboden, J. D. "The Confederate Retreat from Gettysburg." *Battles and Leaders of the Civil War.* Edited by Robert U. Johnson and Clarence C. Buell. New York: Century Company, 1884, 4.

———. "Lee at Gettysburg." *The Galaxy* 11(April 1871).

Johnson, Robert Underwood, and Clarence Clough Buel, eds. *Battles and Leaders of the Civil War.* New York: Thomas Yoseloff, 1956.

Johnston, John White. *The True Story of "Jennie" Wade.* Rochester: Johnston, 1917.

Jones, J. William. *Christ in the Camp: Or, Religion in Lee's Army.* Richmond: B. F. Johnson, 1888.

Jones, Terry L. *Cemetery Hill: The Struggle for the High Ground, July 1–3, 1863.* Cambridge: DaCapo, 2003.

Jordan, Weymouth T., Jr., and Louis H. Manarin, eds. *North Carolina Troops, 1861–1865: A Roster.* Raleigh: North Carolina Department of Archives and History, 1979.

———. *Lee's Tigers: The Louisiana Infantry in the Army of Northern Virginia.* Baton Rouge: LSU Press, 1987.

Kidd, James H., "Address of James H. Kidd, at the Dedication of Michigan Monuments on the Battlefield at Gettysburg, June 12, 1889." *Journal of the United States Cavalry Association* 4 (March 1891).

———. *At Custer's Side: The Civil War Writings of James Harvy Kidd.* Edited by Eric J. Wittenberg. Kent: Kent State University Press, 2001.

———. *Personal Recollections of a Cavalryman with Custer's Michigan Cavalry Brigade in the Civil War.* Ionia: Sentinel, 1908.

Kimble, June. "Tennesseeans at Gettysburg." *Confederate Veteran* 18 (September 1910).

Ladd, David, and Audrey Ladd, eds. *The Bachelder Papers: Gettysburg in Their Own Words.* Vols. 1–3. Dayton: Morningside, 1994–95.

———. "The First Delaware Regiment." *The Bachelder Papers: Gettysburg in Their Own Words.* Vol. 3. Dayton: Morningside, 1994.

———. "Letter of Lt. Egan to George Meade Jr." *The Bachelder Papers: Gettysburg in Their Own Words.* Vol. 1. Dayton: Morningside, 1994.

Lane, James H. "Letter From General Lane." *Raleigh Observer.* November 29, 1877.

Lane (John R.) Papers. Southern Historical Collection. University of North Carolina at Chapel Hill.

Lee, Alfred. "Reminiscences of the Gettysburg Battle." *Lippincott's Magazine of Popular Literature and Science* 32 (July 1883).

"Lieutenant Wheelock, Describes the Battle of Gettysburg." *Ithaca Journal* (July 15, 1863).

Lineback, Julius. "Extracts from a Civil War Diary." *Twin Cities Daily Sentinel* (June 14, 1914–April 3, 1915).

Lineback (Julius) Papers. Southern Historical Collection. University of North Carolina at Chapel Hill.

Lochren, William. "Narrative of the First Regiment." *Minnesota in the Civil and Indian Wars, 1861–1865.* Edited by C. C. Andrews. St. Paul: Pioneer Press, 1891.

Longacre, Edward G. *The Commanders of Chancellorsville.* Nashville: Rutledge Hill Press, 2005.

———. *General John Buford: A Military Biography.* Cambridge: DaCapo, 1995.

———. *Joshua Chamberlain: The Soldier and the Man.* Cambridge: DaCapo, 2003.

Long, E. B. *The Civil War Day by Day: An Almanac 1861–1865.* Garden City: Doubleday, 1971.

Longstreet, James. *From Manassas to Appomattox: Memoirs of the Civil War in America.* Philadelphia: J. B. Lippincott, 1908.

Lyman, Theodore. *Meade's Headquarters, 1863–1865: Letters from Colonel Theodore Lyman from the Wilderness to Appomattox.* Edited by George R. Aggasiz. Boston: Atlantic Monthly Press, 1922.

"Maj. Gen. Isaac R. Trimble." *The Bachelder Papers: Gettysburg in Their Own Words.* Vol 2. Dayton: Morningside House, 1994.

Marsh, Henry E. "The Nineteenth Indiana at Gettysburg." Civil War Collection. U.S. Army Military History Institute, Carlisle, PA.

Martin, Rawley, and John H. Smith. "The Battle of Gettysburg and the Charge of Pickett's Division." *Southern Historical Society Papers* 32 (January–December 1904).

Marvin (Matthew) Diary. Matthew Marvin Papers. Minnesota Historical Society.

McClellan, Henry B. The Life and Campaigns of Major General J.E.B. Stuart. Boston: Houghton Mifflin, 1885.

McClure, Alexander K., ed. *Annals of the War: Written by Leading Participants North and South*. Philadelphia: Times Publishing, 1879.

McConaughy (David) Papers. Special Collections, Musselman Library, Gettysburg College.

McLaws, Lafayette. "Gettysburg." Southern Historical Society Papers 7.

McPherson (Edward) Papers. Library of Congress, Washington, D.C.

Meade, George Gordon. *The Life and Letters of George Gordon Meade*. New York: Charles Scribner's Sons, 1913.

Miller, J. Michael. "Perrin's Brigade on July 1, 1863," *Gettysburg Magazine* 13.

Moe, Richard. *The Last Full Measure: The Life and Death of the the First Minnesota Volunteers*. New York: Henry Holt, 1993.

Moon, W. H. "Beginning the Battle of Gettysburg." *Confederate Veteran* 33 (December 1925).

Moore, J. H. "Heth's Division at Gettysburg." *Southern Bivouac* 3 (May 1885).

Moore, John W., ed. *Roster of North Carolina Toops in the War Between the States*. Raleigh: Ashe and Gatling, 1892.

Moyer, Henry. *General Lee's Headquarters at Gettysburg, Penna*. Allentown, 1911.

Muffly, J. W., ed. *The Story of Our Regiment: A History of the 148th Pennsylvania Volunteeers*. Des Moines: Kenyon Printing, 1904.

National Tribune. June 26, 1884.

Neese, George M. *Three Years in the Confederate Horse Artillery*. New York: Neale Pubishing, 1911.

Nicholson, John P., ed., *Pennsylvania at Gettysburg: Ceremonies at the Dedication of the Monuments Erected by the Commonwealth of Pennsylvania*. Harrisburg: E. K. Meyers, 1893.

Nolan, Alan T. *The Iron Brigade: A Military History*. New York: Macmillan, 1961.

Oates, William C. "Gettysburg: The Battle on the Right." *Southern Historical Society Papers* 6 (1878).

Olds, Fred A. "Brave Carolinian Fell at Gettysburg." *Southern Historical Society Papers* 35. Collection. Library of Congress, Washington, D.C.

Owen, Henry T. "Pickett at Gettysburg." *Philadelphia Weekly Times* (March 26, 1881).

Patterson, John A. "The Death of Iverson's Brigade," *Gettysburg Magazine 5* (July 1991).

Perrett, Thomas. "A Trip that Didn't Pay." Thomas Perrett Papers. North Carolina Department of Archives and History.

"Pettigrew's Old Brigade." Southern Commanders and Staff Officers File. Robert L. Brake Collection. U.S. Army Military History Institute, Carlisle, PA.

Pfanz, Harry W. *Gettysburg: The Second Day.* Chapel Hill: University of North Carolina Press, 1987.

Phisterer, Frederick, ed. *New York in the War of the Rebellion, 1861 to 1865.* Albany: D. B. Lyon, 1912.

Pickett, George Edward, and LaSalle Corbell Pickett. *The Heart of a Soldier: As Revealed in the Intimate Letters of George E. Pickett.* New York: Seth Moye, 1913.

Polley, J. B. *Hood's Texas Brigade.* Dayton: Morningside, 1976.

Powell, William S., ed. *Dictionary of North Carolina Biography.* Chapel Hill: University of North Carolina Press, 1991.

Proceedings of the Vermont Historical Society. Montpelier, 1871.

"Rebel Letter." Newspaper File. Edward McPherson Papers. Library of Congress, Washington, D.C.

Reed, Charles W. *A Grand Terrible Drama: The Civil War Letters of Charles Wellington Reed.* Edited by Eric Campbell. New York: Fordham University Press, 2000.

Report of the Joint Committee of the Conduct of the War, Washington: U.S. Government Printing Office, 1865.

Robertson, James I., Jr. *A.P. Hill: The Story of a Confederate Warrior.* New York: Random House, 1987.

———. *Stonewall Jackson: The Man, the Soldier, the Legend.* New York: Macmillan: 1997.

Roth, Mark. "Gettysburg: Profiles in Courage." *Pittsburgh Post-Gazette* (July 6 2003).

Rosentreter, Roger L. "Those Damned Black Hats: The Twenty-fourth Michigan at Gettysburg." *Michigan History Magazine* (July–August 1991).

Ross, Fitzgerald. "A Visit to the Cities and Camps of the Confederate States, 1863–1864." *Blackwood's Edinburgh Magazine* 96 (December 1864).

Ryder Family Papers. Bentley Historical Library. University of Michigan.

Sawyer, Franklin. *A Military History of the 8th Ohio Volunteer Infantry.* Cleveland: Fairbanks, 1881.

Sawyer, George T. *The Life and Letters of Alexander Hays.* Pittsburgh, 1919.

Schaff, Morris. *Battle of the Wilderness.* Boston: Houghton Mifflin, 1910.

Schuricht, Hermann. "Jenkins' Brigade in the Gettysburg Campaign: Extracts from the Diary of Lieutenant Hermann Schuricht, of the Fourteenth Virginia Cavalry." *Southern Historical Society Papers* 24 (1896).

Schurz, Carl. *The Reminiscences of Carl Schurz.* Garden City: Doubleday and Page, 1917.

Scott, Winfield. "Pickett's Charge as Seen from the Front Lines." *The Gettysburg Papers.* Compiled by Ken Bandy and Florence Freeland. Dayton: Morningside, 1978.

Searles, Jasper Newton, and Matthew F. Taylor. *History of the First Regiment, Minnesota Volunteer Infantry, 1861–1865.* Stillwater: Easton & Masterman, 1916.

Sears, Stephen W. *Gettysburg.* New York: Houghton Mifflin, 2003.

Sheahan (John Parris) Collection. Maine Historical Society.

Shulz, David. *Double Canister at Ten Yards: The Federal Artillery and the Repulse of Pickett's Charge.* Redondo Beach: Rank and File, 1995.

Sixth North Carolina Regiment Casualties Report. *Confederate States Army Casualties: Lists and Narrative Reports, 1861–1865.* Record Group 109. War Department Collection of Confederate Records. National Archives, Washington, D.C.

Smith, Carl. *Gettysburg 1863: High Tide of the Confederacy.* Oxford: Osprey, 1998.

Smith, Derek. *The Gallant Dead: Union and Confederate Generals Killed in the Civil War.* Mechanicsburg: Stackpole, 2005.

Smith, James Power. "General Lee at Gettysburg." *Southern Historical Society Papers* 33.

Sorrell, G. Moxley. *Recollections of a Confederate Staff Officer*. New York: Neale Publishing, 1905.

Stiles, Robert. *Four Years Under Marse Robert*. New York: Neale Publishing, 1910.

Stillson, J. B. "Report of J.B. Stillson." *Christian Commission: Report of the Committee of Maryland*. Baltimore: James Young, 1864.

Stine, James Henry. *A History of the Army of the Potomac*. Washington: Gibson Brothers, 1893.

Strikeleather, J.A. "Recollections of the Late War." *Company Front* 17 (October 1993).

Sturtevant, Ralph O. *Pictorial History of the 13th Regiment, Vermont Volunteers, in the War of 1861–1865*. Burlington, 1910.

Sullivan, John P. *An Irishman in the Iron Brigade: The Civil War Memoirs of James P. Sullivan*. Edited by William J. K. Beaudot and Lance J. Herdegen. New York: Forham University Press, 1993.

Taylor, Michael W. "Col. James Keith Marshall: One of Three Brigade Commanders Killed in the Pickett-Pettigrew-Trimble Charge." *Gettysburg Magazine* 15 (July 1, 1996).

Taylor, Walter H. *Four Years with General Lee*. New York: D. Appleton, 1878.

Thompson, Richard S. "A Scrap of Gettysburg." *Military Essays and Recollections Read Before the Illinois Commandery of the Military Order of the Loyal Legion*. Chicago: Dial, 1897.

Trudeau, Noah Andre. *Gettysburg: A Testing of Courage*. New York: HarperCollins, 2002.

Truluck, Alice Rains. *In the Hands of Providence: Joshua Chamberlain and the American Civil War*. Chapel Hill: University of North Carolina Press, 1992.

Tucker, Glen. *High Tide at Gettysburg*, Gettysburg: Stan Clark Military Books, 1995.

Underwood, Adin. *The Three Years Service of the Thirty-Third Massachusetts Infantry Regiment, 1862–1865*. Boston: A. Williams, 1882.

Wainwright, Charles S. *A Diary of Battle: The Personal Journals of Col. Charles S. Wainwright*. Edited by Allan Nevins. New York: Harcourt, Brace and World, 1961.

Waitt, Ernest Linden. *History of the Nineteenth Regiment, Massachusetts Volunteer Infantry, 1861–1865*. Salem: Salem Printing, 1906.

Walker, Charles D. *Memorial Virginia Military Institute: Biographical Sketches of the Cadets and Eleves Who Fell During the War Between the States*. New York: J. P. Lippincott, 1875.

Wall, H. C. "Twenty-Third Regiment." *Histories of the Several Regiments and Battalions from North Carolina in the Great War 1861–'65*. Edited by Walter Clark. Raleigh, 1901.

Warner, Ezra J. *Generals in Blue: Lives of Union Commanders*. Baton Rouge: LSU Press, 1964.

War of the Rebellion: The Official Records of the Union and Confederate Armies. Washington, D.C.: Official Government Printing Office, 1880–1901.

Webb, Samuel L., and Margaret England Armbrester. *Alabama Governors: A Political History of the State*. Tuscaloosa: University of Alabama Press, 2001.

Weld, Stephen Minot. *War Diary and Letters*. Boston: Riverside Press, 1912.

Wert, Jeffry D. *Cavalryman of the Lost Cause: A Biography of J.E.B. Stuart*. New York: Simon and Schuster, 2003.

———. *Gettysburg Day Three.* New York: Touchstone, 1993.

Weygant, Charles. *History of the One Hundred Twenty-Fourth Regiment, New York State Volunteers*. Newburgh: Journal Printing House, 1877.

———. "Officer Gives View of the Battlefield After the Second Day's Fighting." *New York Sun* (June 29, 1913).

Whitaker, Frederick. *A Complete Life of General George A. Custer*. New York: Sheldon, 1876.

"Whose Father Was He?" *Philadelphia Inquirer* (October 19, 1863).

Wiley, Bell I. *The Life of Billy Yank: The Common Soldier of the Union*. Baton Rouge: LSU Press, 1978.

———. *The Life of Johnny Reb: The Common Solider of the Confederacy*. Baton Rouge: LSU Press, 1978.

"William G. Browning." *New York Observer*, (May 12, 1910).

Wilson, Clyde N. *Carolina Cavalier: The Life and Mind of James Johnston Pettigrew.* Athens: University of Georgia Press, 1990.

Wise, Jennings Cooper. *The Long Arm of Lee: The History of the Artillery of the Army of Northern Virginia.* Lincoln: University of Nebraska Press, 1991.

Wittenberg, Erick J. "An Analysis of the Buford Manuscripts." *Gettysburg Magazine* 15.

Woodworth, Steven E. *Beneath a Northern Sky: A Short History of the Gettysburg Campaign.* Lanham: Rowman & Littlefield, 2008.

Worsham, John H. *One of Jackson's Foot Cavalry.* New York: Neale, 1912.

Wright, James. "The James Wright Letters." Edited by David H. McGee. *Company Front* 1 (1992).

Young, Louis G. "Pettigrew's Brigade at Gettysburg." *Histories of Several Regiments and Battalions from North Carolina in the Great War 1861–65.* Edited by Walter Clark. Raleigh, 1901.

Index

Eyewitness Gettysburg

Expand your library with other titles from
Regner History's featured collections

CIVIL WAR

Backstage at the Lincoln Assassination:
The Untold Story of the Actors and
Stagehands at Ford's Theatre
by Thomas A. Bogar

Lee vs. McClellan:
The First Campaign
by Clayton R. Newell

Lincoln and Grant:
The Westerners Who Won the Civil War
by Edward H. Bonekemper III

The Real Custer:
From Boy General to Tragic Hero
By James S. Robbins

COLD WAR CLASSICS

Operation Solo:
The FBI's Man in the Kremlin
by John Barron

The Venona Secrets:
Exposing Soviet Espionage and
America's Traitors
by Herbert Romerstein and Eric Breindel

Witness
by Whittaker Chambers

THE PRESIDENTS

Cleveland:
The Forgotten Conservative
by John M. Pafford

Coolidge:
An American Enigma
by Robert Sobel

Nixon:
A Life
by Jonathan Aitken

Reagan:
The Inside Story
by Edwin Meese

THE GENERALS

Curtis LeMay:
Strategist and Tactician
by Warren Kozak

George S. Patton:
Blood, Guts, and Prayer
by Michael Keane

Hap Arnold:
Inventing the Air Force
by Bill Yenne

Omar Bradley:
General at War
by Jim DeFelice

Look for these other collections by Regnery History
World War II & Early America

www.RegneryHistory.com